Modernizing the Provincial City

Modernizing the Provincial City Toulouse, 1945–1975

ROSEMARY WAKEMAN

HARVARD UNIVERSITY PRESS
Cambridge, Massachusetts
London, England
1997

For Gabrielle and Jessica

Library of Congress Cataloging-in-Publication Data
   Wakeman, Rosemary.
     Modernizing the provincial city : Toulouse, 1945–1975 /
     Rosemary Wakeman.
         p. cm.
     Includes bibliographical references and index.
     ISBN 0-674-58072-9
     1. City planning—France—Toulouse—History—20th century.
   2. Toulouse (France)—Economic conditions. I. Title.
   HT169.F72T68 1997
   307.1'216'094862—DC21   97-23077

Contents

Illustrations

Acknowledgments

I have many people to thank for this book, written as it was over time in many places. Its roots are in the history department at the University of California, Davis, where the mentoring and friendship of Roy Willis, Ted Margadant, and Dan Brower sustained my research as a graduate student and as a faculty member there. It often seemed a very long distance between the Garonne and Sacramento Valleys, but their intellectual wisdom and superb grasp of urban history provided the bridge that made this book possible. My sincere thanks to Herrick Chapman, Ellen Furlough, Julia Trilling, Tyler Stovall, Suzanna Barrows, Paul Rabinow, Gabrielle Hecht, and H. Roderick Kedward, who read various drafts of the manuscript and generously offered their ideas, criticism, and advice. I have gratefully embraced their suggestions, and the book has profited enormously by them. I thank Tyler Stovall and Julia Trilling for many fruitful discussions on the city. Gabrielle Hecht, Robert Frost, Joe Corn, and my colleagues in the Program on Science, Technology, and Society at Stanford University helped me decipher the history of technology. I appreciate the support and suggestions of the history faculty at the University of Tennessee, Knoxville, especially Russell Buhite, John Muldowney, and John Bohstedt. The staff at the Hoover Institute, Stanford University, as well as the inter-library loan staff at the University of California, Berkeley, were of tremendous help in finding resources. Research for this book was conducted in Toulouse with the aid of grants from the University of California, Davis and the University of Tennessee, Knoxville. I thank the National Endowment for the Humanities for their Travel-to-Collections Fellowship that helped complete the project.

In France, Marcel Roncayolo and André Burguière at the Ecole des Hautes Etudes en Sciences Sociales initially guided my research and graciously led my passage into French urban theory and history. Roger Brunet provided decisive aid in the book's conception. As well as helping me tie the project together, Guy Jalabert at the Center for Urban Studies at the University of Toulouse Le Mirail introduced me to Toulouse when I first arrived as an American graduate student ready to take on the city. Professor Jalabert ushered in a world of amiable, talkative, perceptive Toulousains who made my stays there not simply successful but intoxicating. Each time, it was difficult to leave Toulouse. And so, my heartfelt thanks to Professor Jalabert, and to the extraordinary people at the Préfecture office, the Toulouse Mayor's Office, the Agence d'Urbanisme, the Ecole d'Architecture at the University of Toulouse Le Mirail, the Municipal Library, the Chambre de Commerce and the Chambre des Métiers, at the Toulouse offices of DATAR and INSEE, and at CNES, Airbus Industries, and Aérospatiale. I am particularly indebted to Madame Maillard of the Archives Municipales, who generously contributed her knowledge and support to this project. During my stays at Toulouse, many ordinary citizens freely gave their time and energy to my incessant questions and interviews. And I must admit, in my zeal I attempted to interrogate everyone. I was treated to tours of the French Space Center, lunches at office cafeterias, and street dances, and driven around to see the sights, brought home for dinner, taken to local conferences—all to talk about Toulouse and the changes in its life and landscape. I thank all of these people sincerely for their generosity of spirit and their hospitality and hope that I have represented their city well.

I am grateful to Aïda Donald and Betty Suttell at Harvard University Press for their enthusiasm and support for this book, and to the staff at ESNE for their help preparing the manuscript. My thanks as well to William Truitt for his superb map designs. I spent wonderful hours with Madame and Monsieur Jean Dieuzaide among his extraordinary photographs of Toulouse, and I heartily thank them for their help and generosity. Madame Geneviève Dieuzeide of the Department of Photography at La Documentation Française, as well as Madame Bernadette Suau and Madame Marie-Hélène Ristorcelli at the Departmental Archives of the Haute-Garonne, helped me select illustrations among a plethora of superb photographs, as did Madame Catherine Pra at the Aérospatiale Aircraft Museum and Monsieur Coe at the Mayor's Office.

Finally, my deepest thanks to Tom Wakeman, for his enthusiasm, encouragement, and willingness to read and critique the manuscript in all of its many stages. Our discussions on urban and regional planning provided a constant source of ideas. His exceptional insights and clarity of vision, as well as his love and support, were my inspiration. And to our remarkable daughters, Gabrielle and Jessica, who have spent their childhood patiently listening to tales of Toulouse, I dedicate this book.

Abbreviations

APC	Azote et Produits Chimiques
CDL	Comité Départemental de Libération
CFDT	Confédération Française Démocratique du Travail
CFTC	Confédération Française des Travailleurs Chrétiens
CGT	Confédération Générale du Travail
CII	Compagnie Internationale pour l'Informatique
CNES	Centre National d'Etudes Spatiales
CNR	Conseil National de la Résistance
CNRS	Centre National de la Recherche Scientifique
COEA	Comité Occitan d'Etudes et d'Action
CRS	Compagnies Républicaines de Sécurité
DATAR	Délégation à l'Aménagement du Territoire et à l'Action Régionale
DGEN	Délégation Générale à l'Equipement Nationale
DGRST	Délégation Générale à la Recherche Scientifique et Technique
DPO	Direction Participative aux Objectifs
EEC	European Economic Community
ENAC	Ecole Nationale de l'Aviation Civile
ENSAE	Ecole Nationale Supérieure Aéronautique
FDES	Fonds de Développement Economique et Social
FEN	Fédération de l'Education Nationale
FFI	Forces Françaises de l'Intérieur
FTPF	Francs-Tireurs et Partisans Français
HBM	Offices Publics d'Habitations à Bon Marché
HLM	Offices Publics d'Habitations à Loyer Modéré
IGAME	Inspecteur Général de l'Administration en Mission Extraordinaire
INSEE	Institut National de la Statistique et des Etudes Economiques

LOGECOS	Logements Economiques et Familiaux
MRL	Ministère de la Reconstruction et du Logement
MRP	Mouvement Républicain Populaire
MRU	Ministère de la Reconstruction et de l'Urbanisme
ONIA	L'Office National Industriel de l'Azote
PME	Petites et Moyennes Entreprises
POS	Plan d'Occupation des Sols
PSA	Parti Socialiste Autonome
RPF	Rassemblement du Peuple Français
SDAU	Schéma Directeur d'Aménagement et d'Urbanisme
SFIO	Section Française de l'Internationale Ouvrière
SNCAM	Société Nationale des Constructions Aéronautiques du Midi
SNCASE	Société Nationale des Constructions Aéronautiques du Sud-Est
SNCASO	Société Nationale des Constructions Aéronautiques du Sud-Ouest
SOTOCOGI	Société Toulousaine de Construction et de Gestion d'Immeubles
UDR	Union pour la Démocratie Française
UNR	Union pour la Nouvelle République
ZPIU	Zone de Peuplement Industriel et Urbain
ZUP	Zone à Urbaniser par Priorité

Introduction

During the 1980s, it became fashionable for the French to portray the city of Toulouse as the vision of the French technopolis, the pioneering model for the city of the future. The French magazine *GEO*, for one, devoted an entire issue to Toulouse, its pages filled with color shots of aircraft factories, the Space Center and research parks, and the luminous high-rise office buildings along the allée Jean Jaurès. The city's planned suburbia, with its stylish condos and homes, shopping malls, and parks anchored in a web of highways, was offered to *GEO*'s readers as exemplar of the modern built environment. Even *Le Monde* added its voice to the chorus of praise heaped upon the "city of the future" emerging in the Midi.[1] This was a rather drastic change of heart considering that traditionally Toulouse's reputation was as a boring, unattractive town deep in the bleak, uncivilized territory of the southwest—poverty-stricken, pedestrian, beyond the mainstream of French historical consciousness. How this should be so, how Toulouse metamorphosed from the epitome of backwardness and peripheralization to become an icon of the French future, is the subject of this book.

Toulouse straddles the wild Garonne River that chisels the historic border between the old provinces of Languedoc and Gascogne. For centuries it dominated the culturally rich world of sovereign Languedoc. Molded by a complex and rebellious history, consigned to a historic role as one of France's poorest towns, Toulouse actually defies easy description or characterization. Its contemporary civic imagery may shout devotion to modernism and the future, but evidence of its rich urban past is everywhere. The Cathedral of Saint-Sernin and the steeples of some ten to fifteen churches rise over the city like ghosts of Toulouse's powerful medieval past, relics of the tragic clash between heresy and orthodoxy that cost the city its autonomy in the thirteenth century. The grand palace of the Capitole at the city's heart and the Palais de Justice, the seat of the Old Regime Parlement, attest to its birthright as the administrative and judicial capital of Languedoc. The city's visual appearance is actually unique in France. The signature pink brick and red tile roofs of *la ville rose* seem to resonate with the city's individuality. Sinuous medieval passageways are lined by brick walls the color of red wine that the centuries have woven with intricate patterns of purple and pink moiré. The red brick of Toulouse frames the abodes and the shops, the daily life made up from a wild amalgam of Occitan cultural tradition, modern urban existence, and postmodern consumerism.

Throughout most of its history, Toulouse has been a decidedly unprosperous city. Privation seems to be part of the local legacy. Yet the generations of artisans and shopkeepers who have plied their wares within the sanguine orbit of the city's streets for centuries may now well offer the most elegant of worldly goods in the chicest of boutiques. Nevertheless, the Toulousains will often defend their antiquated customs and habits as inviolate, infusing them with the political defiance of their Radical and Socialist political heritage, priding themselves on the city's infamy as capital of the *Midi rouge*. The Socialist Party controlled municipal government at the Capitole from 1906 to 1971. The streets ring with the echoes of Jean Jaurès, Léon Blum, Vincent Auriol. Toulouse culture is lauded for its temperamental, maverick spirit—especially as a perennial thorn in the side of Paris. Yet the city can't seem to get along without economic infusions from the French capital. It both claims distinctiveness within the galaxy of French cities and offers itself as a future vision of what it means to be French. If the sunlit red brick is used as the symbol for the texture and experience of its urban life, so are the products of its modern industries: the supersonic Concorde, microchips and computers, the Ariane and Hèrmes space rockets. The city's suburban communities, Le Mirail and Rangueil-Lespinet, stretch outward across the Garonne Valley as prototypes of the modernist ideal. With its tangled and impudent heritage still in tow, Toulouse has managed to emerge from the dustbin of history as the new French think tank, wedded to the latest innovations in science and technology, marking the path toward the future.

What this book grapples with is this enigmatic modernist transformation of Toulouse that was mediated through the layers of local culture to produce the multifarious urban environment of the contemporary age. The first part of the book is about modernism in the aesthetic sense of urban design; the second part is about modernization in the economic sense of innovation and development—and how these intertwining motifs were molded and suffused around the old derelict provincial capital. Toulouse was certainly not a city particularly high on the itinerary of modernity. It was not one of the established great capitals strung like pearls across the map of Europe. It was a lost city somewhere in the outback of the French provinces. Precisely because of this, and because of its intensely rich Occitan past, Toulouse is an absorbing case from which to study the exuberance and pathos involved in this pursuit of the modern as well as the tricky and multiform adaptability and resistance of historic urban practices.

The process of modernization at Toulouse actually began in the 1920s and 1930s, was funneled through the Vichy years of the Second World War, and then was vastly accelerated through reconstruction and the economic miracles of the postwar era. The *trentes glorieuses*[2] from 1945 to 1975 was an unprecedented period of transformation and growth. There was a whole conjuncture of spatial, economic, and sociocultural changes that took place throughout France that can be gathered under the general term "modernization." It was propelled by the widespread conviction that economic innovation and progress, that ordered, wholesome living environments, and that the judicious organization of the various social classes were the solutions to the conflicts that had plagued France for two centuries. Modernization was about full employment in newly mechanized industries, decent housing and regulated social welfare programs, and material affluence as the marks of social harmony.

This program was largely carried through by the combined forces of the French state bureaucracy and corporate capitalism. The French reform-minded elites, the pioneering technocrats who made their way into public power by the 1950s, were unquestionably the philosophers of the new. They proselytized in a rhetoric of grandeur about change and the possibilities of the French future. Modernization became a form of manifest destiny, a predestination around which French identity could be rebuilt after the catastrophe of war. The application of their modernist canon, known as Fordism, meant technological innovation, control over labor, steering the country's resources toward automated production and mass consumption in novel industries, and infusing a new will and spirit into French business culture and practices.

Avant-garde modern style in architecture and urban design became heavily associated with this epistemological framework. Modernism became the established art of the city within the capitalist, state-managed economy. It was the aesthetic arm of the rationalist, progressive outlook that infused French public policy and the technocratic agenda.[3] As urban planning, modernism was the *leitmotif* for experiments in a mass-produced

futuristic built environment and for regulating and harmonizing the material basis of urban existence. As two intertwining strategies, economic modernization and modern urban planning were used as the means to launch a
vast program for the reconstruction and reorganization of France, or, in the
bureaucratic argot—*aménagement du territoire*. It was a mighty saga, this
modernist rejuvenation of a country steeped in an eclectic and contentious
history and in a provincial culture that was a byword for "passé." And
indeed the allusions to "the new France" finally flowing with the vital tides
of progress, innovation, order, and efficiency are too numerous to relate,
except to say that without doubt this emergence of the "new" has been one
of the central fixations of contemporary French society.

These questions of modernization and the societal flux that it creates
are intertwined in the most basic sense with questions about the city. As
counterpoints, both aesthetic modernism and economic modernization
were rooted in the leviathan drama of urbanizing. Or, as Michel de Certeau
has so aptly put it, "the city is both the machinery and the hero of modernity."[4] Especially in the case of the French, modernization was experienced
culturally, socially, and spatially as massive urbanization. It was a shift from
traditional rural existence into the city and the whole conundrum that
entails. The adjustments were particularly severe because France managed
to put off city living far longer than any of the other more advanced nations
of Europe. Up to the end of the Second World War, half of French citizens
still lived in the countryside. The provinces were tied together by ancient
and multifarious patterns of rural culture and habit that had persisted and
adapted to the forces of change with remarkable resourcefulness. Large cities
were rare, industrial cities even rarer. France long remained a puzzle of
parochial localisms and regionalisms that defied any rational definition,
resisted efforts at centralization, and claimed either the emotional devotion
or the unending reproach of most of the country's population. Nowhere did
this prevailing rural milieu linger longer than in the southwest, the *pays
toulousain*. The region was a synonym for the pastoral arrangements underlying French culture and society from time out of mind. Up to the 1920s,
Toulouse itself was simply a shabby regional outpost, a *grand village*, of some
150,000 mainly petit-bourgeois landowners and small-time shopkeepers
and artisans furnishing daily goods to upper Languedoc. Its lifeline was its
region.

The first two chapters of this book address the city's historic experience. Chapter 1 follows the history of Toulouse in a brief introductory
chronology, from its founding through the Second World War. Chapter 2

then assesses this history from a more theoretical standpoint. It attempts to grapple with the evolving meanings of region, city, and geographic space that defined Toulouse's history, its culture, and its identity. The categories of region, city, and space in France are a daunting challenge, and I would not pretend to take them up in any complete way. This chapter is limited to the more merciful duty of analyzing how historic urban processes at Toulouse and the question of modernization were mediated through a tangle of perceptions about geography and regional life. They gave the images of progress and spatiality a rich and disputatious character that highlighted the conflicts and incongruities within French society. The green valleys and quaint villages of the *Haut-Languedoc* continue to the present to be a favorite vacation haunt for French families looking to give the modern world the slip and bond with their rural roots. But the impressions of Languedoc and Toulouse as peripheral fields of ideology, politics, and cultural practice have been as ambiguous and controversial as any in France.

In any case, this magic and nostalgic spell of country living can perhaps best be explained by the fact that with the Second World War's end in 1945, the French abandoned their traditional rural predilections and began moving to the cities. Just a short thirty years later, in 1975, 37 million people, or three-quarters of the country's population, resided in cities, and half of these numbers lived in the largest provincial capitals. Toulouse experienced one of the most radical population increases. It mutated from a sleepy regional town to an industrial and scientific metropolis with an extended suburban realm and a population well over 600,000—one of the largest cities in France. Although its growth may have been among the most exceptional, in many ways its experiences were typical of those in urban areas throughout the country. High-rise office and apartment buildings, parking garages, and supermarkets settled into picturesque towns. Crowds of pedestrians, automobiles, and buses clogged narrow streets meant for horse-drawn wagons. Towns and cities spread out like amoebas across the sacred landscape of the rustic countryside. Historic central districts were enfolded in layers of goliath housing tracts, commercial centers, and highways. The French were quite daunted, even obsessed, by the dimensions of this urban revolution. Most future forecasts during the 1960s and early 1970s predicted the urbanization of the quasi totality of the country. The Commissariat du Plan anticipated that "at this rate we will need to construct in one or two generations as many cities as we constructed since the beginning of French history."[5] The "urban question" and the "regional question" took on crisis proportions within public debate.

Modernization and urbanization offered a maelstrom of possibilities. They proffered a vital future of growth, prosperity, and power. They also cut across known cultural and geographic boundaries, clashed with traditional class and social relations, and tore up historic continuity. By virtue of the rupture and disarray it wrought, the sweeping change to city life that commanded so much of the country's attention during the *trentes glorieuses* necessitated as well a radical rethinking of French identity. Indeed, how a city looked, how its spaces and its economy were reconceptualized and arranged, formed the basis around which social and cultural practices were thought about, evaluated, and altered. Fashioning and designing a new image, a new living environment for cities like Toulouse, encapsulated the controversies and friction over this prodigious undertaking of living modern life in France. Much of this study is about the construction of a new urban image for Toulouse and the use of the city's past and its future, its visual landscape and its economy, in a complex debate about modernization and the changing nature of French cultural and social identity. The development of Toulouse was more than anything seen as an opportunity for state technocrats to experiment with modernism and modernization as solutions for one of the more unequivocal specimens of neglect, defiance, and traditionalism in France. Modern architecture and urban design (public housing programs, suburban planned communities and office parks, rational highway systems) were altruistic answers to the disarray and muddle of the antiquated habitat of red-brick buildings.

Two chapters examine the repercussions of these state programs for urban rehabilitation in detail. Chapter 3 assesses the impact of urban planning and public housing programs at Toulouse during the 1950s. Chapter 4 examines the struggle to institute the imperial suburban designs for "Toulouse of tomorrow" during the 1960s. The modernization of the Toulouse economy (industrialization, mass production, and technological innovation) was painted as a benevolent and progressive cure for a backward and archaic cultural environment. Two chapters, as well, are devoted to the repercussions of these economic projects. Chapter 5 looks at the fortunes of Toulouse's business community within the context of reconstruction and the "French economic miracle" of the 1950s. Aviation played such a distinguished role in Toulouse's public culture and its modern economy that it clearly deserved special attention. Chapter 6 examines the city's aircraft as the penultimate vision of modernism, urban power, and technocratic control. Chapter 7 then continues with the revamping of the city's economic culture and its "downtown" through the august modernization programs of the 1960s and early 1970s.

In the hands of state regulatory agencies, then, modern aesthetic design and economic remodeling were the creative forms for the normalization and control of the dangerous, creature-like flow of urbanization that threatened to tear apart the French social fabric. In this sense modernization was more than just a matter of reshuffling the built environment. It was about social engineering and social power. Even the idea of the city, as an object and as a concept, can simply be seen as the spatial and symbolic canvas used to depict the advent of new social classes, new forms of consumer culture, new networks of economic and political authority. For Marxist theoretician Henri Lefebvre, urbanization was the summative metaphor for the spatialization of modernity and the strategic planning of everyday life that allowed state capitalism to survive and reproduce its vital relations of production.[6] The modernist landscape was clearly a social order and a strategy for political power imposed upon the city. The modernization of Toulouse became a subterranean celebration of bureaucratic power and rationality, both in terms of aesthetic design and material production. It was a mechanism for forging a new French identity around modern middle-class elites, their tastes, and their values. The city was filled with the metaphorical allusions, the symbols and representations that the modernist paradigm was always so preoccupied with generating. They revealed its subtext of social and political appropriation. At Toulouse the planned community of Le Mirail, the glitzy Place Occitan, the Caravelle and Concorde aircraft were all so blatant in their symbolism that they effectively revealed the contours of modern power relations hidden just beneath the surface of "urban planning and economic development." They were essentially transparent similes of modernist discourse. The abundance and obstreperous flavor of these symbols disclosed the intensity of the struggle for sociopolitical mastery at Toulouse and the necessity of blanket-bombing a vigorous historic paradigm that had some pretty potent symbols of its own. A whole variety of social and mental constructions—modernist, traditional, revisionist, and composite—were projected onto the historical record, the economic culture, and the landscape of Toulouse in an attempt to influence the phenomenon of urbanity. It was indeed contested terrain.

The reality was that modernism was not applied to a clean slate, no matter what the modernist discourse would have us believe about its power to jettison the past and install a rational and technical model in its place.

Rather it was bestowed upon an existing and well-ingrained urban environment with its own sense of habitability and culture. The local conflicts over
and adjustments to the prescription of this kind of modernist medicine were
particularly acute in the southwest because it had lagged far behind the rest
of France. The region was definitively on the country's geographic periphery. The process of constructing a modern city and a modern economy
necessitated a rupture with the city's older urban community solidarities—
the shopkeeper and artisan world of old red-brick Toulouse. Modernizing
claims to radical difference and innovation tended to simplify the terms of
the debate about French identity and to ignore as invalid and unprogressive
the historically articulated ensemble of city life. The neighborhood networks of Toulouse and their sense of political economy, the city's historic
architecture, the kaleidoscopic ambience of its street life were pronounced
"inefficient and unprofitable," "backward," "derelict," and unsuitable for
the future. The craftsmen, storekeepers, and workers of Toulouse were holding back the regeneration of France. They had to be rehabilitated as modern,
profitable producers capable of competing in a universe based on efficiency
and innovation, mass consumption, and modern market dynamics. The
regulatory and administrative mechanisms for this social reordering and
political conquest were potent and visceral. The landscape of the city, its
community, and its spatiality were at times clearly defeated by the imperialism of state technocrats and corporate elites. There is perhaps no better
example of this hegemonic mastery than the fact that by 1971 the Socialist
dominion so closely identified with Toulouse's political tradition had fallen
to a moderately conservative municipal administration much more in keeping with the state's technocratic agenda.

Yet despite the crusade to intrude urban design models and to rationalize the urban landscape and economy—and the people of Toulouse—in
the image of modernity, there were obstacles. The restraints posed by local
culture, the vagaries of land speculation, the triumph of the automobile,
and a host of sociopolitical vernacular traditions militated against any revolutionary or wholesale intervention. The often hidden and contradictory
elements of the city's historic culture were not necessarily easy for the
avatars of modernism to administer. Instead the various tentacles of modernism were manipulated within a local context to produce a cityscape with
its own inherent logic and which did not necessarily conform to anyone's
standards. The vernacular, historic sense of the city persisted and adapted to
the circumstance of modernism. The local community of Toulouse inter-
jected its own colloquial principles, its own perception of modernization,

into the debate about the future. These local versions of modernization were built on the identities and images that emerged from perceptions of urban place. They were defined by the structures of local experience in the Second World War, the Liberation, and Reconstruction. In this regard, Kenneth Frampton has stressed the crucial difference between a sentimental localism or regionalism absorbed with some simple-minded understanding of a lost history and literature (often sterilized of any political agenda) and a critical regionalism with elements derived indirectly from the peculiarities of a particular place. Traditional culture, he argues, was tied to a sense of place or places that have and are understood through complex sets of associations. It is a level of critical self-consciousness that derives its inspiration from such things as the quality of the local light, the color of the cityscape, or the character of the local topography. It is this strategy of critical regionalism that can mediate the impact of universal culture and modernization and deflect the sharp overtones of conquest, domination, and internal colonialism.[7]

In the case of Toulouse, this kind of critical local aesthetic, overtly political in tone, acted as a foil to the modernist agenda of the French state and opened at least a faint but authentic dialogue about the meaning of modernization itself. The vernacular is visible in the city's color, its indigenous brick, which was an especially expressive and symbolic allusion to the collectivity and community of historic Toulouse. But there were others: the monasteries and churches with their grand spires, the city's squares with their cafes, the Grand Balcon hotel that had been home to the heroes of French aviation, the local markets and street dances that had been a part of the city's historic neighborhood culture. Their evocation found resonance in the political contentiousness and resistance to positivist planning and the technocratic model of the well-oiled and well-controlled city. This local critical perspective embraced its own version of modernization and what it implied socially and culturally for Toulouse.

Indeed, the conceptions of what constituted modernization were derived from a variety of sources within France, both on the left and the right of the political spectrum, from the historic local outlook as well as from the state and from Paris. The outcome was that modernization as it was actually applied in practice was a bumptious process that was often ironic and illegible. It was filled with discontinuities and contradictions. The process was a matter of imposition, resistance, and reappropriation that revealed the tensions between the changing character of local community and state power. The modernist urban image and the modern city were created from the battles, debates, special interests, and compromises carried on by a variety of participants in the struggle to define the future. They opened a whole range of alternatives, a plurality of modernist perceptions and options. Like Kublai Khan in Italo Calvino's *Invisible Cities,* we discover that the fantastic urban visions woven by state technocrats, by local politicians, by small shopkeepers, by aircraft engineers—each in their turn—are all really the same place.[8]

In this sense, the city of Toulouse, as well as the region around it, were both simply discursive concepts between different systems of political and ideological power. The technocratic modernization model that usually emanated from Paris deliberately molded the process of spatial and socioeconomic development at Toulouse. But local Toulouse culture was also capable of influencing the shape and character of the state planning and urban modernization schemes imposed upon it. It is precisely this contentious dialogue over the representation and construction of the modern provincial city, the images of landscape, economics, and sociospatial ordering that were produced from it, that this book attempts to analyze. They are worth examination because they give such sharp material form to the social and political conflicts that shaped contemporary France.

Reflecting on Toulouse, Fernand Braudel bracketed it with Paris as the centers of gravity for the two great sedimentary basins of France, the Aquitaine and the Paris basins, and for the two Frances, the *oïl* and the *oc.* Braudel posed the question that "if history had run in its favor, its language, like that of the Ile-de-France, might have conquered great areas, beyond the Rhône as well as toward the Atlantic. Was Toulouse a Paris that did not succeed? And is it today having its revenge, with its industry and the 600,000 inhabitants of the conurbation?"[9] From the vantage point of its recent success, Toulouse does seem to have arrived unexpectedly from the periphery of French history to recover its birthright as the alternative to Paris, this time as the vision of technopolis. The conjecture suddenly complicates the more usual and tamer image of Toulouse as completely dependent on Paris, conquered yet again by the north, this time by armies of bureaucrats carrying out Parisian regional development programs—the enigma of Toulouse, once again. In any case, the French are fascinated with the phenomenon of Toulouse precisely because it seems to have undergone the kind of alchemy that yielded modernity out of a traditional culture and setting—the kind of transformation that lay at the heart of the cultural and social paradoxes intrinsic to French society.

CHAPTER 1

Red Flower of Summer:
Toulouse before 1945

The City Half as Old as Time

There are two good ways to travel to Toulouse, at least from a historical perspective. The first is to come up from the south, by the ancient route de Narbonne, or National Highway 113 in modern nomenclature. It takes you from the Mediterranean Sea through Languedoc and opens onto the green plains of the Garonne River Valley. This was the route originally followed by the Tectosages, a nomadic band of Celtic tribesmen. Sometime in the third century B.C., they settled along a wide curve in the Garonne River at one of the few places where the water's span could easily be crossed. The steep right bank protected their village from flooding. It was enclosed to the south by the slopes of the Peche David hills and to the east by the buttes of Calvinet along the Lauragais plateau. It was in this protected spot along the river's edge that Tectosage raiders hid the Greek treasure they had stolen from the Temple of Apollo at Delphi (according to legend) at what would eventually become the *Capitole de Toulouse*.

The same "route from Narbonne" was followed by Roman legions who conquered the Tectosage settlement in 121 B.C. in the military campaign to link Spain and Italy. The village, romanized as Tolosate, was established as a garrison town in the Roman frontier province of Narbonnaise. The Romans recognized the possibilities for the primitive frontier hamlet immediately. Centrally located in the Aquitaine basin that dominated southern Gaul, Tolosate became the main transportation and communication hub in the Roman attempt to domesticate its new province. The Romans constructed the Cardo Maximus that extended the route de Narbonne through the town to the Temple of the Capitole. From there, the Garonne River curved through northern Aquitaine and opened into the Atlantic

Ocean. But even more propitious was the artery just south of the settlement where the Garonne and Ariège Rivers fused to form the main route to the passes over the Pyrenees Mountains into Spain. Under Roman command, the town's commerce flourished. Wagons and mules laden with goods crossed the Pyrenees into Spain and trundled down the route de Narbonne toward the Mediterranean and toward Rome. Under Roman tutelage Tolosate became known for its schooling in rhetoric, Greek, and Latin. The poet Martial dubbed it "the city of Pallas," the Roman goddess of wisdom, or "Toulouse, La Palladienne."[1]

Route 113, then, was Toulouse's lifeline to the world of the Mediterranean, whose culture and language, politics and commerce would dominate the city's history. Toulouse faced south. It was a city of the south. Urban identity was forged from this directional heading. Even after it was conquered by the Visigoths in the fifth century, its Roman heritage and Latin culture remained central to its sense of urbanity. By the Middle Ages, this Mediterranean influence had metamorphosed into the distinctive southern civilization of Occitania, known, according to historian Emmanuel LeRoy Ladurie, for its Latinity, a penchant for heresy, and its peripheral marginality.[2] Under the patronage of the ruling houses of Aquitaine, Aragon, and Toulouse-Rouergue, the Midi produced a brilliant flowering of the *langue d'oc* in literature and the songs of the troubadours and some of the finest examples of Romanesque art and architecture. Toulouse lay at the heart of this Occitan dominion. It controlled the eastern Aquitaine basin and waged a fierce struggle for control of the Midi with the Duchy of Aquitaine west of the Garonne and the state of Catalonia to the south. It was in this central Occitanian belt that spread from the Garonne to the Rhône Rivers, controlled by the Counts of Toulouse and of Foix, that the traces of an independent nation began to appear in the twelfth and thirteenth centuries. As its capital, Toulouse had every possibility of challenging Paris for control over the birth of France.

Supported by its Mediterranean trade and its command of the routes into the southwest and Spain, Toulouse's commercial and business quarter, the Cité, flourished. It was filled with throngs of artisans and merchants plying their wares within the chaotic confines of the old Roman wall. The Cardo Maximus was the Cité's trade hub and the craft quarters fanned out around it like worker bees to a queen. Each street bore the name of its art—spinner's street, winder's street, cutler's and weaver's street. As the city's population swelled, the neighborhoods spilled outside the ancient barrier and across the Garonne, where newly arrived peasants and artisans braved the annual flooding to settle the Saint-Cyprien district on the left bank of the river. The city's wealth and prestige were enhanced by its function as a pilgrimage station on the route to the shrine of Santiago de Compostella in Spain. The city's religious life was dominated by its ecclesiastical quarter, the Bourg, that emerged just north of the Cité. There the city's nobility and wealthy bourgeoisie built their residences around the powerful Abbey of Saint-Sernin. The Abbey's magnificent Romanesque basilica, crowned with its octagonal steeple, towered over the city, proclaiming the power and influence of Toulouse as capital of the lands of Oc. The Counts of Toulouse even founded an *état colonial d'oc* at Tripoli in North Africa from the overseas conquests of Raymond IV during the First Crusade.[3] By the twelfth century, the citizens of Toulouse had wrestled free of the Counts and declared the city an independent republic that controlled an extended *patria tolosana*. It was one of the most powerful political and economic realms in the Midi.

But the vagaries of historical hubris fell heavily on Toulouse. Its wealth and independent destiny were thwarted by its own religious proclivities. The city was the center for the most notorious heresy of the Middle Ages, Catharism or Albigensianism. The Bourg was teeming with heretics who fought the Orthodox of the Cité in the streets in what amounted to a civil war. It was an open invitation for intervention by the Church and the French kings in the Albigensian Crusade. More than a sanctified purge of the Cathar rebels, the Crusade was an opportunity to establish French hegemony over the rival County of Toulouse and over the entire fabric of southern Occitan society. Between 1211 and 1219, Toulouse underwent three bloody sieges led by Simon de Montfort and was finally forced to capitulate to the armies of Prince Louis of France. After six months' imprisonment in the Louvre in Paris and a humiliating confession on the steps of Notre Dame Cathedral, Raymond VII, the last Count of Toulouse, was forced to sign the Treaty of Meaux in 1229. Although he was allowed to maintain his authority over the city of Toulouse, most of the County of Toulouse was either taken by the Church or ceded to Louis IX of France. The city's ramparts were destroyed, its moat filled in, its citizens forced to swear an oath disavowing their rebellious, blasphemous deeds. It was a singular history, with all the features of romantic tragedy. Occitania vanished and the Midi was grafted onto the world of northern France. Toulouse became a minor provincial capital within the French king's domains.

The crisis of the thirteenth century has been called the "decisive turning point in the urban evolution of Toulouse."[4] From an independent Occitan capital and a core of resistance to the Church and to the French monarchy, Toulouse was transformed, over the course of this century, into an orthodox Catholic city and the center of royal influence in the Midi. Multiple monastic orders were sent to oversee the city's conversion to religious conventionality. Their cloisters and churches rose over the rooftops in the disputatious parishes: Saint-Etienne, La Daurade, Les Jacobins, des Carmes, des Augustins. Built of brick and peaked with majestic octagonal spires, they endowed the city with its stunning and distinctive skyline. The supreme religious watchdog, however, was the University of Toulouse. It was established in 1229 and turned the blasphemous Bourg into a Latin Quarter known for instruction in religion and law. If Toulouse had lost its independence, it at least gained some prestige as an orthodox religious seat. The main administrative and judicial arm of the French monarchy was the Parlement du Languedoc, which was granted to Toulouse in 1443

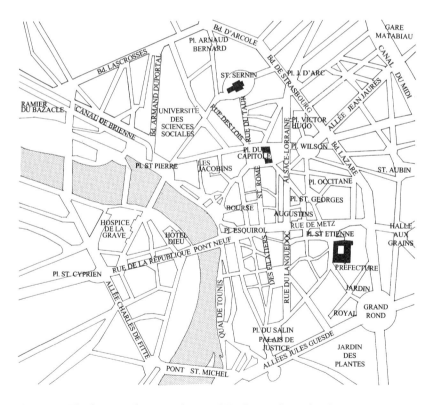

Figure 1. The historic districts of central Toulouse along the Garonne River.

with responsibility for molding the defiant Midi into the framework of the French state. It met in the south of the city, in the Château Narbonnaise.

But despite the French monarchy's efforts at indoctrinating the wayward Occitan capital, Toulouse remained oriented toward its Mediterranean roots. The city was governed by a unique municipal body called the Capitoul, created by the Counts of Toulouse and comprising twelve appointed neighborhood "consuls" whose decisions touched every aspect of city life. They assembled in the sumptuous pink marble, stone, and red brick Renaissance palace on the place du Capitole. The city's Mediterranean commerce (first in pastel, or woad, during the Renaissance and then in wheat during the seventeenth and eighteenth centuries) supported a wealthy merchant class ensconced in elegant mansions in the Dalbade quarter of the old Cité. The tree-lined Canal du Languedoc, constructed in 1681, followed the same time-honored course down the route de Narbonne to the Mediterranean and north along the Garonne to the Atlantic. The Capitoul laid out a Baroque ensemble of royal gardens and formal avenues for the new faubourg Saint-Etienne bordering the Canal. Saint-Etienne became a fashionable residential quarter for the cream of Toulousain high society. A vibrant culture emerged around the university, the city's various schools, and its Académie des Jeux Floraux.[5] Although French was used increasingly in public life under the Old Regime, everyday language remained Occitan. The city's religious ceremonies, its commerce and business continued to be carried out in the *langue du peuple*.[6]

Nowhere are the layers of the city's rich and contentious Occitan history and its southernness so apparent as in its visual imagery. Toulouse had the traditional appearance of a Mediterranean city. In many ways its atmosphere and vistas were more like those of an Italian or Spanish town along the Mediterranean coast than those of a typical French bourg. The quays along the Garonne and the place du Capitole were lined with red buildings with covered loggia. The city's Renaissance palaces and City Hall were massive brick structures, reminiscent of Florence, with Roman arches, defensive towers, and jutting roof lines. The open squares mirrored Latin agoras with bustling crowds and open-air markets. It was the intensity of the city's imagery, its complexion—the impression of Italy and the Mediterranean—that most struck travelers who came upon Toulouse. It was the vision that the venerable Larousse *Illustrated Geography of France*, for example, highlighted even in 1918: "'Roman' Toulouse its admirers call it . . . Midway between the Ocean and the Mediterranean, between the Massif Central and the Pyrenees, the city shines on this little world. Its unruly river evokes the

Tiber . . . the broad horizon of its plain is like a sister to the Roman country-side. And when, at the end of a brilliant day, the western sky turns crimson it is the glory of the Italian sun that one thinks of."[7] If nothing else, its color gave it an exotic, Mediterranean hue. The city has always been constructed with the same material, the red clay extracted from the Terrefort soil around it. The buildings were initially of timber and sun-dried adobe clay. After the great fire of 1463, Toulouse was rebuilt in wood-fired brick with tile roofing. But in any case, it has always been red. That is, except for the period from the 1780s to the 1840s, when most of the buildings were whitewashed in an attempt to emulate the nobler stone facades of Paris. The red brick of Toulouse was considered an embarrassing display of provincial poor taste by the capital's connoisseurs of urban design. The white coating was cleaned off beginning in the late nineteenth century to reveal again the rose-colored brick and red tile that composed such a striking urban setting within the lush green of the Garonne Valley.

That is why the second means of travel to Toulouse may be even more interesting and symbolic. Arriving by airplane, probably from Paris, a true devotee of *le pays toulousain* pays homage to the city's modern alter ego as "the land of flight" and the "cradle of French aviation." But from the exalted vantage point of the sky, the city's long history can also be spotted in the urban vistas. In the early years of the twentieth century, when the first planes flew over Toulouse, the skyline was still dominated by the elegant Occitan steeples of its monasteries and churches. From the sky, the turret towers of the Renaissance palaces were visible. The classical domes of the Hospice de la Grave and Saint-Pierre Church hovered over either side of the tortuous Garonne River, mastered finally by four graceful stone and iron bridges. The ornate pink and white facade of the Palais du Capitole with its *grande place* was discernible as the city's historic heart. The Canal du Midi, its black barges hidden below the trees, meandered down through Langue-doc. But, by plane, it would be the astounding color of Toulouse that would become so apparent—the pink, red, and maroon brick capped by red tile, the crimson and vermilion, the sanguine tints blending in various shades as the sunlight passed over the city. The aged *oustal toulousaine*[8] with their brick facades and wooden shutters could be seen squeezed along the sinuous streets and alleyways, the whole reddish composition densely hugging the river. This was the panorama that the native Toulousain identified with a sense of place. Toulouse was like no other French city. Its color and its Mediterranean style were metaphors for its distinctiveness, its special character. Toulouse was the jewel of old Languedoc. The vernacular red-brick landscape was converted into a social and cultural construction that identified a specific urban character and history. The city's visual demeanor was associated with a collective historic consciousness defined by the community's reputation for rebelliousness, its independent-mindedness, and especially its sociability.

But not everyone has been disarmed by the charms of Toulouse. There exists, in fact, a historic travel literature dedicated to condemning the city as a stain upon the silken fabric of the French landscape. In his not-short-enough stay in Toulouse in 1838, for example, Stendhal rained down indictments against the hapless town: "Toulouse is almost as ugly as Bourges . . . The Capitole is the ugliest building imaginable . . . It is hard to imagine anything uglier than the bridge over the Garonne . . . These loud, rather vulgar, people all pronounce the end syllables on their words . . ."[9] But then Stendhal was a man of the north, *la vrai France* as Michelet put it, and would have had trouble seeing any signs of civilization in such a far-removed

Figure 2. Place du Capitole.

outpost. Michelet himself described the people of Toulouse as simply not French, "more Spanish perhaps or Moor." Henry James found his visit to Toulouse in 1883 just as uncomfortable: "A big, brown-skinned population, clattering about in a flat, tortuous town, which produced nothing whatever that I can discover . . . the people are not so good . . . they have none of the personal richness of the sturdy Piedmontese." But even in his admonitions, James had referred to Italy when trying to capture the essence of the city: "I have not done with my Italian comparisons . . . in the way in which Toulouse looks out on the Garonne there was something that reminded me vaguely of the way in which Pisa looks out on the Arno."[10] On her motorcar tour of France in 1907, American Edith Wharton was no more impressed by the *pays toulousain* nor by the fierce *l'Auta* winds:

> A dull region at best, this department of the Haute Garonne grows positively forbidding when the mistral rakes it, whitening the vineyards and mulberry orchards, and bowing the shabby cypresses against a confused gray sky; nor is the landscape redeemed by the sprawling silhouette of Toulouse—a dingy wind-ridden city, stretched wide on the flat banks of the Garonne, and hiding its two precious buildings [Saint-Sernin and the Capitole] in a network of mean brick streets.[11]

It was a confusing puzzle of derogatory and cheerful impressions that aptly represented the paradoxical nature of what had become by the late nineteenth and early twentieth centuries a fairly unknown city in one of the farthest backwaters of France. Representations of the city's different historical experiences were placed in contradictory juxtapositions. Historical memory itself was perforated with antithetic, ironic images of community, space, and culture. The allusions to Toulouse's preeminent past were everywhere: the Capitole, Saint-Sernin Cathedral, the Assézat mansion, the Dalbade and Jacobin monasteries. Yet the undeniable dinginess of the place was hard to deny. The visualization of France into two geographic communities—north and south, *langue d'oc* and *langue d'oie*—was long-standing by the modern era. Toulouse represented the epitome of southern cultural and economic backwardness. It was "nowheres-ville,"[12] cut off from the north by the barrier of the Massif Central, reigning over a region that had become an economic and social cul-de-sac. Only the locals had any appreciation left at all for the archaism and hidden charms of Toulouse. As geographer Pierre Bonnaud has so aptly put it: "After having failed to assume a great destiny,

Figure 3. La ville rose. The brick and tile of old Toulouse.

Toulouse is like an old person forgotten in an obscure corner of the house, far from the principal rooms of family life."[13]

Toulouse in Decline

In looking for the roots of this grim turn of events, most historians have focused on the French and Industrial Revolutions (the dawn of the modern age) as the perpetrators of Toulouse's demise. This in itself is revealing. To a great extent modern history was associated with the city's decline and its loss of status within the hierarchy of French cities. This perception was pivotal in defining the local meaning of both tradition and modernization and the way each would shape urban identity. The administrative reforms of the French Revolution fatally undermined the city's special rank as a provincial capital by abolishing the province of Languedoc.[14] Toulouse became the simple administrative center for the new department of the Haute-Garonne, a vastly reduced portion of its historic realm. The Mediterranean and Atlantic commerce that had assured Toulouse's prosperity was paralyzed by the naval war between France and Britain and the commercial blockade. The Languedoc "wheat machine" never recovered, and Toulouse lost its extensive commercial network.[15]

But market deficiencies were not the only problem facing Toulouse and the southwest by the nineteenth century. The crop failures and depression of the period 1846 through 1851, which were particularly severe in wheat-growing regions such as Languedoc, provoked a massive rural exodus from the central Aquitaine basin. The richest part of the Toulouse plain, the Lauragais Valley, experienced the greatest depopulation. Then in the 1870s and 1880s, the Midi suffered a "great depression" in agriculture. Farm production stagnated. An atmosphere of lethargy and desertion spread throughout the region.[16] Between 1851 and 1935 the eight departments which today make up the Midi-Pyrénées lost 662,000 people to emigration, nearly one-fourth of its population. Those who stayed routinely moved to the central agricultural belt and to Toulouse for refuge. The city's population increased from 50,000 in 1800 to 150,000 in 1890[17] due entirely to this rural exodus.

Under these troubled conditions, industrialization remained a slow process. Traditionally the city had relied on its state-run factories as an economic foundation: the gunpowder factory and the Arsenal along the Garonne, the cannon foundry in the convent of Clarisses du Salin, and the tobacco processing plant in the old Benedictine convent of La Daurade.

These were the only industries that had profited from the economic disruptions of the early nineteenth century. The inauguration of the Compagnie des Chemins de Fer du Midi, with Toulouse as the hub for nine lines,[18] resulted in a spurt of activity after 1870. A footwear industry was launched; by 1910 it employed 7,000 workers. Two large hosiery firms, Etcheparé and Saler-Puig, set up mechanized production in the city. About 400 workers at the Maison Amouroux built agricultural mowers.

But Toulouse had no real bourgeois industrial dynasties of any size or kind. The Duffour family, with its chemical and fertilizer plant, and the Sirven family, with its printing works, were the only two cases that could possibly qualify in that category. Toulouse was simply not a humming industrial center. Beyond these few large firms the vast majority of the city's businesses were artisan shops living off the local demand for food, clothing, and shelter. Textile, garment, and shoemaking shops, rope-making and leather works, furniture makers, tiny foundries, and construction yards were scattered through the narrow streets. The old medieval Bourse quarter west of the Cardo Maximus (the Grand rue) was the garment district, filled with shirt and dress, lace, and glove shops. Small metal and dye works, ironworks, and brickyards congregated in the Arnaud-Bernard and Minimes districts north of the city.

Regional commerce sustained the city's flagging economy and provided jobs for its growing population. The wholesale and retail markets in local produce and domestic goods prospered unceasingly during the late nineteenth and early twentieth centuries. Toulouse remained the commercial heart of the southwest. There are moments in reading the history and geography of Toulouse when the entire city seems like one immense commercial fair, an image resplendent in Occitan iconography.[19] It was one of the most arresting ingredients in the formation of vernacular urban identity. The mercantile heart of the city was still the ancient Cardo Maximus that connected the place du Capitole with the place des Carmes. Historically known as the Grand rue, and in modern times as the rue Saint-Rome, rue des Changes, and the rue des Filatiers, it was an incontestable shopping bazaar. Clothing, hosiery, boots, furniture, food delicacies and wines, jewelry, perfume, guns and hunting equipment filled the store windows along the sinuous cobblestone path perennially packed with shoppers and *flâneurs*. The Midi's goods were stored and distributed through the warehouse and wholesale districts around Saint-Cyprien and Matabiau railroad stations.

Toulouse was known for its seven great open-air markets, where buyers and vendors clogged the inner districts haggling over every variety of regional product, the merchants crying out their prices in *patois*. The most famous market was on the place du Capitole itself. Each morning tradesmen from around the countryside set up wagons, booths, and multicolored parasols in front of the pink municipal palace to sell a profusion of commodities. Shoppers could find fresh produce and wares at daily markets on the place des Carmes, place de Strasbourg, place Victor-Hugo, boulevard Arcole, place Saint-Cyprien, and the place Dupuy, all in the central city. Wholesale markets started at two in the morning, then retail markets at seven—each taking their turn at the stalls. Each year on the feast day of Jeudi-Saint peasants offered country porks and hams for sale around Saint-Sernin Cathedral. The garlic fair was held Saint Bartholomew's Day on the place du Salin. Produce markets and specialty shops sold the sausage made at Toulouse, the *foie gras* and *confit d'oie,* the apple pastry *à la toulousaine,* and a host of traditional breads and pastries. The cultural sanctity of this local labor-intensive production was such that Toulouse was historically known as the "city of violets," after the flower produced in the northern suburbs, made into candies and perfumes, and then sold in its stores. The Cité's sidewalks, particularly on the place Esquirol and the place du Capitole, were inhabited during the day by street hawkers selling escargot, herbs and vinegar, fritters, cards of wool, cooking pans and utensils, buckets, umbrellas, porcelain, and crystal from their green wooden kiosks and clapboard stalls.

To the east of the rue Saint-Rome were found the great department stores and elegant shops of the rue d'Alsace-Lorraine and rue du Languedoc that had been cut through the congested inner districts as part of the nineteenth-century Haussmann-style renovation of Toulouse. These urban public-works programs, including a municipal streetcar system, were the dividends from the city's growing commercial influence. The modern department stores along the new boulevards (the Maison Universelle, Printemps de Toulouse, and Le Capitole) made the city the luxury center for the Midi. East of the rue d'Alsace-Lorraine was the Saint-Georges district, the quintessence of traditional craft and commercial life in the Cité. South of the rue de Metz lay the garment and furniture shops, the groceries and boutiques of des Carmes. On the other side of the place du Capitole, the rue du Taur rambled into the old Latin quarter to Saint-Sernin Cathedral. There, book dealers and antiquarian shops predominated. Street hawkers sold antiques and second-hand furniture around the cathedral, where passage out to the commercial districts and markets along the exterior ring of boulevards was easy.

The city's traditional markets and fairs were also one of the main institutions for its historic sociability. In whatever epoch they happened to inhabit the city, the citizens of Toulouse were known for the vibrancy of the urban life they created in the streets, the cafés, the markets that were always crowded, day and night, with shoppers, strollers, throngs of people out communing amidst *la ville rose.* The city's visual composition was conceived as the setting for the animated gregariousness of indigenous public life. "The street is a salon," Robert Mesuret wrote in describing Toulouse.[20] The great traditional holidays such as Carnaval were urban festivals that swept up the entire city. Everyone took to the streets in vast parades and celebrations replete with costumes, regalia, and gifts. The regional fairs held twice each year along the allées Villeneuve (now the allée Jean-Jaurès) attracted enormous crowds. For a few days in May and November the avenue was filled with colorful fair booths, illuminated rides and attractions, and exotic articles for sale in a fiesta atmosphere. During the annual masked ball, or *veglioni,* along the allées Saint-Etienne, students paraded an assortment of vehicles decked with flowers. On Arbor Day, schoolchildren marched through Toulouse for the ceremonial tree planting at the park. By the late nineteenth century, the tiny commons around an old stone market had been transformed into the spacious place Esquirol at the juncture of the rue Saint-Rome and the rues d'Alsace-Lorraine and Metz. It was a mecca for the city's social vitality. Some of Toulouse's most fashionable cafes, stores, and theaters were located there. The popular *fin-de-siècle* bistros around the Place Lafayette (now the Place Wilson), the Café de la Comedie, the Grand Café Sion, and the Grand Café des Américains, were filled late into the night with music and dancing.

But it was the working-class artisan neighborhoods that most represented this historic Occitan sociability and the sentiment for popular public culture. By the turn of the century, some 3,000 artisan-proprietors and nearly 18,000 workers called Toulouse home. The local dress of the working classes was still recognizable up to the end of the nineteenth century by the men's traditional red or violet cap, called the *barratine,* common to all the Mediterranean regions. For women, a head scarf covered by a wide-brimmed straw hat, known as the *pailholo,* protected against the southern winds. Artisan neighborhoods such as des Carmes, Saint-Georges, Saint-Auban, and Matabiau fanned out from the medieval core. The *petit peuple* lived in the working-class district of Saint-Cyprien on the left bank of the Garonne that still suffered from periodic flooding or the Saint-Michel faubourg to the south of the central city. Each was a discrete rural village, practicing the tradition of *bonhomie cordiale et joviale* that wove the pattern of everyday routines. Their social life traditionally took place in the streets, in the cafes and markets of the neighborhood, and around the parish church. The men gathered to bowl. Families sat outside their doors, cooking on open braziers in the Occitan tradition, and chatted in the cafes. Neighborhood social cohesion was especially manifested in music and singing

Figure 4. A troubadour on the boulevards of Toulouse, 1954.

and, above all, in *les baloches,* the traditional open-air neighborhood dances. Everyone belonged to a neighborhood choir or singing group that strolled through the streets singing popular romantic serenades in the Italian *bel canto* style or medieval ballads in Languedocean. Every neighborhood held its own parades, street dances, and holiday festivals.

One explanation for the persistence of traditional regional culture and sociability was that the city's working classes were continually nourished by the rural migrants flowing into the city during the nineteenth century. Dispossessed peasants and rural craftsmen brought with them customary Midi habits and language, found jobs in the handicraft shops, or opened their own small *ateliers*. The vast majority of this fluid tumult were dependent on the skill and solidarity of their family units and their own workrooms for survival. But the Toulouse economy was barely able to sustain their numbers. Clearly Toulouse was the commercial capital of the southwest. But commerce in regional goods and luxury items alone was not enough to turn the economic tide. The fact remained that the city had lost its economic dynamism over the course of the nineteenth century. The marginality of the city's location became painfully clear as industrialization shifted the gravitational center of the nation's economy toward the northeast. Toulouse and the entire southwest became isolated and increasingly dependent on local agricultural production. By the turn of the century, privation had become as much a part of Occitan heritage as singing and affability. The standard of living at Toulouse and in the Haut-Languedoc did indeed increase in the second half of the century, for artisans and shopkeepers as well as for workers and hired help. Nevertheless, the *haute bourgeoisie* at Toulouse, mainly merchants and bankers, landowners, magistrates, and members of the legal profession, owned an overwhelming portion of the city's wealth while half the population was close to indigence.[21] Poverty was the norm.

It was precisely at this low point in the city's economic fortunes that the historic pattern of Midi popular culture was becoming vulnerable to the encroaching linguistic and cultural uniformity of modern France. The result was a crisis of identity that is best evidenced in the abatement of the *langue d'oc* and the dwindling participation in local holidays and festivals by the final years of the century. The Toulouse region actually underwent this *déracinement culturel* at a slower pace than the cities of the eastern Languedoc region. Occitan patois continued to be the language of everyday use among the city's working classes despite the fact that French was associated with social mobility and was incrementally replacing native speech. Nevertheless, it is clear that the older cultural traditions associated with the city's life were beginning to expire. After 1890 the population of Toulouse began to stagnate and age as well. By the early years of the twentieth century the city had taken on all the characteristics of an oversized village. Its commercial and artisan shops lined the city streets, its markets opened daily, providing goods and services to the inhabitants of the once powerful *patria tolosana*. Toulouse had become above all else a Languedoc market town in what had become a depressing "outland" of France.

The political reaction to this cultural disintegration and economic decline was strikes, riots, and a turn toward Radicalism and Socialism.[22] Toulouse became *la ville rouge*. The visual spectacle of its red buildings metamorphosed into a representation of the city's leftist political predilections. But as a "red" center for political resistance it remained something of an anomaly—a revolutionary stronghold in what was still the "white" rural countryside of upper Languedoc. More than anything, it was the turn toward both political extremes that most marked the reaction to deprivation and cultural breakdown. The *Midi blanc* and the *Midi rouge* existed side by side. In the midst of a Catholic, rightist ocean, the city became a welcoming island for the new political parties of the left. Under the Second Empire, it was the stronghold of the militant Republican Party and for Radical-Socialism in the Midi. The city was littered with anticlerical Republican journals and newspapers, the most important of which was the daily *La Dépêche*, founded by the Republican Association of the Haute-Garonne in 1870.[23] The Radical Party, at the extreme left of the political spectrum in the 1890s, took over management of *La Dépêche* and used it as the mainspring for their political control of the Toulouse region until 1906. Then, under the influence of Socialist pioneers Jules Guesde and Jean Jaurès (who was a member of the Faculty of Letters at the University of Toulouse and one of the city's municipal councillors), Toulouse began moving further to the left. With the help of the city's nascent Socialist leadership, workers organized themselves into trade unions and cooperative associations.[24] In 1906, Socialist Albert Bedouce was elected the city's mayor. Vincent Auriol's newspaper *Le Midi Socialiste*, founded during the Section française de l'Internationale ouvrière (SFIO) Congress held at Toulouse in 1908, served as the backbone of the new movement. By 1912 the Socialist Party, led by Bedouce, Auriol, Etienne Billières, and Gabriel Ellen-Prévot, captured the majority of the city's municipal offices and its representatives to the French National Assembly in Paris. The Socialists continued their leftist duel with the Radicals for control of Toulouse from 1908 until 1925, when the SFIO gained stable control.

This Radical-Socialist contest was intensified by the experience of the

First World War, largely because the dividing line between them was over allegiance to the great patriotic cause or to pacifism. The Socialists' position was perhaps made more resolute by the fact that the Midi sacrificed, along with the Bretons, a larger proportion of its young men than any other region of France. Nearly 18 percent of those mobilized at Toulouse lost their lives, some 46,000 soldiers. Still, the general population of the city remained patriotic, at least until 1917. Toulouse's distance from the front made it a secure haven for French arms production. The city's old gunpowder and cartridge factories geared up for the war effort, employing thousands of women, rural migrants, and North African, Spanish, and Vietnamese immigrants in the manufacture of ammunition destined for the Western Front. The gunpowder factory alone employed 26,600 people, while another 15,000 worked at the Saint-Cyprien cartridge works. The city's clothing shops switched to making uniforms by mobilizing domicile work done by women throughout the Toulouse region. Refugees arrived from northeastern France. Among them was Pierre-Georges Latécoère, trying to reestablish his family's railroad-car business in the safety of Toulouse. In 1917 he won a government contract for 1,000 military reconnaissance planes to be manufactured at Montaudran just east of the city.

Despite the tragedy taking place in the northeast, the war had brought miraculous opportunities for work to normally impoverished Toulouse. Its isolation had momentarily become its strength. Nevertheless, the rising prices and growing scarcity of basic goods, as well as the mounting military failures, finally provoked a wave of strikes and protests in June 1917. Once wage raises were granted, the situation calmed. But as it did throughout France, the war ended in frustration and, despite the victory, seemed to accentuate the cleavages in Toulouse society.

The war had also clearly stimulated what had been a languishing economy. War production enhanced the local market in ready-made clothes and footwear, machinery and tools, and processed food. Even after the war, once the reconversion of industry was accomplished, the Toulouse economy seemed to maintain its momentum, due largely to its isolated, and therefore secure, geographic locale. The armaments plant continued supplying munitions to the French army. The menace of renewed hostilities convinced the French government to move its new nitric acid fertilizer industry, won from Germany in the Treaty of Versailles, to Toulouse. In 1924 the Office National Industriel d'Azote (ONIA) was installed in part of the old gunpowder factory on the Ile de Ramier. Some of the country's early aircraft manufacturers followed Latécoère down to Toulouse and built the beginnings of the city's aircraft industry. Toulouse became known, in its modern incarnation, as the "city of Isaure," the Greek god of flight. The success of their airplanes brought the hope of the city's heroic renewal and continued economic prosperity. Latécoère himself began experimentation with commercial aircraft and launched the Compagnie Générale Aéropostale. Aéropostale inaugurated the era of breathtaking Mediterranean and trans-Atlantic test flights by the pilots of *la ligne*—Jean Mermoz, Robert Guillaumet, Antoine de Saint-Exupéry. They began their heroic missions from the dirt runways at Montaudran Airport and flew out over Toulouse to Dakar and Casablanca, Buenos Aires, and Santiago, Chile. The city boasted two airports by the mid-1930s, and it had begun work on a new facility at Blagnac to the northeast. The city's older factories (the Maison Amouroux, Société JOB, the Maison BEC, Saler-Puig, and Etcheparé) built modern new plants and expanded their production.

All of this new demand was a byproduct of Toulouse's growing population. It had first been boosted by workers streaming into the city looking for work during the war. By 1921, 175,000 people lived in Toulouse, and their numbers multiplied to 213,000 by 1936. The city's economic support of the Great War, its role as a haven for refugees and as a budding aircraft center, as well as its new inhabitants, all served to end the stifling cultural and social isolation that had kept Toulouse and Languedoc separate from the rest of France. By the early 1920s nearly everyone at Toulouse spoke French, a *français toulousain* that pronounced all letters of a word, including the silent *e*, and sounded like a local twang, or *ong*, to northerners. Most considered themselves French in mentality and outlook. Occitan was rarely spoken in the central city and was even disappearing in the faubourgs. It was only in the artisan and working-class districts that it could still be heard as everyday language. On the left bank of the Garonne, in Saint-Cyprien and beyond, Gascon was still the familiar form. Farther out in farming areas, like Saint-Martin-du-Touch, Montaudran, and Lalande, that were being turned into suburbs, local dialects prevailed although they spoke the "city language."

The other great envoys of modern culture in the interwar years also succeeded in breaking down the cultural isolation of the old Occitan capital. National chain stores like Monoprix, Printafix, Galerie Lafayette, and Bon Marché took up residence along the rue d'Alsace-Lorraine. In 1925, Radio-Toulouse, or TSF, began regular broadcasting from the Schmidt Villa in the suburb of Balma, and its daily programs could be heard virtually everywhere in the city. Sixteen movie theaters operated in Toulouse by the mid-1920s. Among the most luxurious were the Royal, the Olympia, and the Apollo in the new theater district along the boulevard de Strasbourg. Latin dancing, especially the tango, became the rage in the city's cafes and dance halls. Jazz music, the shimmy, and the Charleston were offered at the Kid Cat Club; L'Oasis Dancing on the second floor of the Café de la Paix; and the Fantasio Dancing on the place Arnaud-Bernard.[25] Automobiles streaked through the city's sinuous streets, threatening the horse-drawn hippo mobiles with their blue umbrellas, the wagons, and produce carts. Rugby became the city's obsession. The Stade Toulousain dominated the French national championships between 1912 and 1924, and local rugby matches drew thousands of devoted fans. But as the most compelling sign of modern times, the public was mesmerized by the aerial exploits of the Aéropostale pilots. Bréguet and Latécoère aircraft were tested regularly on the Garonne River and in the skies over Toulouse. Barnstorming pilots traveling the French air show circuit thrilled thousands assembled at the airports and in the city streets to watch "the masters of the air."

Toulouse's leftist political proclivities were also reaching their maturity during the 1920s and 1930s. Radicalism and its standard bearers, Maurice and Albert Sarraut, who controlled *La Dépêche,* continued to exert formidable influence throughout the region and over the Third Republic. But by the mid-1920s, the Socialist Party had achieved extraordinary success in the *pays toulousain.* The Party offered an agenda of internationalism, social democracy, and economic reform on behalf of the working classes. It was a cogent program when offered by the Midi Socialist luminaries who lit the French political landscape in the interwar years. In the 1930s Paul Boncour was elected to the Chamber of Deputies from the Tarn, Hubert Rouger from the Gard, Edouard Barthe from the Hérault, Léon Blum from Narbonne, and Vincent Auriol, Albert Bedouce, and Jean Rieux from Toulouse. In the crucial elections of 1936 more Toulousains went to the polls than at any time in the city's history. With 80 percent participation in local elections, Toulouse registered the Socialist Party's greatest victory for the Popular Front. The delegation from the Haute-Garonne to the Chamber of Deputies included six Socialists, two of whom, Auriol and Bedouce, became members of Blum's government.[26] The city's administration, led by Socialist mayors Etienne Billières and Gabriel Ellen-Prévot, also pioneered some of the most successful early efforts at municipal and social reform amidst the growing political turmoil that subsumed France.

In 1934, local author Louis Gratias tried to capture the essence of Toulouse and what it represented as a city. "At Toulouse," he recounted,

> the richness of coloring blends into beautiful days of a mezzotint hue . . . Toulouse, red flower of summer—the city of golden sun and

song, of violets and lazy days, where the cicadas sing night and day
. . . new forces animate your life. They are found in the antennas of
TSF, the planes taking off from their hangars, the artists and writers
intent on new forms. There is a new atmosphere in the *cité palladienne*—it is a place where one works. There is an immense spirit here
that cannot be stopped.[27]

Whatever that "immense spirit" might have represented (and for
many it represented the winds of Socialist reform), life at Toulouse was, by
the 1930s, a crazy-quilt mélange of traditional and modern. In this sense it
mirrored the abrupt changes that took place throughout historic, provincial
France during the interwar years. Urban identity had been forged from
centuries of local existence. Yet the influence of modernization was already
dramatically transforming culture and society in the cities. A multitude of
interest groups and political factions both on the left and the right took up
the growing debate over the merits and flaws of this rapid "modernization."
It was one of the most politically charged disputes within the context of the
intense social conflicts and the depression increasingly dividing the country
by the end of the 1930s. The process of modernization, and the controversy
surrounding it, was then abruptly sifted through the sieve of the Second
World War, Vichy, and the Liberation, where it would take on an even more
intense complexion.

The Second World War

The experience of the Second World War was, for Toulouse, a watershed in
shaping local consciousness and identity. Collective memory, the meaning
of place and community, were all imbued with the passions and events of
the cataclysm. The war's enduring significance was based not only on the
catastrophe it represented for France but on the particularity of the experience in the southwest. The entire history of Toulouse had shaped the city as
a distinct, maverick urban entity. The Second World War and the Liberation
are legible precisely from the same frame of reference. The molding of a
special, vernacular meaning to the war explains its fervent and long-lasting
influence—on the city and on the colloquial perception of modernization.
There are a number of advantages in recounting and interpreting the war as
part of the process of modernization and as a source for the perceptions and
meaning surrounding it. It dramatizes its tangled composition from within
the structures of local experience. It affirms that modernization, as a trans-

formative framework, was constituted not simply as the penultimate healing of France's wartime wounds (as in the discourse of state technocrats). The process and meaning behind the word itself was invented from within the embattled experience of the war, Vichy, and Liberation.

Initially, Toulouse's location in the southwestern corner of France shielded it somewhat from the political crises rumbling through Europe during the 1920s and 1930s. But as the shock waves of Fascism and political breakdown intensified, the repercussions were unavoidable. For many refugees throughout Europe, desperate to escape political repression, Toulouse appeared yet again as a safe haven, far from the insanity and peril engulfing their homelands. From the late 1920s, Italian exiles sought asylum at Toulouse from Mussolini's police snare. Nazi political persecution and its anti-Semitic campaigns after 1933 added German Jews and German leftist exiles. But by far the most devastated stream of castaways were Spanish Republicans fleeing Franco's reprisals after his victory in the Spanish Civil War. In 1939, thousands of Spanish refugees crossed into France after harrowing escapes through the Pyrenees Mountains. They reached Toulouse as their first sanctuary and, for many of the guerrilla units and leaders of the Popular Front, as a base to continue their struggle against Fascism. The city became the de facto capital of Republican Spain.[28] They were greeted with a mixture of sympathy and hostility. Socialists at Toulouse remained dedicated to the Republic's cause, but the Radicals had turned their support to Franco and the Fascist insurgents. Many of the exiles were interned at ghastly "Concentration Camps for Undesirable Aliens" set up at Le Vernet, Bram, and Septfonds in the foothills of the Pyrenees Mountains. It is estimated that about 100,000 Spanish refugees passed through Toulouse, swelling the stream of desperate strangers hunting for food and shelter in the city. The amplitude of the refugee problem dwarfed local concern about Germany's ultimatum over the Sudetenland and the signing of the Munich Agreement. On the eve of war, Toulouse was focused south on Spain and the massive problems of harboring Spanish political refugees.

The declaration of war in September 1939 did not initially affect Toulouse in any dramatic way, except to amplify the refugee problem yet again. It was mainly a question, during "the phony war," of preparing France's military crusade. The city's cartridge and gunpowder factories, the ONIA fertilizer facility, and especially its aircraft plants geared up for war production. Aircraft workers and technicians from Paris were dispatched to the Toulouse factories. The boom in aircraft and munitions production and the crises of finding, training, and housing over 20,000 armaments workers added to the growing variety of evacuees. But Toulouse remained, if any-thing, indifferent to the distant threat of war. Only a small number of men were actually called up for military service, since the workers in the aircraft and armaments industries were all classified as *affectés spéciaux,* or mobilized workers under military authority. Other than the evening blackouts and the disruption of the regional grape harvest, there was little evidence of hostilities.

The invasion of France on May 10, 1940, came as a rude shock. The panic over the advancing German army was heightened by apprehension over the human waves heading for the safety of southern France. As the Ger-mans attacked west, the Belgian government had evacuated 40,000 army reservists to southern France, many of whom came under the jurisdiction of the Toulouse military region. They were followed by thousands of Belgian refugees. Far more ominous, however, was the panic in France as the Ger-man war machine swept toward Paris. In mid-May, millions of refugees fled south to escape the German assault. France was reduced to pandemonium as cars, wagons, and panic-stricken people jammed the roads, chased by German bombardments and breakthroughs. At Toulouse trains pulled into Matabiau Station day and night, filled with thousands of women, children, and the elderly. Troop trains and truck convoys arrived. Swarms of cars loaded with refugees jammed the roads into the city. In the space of three weeks, some 300,000 to 400,000 people had been evacuated to Toulouse. The historian Philippe Wolff was one of them, and his description of the city is a grim portrayal of men and women confronted with the realities of invasion:

> Masses of cars of all types, from Holland, Belgium, and the north of France, streaked through the streets provoking gigantic traffic jams. The sidewalks were black with people, many of them sleeping on the pavement for lack of shelter. The walls of the Capitole were covered with names and addresses—those of refugees looking for someone.[29]

The insurmountable problems of housing and feeding the withdrawn troops, the evacuees, and the refugees became the essential preoccupation of the municipal authorities, masking even the military situation in France. Thousands arriving at the railroad station were sent through a processing center set up at the nearby Veterinary School, where they were assigned lodging in the city or in neighboring villages. Within the first week of the exodus, every available space in Toulouse was filled. Vacant apartments, auditoriums, movie theaters, schools, and the city's sports park were all commandeered by the authorities as temporary lodging. Mayor Ellen-Prévot made a public appeal for residents to take in some of the thousands of homeless families. Soup kitchens were set up on the sidewalks and emergency hospitals organized. Food disappeared as hoarders and the desperate population cleaned out the markets and stores. In the last week of May, curfew hours were established, the refugees were restricted to their neighborhood of residence, and the mayor's office began publishing warnings against price hikes. But the widespread confusion and scarcity of food further terrified a population already traumatized by defeat.

The announcement of the June 17 armistice was greeted mainly with relief. It was the end of a horrible nightmare. The painful specter of bewildered refugee families searching the city for housing began to evaporate, and routine life was restored. When on July 10 the National Assembly at Vichy abolished the Third Republic and announced the advent of the "new, audacious, authoritative" French State, the deputies from the Haute-Garonne voted unanimously against the measure. But Mayor Ellen-Prévot and the Toulouse municipal government voted their support for Pétain in the hopes of maintaining order and security. The city's leading Socialists followed the mayor's lead and surrendered as well to the Vichy arrangement.

For nearly two years there was little overt opposition to Vichy at Toulouse. The population and the city's administration remained essentially compliant to Vichy policy and the "national revolution." Gérard Cholvy, one of Languedoc's leading historians, suggests that this tacit acceptance can be explained by the enormous drama of invasion and the profound shock of the French defeat.[30] Toulouse experienced this upheaval as waves of humanity pouring into the normally isolated city and the confusion and disorder caused by their arrival. Relief from this chaos was foremost on the minds of the city's dazed and disoriented residents. But for many at Toulouse, Pétain was also a savior who offered both security and the opportunity to revitalize the prostrate nation. His visit to Toulouse in November 1940 was triumphant. Although *La Dépêche de Toulouse* had published excerpts from Charles de Gaulle's "call of June 18th," the paper and its powerful Radical benefactor Maurice Sarraut quickly rallied around Pétain. Throughout the Occupation *La Dépêche* remained a steadfast ally of the Marshal. The July 3, 1940, bombardment of the French air squadron at Mers El-Kébir by the British fleet also won over many Toulousains to the side of Vichy, as well as implicated de Gaulle as a traitor. The first condemnation for treason against de Gaulle and the Free French movement came on July 4 from the military tribunal at Toulouse.

Despite Mayor Ellen-Prévot's submission to Vichy authority, he and the city council were quickly ensnared in the purge against the political left and the backlash against the Third Republic. The *"république des camarades"* was to comprise suitable right-wing reactionaries willing to work under Vichy authority. In September 1940 the city was placed in the hands of the First World War veteran and prominent jurist André Haon, appointed mayor by the Conseil d'Etat at Vichy. In April 1941, seventeen provincial regions were created: six regions within the free zone and eleven regions within the occupied zone. The Toulouse municipality worked under its appointed regional prefect for Languedoc, Léon Cheneaux de Leyritz, flanked by regional intendants of police and economic affairs, all chosen by the Conseil d'Etat. Within the context of this new administrative network, the forces of Vichy totally controlled the city's public life. The Légion des Combattants organized parades at Toulouse. Posters, public oaths, and school pledges all glorified the Marshal as the savior of France. Regionalists at the Collège d'Occitanie and the "Association for the Renaissance of the Province of Toulouse" waxed eloquent on the spiritual and moral virtues of traditional Languedoc. Collaborationist organizations such as the *Parti Populaire Français* held conferences and expositions. As part of the new concern for "authentic regional life," the Jewish refugees hiding in the Toulouse area were rounded up and transferred, along with many of the Spanish exiles from the camps at d'Argelès and Vernet, to new internment camps at Récébédou, in the commune of Portet-sur-Garonne just south of Toulouse, and Noé, a "hospital-camp" built by Spanish refugees about twenty-five kilometers to the southwest. An American delegation toured the camps just after their opening in February 1941 and praised them as "remarkable testimony to the benefits of Pétain's rule." That did not prevent the prisoners from suffering the effects of tuberculosis, malnutrition, and starvation.[31]

The high hopes for Vichy's national revolution and provincial restoration did indeed ironically deviate from the somber reality of war. Under the thin veneer of public ceremonies and administrative rejuggling, both people and work at Toulouse suffered from the requisitioning, shortages, and food rationing that worsened with each year of conflict. The lack of resources—everything from hemp and cotton to lubricants and gasoline— threatened to completely shut down the city's industries. Complaints about the shortage of qualified workers were legion, as were concerns about absenteeism and low productivity. Requisitioning and food taxes appeared in the summer of 1940. Although Vichy attempted to systematize rationing of essential goods, the necessities of life simply evaporated. The Midi received fewer essential provisions than the west or central regions of France. Perennially poor, the population in the southwest could do little to sustain itself. At Toulouse, families managed to boost their rations by raiding the surrounding countryside and by resorting to the black market.

Public approval of Vichy began to dwindle in 1941 and 1942 with the worsening hunger and scarcity. Added to it, Vichy support for the German war effort provoked genuine hostility. Laval's return to power in April 1942 and his *"Relève"* calling Frenchmen to work in German war industries exposed the extent of collaboration and the fallacy of the regime's protection. Protests broke out at Toulouse and Montpellier. About 25,000 people packed the place du Capitole on July 14 and sang the "Marseillaise" despite police charges, fire hoses, and arrests. Vichy lost one of its most ardent supporters when the Archbishop of Toulouse, Monseigneur Jules-Géraud Salièges, rebuked the regime for the deportation of Jews to the death camps. The convoys of cattle cars departed from Récébédou and Noé beginning in August 1942. Despite pressure from Cheneaux de Leyritz to remain silent, Salièges released a pastoral letter condemning the deportations that was relayed throughout Languedoc and read over Radio London. Under the leadership of Raymond Naves, the city's Socialists began to clandestinely reorganize themselves, as did the small Communist Party. The key resistance organizations in the Toulouse region, *Combat, Libération,* and *Franc-Tireur* (FTPF) met in mid-1942 to negotiate merging their growing forces. But the blame for France's predicament could be placed in many directions. The Allied economic blockade was also condemned for food and fuel shortages. Even more troublesome were the Allied military campaigns that seemed to involve little but French losses. Hostility toward the British became more overt once serious Allied bombing of French sites began in 1942. Some 2,000 people demonstrated in Toulouse on June 16 against British bombing and "Communist terrorism,"[32] and once again Pétain was welcomed to the city with open arms.

The situation deteriorated sharply once German military forces directly occupied southern France in November 1942. The German First Army took up residence in the Toulouse region. Some 4,000 to 5,000 troops were billeted in the city. With them came the German Security Services, which set up headquarters in the Hôtel de l'Ours Blanc at Toulouse, and their Gestapo units, which were housed on the rue Maignac. For the rest of the Occupation the city's population suffered the terror and repression that were by-words for Gestapo rule: arrests and executions, deportation of Jews to the camps, raids on resistance organizations by French recruited into special SS units, confiscation of property, and suspension of all public activity. In 1943 the newly formed *Milice,* under the command of local landowner Frossard, began coercive operations against the uncooperative and recalcitrant. Their brazen raids and accusations against local authorities for insufficient diligence finally ended in the assassination of Maurice Sarraut in December 1943. All told, about 600 people were killed, 400 imprisoned, and 1,400 deported to concentration camps during the German occupation of the Haute-Garonne.[33]

At the same time, the Service du Travail obligatoire stepped up requisitioning of Frenchmen to work in German factories. The largest contingent from the Haute-Garonne, over 3,000 men, left in the spring of 1943. By the end of the war the Toulouse region had contributed 9,000 workers to the German war effort. The city's factories and warehouses also supplied armaments for the German military campaigns. The munitions factories, the ONIA plant, and above all the aircraft facilities all worked, either directly or indirectly, for the Germans. In 1943 the last French planes left the Toulouse factory for flight schools. From then on the celebrated Montaudran and Saint-Martin-du-Touch aeronautical centers made and repaired German Messerschmitts and Junkers.

It was the arrival of the Wehrmacht in 1942 and the dedication of Toulouse's aircraft industry to the German cause that provoked widespread fears of Allied retaliation. The British Air Force was bombing industrial and civilian sites in Germany by late 1942. The French factories at Le Creusot, Marseille, Bordeaux, and Lyon were, one by one, hit by Allied raids in early 1944. It was clear that Toulouse's turn was coming. The city underwent four attacks by the British Air Force in 1944. The bomber assaults, the German antiaircraft machine-gun fire, and the explosions and illumination from fires that broke out at every target created a lethal spectacle. The munitions depots and the Arsenal and gunpowder factory were bombed first and exploded into flames. The aircraft factories at Saint-Martin-du-Touch and Montaudran went up, while the airfields and runways at Francazal and Blagnac were demolished. At ONIA, storehouses filled with nitric acid were ignited by phosphorus bombs. Empalot Bridge, the railroad lines, and the main roads out of Toulouse were all cut by huge 2000-kilogram shells. German troops poured out of their barracks and set up mobile antiaircraft batteries in civilian neighborhoods and out along the roads surrounding the city. To screen their positions, they launched flares over unprotected districts that then became mistaken targets for British dive-bombing attacks. The neighborhoods of Empalot, Champ du Loup, Calvaire, Saint-Agne, Peche-David, and Braqueville suffered heavy damage and human loss. Close to 200 civilians were killed and countless wounded. More than 5,000 buildings were severely damaged or destroyed. The city's industrial base was ravaged.[34]

At the German Consulate and at Gestapo headquarters, archives and papers were quickly burned. The Allied landing at Normandy on June 6 and its invasion of Provence on August 15 spelled the end of the Nazi grip on France. With orders to retreat to the Rhine River, the Germans began to evacuate Toulouse along the route de Narbonne south through Languedoc. All available vehicles, even bicycles, were requisitioned and formed into convoys for the withdrawal. The pullout was accompanied by continued destruction intended to impair the Allied campaign. Remaining munitions, the city's general storehouses along the Canal du Midi, the telephone centers on the boulevard Riquet and place Saint-Aubin were all wrecked. Violent explosions rocked the main post office, where the Germans blew up the telegraph service. Threats to blow up all the bridges across the Garonne raised the fear of the complete destruction of the city.

The confusion of authority, the general panic, and pent-up hostility furnished the opportunity for spontaneous reprisals and pillaging.[35] The general storehouses and the city's slaughterhouses were quickly looted of any remaining meat, butter, and preserves. A crowd of several thousand carted off the food provisions in the German warehouse at Saint-Cyprien railroad station and burned the sheds. At Gestapo headquarters on the rue Maignac, crowds broke past the barbed wire and raided the offices and neighboring homes of the luxury items so coveted during the lean years of war. The hunt for "collabos" began as the Germans retreated. Shots rang out in the streets. Rumors and stories of gruesome discoveries and vengeance circulated everywhere. The atmosphere of panic, disorder, and retribution was intensified by the city's isolation. After the initial August 15 landings in Provence, American and French troops moved north and west, liberating Montpellier, Marseille, and the Rhône Valley. The southwest was left on its own. Toulouse was one of the largest cities to liberate itself without any assistance from the outside. With the transport and communication systems in ruins, it was completely cut off from the rest of France.

The southwest possessed a strong regional network of disorganized resistance movements (designated R4 for the Aquitaine region) that had struggled for some form of coordination during the difficult years of 1942 and 1943.[36] By 1944, the Comité Départemental de Libération de la Haute-Garonne (CDL), controlled in the main by the Socialist underground, was spreading its authority over the vast array of military, paramilitary, and political resistance organizations. In August its members pledged themselves to the Conseil National de la Résistance and to de Gaulle's strategy of national insurrection. In October 1943, de Gaulle had named twenty Commissars of the Republic and fifty departmental prefects. Jean Cassou, the head of the Mouvements Unis de Résistance in the free zone and the Comité Régional de la Résistance in Languedoc, was named Commissar for Toulouse. The local military forces of the Forces Françaises de l'Intérieur (FFI), led by Colonel Serge Ravanel, numbered around 44,000 on the eve of the Liberation.[37] The Communist underground had also established itself as a formidable power within the local resistance and could count on support from branch organizations such as the National Front and the FTPF,[38] from the Spanish guerrilla units who were particularly powerful in the Toulouse region, and sympathy from Ravanel and the FFI.

On August 14, Ravanel gave orders for the insurrection to begin. At the same time the Communist underground called for the citizens of Toulouse to launch a revolutionary general strike. Local FTPF units and the FFI attacked truck convoys awaiting evacuation at Matabiau railroad station, avenue des Minimes, place Arnaud-Bernard, at the Grand Rond, and at Saint-Cyprien.[39] The night of August 19, the FFI and FTPF brigades improvised barricades along the main roads into Toulouse and defended the city against the German columns passing through in their retreat from Languedoc. Some thirty-six Resistance volunteers died in the defense of the city. De Gaulle's commissar Jean Cassou was seriously wounded, and Lucien Cassagne, secretary of the clandestine Socialist Party, was killed in a German attack on Cassou's car near the boulevard de Strasbourg. Both would become Toulouse's martyrs of the Liberation. But in retrospect, the fighting was really minimal. Even Pierre Bertaux, perhaps the principal beneficiary of the "insurrection," argued that Toulouse was really liberated by the Germans, who simply left in the face of defeat.[40] By morning, they were gone. On Sunday morning, August 20, Bertaux, who replaced Cassou as the new Commissar de la République, took possession of the prefecture on the place Saint-Etienne while Raymond Badiou, head of the Comité de Libération de Toulouse and the city's new mayor, took over the Hôtel de Ville. Radio Toulouse was occupied and the "Voice of the Resistance" took to the air. Proclamations were posted on the streets: "THE ENEMY HAS ABANDONED

THE CITY—TOULOUSE IS FREE." The next day the first newspapers of the Liberation appeared, their front pages covered with the names of cities throughout France liberated by the Allies and the FFI. A crowd of 30,000 deliriously joyful, emotionally overwhelmed people appeared at the place du Capitole to greet their new leaders and to sing the "Marseillaise" "from the bottom of their souls."[41]

CHAPTER 2

Regionalism, Municipalism, and Modernization

The drama of the Second World War, the Vichy Regime, and the Liberation were a watershed in French historical consciousness. They divided the country along a series of social, political, and spatial axes that illuminated the deepest historical fissures tearing at French society.[1] A good case in point is the city of Toulouse itself. Its dubious reputation as "no-wheres-ville" was ripe with meaning during the war years. Toulouse was the farthest urban outpost from the Nazi threat, stuck out on Charlemagne's March, at the edge of the French frontier, an imperfect but reliable hiding place in a hideous occupation that left few choices. Once the Liberation began, the city was left to its own devices by both the Germans and the advancing Allied armies. It was too far removed from the mainstream of events to warrant any strategic defense or recapture. Indeed, Toulouse's modern history, including its experience with Vichy and the Liberation, has always been informed by the meaning and context of its regional geography and its spatial peripheralization. The city was linked inexorably with the region around it for its historic culture, for its identity, and for its viability. But exactly what constituted a "region" and what role the city played in it were open to impassioned controversy. Theories about regionalism and about urban functions abounded in France. Each was fiercely defended as the embodiment of truth. This chapter considers the historical experiences and urban processes that shaped Toulouse, both within the context of its immediate local setting and within the explicit political debates about the meaning of region, city, and geographic space in the quest for modern France.

As an object of debate, the idea of the region was invented and rein-vented by competing groups within French society over the course of the late nineteenth and twentieth centuries. Like the idea of the city, it was a discursive concept between diverse systems of social and political power. The weight of geography was so strong that the "region" was the ideological space in which many of the country's political and social battles were fought. Even a superficial examination of France brings to light the grounds for this exaggerated concern with the country's territorial realms. Plumbing the depths of French history meant descending into a vortex of pluralist cultures. Layers of ambiguously defined yet defensively "authentic" regional identities were what constituted the entity called France. There was, of course, the gross division between north and south. The lands of Oc in the south were carved into the provinces of Gascogne, Limousin, Auvergne, Languedoc, and Provence. Each was further partitioned into a myriad of indigenous local languages and societies framed by the geography around them. Cities like Toulouse practiced a nonconformist municipalism under which an array of autonomous neighborhood-villages thrived. Given the fractious divisions that peppered the landscape, the very constitution of the nation was bound up in the struggle to define and order geographic space. It was an effort to pin down, one way or the next, the meaning of both the *pays* and the nation. The Revolution of 1789 may have replaced the historic regional provinces with a rational system of departments controlled by prefects appointed at Paris, but the creation of agreed-upon democratic institutions and a national culture was a long and arduous task. The conceptualizations of the relationship between the nation, the region, and the city were thus a pivotal part of the broader debate about the construction of French identity and the future of France.

As a panoramic vision, modernization offered a resolution of this spatial dissonance. Indeed, the seductiveness of the modernist mission for France was that it offered a mechanism for national unity. It was a way to inscribe the vast array of ancient, pluralistic cultures with an agreed-upon national creed. If the manifold localist versions of Frenchness could be merged into the collective project of modern rejuvenation, then the nation's political and social wounds would be healed. Hence, theories about modernization inevitably revolved around notions of restructuring the national territory and about cities and regions. Progress seemed to imply a geographic refashioning, or reconstitution, of the provinces, as if solving the puzzle of particularisms was the alchemy that would revitalize France. This hand-and-glove relationship between progress and spatiality specifically differentiates the French approach to political economy and modernization from Anglo-American or German strategies.[2]

Even more, the images of progress and geography that came to encompass the notion of modernization were themselves girdled in the plural-ist confusion of French territory. The scramble for modernization, and the question of who would control it, embraced the full range of political and intellectual interests, on the right and on the left, in Paris as well as in the provincial regions and their cities. There was a rich mixture of opinion as to what constituted French identity and what path the region and the nation should follow in the quest for a modern destiny. Modernization was thus both context and conjuncture in the struggle to create a "true France" from its puzzle of localisms. It offered a definitive setting in which French politi-cal and cultural synergy could finally be attained. Yet as an experience the tangle of meanings and influences assigned to the phrase "modernization" sharpened the very social, political, and spatial ruptures that historically imperiled the nation.

In the case of Toulouse, there were distinct "white" and "red" ver-sions of regionalism and modern renewal. During the first half of the twen-tieth century, modernization was effected within the context of Socialist municipalism, within the apparatus of Vichy administration, and within the euphoria of the Liberation. Each variation had a distinct social agenda, a finite vision of urban and regional life and of the French nation. Each left its mark on the city. Ultimately, however, the fight over modernization and its meaning represented the decisive struggle between local interests and the French state. There was a vitalist, moral mantle to the modernist enterprise once it became a mechanism for national consolidation and the centralizing state's manifest destiny. The state's discourse equated the country's weak-nesses with the regional-particularist clutching to outdated customs and values. By extension, then, any defiance by localist *mentalité,* any refusal to modernize, embodied the kind of nefarious betrayal of national solidarity that was holding back France. Toulouse, with its conspicuous red-brick architecture and its just as "authentic" cultural and political habits, became a metaphorical crescendo of particularism, rigidity, and the refusal to adjust to modern national norms that held the country hostage. It was a derelict historic capital reigning over a backward, deficient region—one of the poor-est cities in France. The term invented for this economic and psychic mal-ady was "underdevelopment." The word seemed to stick to the city like a scourge, nullifying anything worthwhile about living in the old capital of Languedoc. Toulouse's painful inadequacies were associated with the lack of productive forces and the unprogressive mentality understood as peculiar to the south. By the end of the war, the Pétainism espoused by many of the city's most powerful citizens added yet another disgrace to the long list of offenses leveled against the reactionary mentality of "the other France." At the same time, the city's infamous reputation as a leftist hotbed made it even more threatening to any sense of national identity. One way or the other, a proper modernization and spatial ordering of Toulouse and its region were essential to national cohesion and the triumph of the state.

The Roots of Regionalism

Since the nineteenth century, a cacophony of geographers, economists, historians, and publicists have studied and spread the doctrine of regionalism.[3] Pierre-Joseph Proudhon, Frédéric Le Play, and Maurice Barrès were perhaps the most famous of them, but theorists and projects of every flavor and opinion knew momentary notoriety, both on the local and national levels. There were in fact a variety of regionalisms, each offering a vision of renewal and modernization that would forge a unified French nation from the country's particularist traditions. The cause of regionalism was initially a movement of the extreme right, of the "whites": monarchists and archconservatives, the Church among them, who abhorred the political centralism and rationalism that were the legacy of the French Revolution. Regionalism thus flavored the whole dispute between republicanism and royalism that plagued the early years of the Third Republic. The "white" vision of the region centered around its historic, artistic, and intellectual "authenticity." The Montpellier royalist newspaper *L'Eclair,* one of the most important organs for Occitanism, argued that a France parched by abstraction and rationalism would be revivified by the splendid mosaic of provinces and local traditions that represented the true *patrie.*[4] In a 1907 article in *Action Française,* Charles Maurras argued that the economic interests of the Midi had never suffered so much as under the preponderance of southern republicans elected to Parliament. The regions, endowed before 1789 with abundant liberties, had experienced only decay with the adhesion to a democratic system that cloaked subjection to centrist doctrine.[5]

This type of regionalism was largely cultural and spiritual in orientation. It was clearly manifested in the 1907 revolt of the wine growers in lower Languedoc, where Ferroul, the mayor of Narbonne, and Marcellin Albert, the coffeehouse keeper who led the strike, reached into the right-wing tradition of mystic union and Provençal-Occitan heritage, including the *félibréenisme* of Mistral and the idea of a *"nation méridionale,"* to legitimate their cause.[6] Political separatism was the mission of the most resolute followers of this siren call of Occitanism. It required the sleight-of-hand invention of a cohesive regional entity out of what was, by the modern period, a diverse mix of local territories, each with its own separate culture and linguistic features—even if they did share Occitan roots. In any case, this "white" exaltation of particularist tradition was rapidly losing its grip by the early years of the twentieth century. After the crisis of 1907, the political influence of the right declined throughout Languedoc. The great political battles of the nineteenth century between "whites" and "reds," Catholics and secularists, *langue d'oc* and *langue d'oie* were passing. Momentarily encouraged by the appearance of new "ethnic" nations in Eastern Europe after the First World War, a *Ligue de la patrie méridionale* was formed in 1923 and demanded a regional government. But these movements remained marginal, essentially literary or folklorist, preoccupied with reasserting a *méridional* culture and exalting "the qualities of the race." Except for the extreme right and small artistic circles, the *déracinement culturel* taking place throughout the Midi was greeted with acceptance by most of the population. The regional press and politicians expressed little anxiety about the decline of Occitanism taking place through the public schools and military service and through the influence of French administration and the suffrage.

At any rate, Toulouse was not the domain of the conservative "whites" as was lower Languedoc and cities like Montpellier. The traditional upper-crust elites of landowners, lawyers, and judges remained Catholic and supported the emergence of some right-wing political organizations. Royalist clubs and extreme right-wing movements such as the Union Sociale du Midi and Action Française exercised some fringe influence over city politics. Debates about Occitanism were confined to small coteries of devoted regionalists. The Académie des Jeux Floraux remained their cultural orbit. Associations such as La Ligue "Oc," Le Travail, and L'Archer wrestled with the definition of a Toulouse school of artistic style. But from 1900 Toulouse was steadily becoming a bastion of the left. The Radicals who governed Toulouse at the turn of the century, and then intermittently until 1925, oversaw the last stages of the argument over the survival of traditional Occitan culture. In the Radical agenda, the disappearance of regional particularisms was seen as a guarantee of the unity and indivisibility of the Republic. The Radical bastion *La Dépêche* exalted the French language and national unity against the *félibréenne* enterprise of Mistral's Provence. Although Occitan literature received international recognition with the awarding of the Nobel Prize to Frédéric Mistral in 1904, the Radical-run Toulouse municipality and *La Dépêche* offered little support to the speakers of d'Oc.[7] Nor had the Radicals any interest in tampering with the structure of the Republican state by offering some new version of regional administration. Rarely was regionalism raised by Radicals as a possible solution to economic problems. Doumergue and Laffere, the Midi's Radical vanguard, condemned regional particularism as a defamation of the Republic and warned that its proponents would be expelled to the margins of the national community.

Despite the Radical admonition of Occitanism, there was nonetheless a left-wing politics of spatiality and regionalism that had developed from the struggles of the late nineteenth century. Occitan publicists August Fourès and Louis-Xavier de Ricard had launched the almanac *La Lauseto* in the 1870s that espoused a *félibréenisme du gauche*. It was ingrained with an anticlericalism, a devotion to humanism and social progress, and a Latin-Occitan patriotic fidelity on behalf of the people. It was an ideology of resistance against the forces of oppression (the Church, the French monarchy, the French state) that had wiped out the independent culture of the *petit peuple* of the Midi. The work of Proudhon figured prominently in this marginal literary movement. His critique of the combined despotic forces of the centralized French state and monopoly capitalism confirmed the abrogation of local liberties and the fear of "proletarization" by northern business interests. It echoed the protestations within the *compagnonnage* and among the *poètes-ouvriers* that were the traditional Occitan expressions of "the people." At the same time, his critique of capitalism molded regionalist thinking into a more modern political form and paralleled as well the introduction of syndicalism and socialism into the region.

Proudhon's federalism also offered a denouement in regional terms. The progression of this left-wing political discourse on regionalism can be seen, for example, in the federalism espoused by Paul Ricard and Charles Camproux, who launched a Parti Provençal in 1935. Although it remained largely an intellectual exercise by a new generation of regionalists, the party spread to Toulouse, Montpellier, Barcelona, and Valencia and received some support from the Popular Front. In his Per lo Camp Occitan, Camproux offered an Occitan distillation of Proudhon, arguing for both a French and a European federalism based on economic regions and natural markets of exchange. Within these regions, peasant proprietors, workers, artisans, and shopkeepers would become "small capitalists," dividing the wealth equitably and humanely while the imperialism of large-scale capitalism would simply die away.[8] Although Camproux's populist ideas were far from Marxism, the Parti Provençal was vehemently antifascist and attempted a socioeconomic analysis and a political agenda more in line with contemporary left-wing thought.

The Socialists who increasingly dominated Toulouse's municipal politics from 1912 on were, as well, less anxious to defend the Third Republic against the waning forces of regionalism. Although Socialism was internationalist by ideology, at Toulouse it was often expressed simply as a more zealous extension of radicalism, and the dividing lines between them were often blurry. Perhaps more importantly it was the Socialist humanism of Jean Jaurès and the critiques of Jules Guesde, rather than Marxism, that informed the developing debate on working-class politics in Languedoc. Jaurès himself gave little support to the cause of Occitanism, nor did the early Midi Socialists take up the banner of regionalism as the solution to working-class ills.[9] Nonetheless, the defense of the left was increasingly seen in regional terms. Politically progressive and socially conservative, the workers and *petits peuples* often understood Socialism as a defense of the world of craft and independent workers rather than as an international class struggle. They practiced more of a "reactionary leftism," or, perhaps more precisely, a "militant particularism," designed to protect the traditions of their own regional economic culture. Adherence to the left expressed an adhesion to democracy, anticlericalism, pacifism, a reformist program on behalf of the working man, and the defense of regional interests. They were the ethics of the *petit patron,* the artisan, and the peasant proprietor who dominated Toulousain life. Socialist tradition was increasingly linked to a belief in the *Midi rouge*, a visceral attachment to the left as proper to the region's political spirit. These were the dominant occitan values by the early twentieth century.[10] It generated a more modern strain of culturalism that can best be detected in the literary review *Oc,* initiated by Toulouse doctors Camille Soula and Ismaël Girard in 1923. The review called for the reform and update of the *langue d'oc,* one that would make it a modern language rather than a *passéiste* nostalgic reverie. *Oc* was published jointly with militant Catalan organizations in Barcelona and became the organ of the Society of Occitan Studies, founded in 1931. But, in any case, there was little public sympathy for this kind of particularism in an era dominated by the great forces of Marxism and Fascism. Although the *Midi rouge* was flexing its muscle, the left itself would not take on the cause of regionalism until the end of the Second World War.

The theme of community or municipal liberties was deftly woven into this strikingly leftist representation of regional distinctiveness. Occitan culture was associated with a collective practice of democracy and free thought whose roots harkened back, depending on the theorist, to the Middle Ages or to the Enlightenment. The most powerful symbols for Toulouse were the flowering of municipal independence during the triumphant twelfth century and the fact that the city was already practicing an early version of municipal democracy under the Old Regime. Its municipal "Capitouls" were chosen from lists of candidates representing the various districts.[11] Based on these Occitan roots, municipalism at Toulouse was understood as a responsive form of political empowerment. It was a channel for populist interests linked specifically to urban culture and community. The modern version of this municipalism actually began during the Third Republic in 1884. The cities of France received the right to elect municipal councils by universal suffrage, with the power to choose the mayor and his aides (although local affairs still remained under the tutelage of the Conseil d'Etat).

Except for the brief period under Vichy, the Toulouse Municipal Council acted both as an effective and a remarkably stable force for urban democratic politics. The blanket suffrage extended to all of the city's residents singularly legitimized its power. Even more importantly, the Municipal Council acted as an authentic, traditional tool of popular democracy, both by the populist social background of the councillors themselves and by the fact that they were chosen to represent the traditional puzzle of neighborhood-villages that made up the city. More than any other institution, the Municipal Council directly represented the interests of the people of Toulouse.

However, despite its populist roots, or perhaps because of them, the city's government could easily break down into duels between vested neighborhood interests. It was difficult to see any benefit in associating the common good with some larger understanding of community defined by a notion of "Toulouse." The neighborhood possessed a name, an identity, a form of sociability and culture that, in the early years of the twentieth century, far surpassed any notion of a larger urban totality. It was the diversity of neighborhood spaces, the pluralist texture of daily life, that shaped urban existence. The political landscape was the neighborhood network outlined by historic passageways and boundaries. "Village" loyalty was its own form of particularism, with municipal representatives each wedded to a minisystem of neighborhood corporatist interests and to the defense of their own quarters.[12] Historically, these neighborhood networks had been built around professional societies, religious associations, and artisan brotherhoods. But by the early twentieth century, secular and political leagues such as the Jeunesses Laïques et Républicaines and the Jeunesses

Socialistes, or Gardes Rouges, were forming around neighborhood cafés, bowling clubs, and musical societies. They staged their own balls and political *fêtes* and offered an alternative, and more politically modern, system of patronage. Within this powerful sphere of precincts, the mayor continued to function as a popular local notable, something of a good-natured symbol of the city's traditional interests.[13] This particularist version of municipalism was most associated with Radical hegemony at Toulouse from 1888 to 1925 under such mayors as Raymond Leygue and Paul Fuega.

Municipalism and Modern Urban Reform

This customary portrait of Toulouse as a labyrinth of robust neighborhoods was losing its validity by the early years of the twentieth century. The waning influence of the traditional *quartier* was one of the clearest indications of the cultural excision taking place throughout Languedoc. In the early 1920s, the city was still nominally functioning under a street plan sketched out in 1842. Other than the boulevard projects constructed under Haussmann's influence during the late nineteenth century, nothing had been done by way of urban renovation in the inner districts. Given the population increases during the nineteenth century and then again during and after the First World War, the historic neighborhoods were simply obsolete and in chaos. Most of the city's streets, its public utilities, and transportation were privately owned and outside the municipality's jurisdiction. Basic infrastructure was in disrepair. The decrepit water and sewer utilities threatened public health. Housing was scarce and dilapidated.

The development taking place around the old districts and faubourgs was even more chaotic. By the 1920s, Toulouse was spreading out through the surrounding countryside in a frenzied race for cheap housing. Suburban expansion fractured the fixed notion of Toulouse as a system of inner neighborhoods and blurred the boundaries between urban and rural authority. The combination of the Canal du Midi and the marshalling yards and warehouses at Raynal made the northern districts prime locations for the city's early industry. Fumes and smoke blackened the sky over Minimes, Négreneys, and La Salade and, beyond them, the northern communes of Fenouillet, Launaguet, and Aucamville. Working-class communities sprouted early around the ancient convents and churches of this northern *gardiage*. By the interwar years the area around the avenue des Minimes and Highway 20 to Paris was crowded with a hodgepodge of wood or stucco dwellings. Farther out, shacks of corrugated iron or reused wagon parts composed isolated "tin cities." The most infamous was at Grand Selve at Launaguet, where workers and the poor endured life in shanties and covered wagons without basic utilities or services.[14] On the left bank of the Garonne, Saint-Cyprien spread incrementally westward past the octroi walls. One- and two-story suburban-style stucco houses, topped with their tile roofs, lined the streets in tedious procession. Farther out, *pavillons isolés,* flanked by vegetable gardens and homely rabbit-hutches, became gradually more primitive as they turned up around old country hamlets. The most extensive of the suburbs, however, was to the southwest of Toulouse, where from the 1930s on, workers from the ONIA plant, the gunpowder facility, and the Francazal airbase and military garrison spread out to the adjacent communes in search of a place to live. An assortment of slapped-together allotments, or *lotissements,* stood in drab clusters along the roads and around villages. As in all the suburbs surrounding Toulouse in the great arc swinging from the north of the city westward down to the southern districts, a confusion of habitat reigned. Pigeon coops and henhouses, old barns turned into garages, unkempt vegetable gardens and farm plots, and makeshift tin cities were jumbled into the encroaching squeeze of urban development.[15] Construction was poor in quality and incoherent. Water and sewer lines, electricity and plumbing, even usable roads were unavailable luxuries to the working-class families who ventured out past the perimeters of the octroi walls and the inner faubourgs in search of suitable housing.

As long as the old neighborhoods reigned supreme in Toulouse's political morphology, there was little chance of improving urban existence or supervising this uncontrolled expansion. Any type of coordinated city management risked their power and independence. The Radical Party that controlled Toulouse through the early years of the century steadfastly protected district interests against any threat of citywide regulation. It was simply seen as a ghastly assault on private and particularist rights. Nevertheless, urban growth and disarray themselves had broken down the older networks of neighborhood political patronage. Their demise provided growing strength for the Socialist Party and for the Socialist effort at pioneering modern urban policy. The Socialist Party at Toulouse had, from its inception, made a more interventionist city government and some form of urban planning a part of its political agenda. Albert Bedouce, the city's first Socialist mayor, created a Service du Plan in 1908 that opened the debate on the creation of a coherent outline for modernizing Toulouse. But little was actually accomplished until the Socialist government elected in 1925 under the leadership of Etienne

Billières carried through a series of reforms. They introduced modern municipal management in the commune of Toulouse and sketched out a framework for planning from a citywide point of view.

Billières presented "Les réalisations de la Municipalité Socialiste de Toulouse" to the Thirty-First Congress of the SFIO in 1933 in Grenoble. They were a key part of the broader Socialist agenda for social and economic reform based on working-class interests and Socialist Party leadership. For Socialist reformers, creating the modern city meant constructing a space for social progress. But these initiatives were still implemented within the context of the local Toulouse setting, where demonstrating Socialist ability to manage a city and adroitness at attracting supporters from within the old neighborhood network were perhaps higher priorities. A vast amount of road and street repair and an extension of public utilities were carried out during the late 1920s and 1930s by Albert Bedouce, as Commissioner for Public Works. In an attempt to broaden municipal authority, private roads in the city were declared public domain, and electricity services were made the responsibility of the *régie municipale de l'électricité*. They were part of an enlarged network of public *régies* and *ateliers* that vastly extended the city government's leverage and increased the number of municipal employees by over 3,000 by 1937.[16] A new municipal library, the largest swimming pool in Europe, a wide variety of public bath houses, public toilets, new post offices, schools, and kiosks were all built. They were meant for the health, education, and social benefit of the city's working classes. The new Offices Publics d'Habitations à Bon Marché (HBM) and a workers' cooperative for building and public works constructed Toulouse's first garden-city projects and public-housing programs.

The designs for these projects were overseen by city architect Jean Montariol. In favoring Montariol's work, Billières' administration manifested the complex character of the left at Toulouse, rooted both in regional culture and in the modernism associated with social reform. A native Toulousain, Jean Montariol studied at the Ecole des Beaux-Arts at Toulouse, as well as with Deglanes and Nicod at the Académie des Beaux-Arts in Paris. He practiced the kind of mixed modern-traditional style that effectively personified the mélange of architectural types constructed at Toulouse during the 1920s and 1930s. In general, the rather preposterous stew of Classical, Expressionist, Art-Deco, Regional, and Modernist designs that materialized throughout the city reflected the impassioned competition in the transition away from historicist and traditional motifs and toward pure modernism. Orthodox regionalists asserted the viability of colloquial architecture based on the scientific analysis of local culture. Regional building forms were an expression of local spirit, in harmony with the sense of place, ethnology, and history. Principal among the defenders of regional building types were the members of the Société des Toulousains de Toulouse, the outspoken private association devoted to the defense of traditional Toulouse construction in brickwork, rock, and adobe with its picturesque Gothic, Renaissance, or eighteenth-century decoration. There was an upsurge in these regional motifs during the 1930s, most of it in the town homes of wealthy bourgeois families entrenched in the Occitan movement. The designs were inspired by the loggias and mirandas, the brick and tile, the Roman arches and jutting flat roof lines associated with Languedoc Toulousain. On the other hand, purist modern motifs were being introduced to Toulouse at precisely the same time by architects, such as Robert Armandary, working on designs for apartment buildings, storefronts, and public buildings.[17]

Montariol himself designed nine public-housing projects and nine city-garden projects that fall squarely between these architectural extremes.[18] His HBM public-housing projects in particular emphasized modernism's signature high-rise linearity and the use of concrete and flat-roof design. The HBM rue des Récollets in the working-class quarter of Empalot, for example, and the HBM allées Charles-de-Fitte at Saint-Cyprien both loomed over the squat red brick buildings like white giants six stories high. Their facades were done in a simplified classical design. All of the HBM housing projects were constructed either at Saint-Cyprien or in the working-class districts that had grown up along the outskirts of the central city. Montariol's garden-city projects, on the other hand, were modeled after the traditional regional building styles, in stucco with brick facades, loggia-styled porches, and tile roofs. It is difficult not to interpret them as reflections of the particular style of the left at Toulouse, embedded as much in the defense of the region's working-class culture as in internationalism. They read like architectonic distillations of Socialist progressivism and regional custom. Indeed, forums such as the review *Art Méridional*, published at Toulouse by Jean-Louis Gilet during the 1930s, debated the merits of regional design and construction as modern architecture and as a common idiom for the future.

As garden cities, the Toulouse undertakings were only barely articulated ensembles of one or two dozen small dwellings each along the fringes of the city. But like the HBM projects, they were among the first attempts to ameliorate the sad problem of "popular housing." In this context, their central heat and indoor plumbing, modern kitchens, and separate bedrooms were perhaps more appropriate measures of modernist reform efforts than was their architecture. They were built as exemplars of modern habitat, to advance the quality of life for the city's workers, and to remedy the social injustices that had poisoned urban social relations. At Toulouse, they were initiated within the circumstance of the first substantial efforts at progressive reform and urban modernization by the Socialist municipality.

The Socialist efforts at Toulouse paralleled the kind of reforms debated throughout France by a new intellectual elite of social scientists and urbanists. The need to socially stabilize the Third Republic drew theorists from a variety of backgrounds into the debate about cities and social existence. Reformers at the Musée Social in Paris founded the Section d'Hygiène Sociale and the Société Française des Urbanistes in the years before the First World War. The Institut d'Urbanisme of the University of Paris was established in 1919 with the urging of Socialist Henri Sellier.[19] The war's destruction produced the first legislation on reconstruction and urbanism. The Cornudet Law of 1919 and 1924 required cities with populations of over 10,000 to establish a city plan. Albert Bedouce had been one of its principal advocates. At Toulouse, after the long debate initiated by the Service du Plan, the Socialist administration finally appointed Léon Jaussely in 1926 to design a modern city plan in accordance with the Cornudet Law. Jaussely was a distinguished native son in the field of urban design. As a student at the Ecole des Beaux-Arts, winner of the Grand Prix de Rome in 1903, and member of both the Section d'Hygiène Sociale and the Institut d'Urbanisme, he had worked with Tony Garnier, Eugene Hénard, and Henri Prost.[20] His plan for Toulouse was never actually approved, but in many ways it remained the bedrock upon which land-use planning and urban design would subsequently be carried out after the Second World War. True to the modernist Beaux-Arts ideal, Jaussely introduced the rationality of zoning and urban boundaries, the careful regulation of building design to maintain uniformity, and the use of the boulevard as urban renewal.

Toulouse was divided into four zones. Historic Toulouse was at its heart. New boulevards were to cut through the congestion and the dilapidated districts, while still paying heed to the preservation of the city's monuments and historic treasures. In Saint-Cyprien, two new avenues would break through the working-class districts from the place de la Patte d'oie to the Garonne River. The main thoroughfare from Saint-Cyprien to central Toulouse, the rue de la République, was to be widened. Once it crossed the pont Neuf on to the right bank, it would break into two wide arteries through the old districts, one to the place des Carmes and the other connecting with the allée Jean Jaurès. The boulevards were meant to give Toulouse a classical composition based on contrived axes and to give it linearity and monumentality.[21] The zone surrounding this historic core corresponded to the old faubourgs and was designated specifically for apartment buildings and collective housing. From it radiated outward a zone for suburban residences and villas. Then zoned areas along the outskirts were reserved specifically for industry. The city was thus given the concentric planning motif that would dominate its modern expansion. The whole ensemble was to be encased in a concentric highway to relieve the growing street congestion and open up the city. Even in the peripheral areas outside the traditional boundaries of Toulouse, the municipality would carefully regulate building and road construction.

The problems of urban sprawl and land speculation were particularly noxious to Socialists and progressive-minded urbanists like Jaussely, who saw the urban amoeba spreading across the countryside as a clear indication of the mayhem of unchecked capitalism. At Toulouse, typical of large cities, urban expansion was left entirely in the hands of private interests who indiscriminately bought up rural parcels along the city's outskirts and subdivided them into small, hit-or-miss suburban allotments. Families devised and retrofitted all variety of structures in the scramble for shelter. In response to these same conditions, a "Paris region" was created by the government in 1932 and overseen by Henri Prost in the hopes of controlling the suburban sprawl around the capital. The first Congress on French Urbanism then met at Bordeaux the next year to discuss the growing urban chaos in the provinces and the necessity for some form of intercommunal cooperation in areas hit by urban blight. The obvious solution was to apply the idea of the Paris region to the rest of France's cities in the form of *projets régionaux d'urbanisme* (1935). Toulouse's Socialist government attempted to apply the formula by defining a "greater Toulouse" composed of eight communes, thereby extending some municipal control over the spreading anarchy. The effort was turned down by the Conseil d'Etat because it did not include all the communes thought to be within the city's sphere of influence.

Although most of these interwar efforts at urban modernism remained in the realm of the theoretical, they nevertheless initiated the first real public debates over the principles of urbanism as a science pertaining to health, hygiene, and social and economic organization that dominated progressive programs for change. These early efforts also opened up the arguments about the application of modernism to historically bound cities such as Toulouse. In any case, the improvements at Toulouse were introduced within the context of a modernized version of municipalism practiced by Socialist reformers. They identified themselves with a mixture of internationalism and regionalist democratic and humanist ideals.

The Region as Economic Space

There was, however, yet another conception of regionalism that found a growing base of public support during the interwar years. It was a new brand of regionalist doctrine advocating the scientifically based reorganization of France around natural systems of trade and commerce. No longer armed simply with the folklorism and the return to provincial authenticity espoused by the older forms of regionalist ideology, modern regionalists saw in their program the key to forging a new, modern France. Economic development, a more flexible and efficient administration, and the strengthening of social bonds would all be facilitated through a rationally drawn set of regions. The new social sciences would provide the keys to this reform. For example, the Fédération Régionaliste Française, established in 1900, was supported by many of the leading political figures in the Third Republic. Its program was a supposedly apolitical agenda advocating economic, intellectual, and administrative decentralization along regional lines.[22] Reconstruction after the First World War created further concerns about streamlining an antiquated administrative system based on the traditional dominion of independent communes and departments. By the 1930s, regional administrative units of one kind or another had appeared: regional organizations for transport and for the construction and administration of hospitals and sanatoriums; economic regions delineated by the census office; agricultural inspection regions; academic regions; military regions; and more, although their assignments were very limited.[23] The ideological origins of the increasing array of regionalisms were as diverse as the projects themselves. Nevertheless they all shared the same concern with more efficiently arranging the country's geography as a sign of efficacy, progress, and national union.

It was particularly in the realm of geography that this neoregionalism was argued most persuasively. Geographers Paul Vidal de la Blache and Henri Hauser contended that modern economic practices would, over time, naturally mold regions from the historic provinces of France. In his influential article "Régions françaises," published in *La Revue de Paris* in 1910, Vidal distinguished the city as essential to this shaping of modern economic spaces. A regional geography was evolving around the large French cities, which acted as the commercial and industrial engines within their spatial domains. Progress and modernization would seep down into *la France profonde* via this network of dynamic urban "growth poles." For social scientists such as these, whose work received increasing attention in the 1920s and 1930s, natural economic regions could then be used as the basis for administrative circumscriptions.

The role of the city as the central node, the guiding economic nerve center around which regional life would be organized, held open great hopes. The rigid administrative straitjacket that usurped all local initiative could be replaced with a new commercial management spirit, emanating from the revitalized cities of France. For Vidal, this transformation was essential to France's acceptance of the realities of modern life and to the next stage in the country's development. The great urban centers would provide the unifying web around which France and its regions would be built.[24] The necessity of "modernizing" was thus seen in terms of the restructuring of the national territory, of geographic space, according to the rational economic prerequisites of markets, capital, infrastructure, industry, and commerce. France would then conform to the temper of competitiveness and adaptability necessary to the twentieth century.

This particular conceptualization of regionalism was supported by business elites, who saw in it a more efficient mechanism for creating markets and influencing government regulation of the economy. In a certain sense they saw themselves as the inheritors of the tradition of regional community and the vanguard for regional rights, now garbed in a more progressive form. One of the most effective agents for this change in perspective was the Chamber of Commerce. Founded in 1902, the Toulouse Chamber's role, typical all over France, was essentially that of managing the city's customs warehouse and commercial bodies, as well as seeing to the development of basic airport facilities. It was firmly under the control of the traditional business community, that is, the commercial and craft interests, the few large-scale industrial enterprises, that dominated the Toulouse economy. From the interwar years on, the Chamber continuously elaborated its administrative and consultive role in championing economic modernization and the new regionalism. It was also the provincial Chambers of Commerce that had offered one of the earliest plans for regional economic development. The proposal was initiated during the First World War when the Chambers offered the Clemenceau government a consultive regional union that would facilitate participation in the war economy. Economic regions were constituted under the direction of Henri Hauser, who based his designation of *"grands centres urbaines, pôles industriels et commerciaux,"* around which local businessmen should organize themselves, on his own work and that of Vidal de la Blache. Toulouse was designated as the central city for the IXth Economic Region in 1918, called "Toulouse and the Pyrenees." Under its leadership were grouped the Chambers of Commerce at Tarbes, Auch, Foix, Montauban, Rodez, Albi, Castres, Mazamet, and Cahors. The area spread from the department of Lot to the Ariège in an exact rendering of the later Midi-Pyrénées Region.

At its heart was the Toulouse Chamber of Commerce and its president, Hubert Lagardelle. It created an early "Office of Industrial Studies," a subcontracting exchange for small businesses, as well as organizing an International Colonial Exposition in 1931 that accentuated the city's traditional trade with North Africa. The Chamber and the city's various merchant associations, allied with the press and municipal leadership, were also instrumental in promoting mass spectator sports and citywide entertainment. Organized as exalted forms of city boosterism, these spectacles were commercially profitable and helped to establish collective urban rituals and experiences shared by the community as a whole.

Perhaps the most emphatic sign of this renovated regionalist conviction was Toulouse's intense competition for mastery over French commercial aviation during the 1920s. The Chamber of Commerce and the IXth Economic Region, in league with the Municipal Council, the departmental Council for the Haute-Garonne, and *La Dépêche,* waged a veritable influence war with Bordeaux and Marseille over the drawing up of France's network of air lanes. The struggle was essentially over the economic and commercial blessings to be reaped from designation as the southern *tête de la ligne* for the routes from Paris and to North Africa, Spain, and South America. As the established aviation center, Toulouse was seriously threatened by the upstart maneuvers of its powerful rivals for a piece of the commercial action. It was the Toulouse Chamber of Commerce and the IXth Economic Region that worked with the Comité Français de Propagande Aéronautique in an attempt to protect the city's interests. Despite the combined exertions of Hubert Lagardelle, Albert Bedouce, Albert Sarraut, and Vincent Auriol, the Toulouse contingent was unable to withstand the assaults from the regional business interests organized at Bordeaux and Marseille. In a memorandum to the French administration, Bordeaux's Compagnie Atlantique de Navigation Aérienne, backed by its Chamber of Commerce and economic region, as well as by its most powerful newspaper publisher (Capon of the antiradical *La Petite Gironde*), argued that Toulouse could not possibly be the head of the line because "its economic importance was not on a par with that of Marseille or Bordeaux. Our company has no future at Toulouse. *La ville rose* should be a supply and construction center and *déclassé* as a port of entry to North Africa."[25]

These kinds of assertions that Toulouse should be reduced to a supply depot on the Bordeaux air network brought retaliatory cries of fury from Toulouse business and political elites. It was an eerie echo of the Languedoc-Gascogne clash for leadership over medieval Occitania. The modern struggle was played out in interregional conferences, aircraft company memoranda, and backroom political influence mongering. Although Toulouse lost the main battles over the commercial air lanes, it maintained a fair portion of mail and commercial routes as well as aircraft factories due largely to continuous lobbying by its Socialist-Radical municipal leadership. The Chamber of Commerce was instrumental in constructing two fully functioning airports for the city by the 1930s that gave it the infrastructure essential for its claims as a French aviation capital.

Although the IXth Economic Region had limited power in the interwar years and only received actual legal sanction in 1938, it was clearly being utilized as an expedient tool in the arsenal of local prerogatives. It represented the appearance of local business elites as central players in the drama of progress and the administrative reshuffling of geographic space. They espoused a robust new form of regionalism steeped in the ideological and scientific doctrine of economic modernization.

Modernization under Vichy

The Vichy years added yet another tier of practices to urban-regional reform and economic revitalization. Among the competing agendas within Vichy ideology was the project to destroy the administrative structure carried through by the French Revolution. It would be replaced with a *restauration des provinces*. This interest in reviving the "authentic" provincial *généralités* of the Old Regime was based on the strong neomonarchist doctrine that pervaded Vichy thinking. It was part of the imperative to construct an authoritarian and hierarchical administrative system capable of reinforcing control from the central Vichy powers. Like work, the family, and country, this provincialism became official policy in July 1940.

While the call for the *restauration des provinces* provided a dramatic folklorism for Vichy propaganda, the interpretation of history was very imprecise when Vichy officials actually carved out the regional administrative puzzle of France. Commissions de Propagande Régionaliste were instituted in September 1940 with the primary task of delineating the country's future regions. The Commission de Propagande de la Région de Toulouse evinced the ambiguous nature of the project by endlessly debating exactly what did constitute the region of Toulouse. In April 1941, Vichy provisionally carved the Toulouse region from the IXth Economic Region with the addition of the department of Lot-et-Garonne and the portions of the Landes and Basses-Pyrénées left in the Free Zone. The departments of the Tarn, the Aude, and the Pyrénées-Orientale were given to Montpellier. However, the local Commission de Propagande zealously hung on to the three departments in its own definition of Toulouse's region and insisted that only a public opinion poll could be the final judge of territorial acquisitions. While some local authorities on the Commission argued that the "intellectual, artistic, and historic affinity" between the departments should be the determining factor, others opted for economic networks as the critical determinant.[26] What seemed to be at stake in these discussions was the future social construction of the new *pays toulousain* and the possibility of realizing some measure of economic modernization and prosperity out of the older "spiritual" community intrinsic to the myth of Occitanism.

In any case, the Vichy government created seventeen regions on the basis of their "geography, production, and population." Their boundaries were largely based on the work of Vidal de la Blache. Vichy thus drew upon contemporary neoregionalist doctrine on economic zones of influence and the centrality of the city as the basis for recognizing geographic spaces—as well as on the older folklorist delineation of the "natural" regions of France. Within this hybrid geographic construction, Vichy attempted regional policy as a mechanism for reinforcing the authority of the state. At Toulouse, Prefect Cheneaux de Leyritz exercised authority over agricultural and industrial production within the region, provisioning and the fixing of prices, work, transport, and general infrastructure. The power of the regional prefect over economic questions thus appeared to be considerable. But in reality, regional decision making was very narrowly defined. Central government officials at Vichy remained fiercely defensive of their authority and power.[27]

The regional framework, however, did provide the opportunity for conceptualizing economic modernization within the context of geographic space. For the technocrats of Vichy, modernization constituted an essential part of the national revolution, in spite of the regime's nostalgic turn of mind. The word "modernization" was interpreted to mean the need for new administrative and economic elites, the will to adapt to the changing nature of capitalism, and the affirmation of the Nazi new world order. The Délégation Générale à l'Equipement Nationale (DGEN), created in April 1941, was charged by the Darlan government with establishing a ten-year development plan for France. The DGEN called for a determined effort at spiritual, moral, and material regeneration. The planners looked ahead, not to simply reconstituting a traditional France but to overhauling the structure of the economy, embracing technology and competitive industry, modernizing the rural sector, and creating a high standard of living. This conglomerate of modernist ideals was encapsulated in official discourse by the phrase *aménagement du territoire*. It was translated as a reorganization, or refashioning, of French territory.[28] A study of industrial concentration was launched in 1943 by a team of economists, geographers, and historians led by engineer Gabriel Dessus. The final report, based on regional evaluations, set up a classification of French cities based on population for the purposes of determining centers capable of welcoming new industries. While older cities such as Toulouse and Bordeaux were seen as unfavorable settings for industrial development, the DGEN endorsed the idea of invigorating the regions with smaller "corporative cities" built around selected modern industries.[29]

In keeping with Vichy's modernist agenda and the DGEN's economic plans, Cheneaux de Leyritz, the IXth Economic Region, and the Toulouse Chamber of Commerce initiated a policy for the restoration and industrialization of the southwest. The prefect's program recognized the efficient circulation of goods, free markets, and uniform prices as the first stage in the economic organization of the region.[30] The Commission de Propagande began a survey of the region's economy, compiling economic statistics and investigating the availability of energy sources. The discovery of natural gas at Saint-Marcet, less than a hundred kilometers from Toulouse, in July 1940 bolstered hopes for their plans. In 1941, the Société Nationale des Pétroles du Languedoc was formed by Vichy to exploit the new-found reserves. But only one pipeline was constructed by 1944, while a second was finished at the end of 1945. Electrical power plants in the Pyrenees were previewed for construction, and plans were made for a massive hydroelectric plant at Vignemale.[31] In anticipation of the new energy sources, the Commission de Propagande staged the *journées de l'électricité* at Toulouse in March 1941. Vichy officials met periodically with the Commission and with the board of the IXth Economic Region to confer on issues of economic development. The Commission also supported a number of committees responsible for invigorating Occitan culture, created a Regional Bureau of Toulouse, and instituted a fairly far-flung regionalist propaganda campaign in the schools and University, on the radio, and through posters, festivals, and parades.[32] Much of this was largely ceremonial and, certainly within the context of the Occupation and war, was pure fantasy. In reality, "economic development" often meant that Cheneaux de Leyritz supervised the paucity of provisions to be distributed around the region. Nonetheless, Vichy's *restauration des provinces,* both in the cultural and economic sense, worked to open up the debate on regionalism and to crystallize a mythic discourse around the idea of a collective regional consciousness.

The DGEN also set out an administrative framework for a policy on urbanism. A Technical Service for Topography and Urbanism was established in 1941 and a Code on Urbanism adopted in June of 1943. Although, again, little could actually be accomplished during the war years, the Code on Urbanism was an essential text that remained the foundation for French urbanism until 1958. Under Vichy it set up a series of urban regions identical to the administrative regions, as well as state commissions on urbanism that sanctioned intervention in city design and planning. The DGEN also received authority to approve and oversee intercommunal and communal development projects. Theoretically, the most powerful of these administrative tools were the *Groupements d'urbanisme,* which were to be organized by the communes surrounding a city to facilitate modernization projects.[33] Creating a *groupement d'urbanisme* was no easy task. The Code on Urbanism defined as a "group" those neighboring communes, whether or not they claimed common borders or were within the same department, that shared common interests. Those interests were defined as economic and demographic. The impetus was clearly to claim as much territory for state decision making as possible. The Inspector General of Urbanism at Toulouse approached the Vichy-appointed Municipal Council in 1944 with a list of thirty-three communes. Although the Council could argue for the incorporation of sixteen of them into a *groupement d'urbanisme* (those communes bordering on Toulouse that generally conformed to the city's outlying industrial and aircraft districts), the remainder did not, in the general opinion, have clearly established "links" with Toulouse.[34]

In the meantime, the Municipal Council did initiate an urban plan solely for the commune of Toulouse. To comply with the Code on Urbanism, in July 1942 it hired architect Charles-Henri Nicod, a graduate of the Ecole des Beaux-Arts and winner of the Rome Prize in 1907, to design a plan for the embellishment and extension of the city. It was to be the expression of Vichy's conception of the city as the historic administrative and commercial capital of the resurrected region of Languedoc. However, Nicod was clearly to build on Jaussely's efforts to introduce modern urban reform into the historic mélange of Toulouse's built environment. The Nicod Plan was supported by a local Comité consultatif du Bureau d'Esthetique Urbaine composed of representatives from the board of local architects and the craft association in building and public works.

Vichy itself denied the efficacy of modernist architecture and instead championed regionalist building forms as a populist craft. The Vichy years were a field day for enthusiasts of historicist and rural motifs, who saw regionalist forms as the natural expression of local culture. One of Toulouse's most prominent historians and most active members of *Toulousains de Toulouse,* Pierre de Gorsse, was appointed by the prefect to oversee the rebirth of native building styles through the Regional Commission's committee on regional architecture and aesthetics. Toulouse Gothic, Renaissance, and Classicist motifs as well as rural peasant designs were all paraded forth as the images of historic Occitan culture and a newly reclaimed regionalism. Like the rest of Vichy's plans and dreams for reactionary renovation, these conceptualizations were never more than contemplations or blueprints. The significance of Vichy's revivalist formulas lay in their ready availability at the Liberation and in the shared dream of both Vichyites and Liberation leaders for a rebirth or a deliverance of France from the corruption and inadequacies of the prewar years. That common goal, regardless of the radical differences of application, made possible the construction of reforms based on the modernizing goals of the recent and, once purged of its collaborationist poison, very usable past.

Modernization and the Resistance

Once the Resistance forces had successfully liberated Toulouse from the Nazi yoke in August 1944, their celebrated unity was short-lived. The multiplicity of local Resistance groups was itself a source of confusion and agitation. Military powers, reemerging political parties, patriotic militia and the Forces Françaises de l'Intérieur (FFI), local committees of liberation, and the Commissar of the Republic all vied for political control over Toulouse. There was little coordination within this maze of operations. Protests amplified against the overly zealous methods of the FFI units and their frequent recourse to violence.[35] The Communist Party continued its call for revolution and began infiltrating local factory and union committees. The

Spanish Republican guerrilla units added to passions by using Toulouse as a base for intervention against Franco's Spain. There was a particularly tense conflict between the Comité Départemental de Libération (CDL), which represented local Resistance forces; the FFI units under Colonel Ravanel; and the Commissar of the Republic, who represented the state. Although as the new Commissar Pierre Bertaux acted as de Gaulle's consul, he was at first not even able to secure control of his own office at the Capitole.

Under these conditions, order and security remained an elusive goal for weeks. The confusion was aggravated by the fact that Toulouse remained isolated from the rest of France even after the liberation of the south. The first regular link with Paris was only established in September. The first regular connections with de Gaulle's administrative network only began in January of 1945. From August, then, until weeks after the Liberation, Toulouse was on its own. The fact that it had liberated itself and remained free of outside influence was, according to historian Le Roy Ladurie, a decisive experience that dominated the city's postwar political life. It provided an atmosphere for radical reform that simply did not exist in other areas of France.[36] The new local authorities, in their plenitude, took the initiative in implementing the "revolutionary" program of the Conseil National de la Resistance (CNR).

The revolutionary aspirations of the Resistance were in fact a profound desire for change. The Liberation was accompanied by an intense, passionate belief in deliverance, in all possibilities for the future. In the momentary disappearance of *La Dépêche,* nine Liberation papers published daily editions at Toulouse, all of them committed "to the ideology of revolution by law under the banners of socialist humanism and the tricolor."[37] A new society was to be created out of the ashes of defeat, a regime of "justice and liberty, the end of exploitation, the blooming of each individual, an economy at the service of the people, a fraternal and united society." This was not a precise ideology so much as a mélange of sincerity and idealism heightened by the emotional intensity of the liberation.[38]

At Toulouse the unifying framework was the program of the CNR drawn up in March 1944, which had unanimous support from the local Resistance. The program's ambitious economic objectives included a planning-based growth to ensure general prosperity, worker participation, and strategic nationalizations. It proclaimed the right to work (which included retirement and social security) as well as to leisure and education. It charged the Resistance with providing the new leadership for a reconstructed France. These directives were carried through at Toulouse by a variety of squabbling

Resistance forces preaching the rhetoric of unity, buoyant with the support of the city's population, and initiating measures in the spirit of the revolutionary moment of deliverance.

In terms of the social revolution, it was the local aeronautics industry, the nationalized Société Nationale des Constructions Aéronautiques du Sud-Est (SNCASE), and private companies such as Latécoère and Bréguet that served as the experimental laboratories for the creation of new social relations in the workplace. "Committees of Liberation in Factories and Businesses" were organized in the aircraft factories and in most of the large Toulouse businesses during the first days of the Liberation. All of the Committees were dominated by the local Resistance, particularly by the Communist organizations, which began to execute measures in direct conflict with the legal structure being reconstituted by the government of liberated France. They purged administrative staffs, particularly in those firms known to have collaborated with the Nazis. They began to reorganize administration, appoint directors, and assume control over production and marketing in a usurpation of state authority and the rights of private ownership. At SNCASE, the Committee of Liberation proposed the total reorganization of the factory. The Committee was to have control in virtually every area of administration, personnel, and production. The same reforms were initiated at Bréguet, where the Committee demanded that Pierre Bréguet appoint a new director for his factory at Toulouse. At Air-France and ONIA, the Committees themselves appointed new directors and initiated company programs. The Committees were also active in demanding administrative purges in the municipal services and public utilities. Bertaux stepped in to control the "social revolution" by negotiating the Accord de Toulouse (September 12), which legitimized the Committees and specifically defined their powers.

In all these spontaneous reform movements, *autogestion,* that is, self-management and policy making by employees, dominated the goals. The reforms were about the transfer of power and authority to workers and employees. Rarely did they raise the issue of legal nationalization or even the expropriation of private firms. It was the immediacy of the situation that concerned them. The companies were to be taken over by the workers to service the desperate population and to expedite production for the war to liberate France. It was the strong patriotic sentiment, the sense that the struggle to free France necessitated the militarization of the factories and required passionate work by everyone, that most characterized the Committees' purpose. They were often led by veteran Resistance fighters imbued with the emotional comradery of the Liberation. Their cause was France, and although their reforms were clearly influenced by traditional working-class politics and revolutionary ideology, the call for solidarity with the Commissar of the Republic and with the Fourth Republic was as likely a refrain as the call for revolution.[39]

On August 29, the city's Committee of Liberation, presided over by the new mayor Raymond Badiou, with representatives from all the various Resistance groups, demanded the institution of one of the key points of the CNR program: "the return to the collectivity" of public enterprises—gas, electricity, and public transportation. The new prefect of the Haute-Garonne, Pierre Cassagneau, delegated his powers of procurement to the city. The Municipal Council promptly took over ownership and management of the new Régie des Transport Commun de Région Toulousaine, the Régie Toulousaine d'Electricité du Bazacle, and the Régie Toulousaine du Gaz. Each was given a corporate administrative structure based on self-management or *autogestion,* with the duties of administration and the execution of policy strictly separated. The Management Committee for each public enterprise was elected by the personnel. The profits were to be shared for the benefit of the city's population. Working conditions, and especially salaries, were improved immediately by the Municipal Council. In fact, a general reorganization of municipal administration was quickly adopted and the salaries of municipal employees raised, with a special "Liberation bonus" awarded to each "in the spirit of social concern."[40]

In July 1945 the Municipal Council annulled the nominal *groupement d'urbanisme* of eight communes created under Vichy's command and voted a sweeping incorporation of all thirty-three communes into the urban zone of Toulouse, a vast area that would now be under its direction in terms of planning.[41] The city's Chamber of Commerce, under the direction of Gabriel Barlangue (who also served as the president of the IXth Economic Region), established specialized commissions in aviation, tourism, and transport to plan for the development of the Toulouse metropolis. To recover the city's role as aircraft capital, the Chamber of Commerce and Municipal Council resurrected plans in November to construct an international airport at Blagnac that would have a direct rail link to Matabiau Station. The Canal du Midi was to be renovated and the region's tourist facilities updated.[42] To the leaders of the Resistance, these measures were the first steps in the economic revolution launched by the Liberation. The Socialist newspaper *L'Espoir* "saw in the municipalization of the Toulouse tramways the beginning of a triumphal march toward the socialism of the future." The Christian Democratic *La Victoire* put great store in the Accord de Toulouse as the "chart for the future society." There existed then a consensus about the strategy of a rupture with the past that was adopted and applied at the Liberation in the specific, local context of established municipalism.

Pierre Bertaux instituted his own revolution by taking up the cause of economic modernization at the regional level. Bertaux argued that the region was not a Vichy institution. It was a fact, an indispensable necessity for the success of reconstruction in France. The region, according to Bertaux, should become the framework for France's future modern economy. The department simply had no validity from this point of view. Reconstruction provided the opportunity for decentralized decision making, for empowering local authorities and revitalizing the provinces rather than giving the impression that "forty million Frenchmen were to be entirely managed by Paris." Bertaux wrote in his memoirs of this report:

> I was polite. I wanted to write "managed by a Parisian clique." But I wrote without malice. I thought those who, in Paris, endeavored to administer France were competent, of good faith and immense willingness. But I thought that they worked in a vacuum, in an abstract sphere—the airy island in *Gulliver's Travels* came to mind—where one quickly loses any contact with concrete human realities. They only experience the provinces as *"sur le tas."*[43]

Whereas Michel Debré conceived of the regions and their commissars as "large departments," instruments of executive power that overrode local hierarchies, Bertaux thought that the region should exercise real responsibility and control based on personal links and participation in the provinces. Vichy's attempts to restore the Old Regime provinces were a failure, but Bertaux argued that "a certain amount of particularism doesn't frighten me, if it reanimates life in the provinces."[44]

Regional reconstruction commissions had been independently organized by Commissars in a number of cities after the Liberation, notably at Reims, Lyon, Marseille, and Montpellier. Raymond Aubrac, Commissar at Marseille, had initiated the first regional economic council in November 1944. Yves Farge followed the Marseille initiative and organized a Regional Commission for Economic Reconstruction at Lyon in December. In October 1945, Bertaux organized a Conseil Économique Régional at Toulouse that was assigned the task of creating a plan for reconstruction and cataloging the region's resources.

Bertaux and the Conseil Économique Régional looked to the Soviet

Union and also to the American Tennessee Valley Authority Project as models for the "recasting and modernization of the economy of the Toulouse region." The Conseil's membership was composed of officials from the departmental General Councils, the mayors of Toulouse, a rural commune and a working-class commune, local union and business association representatives, and faculty from the University of Toulouse. The Conseil Économique Régional adopted the reconstruction programs proposed by the Toulouse Chamber of Commerce and Municipal Council. It set up work commissions which were to present plans to renovate the region's agriculture, industry, and commerce.[45] And it received the support of the region's most powerful ally in Paris, Vincent Auriol, who had become president of the National Assembly. Midi Socialist Auriol believed "the region is the living cell of the country and should receive a large measure of autonomy,"[46] including a financial footing. André Philip, Minister of Economy and Finance, and François Billoux, Minister of Reconstruction, came from Paris to attend its few sessions.

But this type of viable regionalization actually found little support in Paris. When the appointments of Commissars were made by de Gaulle's government in 1944, their responsibilities were clear. They were to establish legal state authority as quickly as possible in their local domains. The Commissars were meant to represent the Jacobin conception of the state that was threatened by the revolutionary aspirations of the Resistance and the fragmentation of the country. They were provincial envoys committed to the reconstruction of the machinery of the centralized state. Nevertheless, it proved difficult to maintain this centralist unanimity when it came to making the appointments. Debré was forced in some cases to acquiesce to local Resistance movements. This had been the case at Toulouse, where Edouard Dupreux was initially appointed in Paris. The choice was abruptly circumvented by the Liberation vanguard in the southwest, who insisted on the appointment of its leader, Jean Cassou, who would be more supportive of the locally inspired revolutionary programs. Pierre Bertaux, who took Cassou's place, was also a leading local Resistance figure and had refused to leave the southwest to take up an offered appointment elsewhere in France.[47]

Thus despite the fact that de Gaulle and his executive prerogatives had designed the commissar system to extend centralized state control, the individual Commissars themselves, particularly in the south, were far more attuned to popular impatience with reform and to the ability of local Resistance forces to implement the CNR program themselves. The program of the

CNR had initiated the mission of revolutionary reform. Hervé Alphand, who had written the CNR postwar goals, stressed the equitable division of wealth, the elimination of powerful private interests, full employment, and planning as essential to the renewal of France. The factory committees established at Toulouse, the expansion of Municipal Council and Chamber of Commerce jurisdictions, and the construction of a Conseil Économique Régional committed to planning and economic development appeared to fulfill these goals and to establish a concrete framework for local involvement in reconstruction. The south had a particular stake in rectifying the economic imbalances that had produced such atrophy in comparison to Paris and the north. Liberation and reconstruction provided the opportunity to contribute locally initiated reforms in an inspired democratic fashion. The Commissars in the south often carried out these measures without waiting for directives from Paris.

Yet despite these inspirational plans, the Resistance was unable to fulfill the desires of the local population at Toulouse, or for that matter in any of the regions of France. The excitement of Liberation was brief. Even by the end of September 1944 signs of deterioration within the Resistance began to appear. The fragile unity broke down under the weight of its own internal contradictions and the accumulation of difficulties it faced. Food, security, and stability eluded Resistance leadership. The extreme harshness of the winter of 1944 and the disappearance of even the most basic food commodities were made all the more unbearable by the visionary reform projects that had yet to be put into practice. The patience, hopefulness, and goodwill of the city's population grew thin.

The Commissars in particular walked a fine line between adherence to the goals of the local Resistance and their Communist supporters and to the central government directives which began to filtrate down to the local level. De Gaulle increasingly called for fidelity, for order, for union rather than for insurrection and revolutionary reform.[48] It was clearly to reestablish the authority of the state in the wayward provinces that de Gaulle toured France in September and October 1944. When he reached Toulouse on September 16 it became clear that he would give no endorsement to the Resistance forces of the infamous *Midi rouge*. He preached the necessity of order and fidelity to the French state. Cassou was admonished in his hospital bed to reestablish order as his first priority. Bertaux was told to find a local military authority capable of forcing some measure of control over the quarrelsome local liberators. Insurgent Communists were purged from the new administrative system. Resistance leverage was removed by handing over all their power directly to the CDL. Colonel Ravanel and his FFI resistance units were pushed aside. Instead, General Collet was nominated by de Gaulle as head of the Toulouse military region.

But it mattered little in the long run, because by March 1946 the Commissars themselves were purged from the state administration. The notion of independently generated local reform was tainted with the reputation for particularism and regressive traditionalism that had led France down the awkward road of Vichy collaboration. The autonomous movements toward modernization initiated as part of the Resistance program threatened the bonds of the French state. In any case, the 1930s and 1940s had clearly demonstrated the variety of sources and denotations, as well as political and social agendas, behind the elusive object of faith—modernization. The tensions involved in the progressive construction of a lexicon of meanings for that term, within the context of diverse currents of regionalism, could generate rupture and dispersion as well as consolidation in the struggle to revitalize France. The meanings of Toulouse, as place and as culture, were themselves multifold and mercurial. Perceptions about the future of the capital of Languedoc and about its spreading form and municipal identity refracted the ideological currents and disputes that swept across the French political stage. A mixed bag of "urbanisms," each with its conviction on local culture and the vernacular, leveraged notions of progress at Toulouse. The city was a space of multiple social and political meanings. The nature and form of urban life itself became the terrain on which the struggle over the future of France would take place.

CHAPTER 3

Constructing Modernism in the 1950s

Although hostilities had officially ended in 1945, the war continued to dominate life at Toulouse in the late 1940s. The cafes and movie theaters began to reopen in 1946, and the city streets took on a more routine air. But food shortages, rationing, and the lack of basic necessities haunted daily existence. The city's newspaper greeted the normally bountiful feast of the Epiphany in 1947 with the headline, "A somber Sunday; no meat, no fish, little pork . . ."[1] The black market flourished. Rising inflation added to the general malaise. Just before the war, bread at Toulouse cost 3 francs. By 1947 the price was at 15 francs, and then it doubled over the year to 30 francs a loaf in 1948.[2] Since less than half of the city's population was actually working, the question of survival was dire. Even those with jobs sank into acute poverty. In 1946, average salaries in Toulouse were the lowest of any large city in France.[3]

On top of the deprivation, safety remained a constant worry. Groups of armed Resistance fighters and guerrilla units, desperate foreigners, many of them reduced to banditry, filtered through the city. Police units were stretched bare in the pursuit of stolen ration cards, hoarding, and illegal trafficking in food and weapons. Break-ins tormented stores and banks. Sabotage was immediately suspected when fire swept through the remaining buildings at the ONIA fertilizer plant in 1946, destroying what had been left from the Allied raids. Then, a few days later, the main post office burned. To add to the distress, the city's 60,000 street lamps were destroyed in a warehouse fire and there was nothing to replace them. Toulouse was plunged into darkness each night in a virtual continuation of the wartime blackout. Police cars patrolled the streets nightly, checking identity papers and automobiles. Roadblocks were set up on the main roads to control traffic and to limit the flood of strangers passing through the city. The strike waves of 1947 added further to the daily vulnerability. In June the city's gas and electric utilities and public transport went down as workers walked out. Banks closed in support of the strike. The state aircraft plant was paralyzed for weeks.

So the wartime adversity dragged on in the instability and privation suffered daily years after the fighting had ceased. Food supplies and rationing tormented departmental and city officials. The Municipal Council quarreled bitterly over the distribution of the few funds available. Left-wing unity threatened to break down over the difficult decision to cut costs to the bare minimum in the face of enormous public need. The scarcity was aggravated by the increase in population. Overall, the city itself had gained 50,000 new residents during the war, increasing the population to 260,000. The historic central districts were bursting with the human tide that had washed onto the city's doorstep in the midst of wartime calamity. The old *oustals,* already in a severe state of neglect before the war, withered under the strain. Finding a place to live became a Promethean task. This was not a problem specific to Toulouse. Everywhere in France, the massive housing shortage threatened to derail any hopes for reconstruction and a return to normalcy. In the minds of public officials, solving the housing shortage quickly became equated with maintaining "social peace." However, by the late 1940s Toulouse did have the dubious honor of possessing some of the worst housing in France.[4] Building construction had begun a rapid slide downward during the depression of the 1930s and then again during the war and Occupation. In the disastrous year of 1945, no construction at all was done at Toulouse, and the recovery was slow throughout the late 1940s. People found shelter anywhere they could. In 1946 a group of homeless families wrote to the city's newspaper demanding the conversion of municipal buildings into lodging for the homeless, because despite the official appearance of a Public Housing Office, virtually nothing had been accomplished by the city government.[5]

The desperate search for housing spilled over into the western and southern districts around Toulouse.[6] They were close to the ONIA fertilizer plant and the gunpowder and aircraft factories where work had been found during the war. At Braqueville, the fumes from the war-torn ONIA plant clouded the sky over the Garonne. At Francazal and Saint-Martin-du-Touch the grotesque remains of the bombarded aircraft plants and airbases made for a dismal atmosphere. The gunpowder factory lay in ruins. Many of the residential districts around them had also been ravaged by the British bombing attacks. As a result, working-class faubourgs like Saint-Cyprien on the left bank of the Garonne felt the pressure of homeless workers searching for cheap flats and proximity to possible jobs. But with some 15,000 Spanish and Italian refugees harbored in the outlying districts, even there available housing was scarce. Families streamed westward beyond Saint-Cyprien to the villages at Tournefeuille, Purpan, and Colomiers. These western outskirts contained the largest suburban housing stock around the city, mainly old rural bungalows and nominal dwellings of one kind or another. Their quality was certainly no better than in the city, and in many cases far worse. Nonetheless, in the hopes of stumbling on any kind of lodging, suburbanization to the west of the city was spreading twenty to thirty kilometers out to the communes of Noé, Sainte-Foy-de-Peyrolières, and Grenade.

To the south, the population of the faubourg Saint-Michel was packed with laborers. They spread out toward the rural villages of Croix-de-Pierre, Saint-Agne, and Saint-Roch. There was actually little usable housing in these outlying southern districts. People found shelter in the flimsy shanties and "tin cities" strung along the rural roads. The internment camp buildings at Récébédou were donated after the Liberation to the public-housing office, which converted them into private rooms for Spanish refugees and low-income working-class families. Others hastily erected wood shacks for shelter and then slowly converted them into brick cottages. Eventually, the spreading highway community was taken over by private developers who cashed in on the crisis by selling the inevitable hodgepodge of allotments and cheap tract homes.[7] But the further the reluctant suburbanites ventured out into the countryside, the more they were on their own in terms of basic utilities and amenities. Although the southern and western districts especially felt the population pressure, the city was as a whole surrounded by every conceivable kind of makeshift dwelling hastily constructed in the effort to house the refugees, evacuees, and workers pouring in between 1920 and 1945. Everywhere around Toulouse the chaos of war and the struggle to house and feed the growing population prevailed. But in the face of crying need, there was little hope of providing adequate shelter for any of the thousands looking for it. The result was a city crying for repair, with a population in desperate need, but without the funds to accomplish any of it.

Beyond the crisis of financial dearth, the city's municipal administration was entangled in the political crises of the reconstruction years. The new mayor, Raymond Badiou, was president of the Comité Local de Libération and a personal friend of Pierre Bertaux. A graduate of the Ecole Normale and a lycée professor at Toulouse, Badiou was a member of a new generation of Socialists untainted by compliance with the Vichy Regime. Badiou, Paul

Debauges, Achille Auban, and Vincent Auriol emerged after the Liberation as the Midi Socialists most associated with carrying through the Resistance reforms within the context of the state administrative structure finally imposed on Toulouse. Auriol's election as President of France in 1947 sparked the euphoric possibility that *la terre occitane* and its tradition of Socialism would emerge as formidable powers in guiding postwar national politics. Similarly, Badiou's appointment as mayor of Toulouse heralded the resurrection of the Socialist Party and its investiture with the new municipal powers bestowed at the Liberation. With the city's transportation systems and utilities now under public control and with its jurisdiction expanded to the thirty-three surrounding communes of the *groupement d'urbanisme,* the municipal government appeared to be in a felicitous position to undertake the reconstruction and planning of Toulouse along the lines of the Liberation's progressive ambitions.

But the shift from the grand alliance of the Resistance to the machinations of traditional party politics that took place from 1946 to 1948 crumbled the Liberation hopes for social and economic rejuvenation. The municipal administration found itself plunged into confusion. A widening schism opened between the electoral struggles and tactical alliances of the recast political parties and the aspirations and profound needs of the general public. The Communist Party emerged from the Resistance as a new municipal political force of extraordinary power. With cells in the city's factories and trade union and electoral support in working-class districts like Saint-Cyprien, Minimes, and Négreney, the Party relentlessly pressured for the continuation of the Liberation's program of revolutionary reform. The initial prominence of the Communists after the war was heightened by the role they had played in relaunching aircraft production under the worker committees. Communist Charles Tillon had also been appointed French Air Minister with power over Toulouse's future as an aviation capital. When the Communists were suddenly banished from government in 1947, the grand alliance of the left was fractured.

Though it found itself increasingly isolated, the Communist Party, and the Resistance program it represented, continued to exert formidable influence over the city. Badiou was reelected as mayor in 1947 only with the help of the Communist vote—just before they were eliminated from municipal administration by Socialist and Mouvement Républicain Populaire (MRP) censure. Despite its formal exile, the Communist-Resistance block emerged with the most local votes in the 1947 legislative elections to the Chamber of Deputies. With ten seats on the Toulouse Municipal Council, the Communists were strong enough to command two appointments as mayoral adjuncts. Their political prestige waned very slowly during the 1950s, which gives evidence of the psychological and political weight that the memory of the Resistance carried in Languedoc. They continued to control ten seats, or about a quarter, of the Toulouse Municipal Council throughout the 1950s and remained a formidable presence in city politics, with leaders such as Jean Llante, Georges Ducel, and Simone Gardès.

Badiou found himself in the increasingly awkward position of inter-mediary between the failing left-wing Resistance alliance, the Communists, and the emerging centrist and right-wing political parties. By 1948, the mayor and the Socialist Party were a minority in the Municipal Council. Badiou was able to resuscitate his power only by turning to the right for his political alliances. A fragile accord was devised between the Socialists and the centrist MRP that initially provided Badiou with the barest of mandates at City Hall. To bolster their strength, the Socialists increasingly offered municipal appointments to the MRP, the resurrected Radical Party, and even to the Gaullists of the Rassemblement du Peuple Français (RPF). The reemer-gence of *La Dépêche* in 1947 under Jean Baylet and the preeminent leader-ship of Bourgès-Maunoury gave the city's Radicals substantial clout despite the stain Pétainism had plainly left on their popularity. They kept up a vociferous campaign against Socialist dominion in the pages of *La Dépêche* during the 1950s, and succeeded in laying claim to twelve seats on the Municipal Council by 1953 through an alliance with the center-right. By the late 1950s, however, the Radicals were clearly in decline, their political turf usurped by prominent Socialists and by centrists. Despite the threat posed by all these emerging political rivals, the Socialists managed to steer an awkward course through the 1950s by resorting to ephemeral alliances with the right. The strategy was, after all, a dicey proposition given that Toulouse was historically a bastion of the left. Caught in the web of entan-gling political affiliations and the ineffectual "party system" of the Fourth Republic, completely without adequate funding, Toulouse's municipal ad-ministration was incapable of independently responding to public need and resolving the city's difficulties. The city's government spent less on each of its citizens than any other large city in France.

Planning Postwar Toulouse

Despite the lack of means, there was no shortage of interest and ideas on urban reconstruction, both at Toulouse and in France in general. In November 1944, de Gaulle's provisional government created the Ministère de la Reconstruction et de l'Urbanisme (MRU) with Raoul Dautry at its head. Dautry was a well-known and enthusiastic supporter of modernism and the planned city. He officially proclaimed 1945 as the "year of urbanism" and declared that all postwar reconstruction projects take into account the future of the built environment and the creation of a "new France." The administrative structure and urban policies originally set out by the Vichy DGEN were quickly transferred to the new MRU. The 1943 Code on Urbanism remained intact, as did the DGEN emphasis on *aménagement du territoire* and the necessity of creating specific urban plans for each of the French cities. Only Vichy's nostalgic admiration for the past was jettisoned.

Within this purified administrative agenda, an emotional debate ensued on the merits of modernism proposed by Le Corbusier and on the idea of the functional, planned city laid out and coordinated by state-appointed architects and urbanists. Reconstruction projects that favored traditional provincial architecture were labeled as symbols of Vichyist ideology. What remained unclear was how to integrate modernist design into the unique character of the individual French city and how to avoid the banality of an "officially" sanctioned architecture. Cities destroyed during the war received first priority at the MRU. Their reconstruction projects laid the basis for state supervision of local development. Although the local municipalities and mayors could choose their own architects and plans, all urban designs were carefully scrutinized by a Commission Nationale des Plans d'Urbanisme composed of a wide array of architects, urbanists, and state administrators.[8] Paris was to have the final say on the reconstruction of urban France. Those cities that had luckily avoided the worst of the wartime destruction, Toulouse among them, waited behind for their turn at Dautry's MRU gauntlet. In 1946 the administrative services of the MRU set up their Toulouse outpost on the rue des 36 Ponts close to the Municipal Gardens and the Grand Rond. Edouard Weiler, an architect who had spent most of his career in Paris, was appointed as regional inspector in the Toulouse office.

Toulouse already had at its disposal the planning blueprint initiated by Vichy Mayor Haon and the Municipal Council in July 1942. Charles-Henri Nicod had been appointed to expand upon Léon Jaussely's work in an effort to manage the city's uncontrolled growth. Nicod's plan finally appeared in 1947 and began the long rite of passage through the MRU's bureaucracy. The original plan was an interesting mixture of modernist and traditional principles. It demonstrated that despite the enthusiasm for revolutionary design at the MRU, many of the urban plans produced during the reconstruction years were actually quite orthodox in composition. Ultimately, Nicod's project bore the double imprint of Jaussely and of Mayor Raymond Badiou. As a Midi Socialist and humanist educator, Badiou's interests lay in preserving the traditional functions of Toulouse while rationalizing and revitalizing what had clearly become a muddle of decay and overuse. Badiou's understanding of urban planning was rooted in the municipalism carried out by Toulouse's Socialist government of the 1930s. For the Socialists, the catastrophe of dilapidation and unhealthy slum conditions in the center and suburban sprawl on the periphery were tragic examples of capitalism run rampant. A policy of conservationism, urban renewal, and controlled planning would restore Toulouse as regional capital and encourage the city's role as intellectual, commercial, and political center of the Midi.

However, according to Badiou, limiting growth was essential in order to avoid siphoning all development in the surrounding countryside into an urban monster. A maximum population of 200,000 was best for Toulouse; otherwise, the price of expansion would be highly dangerous to the quality of life. Instead, economic development should be spread throughout the towns and cities of the southwest so that Toulouse would oversee a rich and prosperous region.[9] Badiou was clearly an exponent of controlled growth and functionally based planning as the best form for modernization to take. His administration offered a vision of Toulouse embedded in a rich network of towns and villages that spread growth and productivity evenly and equitably throughout the Midi.

Thus, in Nicod's Plan, the metropolis was given a strict legal perimeter beyond which there was to be no development. In terms of physical size, Toulouse was one of the largest urban communes in France—covering 11,943 hectares. The city had historically been built up very tightly around the original Roman-medieval core along the Garonne, and there was plenty of room in the communal territory for expansion. Despite suburbanization, in the 1940s and 1950s vast areas of the commune were still rural. The Nicod Plan set the development limit at the 3,025 hectares surrounding the city, a little more than one-quarter of the commune. All construction was to take place within this area. Nicod then concentrated on a clear design for the central city as regional capital. His vision was of Toulouse as the historic heart of government, learning, and business within Languedoc. The needs of the city's public administration and its scholarly heritage were given first priority. Urban renewal would encourage the reemergence of the city's vibrant commercial economy. Toulouse would be restored to its full heritage based on the Beaux-Arts tradition of formal grandeur, symmetrical axes, and hygienic improvements.

Nicod proposed a broad boulevard crowned with a monumental entry at the place Arnaud-Bernard in the north of the city. The boulevard would cut down through the Bourg, setting off the bell towers and facades of Saint-Sernin Cathedral, the Eglise du Taur, and the Jacobins ("the pearl of Toulouse," in Nicod's words) and ending with an architectural ensemble of administrative buildings surrounding and complementing the Capitole. This monumental center would act as a Palais Royal, with government offices and luxury shops interlaced with open gardens. The new artery would wipe out some of the worst slum districts of the old Latin Quarter. From there it would extend "beautification" down through the Cité. The overhauled commercial districts around the Hôtel Azzésat ("whose graceful tower would become visible once more") and the restored quais along the riverfront (long neglected by city officials) would integrate the Cité into a newly renovated and modern Toulouse. "The first consideration," according to Nicod, "was to safeguard the historic, picturesque character of the old city and to highlight its numerous monuments, while still taking into account the need for new transportation arteries."[10]

To connect the new administrative center at the Capitole with the prefecture and the law courts at Saint-Etienne, an architectural ensemble would be created from the slum clearance of Saint-Georges, the decayed commercial district that acted as a depraved barrier to the virtuous integration of Toulouse's governmental functions. It would become the new business center of the Cité and revivify the old district. A second boulevard system would emanate from the place du Capitole through the place Wilson and down the allée Jean Jaurès to the new residential quarter of Joliment. What the Nicod Plan had in mind then was the monumental ordering of historic Toulouse. The mechanism of the boulevard would unite the Bourg and the Cité in a manner only the medieval Counts of Toulouse would have fully appreciated. And for the first time since the mighty days of the Renaissance, the Garonne riverfront would be an integral part of the city, garnished with promenades, cafes, and restaurants.

The renovation projects were designed to blend monumentality and historic preservation with a modernist formula for wiping clean the *désagrégation* wrought by chaotic growth. If the Plan was traditional in its vision of Toulouse and if it promoted an ambiguous mélange of architectural preservation and slum clearance, it was also clearly within Dautry's vision of modern urban management. The city's administration had designated a clear urban zone that would benefit from reconstruction and urban renewal. Both the extension of municipal authority over utilities and transportation and the Plan's legitimization as a public good through the auspices of state support ensured that "the city" as a technical construction would be carefully and properly delineated. Nicod did not attempt any kind of regressive drift into nostalgia. That he saw the benefits of slum clearance and a "cleaning out" of those districts in the path of his boulevards, that monumentality was at the core of his design, demonstrated an advocacy of modernization that paralleled state interest in executing the rational city.

There was actually little chance that any of the Nicod Plan would be put into effect, at least not immediately. In fact, the grandiose aesthetic ambitions of the Plan in the face of the city's dire need for housing angered local activists. Concerned with the complete breakdown in any building construction and the growing power of public officialdom over urban development, the Order of Architects for the Toulouse region and the local building contractors' union reproached Mayor Badiou for his insistence on Nicod's grand scheme. Its emphasis on historic preservation and building regulations shackled construction. Its monumental visions did nothing to alleviate the slum conditions in the central city's worst districts. Instead, according to the building unions, simple and practical health regulations should be established. Open land should be requisitioned by the city for badly needed residential construction. The worst slum districts should be immediately demolished. In their estimation, the Nicod Plan represented an abuse of municipal power and paralyzed any private initiative. Any plan for the city should be consultive rather than imperative, and the city's historic character should be preserved not by the mayoral staff but by a special commission composed of local architects.[11]

Public Housing and the Built Environment

By far the most important immediate consequence of the Nicod Plan was the barrier it created around the city to prevent further suburban construction. With Toulouse already in the midst of a severe housing crisis, it meant that availability of the *pavillons isolés* and the cheaply built working-class allotment housing scattered around Toulouse was cut short. The policy momentarily aggravated an already serious situation. More important, it portended a drastic change in the form of construction, toward high-density, large-scale housing structures within the new publicly controlled perimeter of Toulouse. This policy was clearly supported by Dautry and the MRU, which saw reconstruction as an opportunity to test modern building styles and materials as the new form of the urban environment. Dautry and his successor as Minister of Reconstruction and Urbanism, Eugène Claudius-Petit, were both ardent admirers of the urban theories of Le Corbusier. They vehemently rejected the traditional, haphazardly developed urban environment as retrograde and dangerous, risking the worst in social dissension. The city as formed by historical accident was renounced as the culprit behind economic injustice, social strife, and political instability. The planned, functional city that fulfilled the basic human need for a healthy lived environment was the solution to these obstacles. Housing was to be considered as the foremost economic and social indicator of well-being. Modern dwellings and living norms were to be prescribed by the state in a public-housing program based on standard of living—defined by equipment rather than by class. Rapidly built high-rise apartments offered the most efficient and rational way of fulfilling this obligation, thereby ensuring social tranquility. The result, according to the protagonists at the MRU, would be an urban environment conducive to the social renewal and regeneration of France along modernist lines.[12]

Edouard Weiler, appointed as regional inspector for the MRU at Toulouse, spelled out the modernist agenda in a series of articles appearing in the newspaper *La République du Sud-Ouest* in 1946. First, the nostalgia for historic patterns had to be expunged from the French mentality. The foolishness of looking back toward traditional regional motifs becomes obvious, he pointed out, if you talk with any local peasant, who will be dumbfounded at your admiration of his humble abode and dreams himself of a little villa in the worst suburban style. The retrograde attitudes of the French were deplorable. In fact, the French were becoming known for their denigration of anything new. Modernism's real appeal was as an antidote to this reactionary and traditionalist ideology that under Vichy had led France down a path of doom. Weiler concluded that "We can't confuse tradition with paralysis. We will badly dress the wounds of the French house if we persist in this morbid manner of making everything pretty 'just like our ancestors'—narrow, small, with common walls and little windows." It was time to clean out these false conceptions of living space and think instead of the recovery of the country, the power of the young, of renovation, of the birthrate. In this regard, he argued, it was impossible to deny the beauty of the modern high-rise residence. It offered efficiency and the best of comforts: central heating, up-to-date bathrooms and kitchens, elevators, and garbage facilities. Interspersed amidst greenery and gardens, high-rises offered their inhabitants the healthy virtues of sunlight and pure air.[13]

There is no doubt that the majority of the city's inhabitants, desperate for decent housing, praised and supported the government's social programs and its building construction policy. In the late 1940s the MRU's revolutionary modernist agenda was a counterpart to the progressive public-housing projects inaugurated by Toulouse's Socialist government in the 1930s. Even more importantly, it appealed to the Liberation demand for social justice and for rapidly built, low-cost dwellings that would be democratically and equitably available to everyone. The start-up of building construction in any style was understood as an improvement over the paralysis that kept thousands either homeless or poorly housed with little hope of bettering their condition. But the verticality and form of officially sanctioned modernism still appeared a daunting challenge. Besides, construction was now caught in a web of frustrating municipal and state regulations that dramatized the debate over traditional and modern style. In a 1949 newspaper article, a local critic took the opportunity to jab at the layers of state and municipal control that had been newly spread over the critical housing scarcity: "So you want to modify, expand, or embellish your house? First you need the approval of the Office of Aesthetics. You want to build on an open lot? Wait! you are told. Be patient! You can't build anywhere that's contrary to the city's urban plan."[14] There were also groups within the city who vehemently disputed Weiler's denunciation of traditional building modes. The Brickmakers' Association, for instance, began their 1949 exposition expounding the charm of the "city of Isaure where the afternoons are flooded with the warm light reflected on the walls and monuments." While grandiose plans were being made for the renovation of Toulouse with prefabricated cement structures, no one was speaking about the merits of simple construction in brick. "If Toulouse, city of brick, wants to safeguard its character and remain the 'cité rose' of municipal diatribe, then public buildings and simple residences had to respect tradition and the elementary rules of local aesthetics."[15]

What the combined efforts of the MRU and the municipality offered by way of solving the "social crisis" of housing was the first of the high-rise public-housing projects. In 1947 the government's old Habitations à Bon Marché (HBM) program was relaunched and by 1950 became the Offices Publics d'Habitations à Loyer Modéré (HLM). Its financial resources were then strengthened by the Minjoz laws of 1949 and 1950. With this system of state aid in place, the Office Public d'HLM at Toulouse received the first loans (in 1949) for 340 flats to be built at three sites: Joliment, Empalot, and Madrid. All three were expansions of the *logements collectifs* built at these sites under Montariol's supervision during the 1930s. At the same time the military camps at Récébédou, Bourrassol, and Cépière were to be renovated to provide housing for 450 more families, most of them working at the two weapons facilities. The state housing authorities also provided the ONIA plant with loans to construct a *cité ouvrière* at the site of Papus, on the left bank of the Garonne, which would contain 300 flats for its employees. Alongside the building projects, the city would also begin reconstructing the districts destroyed in the wartime Allied bombardments. All of this, André Daste, the mayor's adjunct, proudly announced, "would provide ample work for Toulouse entrepreneurs over the coming eighteen months."[16] The MRU and the mayor's office fully realized that, despite this auspicious start, the projects would do comparatively little to solve the severe housing crisis plaguing the city and, for that matter, plaguing all of France. They were simply the prelude to the towering waves of administrative regulations and building programs that clattered out of the state bureaucratic machinery with increasing amplitude in the early 1950s.

The new housing programs were fully integrated into local planning schemes. They were provided with legal muscle through the Land Law (1952), known at Toulouse as the infamous Article 151, which conferred upon local public powers the right to expropriate any land necessary for the construction projects. Nicod sat down with MRU officials to adapt his plan to the new state policy. Given the paucity of local funding and the increasing dependency on state subsidies, Nicod's Beaux-Arts designs were substantially scaled down and modified to reflect state guidelines. The monumental beautification scheme for the old city was essentially dropped as utopian and unachievable. The inference was that preservation of the historic quarters was not particularly high on the state modernist agenda. Urban design, in the formal sense, was simply sacrificed to the housing projects and planning of living norms that were the principal objectives in the Ministry's sponsorship of city development. The Nicod Plan was then adopted, in revised form, by the Departmental Commission on Urbanism and by the Municipal Council. It was then sent back up to Paris for final clearance in 1955. Clearly, the MRU now laid down the framework to which the urban plans and projects would adhere. Although there was room for negotiation by municipal governments, it was difficult to argue with the purse strings. Perhaps even more importantly, by virtue of their approval of the diminished Nicod Plan, the central administration had jettisoned traditional urban precincts created around neighborhood, historic districts and networks of local authority. It replaced them with zones based on type of habitat or functional specialization. Local territory was to be managed by the central powers according to national norms. That policy was to be carried out through technical regulations and the awarding of construction permits within a new system of spatial jurisdictions, with recourse to outright expropriation when necessary.

Over the course of the 1950s, Empalot and Joliment formed the core of an expanding series of public-housing projects constructed around the old city, but well within the development perimeter drawn by the Nicod Plan. The expropriations, financing, and construction programs were carried out by the Société Toulousaine de Construction et de Gestion d'Immeubles, or SOTOCOGI as it was locally known. It was essentially an investment vehicle that was also responsible for providing loans to renters in the expropriated districts to purchase residences in new buildings. The Joliment project already had a long history by the time it was incorporated into postwar reconstruction. In the 1920s, Léon Jaussely's plan for Toulouse had called for a new boulevard axis extending from the place Wilson up the sixty-meter-wide allée Jean Jaurès and beyond to the Plateau de Joliment, where a sumptuous new residential neighborhood would be built. It opened the possibility of extending the city out along one of its most impressive boulevards. The Nicod Plan embraced the Joliment idea, adding the creation of a substantial public garden that would harmonize with the place Wilson and the place du Capitole. The decision in 1948 to construct one of the first public-housing projects at Joliment thus fit into a well-established design for the city. The municipal and departmental HLM offices built 284 flats in a dozen whitewashed high-rise apartment buildings at Joliment by 1956. From that point, private real-estate developers worked in coordination with the city to create a *"grand ensemble"* at Joliment based on a state-sponsored *plan-masse,* or design layout, that authorized the infrastructure and services necessary for the newly created community. By 1960, some twenty-two high-rise apartment structures had gone up, with seven of them containing more than 100 flats apiece. A commercial center was constructed at the center of the district and schools along the periphery. The composition was enclosed by a semicircular parkway that linked it to the allée Jean Jaurès and to central Toulouse.

The Empalot project as well originated in the interwar years. Although the area was farther out from the central district, it had been the site of two public-housing projects of the late 1920s and early 1930s. Montariol's buildings on the rue des Récollets and Saint-Roch were six stories high, constructed with reinforced concrete in white and cream. They had been exemplary representations of modernist social reform in the interwar years. Empalot was bordered by the infamous Champ du Loup, site of a municipal dump and a myriad of makeshift unauthorized "housing" hastily constructed by poor families during the 1930s and 1940s—also exemplary representations, but of the housing shortage and chaotic growth that plagued most of Toulouse.

Both the public-housing projects at Empalot and its neighboring slum were destroyed by the wartime aerial bombardments, unwittingly clearing the area for more planned development. After recourse to Article 151's power of expropriation, particularly in the Champ du Loup, eleven modern concrete apartment buildings of seven to ten stories were constructed between 1950 and 1955 to form what was known as the Cité Daste. Empalot then received a *plan-masse* in 1956 meant to create an urban "ensemble" as expansion continued. The Empalot-Poudrerie apartment complex was

Figure 5. The Empalot, Cité Daste public housing project.

erected between 1955 and 1958. Towering cement blocks of thirteen stories, Empalot-Daste, were added in the early 1960s. A commercial center was constructed at the district's main intersection. Schools and a social center were added to the complex. It rose out of the red Toulouse landscape, housing some 20,000 new residents—its height, linearity, and angular milky-whiteness a compelling image of the future habitat planned by state modernism.

Although Empalot and Joliment were the largest *grands ensembles* at Toulouse,[17] the municipal HLM program also constructed smaller public-housing projects during the 1950s for working-class families and those with fewer resources. In the midst of the working-class district of Saint-Cyprien, the 400-flat Cité Roguet was built by departmental architect Viatgé. It was dominated by a massive concrete apartment tower of twenty stories jutting out above the city. Rangueil-Saouzeloung to the southwest of the city contained more than 600 flats in concrete apartment blocks. Bordering the Garonne to the north of Toulouse, the old 1930s Madrid public-housing project was renovated and expanded. Négreneys-Mazades just north of the Minimes industrial district offered another 600 flats in six-story-high apartment blocks of whitewashed concrete. The public-housing projects were joined by a variety of privately developed high-rise apartment buildings. In 1953 the MRU announced the creation of the *plan Courant* designed to facilitate the construction of low-cost housing projects, Logements Économiques et Familiaux or LOGECOS, in French cities by providing state subsidies and loans to private investors from the Crédit Foncier. By the mid-1950s private apartment buildings of eight to fifteen stories were being constructed on vacant property surrounding Toulouse, particularly along the circle of nineteenth-century boulevards that enclosed the old city and along the main avenues out of town. A modern eighteen-story apartment house towered over the allée Charles-de-Fitte on the left bank. Along the allée Jean Jaurès, ten- to fifteen-story concrete buildings rose above the traditional four-story brick buildings in traditional Toulouse style. A full ensemble of apartment buildings was privately constructed along the avenue Jean Rieux at Côte Pavée east of the city in a district known for its "good air" and gardens.

Altogether, 10,000 buildings were constructed at Toulouse between 1948 and 1961 in a housing market that could only be described as frenzied. The construction provided 30,000 new apartments for the city's desperately needy and rapidly growing population. The expeditious delivery of high-density, low-rent housing was the solution offered by public agencies and private real estate to the national crisis of finding a place to live. Over 60 percent of these new dwellings were within massive *immeubles collectifs*. By the end of the 1950s, more than 60,000 people, one-fifth of the city's population, were living in 224 new high-rise apartment complexes, the majority divided between HLM and *plan Courant* projects.[18] The practical justifications for high-density housing were summarized by a local real-estate promoter: ". . . these islands of grouped apartment buildings, surrounded by greenery, represent the most economic means of housing in the most comfortable manner, the largest number of individuals in the shortest time."[19] It was the functional, practical argument that most suited the housing program.

All of these public and private housing projects offered desperately needed alternatives to the neglected and overcrowded conditions in the historic districts. Most of those who moved to the apartment complexes, particularly during the 1950s and early 1960s, were young working-class and blue-collar families leaving skimpy hovels in search of a better life. In an oral history of Empalot, resident Monsieur Calas remembered that until 1958 he and his wife and four children lived in a two-room *maison toulousaine* behind Matabiau railroad station. There was no bathroom. The water closet in the courtyard was shared by three families. They were overjoyed when they received the news that a rented apartment awaited them at Empalot.[20]

Although the complexes lacked basic commercial services and social amenities, they were a miraculous improvement over the miserable options otherwise available. The flats were comfortable and modern, with up-to-date kitchen and bathroom facilities, heating, and the standard French windows open to light and air. Monsieur Calas recalled: "I opened the door and saw a large room flooded with light. There was a glass door and two windows. There were three bedrooms and, the height of luxury, a WC and bathroom." These remarkable interiors were key representations of the state ideal of utility and quality habitat. This was the new definition of the modern and harmonious urban environment.

The demand for housing was so intense that building permits and contracts were approved for construction with little thought to a more planned setting. Construction simply remained well within the development perimeter established by the Nicod Plan, essentially within three to four kilometers from the place du Capitole. The high-rises rapidly created a virtual wall of concrete around old red brick Toulouse and towered above the ancient *oustals toulousaines* in the most uncompromising form of architectural modernism available. Their straight, angular, unadorned facades of bare framing and reinforced concrete were left exposed or whitewashed. There was not a sign of red brick in their construction. Unadorned windows (bereft of traditional wooden shutters), narrow recessed balconies, and open walkways protected with metal or colored plastic were stacked upwards in a geometric configuration that left no doubts about the rationality and calculation implicit in the new form of the built environment. As they reached new heights of eighteen and twenty stories and spread in great rectangles across whole blocks and districts, the image of Toulouse appeared to be metamorphosing right before the eyes of its astonished citizenry.

Local debate over the merits of urban planning, the Nicod perimeter, and the *immeubles collectifs* raged in Municipal Council meetings and public forums. Behind them lay more difficult issues of statism versus municipalism, communalism, and private-property rights. The situation was not lost on the center and Radical factions in the Municipal Council. They steadfastly defended the proprietor's right to build on his land against the encroachment by public regulation. Paul Ourliac, centrist member of the Municipal Council, argued that the villainous perimeter encouraged speculation in real estate, since all land within the cordon would become instantly valuable as that outside it became worthless: "It's the same old policy as that practiced by Baron Haussmann eighty years ago—the policy of the accordion; periodically inflated and then deflated, the boundary offers endless opportunity for speculation."[21] The application of Article 151 in particular (the government's right of land expropriation) appeared to many as the epitome of the state's strong-arm methods in regulating urban growth and the form of the built environment. It was the ultimate usurpation of private proprietorship by a dictatorial state bureaucracy. These debates on the impact of the Nicod Plan offered a graphic assessment of the vagaries of urban planning, particularly as it was applied to local circumstance. The frustration over state-hatched urban policy and its simplified norms was expressed in Ourliac's remark that "I have absolutely no appreciation for the Inspector General of Urbanism when he tells us that 'we work well *en bloc,* we're not concerned with detail.'"

The question of land and building rights was tied up with the issue of living preferences and the single-family dwelling, the *pavillon isolé,* that dotted the Garonne Valley at a respectable distance from the city. Public authorities at all levels were aware of the traditional ideal of the suburban cottage with its tiny plot decorated with butane tank and vegetable garden. When private landowners insisted on their right to build, it was this kind of suburban bungalow they had in mind. As Ourliac put it:

> Everyone on the Municipal Council supports a housing policy. Where we diverge is on the most desirable form of housing. Some prefer the *cité collective* like the "Cité du Fada" at Marseille, and others prefer the individual house, the "cottage" built in the semirural zone seven to eight kilometers from the city. Perhaps it's an idyllic view, but it is the one most prefer.

In a semiofficial poll taken in 1953, 80 percent of the respondents said they would like to live in a single-family house in the suburbs.[22] It was a difficult dream to square with the *immeubles collectifs* rising around the city.

The discord embodied radically different notions of sociability and the lived environment. The suburban cottage represented the traditional petit-bourgeois investment in a "landed estate." It was the embodiment of individualism and of a certain kind of regionalism par excellence. Suburban architectural styles had been as wrapped up in various conceptions of re-gionalist architecture as had their urban counterparts. Picturesque gable cottages in Basque and Catalan and Mediterranean peasant styles filled the fantasies of suburbia for many a *petit propriétaire*. In fact Montariol's small garden-city projects constructed in the suburbs of Toulouse during the 1930s were the epitome of this ideal. Cottage construction also endorsed the expansion of Toulouse through private real-estate speculation, the arena of the small-time capitalist and building contractor, as a public good associated with the city's general prosperity. Radical leaders such as Henri Galaman vowed to do battle against *les collectivistes* by snatching the Capitole from the Socialists and Badiou and inaugurating a prudent and wise administra-tion in place of "these illusory and pernicious urban utopias."[23]

The mayor retorted that the Socialist agenda was to provide decent housing for the city's working classes rather than succumb to suburban blight in the name of private property and petit-bourgeois self-interest. The Toulouse municipality simply did not have the financial resources to spon-sor the housing and urban development programs necessitated by the popu-lation increases of the 1940s and 1950s. The solution was to impose a planned urban environment that offered the city's inhabitants modern, comfortable housing near the central city through the equitable financial sponsorship of the state, the municipality, and private real-estate partner-ships. Nor did Badiou's Socialist Party have the political clout to neutralize the growing Radical and centrist critique of the city's management. The Radicals' most formidable assault against Socialist dominion at the Capitole came precisely during the mid-1950s, when the debate on Nicod's perimeter and the public-housing programs was at its height. With twelve seats on the Municipal Council, their coalition's condemnation of high-density housing and controlled growth had substantial muscle. For Badiou, siding with the MRU bolstered his position within the maelstrom of local politics.

State planners themselves, however, could afford to be more straight-forward about the multitudinous complaints lodged against their plans for Toulouse. Georges Lacroix, an engineer with the Ponts et Chaussées, was appointed by the Ministère de la Reconstruction et du Logement (MRL) as the principal investigator for the public inquiry on the Nicod Plan. It was Lacroix who was to formally answer the objections in an official government report. He began by reminding the Toulousains that past efforts at urban planning by the municipality, the Jaussely plan for example, were not very encouraging. The shortage of finances, the political battles between private interests and the municipal administration was particularism at its worst. "A strong hand must have recourse to measures of authority . . . After all, works of urbanism require firmness—history shows this—and one shouldn't become overly agitated at the opposition between public and private interests." Although the population had displayed a preference for a certain type of habitat:

> We would like to emphasize that if numerous claimants have in-sisted on the advantages of individual residences and the inconve-niences of collective habitation—not one has said to us in any way, "I live in an apartment building, my life is impossible. I want an individual residence." Unless we have erred, none of the 1483 claims have come from individuals within apartment buildings—al-though there are 10,500 dwellings of this kind at Toulouse.[24]

In terms of the aesthetic conflicts that the buildings presented in the city-scape, Lacroix admitted that modernism marked a revolution for Toulouse and that its application was marked by oversights and careless yielding to pressure from speculative interests. But their contribution to the housing stock was too important to deny. It was simply a matter of a more intelligent application of the building regulations rather than a flaw in the mod-ernist policy.

But it was not that easy to push aside the question of aesthetics. The application of modernist architecture to a city already steeped in its own vernacular understanding of visual imagery and building design appeared to many as a crisis of urban identity that risked the *défiguration* of Toulouse. Although the Nicod Plan strictly regulated building construction in the central city in order to conserve its historic character, the actual extent of high-rise building in or near the center far exceeded the Plan's original intentions. Regulation and the proliferation of bureaucratic control did not necessarily ensure the kind of "firmness" described by Lacroix. The departmental Commission on Urbanism and the departmental offices of the MRL, both responsible for building permits, were accused of openly flouting the height regulations whenever private contractors pressured them to do so. The primary objective of the MRL was to construct the 40,000 dwellings officials estimated would be needed over the next ten years at Toulouse.[25] The result was that high-rises quickly crept into the sacred historical districts between the Canal du Midi and the Garonne River.

Concerned citizens desirous of protecting the traditional aesthetic features of Toulouse found themselves nervously avowing the benefits of modern housing construction. At the same time they pleaded for protection of the historic Latin-Occitan imagery of pink-bricked Toulouse against the blocks of yellow and white cubes that were spreading everywhere. The city's historians, along with members of the university faculty, the local Building and Public Works Association, and various activist groups kept up loud public campaigns to follow the letter of the Nicod Plan and its preservation of historic neighborhoods. Lucien Babonneau, an engineer at the University of Toulouse, and Pierre de Gorsse, university professor and one of the city's most well-known historians, led the aesthetic attack on modernism. They were both members of the Société des Toulousains de Toulouse, the association dedicated to conserving the city's historic riches. Their publication, *Auta*, was filled with diatribes against the high-rises and with lamentations for the historic buildings demolished in the cause of modernist planning. Babonneau appealed to history, aesthetic tastes, and urban harmony in decrying the destruction of Toulouse's traditional countenance: "The foamy pink of the Roman tile roofs, the low houses, the sea of ocher, violet and crimson from which rise the city's churches with their steeples, the domes and towers . . . Like it or not, this is the look of Toulouse. It is the primitive charm that gives it such originality . . ." But all of this now was infected by warts.

> The warts are these massive blocks that ruin the graceful towers that rise above the undulating brick . . . First they were six to eight sto-

ries, then twelve to fourteen, and now we have a skyscraper of thirty stories! . . . If we do not take care Toulouse will have the inhuman atmosphere of a New York or Chicago. We will wake one morning with the steeple of Saint-Sernin obscured by a skyscraper.[26]

The tirades against the repulsiveness of the public housing projects became as much a part of local lore as the nostalgic poetry to the inner city's faded beauty. In a series of editorial satires during 1960, for instance, *La Dépêche du Midi* assailed the high-rises for the damage they inflicted on the city's panorama. A guide leading a tour of Toulouse arrives at the outskirts of Saint-Cyprien and launches into a scathing condemnation:

> . . . and now you will see, on our right, the greatest horror of Toulouse. Look at these ghastly white buildings, worse than rabbit cages. Toulouse was once called "the rose-colored town"; now it should be called "the motley-colored town." The tourists strain their necks

Figure 6. Saint-Sernin Cathedral and the old city surrounded by "walls of concrete."

and look in disgust at the building. One woman asks: "But do you mean people actually live here?"[27]

But the emotional outbursts over the changing color of the city were more than just an issue of retrogressive aesthetics and nostalgia. The rose color of Toulouse had historically been the symbol of the city's social and political values and its collective public life. It provided a sense of place, habitability, and identity. The visual imagery of Toulouse's soft pink and violet hues represented the *joie de vivre* that was possible in the city of Isaure. Rose was the color of the city's intellectual and artistic heritage. It was the color of its political independence. The congested, bleak districts and run-down lodging that were the reality in Toulouse during the 1950s rather refuted this spell of *la ville rose*. But the call to the vernacular landscape was vocalized as a formidable weapon in the struggle against state-controlled modernism. The whitewashed cement apartment blocks, the stark high-rises were understood as an assault on regional culture and the unique character of urban life that it had produced. Reconstruction and public-housing assistance seemed to require a material reconfiguration and style of living at complete odds with the past. The city now seemed vulnerable to the merciless rhythms of modern urbanity. The eighteen-story apartment tower on the allée Charles-de-Fitte in Saint-Cyprien was particularly repugnant to the preservationists. For Babonneau it was "a catastrophe. It completely disfigures the right bank and the view of the river—a scene that had likened Toulouse with Florence . . . It is a colossal mistake, a flop that insults Latin civilization."[28] For Pierre de Gorsse it was

> an architectural mastodon . . . These successive deviations of the building codes that are demanded of us day after day, hurried and under pressure, within meetings with overfull agendas, risk, if we do not take care, giving us a future Toulouse which the Toulousains themselves will no longer recognize and which tourists will no longer care to see. If this is what we are looking for then we must renounce the effort to conserve Toulouse as the "city of art" . . . We demand that the authorities of the Beaux-Arts, the experts on urbanism, the municipal administrators responsible for urban development, make the Nicod Plan a living reality rather than a corrupted tool.[29]

Nicod remained loyal to his original urban design for limiting the growth of the city, enhancing its traditional urban functions, and avoiding the tragedy of uncontrolled suburban sprawl. In the 1957 analysis of his plan, he concluded that

> essentially Toulouse has progressed at the expense of its region. It is already giving the impression of an enormous head attached to a degenerating body. A stable future can be created around a regional capital with a network of prosperous local towns throughout its hinterland. Without this Toulouse will be reduced to the rank of a dead city, an archaeological museum, in a region functioning simply as a national park for tourists and vacationers.[30]

There was more than a hint of bitterness in this statement. His plan had been supplanted by the voracious need for housing. It had also foundered on the reefs of financial scarcity and on the reality of the state's control over the purse strings. Ultimately, however, the Nicod Plan sponsored by the Badiou administration simply did not accord with a variety of private interests in the city—real-estate developers, private businesses, and homeowners—who resented planning regulation and the strict limitations on growth and expansion, to say nothing of the very public revulsion against purist modern style. Nor did it accord with the state agenda for reconceptualizing urban space and habitat according to modernist norms. Nicod and Badiou had fought to modernize Toulouse in the spirit of its traditional form and society. The state, on the other hand, had every intention of dismantling them as retrograde and politically menacing.

The Battle for Central Toulouse

The chief urbanist at Toulouse during the 1950s, Coquerel, attempted to calm the apprehension about the demise of historic Toulouse at the hands of modernism by reassuring the protectionists that nothing had changed in terms of the safeguarding of the central city. "We will try," said Coquerel, "to extricate the neighborhoods from these apartment towers and to find building projects that are suitable for specific blocks and neighborhoods."[31] Even so, the fact was that very little of the exalted plans for historic Toulouse that had been outlined by Nicod had actually been carried through. The state's adamantly modernist policy was clear in its general neglect of renovation and its miserly financial support for traditional housing in the city's center. Modernism was a ruthless break with the past. Its adherents condemned the haphazard growth of the historic city for leaving little but problems in its wake. There was simply no room for compromise with the caprice of historical experience.

The tardiness of any real planning in the old city during the 1950s was particularly damaging given the congestion and overcrowding that were withering city life. Just after the war, in 1946, over 51,000 people were living in the old districts of central Toulouse. It was the largest number that had ever lived there. By 1954, despite the appearance of the first of the public-housing programs, the central city was still home to 49,000 people who represented over 19 percent of the city's population.[32] Except for a few areas such as the place Wilson, the place Victor-Hugo, and the rue d'Alsace-Lorraine, residential housing continued to take precedence over everything else, including commercial and office space. The expanding population of Toulouse continued to press the local housing market to its limits, even in the oldest districts, well into the late 1950s. Only then did the historic districts begin experiencing some decrease in their resident population. Most of those leaving were younger families. By 1962, 41,000 people remained in the *oustals toulousains* of the central city. Most of them were *petits patrons* and *petits commerçants* whose shops and ateliers were the trademark of the city's collective life. This was particularly true in the districts of the historic Cité between the derelict quais of the Garonne riverfront and the slums of Saint-Georges.[33] Its inhabitants were older, many of them poorer, less capable of moving to the rising apartment blocks. They lived alongside the city's foreigners, thousands of Spaniards and Italians, who could afford the low rents for the antiquated flats of the central district.

Given these population pressures, the dilapidation in historic Toulouse was forbidding. The vast majority of the central city had been constructed sometime before 1871. Only a minority of the *oustals* had undergone any type of modern renovation. Electricity, gas, and water were available in most of them by the end of the 1950s, but less than half were equipped with indoor bathrooms. Precious few had bathtubs, central heating, or telephone service.[34] The general state of disrepair made the line between slums and the better districts difficult to find. The faded brick, the sagging roofs, and run-down wooden shutters had lost all charm and instead simply represented the general neglect of the inner districts that characterized the policy to "modernize" the city after the war.

The streets and city squares had also been passed over. This was perhaps a more difficult collective bone of contention, because the growing number of automobiles made traffic and general congestion on Toulouse's "picturesque narrow streets" almost unbearable. If anything, the difficulties of maneuvering the city streets in the automobile age made the historic central districts seem even more grossly outdated. While in 1955 there had only been about 38,000 automobiles circulating through Toulouse, just five years later, in 1960, there were 75,000 cars attempting to journey along the city's main arteries.[35] The rue d'Alsace-Lorraine and the boulevards Strasbourg and Carnot that ringed the city's most important commercial districts were in 1957 described by Nicod as "at the limits of their capacity."[36] Trucks traveling from the route de Narbonne and the route d'Espagne were forced to negotiate the city streets before picking up the highway to Paris north of town. They rumbled down the rue Alsace and the rue du Languedoc day and night to the consternation of the city's residents. The historic sociability and color of the city's markets were difficult to appreciate amid the traffic jams, horns, and general chaos that awaited dauntless shoppers. Even more upsetting to local residents and devotees of Toulouse was the snag created by parking all the vehicles that crawled through the inner districts each day. Public and private garages and wide sidewalks offered space for some 6,000 to 7,000 cars that clogged traffic and sidewalk arteries and spelled doom to the city's historic street life.

Road repair and clearance projects were initiated almost immediately after the war and continued through the 1950s. Although they remained comparatively meager efforts, they fueled the ire of citizens certain that historic Toulouse would be lost in the trample toward modernism. A 1947 renewal project to construct an arcade between the boulevard Strasbourg and the rue Austerlitz demolished the famed Café Sion, one of the largest luxury cafes in France at the turn of the century. Its enormous window frontage and sumptuous decoration made it the epitome of fin-de-siècle modernism and Toulouse's traditional public life. "But progress always demands this extortion of the past. This time it is the grand Café Sion that disappears . . . this establishment represented the joyful lifestyle led by our forefathers," commented a melancholy letter sent to the city's newspaper.[37]

There were even more visceral alterations of Toulouse's image. At the river's edge, the city's historic windmill and the Garonette, a tiny canal that ran parallel to the Garonne, had once been one of the most picturesque areas of Toulouse. In 1926 Alex Coutet described the ". . . absolute tranquility that reigns over this stream . . . la 'Garonette' is rich with pretty little unexpected scenes."[38] But in 1940 the old windmill was destroyed by fire and the Garonnette had become an odorous sewer of semistagnant water. Nicod's Plan had envisioned renovating the area with a linear park running along both sides of the embankment. But instead, the stream was simply filled in during the 1950s and made into a dead-end alley used for parking space.

Clearing for parking facilities took even more unforgiving forms. One of the few early efforts to carry out a central district "renewal" project was the construction of the parking garage on the place Victor Hugo. The ghostly remains of an iron and glass *halle au marché* were all that was left of what had been one of the city's main market squares. The decaying structure was completely cleared in 1957 to make way for a modern five-story parking garage that included an Esso gas station and a "supermodern" market bazaar in the dark interior on the street level.

The planners and engineers responsible for renovating the French city in the 1950s saw the solution to the old district's worsening plight in terms of spatially designed functions that were put into practice through zoning. The inner city was to act as the commercial and administrative heart of Toulouse. This was its historic role. It had also of course been home to the vast majority of the city's inhabitants since the dawn of time. It was this residential character of Toulouse that was to be dismantled. The inner districts were to be cleared of their exhausted housing stock and their occupants, in order to make way for renovated commercial and administrative centers. Inner-city residents would be "relocated," in the language of state planning, to the residential zones of the *immeubles collectifs.* In 1957, Nicod himself continued to call for the complete demolition of the worst inner districts. Their residents were to be driven to the suburbs, leaving the cleared areas to be restored as commercial and administrative centers designed around monumental urban motifs—one of which would be the construction of 25,000 parking spaces.

The question of the renovation of the inner city into a new business core came to a head over the proposed renovation of the slum district of Saint-Georges. Saint-Georges was composed of seven infamous hectares of decayed housing. Despite its run-down condition, it represented one of those tiny popular quarters that many of the native Toulousains, not least among them the Saint-Georges residents themselves, considered to have some historic value as well as some hidden charm. In a rather dubious claim to historic legitimacy, the place Saint-Georges was known for the famous execution of Calas during the eighteenth century at which Voltaire had attempted to intercede. The *plassa de Sant Jordi,* or place Saint-Georges, had been the location of an ancient church dedicated to the patron saint of the Catalans. The streets and alleyways around it had evolved from the incoherent, rambling paths worn over the course of the centuries. Sinuous and narrow, dotted with a few woeful trees and benches, they provided a charm-ing puzzle for the summer evening strolls that had been so popular with the city's residents. The district's buildings perhaps lacked any unique claims as artistic treasures but nevertheless typified the traditional architecture that had come to personify Toulouse. Jean Coppolani could point to a curved house located in a courtyard on the rue d'Astorg, "one of the prettiest creations of the early nineteenth century," with a wall the color of wine.[39]

But even so, in truth by the 1920s Saint-Georges' reputation as an *îlot insalubré* had made it one of the most unsavory districts in Toulouse. Its demolition, for the sake of the city's social and hygienic welfare, was the goal of every planning effort of the twentieth century. Its buildings were considered not only unhealthy but dangerous. Many of them were built around decrepit inner courtyards with narrow passageways, malodorous leaks of contaminated water, and little light and air. In the worst of the buildings, rooms were without windows and the courtyard pump and water closet were the only utilities. By the end of the Second World War, the buildings were divided into 1,700 accommodations, the worst in Toulouse, that housed 3,700 mostly elderly, penniless inhabitants.[40] Junk stores and odds-and-ends shops, shoe repair, plumbing and tool trades lined the seedy streets. An indigent population of unemployed newly arrived foreigners, beggars, and homeless inhabited the district's square or found temporary lodging in its two dozen cheap hotels.

The area had been slated for slum renovation within the Nicod Plan. Demolishing the derelict district in favor of an open plaza with gardens, with new streets and parking facilities, with modern office and commercial space, would, argued Nicod, open up the inner city to light and air as well as solve some of the commercial district's serious congestion problems. The real importance of Saint-Georges lay, however, in its location between the place Wilson–allée Jean-Jaurès district and the administrative quarter of Saint-Etienne. Essentially, as it stood, Saint-Georges blocked any integration of these two districts into a new *centre d'affaires* for Toulouse, one that would reverse the failing economic fortunes of the old city. It was as an office, administrative, and commercial zone that the Saint-Georges neighborhood stood to most benefit Toulouse. "It's impossible to decently conserve all of this artistic capital," state investigator Georges Lacroix argued. "We have to accept doing something with the defunct part of it, of pruning those areas which are too old and too mediocre in order to make way for the new . . ." Lacroix was well aware of the local uproar that would ensue over the destruction of even the most desolate of the historic districts and admitted that the Saint-Georges renovation project would be "an interesting experience."[41]

In 1956 Badiou's administration, with the blessing of MRL, proceeded to design a blueprint for rehabilitating Saint-Georges. The *plan-masse*, designed by the architect Hoym de Marien, was the only major slum-clearance project attempted for the historic core. The neighborhood was to be entirely razed. In its place a broad central plaza would be laid out over an underground commercial center and parking garage. Altogether some 700 new buildings were to be constructed. Classy office buildings, luxury apartment complexes, and shopping galleries would set off a showcase complex of modern urban renewal. The shabby *oustals*, the cobblestone streets, the aged and the poor were all to be swapped for a scheme that exclaimed the benefits of modern urban design. The neighborhood's residents would be evicted and, as compensation, offered new homes in the state housing projects going up along the city's periphery.

The project was carried out under the auspices of a bureaucratic tour-de-force known as Toulouse-Equipement, a joint public-private *société d'économie mixte* redevelopment venture. It was created to coordinate the regulatory webs spun by municipal, departmental, and national agencies and to support private business investment in what were exceptionally expensive modernization projects.[42] The bureaucratic streamlining of Toulouse-Equipement was clearly meant to override the conflicting claims, bickering, and financial dearth that had too often choked the success of municipal management. But it smacked so heavily of *dirigisme* that it instantly became yet another symbol among local oppositional forces of the public tyranny that seemed to go hand in hand with the modernization of Toulouse.

When the plan for Saint-Georges was presented to the Municipal Council for approval in the summer of 1959, the fracas began. In front of a chamber packed with furious Saint-Georges residents organized into a Comité de Défense and a host of both outraged citizens and plan advocates, Communist representative Jean Llante accused the mayor of forcing "this monster fabricated by Toulouse-Equipement" down the Municipal Council's throat. "It took three years to produce, and we're supposed to analyze it in a couple of hours . . . The city's administration promised to include two representatives from Saint-Georges on the planning committee, but Toulouse-Equipement deliberated on the neighborhood without consulting anybody."[43] Despite the swing to the political right, with ten of thirty-seven representatives on the Municipal Council, the Communist Party was still a force to be reckoned with—as was Jean Llante himself, a Resistance hero and a recognized champion of left-wing democratic municipalism. The question was one of local democratic authority versus bureaucratic initiative. "Who were the delegates to the Toulouse-Equipement meetings?" Llante grilled Badiou's administration with the encouragement of a cheering gallery. "The Toulouse-Equipement dossier seems to have a certain orientation. Do you honestly believe that only 316 families want to remain at Saint-Georges as this report attests?"

There was also the sensitive issue of property rights. Llante accused Toulouse-Equipement inspectors of terrifying neighborhood apartment owners, grocers, and artisans with their interrogations and regulations. The local Union des Propriétaires advised Saint-Georges property owners not to work with the interlopers who would declare any building derelict that stood in the way of their plans. E. H. Guitard, director of the Bureau d'Esthetique Urbaine, protested the handing over of the district to commercial interests. "Jesus chased the money changers from the temple. Now they are taking their revenge."[44] Llante and the rest of the Communist councillors, along with Socialist and Radical support, steadfastly insisted on the necessity of sponsoring a public inquiry before the Municipal Council exercised its right, regardless of the departmental prefect's consent, to approve or reject the plan. Communist Simone Gardès bluntly asserted, to enthusiastic applause, that "these grandiose plans of yours are beautiful. They are indeed visionary. But you know very well, Monsieur Badiou, that under a capitalist regime, they are always carried through on the backs of the little people."[45]

The concern for "the little people" was tangled up in the differing images of Toulouse that underlay the painful debates over the Saint-Georges project. Quite clearly, the modern vision offered by Badiou's administration and the Nicod Plan was that of an inner city, cleared of its residential decay, that would blossom as the Midi's commercial and administrative center. They were functions, after all, at the historic heart of Toulouse. The Toulousains themselves were to find modern domestic bliss in the high-rises constructed along the periphery between the central districts and the hated cordon sanitaire. This image of modern Toulouse, carefully planned and divided into functional zones, did not, however, accord well with yet another historic image of the city, that of the culture of neighborhoods, the irregular puzzle of ancient streets, and the daily rhythms of the generations of *petits commerçants* and *petits patrons* who had called Toulouse home for centuries. There were more than enough of these *quartiers* left in the old city, even with the downfall of the most decrepit of them, to continue sanctifying this perception of *la ville rose*. But the demolition of Saint-Georges at the hands of modernism brought out the deepest fears of annihilation of a nostalgic world that was indeed in danger of passing. The relentless dismantling of traditional spatial arrangements barely hid the social excision that was its subtext.

By the late 1950s, it was the extreme left that had inherited the mantle of protecting this sense of regional habitability and culture. For the Communists, the world of old Toulouse represented the authentic popular culture of the Occitan working classes. The party articulated their sense of alienation and demise at the hands of state technocrats intent on a coercive campaign of modernization. The outraged Llante was best at articulating the inhumanity and distress associated with the "forced removal" from Saint-Georges. He accused the pen-pushing modernizers at Toulouse Equipement of hovering like vultures over the remains of the artisanal world. "Their report states that 1,214 families need to be relocated. But Toulouse-Equipement predicts that fourteen of these families, composed of old couples, should be dead by then, which leaves only 1,200 to take care of. At least they're providing work for the undertakers!"[46] The fact that Saint-Georges was to be refashioned into a luxury commercial and residential zone offered little compensation to those the Socialist newspaper *L'avenir* called "deportees."[47] The local population was convinced it was simply an attempt to get rid of them as unwanted vestiges of a former world. Referring to the planned plaza as the "place Toulouse-Equipement" or the "place Bazerque," the residents, along with their Communist supporters, fumed over their banishment into the pigeonholes, or *"bazerquage,"* of Lazaret, Joliment, and Empalot.

Emotions were further fueled by a major financial scandal that broke out in 1958 involving the SOTOCOGI's management of the cité de l'Hers and Rangueil-Souzelong public-housing projects. It cost the municipality millions and threatened families with the loss of their investments in the HLM flats. By 1960, some of the agency's speculators had already been jailed for fraud. It was further proof that the spiderweb of state agencies did nothing to protect the public interest—particularly the interests of low-income families least able to defend themselves against the forces of bureaucratic manipulation. In truth, very few of the Saint-Georges residents could afford the rents anywhere else at Toulouse. They were poor and old, and it was upsetting to disturb them even under the best of conditions.

Perhaps most telling in terms of the conceptualization of modernization was the fact that the Saint-Georges project became one of the most

prominent political footballs in the contest between rival aspirants for control of Toulouse. It was one of the most significant local issues fought out
during the transition between the Badiou and the Bazerque municipal administrations. In the midst of France's political crisis of 1958–59, Socialist
Louis Bazerque succeeded Badiou as mayor of Toulouse. He made no secret
of the fact that he had inherited an urban-planning scheme that he was
personally uneasy with. Given this skepticism about a project that was
too far along for him to prevent, supporting the cries for a modification,
a "humanization" of redevelopment, was an easy political maneuver and
one that distanced him from Badiou's urban policies. But in the painful
process of negotiating the riddle of obstacles that plagued Saint-Georges,
Bazerque's attitude toward the old city became crystal clear. Defending
Toulouse-Equipement against accusations that it terrorized the neighborhood, Bazerque thundered at the Municipal Council that "the director of
Toulouse-Equipement is not driving anyone crazy, he doesn't go around
saying that overnight we're going to destroy the neighborhood and kick
everyone out. But I'll say it for him! I'll declare it! Toulouse is a terrible city!
This whole uproar is completely out of hand!"

Pierre Baudis, Bazerque's first adjunct and eventual successor, had
voted against the original plan because of Toulouse-Equipement's attempts
to railroad slum clearance without adequate protection for Saint-Georges'
property owners and because of the exorbitant costs of reconstruction.
Baudis demanded that the residents be relocated in low-cost public housing
in the central city rather than being banished to the *immeubles collectifs*. He
wanted a special relocation commission set up that would include representatives of the renters and property and business owners from the district.
As erstwhile champion of the forgotten community of needy occupants,
politically centrist Baudis stood with the Communist opposition in insisting upon written guarantees that the residents be treated fairly and that the
whole process of removal be vigilantly scrutinized to purge any injustices
perpetrated against the rightful claimants.

Sitting in the Municipal Council chamber, Badiou listened as his plan
was ground up in the machinery of political dispute. The oppositional
forces rapidly succeeded in forcing modification of the Saint-Georges *plan de
détail*, particularly once it became clear through two official public inquiries
and thousands of letters to the mayor and Municipal Council that indeed
the majority of Saint-Georges residents and property owners resolutely rejected the project. In January 1959, the residents of Saint-Georges marched
in public protest to the Nouveautés theater, where before a packed house

they publicly expressed their consternation with the plan. Madame Dreuilhe, one of the most outspoken neighborhood activists, gave an emotional appeal for reconsideration of the quarter's demolition: "This brotherly feeling, as if we are all related, will we still have it? What will be there after deportation? Theaters, luxury stores, parking garages will replace our old homes."[48] The Union Régionale de la Propriété Bâtie; the Société des Toulousains de Toulouse; Jacques Maziol of the Gaullist Union pour la Nouvelle République (UNR); Pierre Baudis of the centrist Independents; Professor Ourliac from the University; a host of municipal councillors; neighborhood organizers from Marengo, Champ-du-Loup, and Croix-Daurade who had fought the same battles with modernization—all stood with the embattled residents of Saint-Georges. In July, just before the Municipal Council's vote on the project, a crowd of 4,000 overwhelmed the Salle du Sénéchal in the Capitole to hear fiery speeches by a host of civic leaders decrying the ruin of the "still robust world of our fathers." Professor Marty from the Law Faculty exposed the crimes of the modernists: "We aren't retrograde! Nor are we standing around dreaming of the Toulouse of the year 2000. It's my true belief in these circumstances! We have no idea what the future city will look like. But we are here now!"[49] With thousands standing outside the Municipal Council chamber on July 7, the Socialists passed the Saint-Georges plan against the opposition of the Communists, the Independents, and the MRP.

But the popular protest was triumphant—at least in part. The area slated for demolition was cut back, and the amended plan endorsed the conservation of more of the streets and buildings of the old district. An evaluation of the Saint-Georges project was sponsored by the regional prefect and carried out by state engineer Granet from the Department of Public Works. Granet's report concluded: "A choice has to be made between slum clearance or renovation. We choose the latter." The compromise directed de Marien to modify his plan by cutting back the area to be demolished and shrinking the priority given to office, commercial, and luxury hotel construction. In their place, public-housing projects and an artisanal center would conserve the historic character of the district. Some of the sinuous alleyways were to be refurbished as pedestrian promenades. Small open plazas would be resurrected for *petits commerçants* and artisans. The dramatic fabrication of Toulouse as a glamorous regional capital shriveled in the face of the vernacular. Business and flat owners already located at Saint-Georges would be offered first choice in the new commercial galleries and residential high-rises. A special HLM relocation program was created to help move the

Saint-Georges residents that included special aid for the elderly. Toulouse-Equipement was reproached for its heavy-handed policies, which should, according to Granet, be replaced with a far more patient, humanistic approach to the difficult problem of resettlement.

The whole project continued to be mired down in the innumerable arguments raised against it over individual indemnities, the cost of construction, and the difficulties of residential relocation. Once the "removals" began to take place, Toulouse-Equipement was faced with the indelicate job of convincing the intractable residents of the district that selling their property to the state was somehow in their best interests. Few of the sales were amiable, and Toulouse-Equipement resorted to expropriation, with the resultant wrath of the local property owners' association, far more frequently than was politically prudent. Between 1959 and 1974, 269 buildings were either purchased or expropriated, 257 of the neighborhood's trades were bought out, 2,424 people were removed by the public authorities. Few of the businesses survived extradition from their traditional workspace. The majority of the families were found homes in the apartment blocks along the periphery of Toulouse, at Bagatelle or La Faourette, where the rents were far higher than at Saint-Georges. Only sixty-four families remained at Saint-Georges in a new HLM apartment complex that was constructed as part of the effort to mollify the aggrieved citizenry. It was designed by architect François Castaing, the director of Toulouse-Equipement, in what had to be a public atonement for the agency's modernist condescension. With the help of the Bureau d'Aide Sociale, a senior citizens' residence was also built across the river in Saint-Cyprien for the poorest and oldest of the former Saint-Georges dwellers.[50] But their deportation was experienced as a terminal psychic uprooting from the neighborhood and daily life that had sustained their later years.

When the revamped district was finally unveiled, the rakishly modern place Occitan, surrounded by a sentinel of glass towers, stood forth as the site most symbolic of the new Toulouse. It floated over an underground parking lot and a commercial arcade overflowing with enticing wares. All of this was just adjacent to a refurbished, but smaller, Saint-Georges neighborhood. A more incongruous statement of the battle over slum clearance could not have been devised. The fact that the high-rises integrated red brick into the masonry and that the plaza was named in accordance with Toulouse tradition were little consolation. They exuded the opulence and glamour that was meant from the beginning to provide Toulouse with a new modernist image. The place Occitan would, according to its promoters, "eventually be even grander than the place du Capitole."[51] The Résidence Saint-Georges, the Résidence Le Donjon, the Hôtel Mercure were designed to attract a wealthy clientele, as were the luxury shops that moved in to the surrounding neighborhood. The rents in the entire Saint-Georges district skyrocketed. Local urbanist Guy Jalabert accused the project's designers of falsely "historicizing" the whole district, which had, in fact, become the dominion of a prosperous leisure class. As the new *boulevardiers,* they alone patronized the upscale neo-artisan shops, luxury boutiques, and trendy restaurants of the new Saint-Georges. It was faux-Occitan, an abstracted playground setting—fictionalized and depoliticized—carved out of the residue of the historically indigenous Cité. "None of it hides the social logic," Jalabert argued, "that has given the most affluent people control over the central city while the poorest and oldest, the immigrant workers, are kicked out to the periphery."[52]

Urban renovation and public-housing programs, such as those accomplished at Toulouse during the 1950s and 1960s, were indeed coercive systems for shifting the social landscape. They evidenced the fierce struggle for control over urban space that took place as France modernized. The transformation of French cities, the consolidation of capitalist structures and space, could be a conflict-laden and wrenching experience, especially when it was engineered by the state. This was particularly true because modernization always took place within the context of local experience and collective consciousness. And even these were fraught with idiosyncrasies and discord. Certain protaganists for Toulouse understood state regulation of land use, neighborhood renewal and housing programs, and modern style itself as assaults against vernacular society and culture. Others issued their own modernist canon within the vernacular idiom. Both local and state elites articulated "modernist" visions as political gambits. Alliances and the forms of local resistance were shaped, then reshaped by the ongoing struggle to define the meaning of modern Toulouse.

Although the forces of French modernism became increasingly statist and dogmatic, the local environment did succeed in retaining some measure of control over its future. Saint-Georges was the only large-scale slum-clearance program attempted at Toulouse. No clear-cut pattern of modern urban design emerged, despite the persistent attempts by both the state and local officialdom. Instead, the space and image of the city reflected an amalgam of tensions, a plurality of modernist perceptions and options that were at times ironic and contradictory.

The New Regionalism

Slum-clearance and public-housing programs were perhaps the most visible and controversial forms of modernism applied at Toulouse. But the spatial and social ordering of the French landscape extended far past the urban habitat. Postwar reconstruction was conceived as a geographic rearrangement of heroic dimension. It struck at the very heart of the particularist malignancies that were charged with the country's ignominious wartime defeat. The provinces and their fractious regional degeneracies were to be soberly arranged and brought under state control. Toulouse was set within a regional frame of reference that not only determined its character and function but ranked it within a strict spatial hierarchy determined by state elites. City, region, and nation were joined in a pyramidal framework constructed around modernist norms. This was the spatial blueprint, the map of the new France. It would be purged of any of the particularist traits, any of the social and political strife deemed threatening to national consolidation.

The state technocratic corps had been formulating the conceptual foundation for a new version of regionalism since the late 1940s. The original local efforts at regional economic development, sponsored by the Commissars de la République during the Liberation, had disappeared along with the commissars themselves.[53] Pierre Bertaux and his Conseil Économique Régional were far too independent, far too infused with the Resistance euphoria for reform to survive within the context of reconstituted state authority. In general, local efforts at defining the meaning of regionalism were dispersed and somewhat tenuous during the 1950s. Occitanism as a cultural construction had largely become the domain of the left. But it was a dubious and isolated struggle carried on by fairly remote associations such as the Institut d'Estudis Occitans founded by Jean Cassou and Charles Camproux around a group of local Resistance writers. Only the Communists and extreme left actively took on the political cause of the alienation of Occitan working-class culture, and even their adherence was equivocal. Given the postwar aversion to both "regional authenticity" and the extreme left as menacing to national harmony, there was little chance that this culturalist perspective would be revived as an influential force.

The Chamber of Commerce and local business leaders at Toulouse were a far more effective local voice in the debate about reconstruction and regional modernization. Through the medium of the IXth Economic Region, they set in motion at least some of the economic development programs advocated by the defunct Conseil Économique Régional: a tourist commission, an industrial commission, a regional economic council. In this regard, the business elites at Toulouse shared the same concern about overcoming social cleavages and economic shortcomings through regional development that came from mayors, Chambers of Commerce, and industrialists throughout the provinces. An array of clubs and associations popped up across the French landscape committed to solving regional economic inequities as an integral part of reconstruction and modernization. These local ambitions were a crucial catalyst in pressing a cautious government into the arena of regionalism.

Nonetheless, state policy toward the provinces continued to push aside democratic initiative and reinforce the centralizing reflexes that were seen as imperative to the reconstitution of the country. Five months after suppressing the regional commissars in 1946, the state appointed new regional economic inspectors. Then, in response to the strike waves in the fall of 1947, the government designated Inspecteurs Généraux de l'Administration en Mission Extraordinaire, or IGAMEs, to maintain order and oversee prefectorial administration throughout the provinces. The twelve departments around Toulouse formed the Fifth Administrative Region, overseen by IGAME Louis Périllier.[54] This early state version of regional authority was based entirely on the immediate need to reestablish control over France. Within the context of the budding Cold War, the IGAMEs were *hauts fonctionaires* wresting back political jurisdiction from the forces of Communism and the Resistance. They were sent to "normalize" France under the spreading shield of the American umbrella and its Marshall Plan.

However, administrators at the MRU had also inherited the regional industrial studies carried out by the DGEN. Both Raoul Dautry at the MRU and Jean Monnet at the Commissariat Général du Plan clearly supported a geographic redistribution of economic wealth within the context of the *"économie concertée"* and reconstruction. In 1947, geographer Jean-François Gravier published the MRU's report on the spatial mapping of the French economy as *Paris et le désert français,* a scathing attack against the urban monster of Paris that had sucked dry the provinces and made them into a cultural and economic "desert."[55] Gravier's book was highly influential during the early postwar years. By 1949 a Direction de l'Aménagement du Territoire (the term coined by the DGEN) had been created under the auspices of Eugène Claudius-Petit, who took over control of the MRU in 1948. Claudius-Petit introduced the principle as political policy in a February 1950 speech to the government entitled *"Pour un plan national d'aménagement du territoire."* It outlined industrial decentralization, the protection of the environment, and agriculture as the tasks necessary for "a better distribution of the populace across the geography of France."[56] It was initially conceived in terms of a national fund, or the Fonds National d'Aménagement du Territoire, for investment in infrastructure and industries in the provinces. But the gestation period for the new covenant of *aménagement du territoire* was far longer than that for urbanism and the state housing programs. Regional development remained a modest endeavor until the mid-1950s, when, under the guardianship of Etienne Hirsch at the Commissariat Général du Plan, Pierre Mendès-France, who served as premier in 1954–1955, and Edgar Faure at the Finance Ministry, the state's role began to take on more definition.

In 1955 and 1956 "regional action programs" and twenty-two "program regions" were drawn up by high-level officials at the Commissariat Général du Plan. The geographic puzzle was largely left as it had been created by Vichy, under the influence of Vidal de la Blache and Henri Hauser—the regions would naturally create themselves, little by little, around the great urban agglomerations and their spheres of influence.[57] However, the Commissariat also tried to shape the new regions around the more far-flung administrative jurisdictions of the IGAMEs, simply to harmonize the expanding apparatus of state power.

Toulouse was designated capital of the Région Midi-Pyrénées. It was composed of eleven departments, including the departments of the Aude, Pyrénées-Atlantique, and Pyrénées-Orientales, which gave the region control of the Pyrenees Mountains and access to both the Mediterranean and the Atlantic Oceans. The region was the largest drawn up for France, one reason for its fairly rapid reduction in 1960. It was scaled back with the loss of the Aude and the Pyrénées-Orientales to Montpellier and the Pyrénées-Atlantiques to Bordeaux. In this form it was an exact replica of Vidal de la Blache's 1910 version of the Midi-Pyrénées and came quite close to the region drawn up under Bertaux as Commissar de la République. Nonetheless there was genuine local concern that the Midi-Pyrénées was simply an artificially contrived administrative space, the work of Parisian technocrats, and that it lacked any historical or economic cohesiveness. It was superimposed over the whole of the Comte de Foix, half of the old provinces of Guyenne and Gascogne, and the western fragment of the old province of Languedoc. There was somewhat dubious acceptance of what appeared to be yet another arbitrary dissection of Midi historical geography by Paris. For many, the Midi-Pyrénées remained a "phantom" constructed more by political deceit and administrative dim-wittedness than by genuine concerns over historic or economic geographic unity. In fact Toulouse would have difficulty maintaining economic mastery over the region's periphery. The Chambers of Commerce at Pau and Tarbes in the Adour basin launched efforts at constructing their own region, while the area south of Aveyron looked more toward Montpellier for economic leadership.[58]

The Midi-Pyrénées took its place among the imaginary circumventions of spatiality and geographic territory that had marked regionalist endeavors since the early twentieth century. What made it particularly consequential, however, was that it was the invented regional constellation in which the state conceptualized its official program for the modernization of Toulouse. Unfortunately, the state's agenda clearly deviated from Badiou's conception of the city's future. Badiou's planning was rooted in the local tradition of Socialist municipalism and its "humanistic" approach to modernization. It emphasized Toulouse's traditional commercial, intellectual, and administrative functions and the benefits of controlled growth within a balanced regional network of towns and villages.

By the late 1950s, the program sponsored by state planning agencies concentrated instead on the industrialization and rapid expansion of Toulouse as the region's economic nerve center. The energy source for industrial development in the southwest was to be the natural gas deposits at Lacq in the foothills of the Pyrenees Mountains. Its production, plus the hydroelectric resources of the Pyrenees, as well as the possibility of research into liquid hydrocarbons, promised abundant energy for new industry. "Lacq!" a local magazine article exclaimed. "It is one of the most solid reasons for believing in the industrial future of our city."[59] The initial "program for regional action," written in 1958 by a legion of state and local administrators led by IGAME Louis Périllier and regional Prefect Emile Pelletier (both appointed in Paris), named aeronautics and chemicals as the two fundamental growth industries of Toulouse. They would be deliberately expanded by state fiat as the particular "vocations" of the city. The southwest would be pulled out of its economic doldrums through the planned industrialization of its new "economic pole"—Toulouse.[60]

Whatever consternation and skepticism the public and the municipality might have felt about this new era in the city's history launched rather dogmatically by state planners, the immediate benefits overrode them. In 1956, the city's main distinction among its urban counterparts was still its low salaries and income. Nearly 75 percent of the city's wage earners made

less than the national average of 413,000 francs per year.⁶¹ This depressing situation was further aggravated by the recession that plagued France
throughout the 1950s, but which was particularly severe in the Midi. The
president of the local Regional Economic Council, Emile Roche, argued that
if nothing else the state program offered an immediate way out of unemployment and a sagging economy. Jobs would be needed for soldiers return-
ing from the Algerian War. State investment could be used for badly needed
infrastructure.⁶² These rationalizations were bolstered by the criticisms of
Badiou's modernist agenda and especially of his construction boundary. The
objections to his limited-growth approach had become a torrent by the late
1950s. The new state policy of molding Toulouse into an industrial "growth
pole" within the new Midi-Pyrénées region was far more in keeping with the
expansionist mentality of the city's business and propertied interests.

In October 1958 an embattled and unyielding Raymond Badiou resigned as
mayor of Toulouse and walked away from the Capitole. He renounced his
membership in the SFIO in opposition to the Socialist Party's support for
Charles de Gaulle and the creation of the Fifth Republic. His departure from
City Hall was a feature of the complicated political crisis of 1958 and 1959.
It was played out at Toulouse in a turbulence of issues and events: the
Algerian crisis and the reappearance of de Gaulle, the breach in Socialist
unity that this turn of events provoked, the controversy over the Saint-
Georges project and Nicod's city growth boundary. The mayor's resignation
in the midst of the public ruckus over his planning policies and the coun-
try's profound political instability came as something of a rude, as well
as for some a gratifying, shock. Badiou joined with the Parti Socialiste
Autonome (PSA), along with his personal supporters and fellow dissidents
at Toulouse, in protest against Guy Mollet's brutal takeover of the Socialist
Party (SFIO) machine.

   Clearly, Badiou's shift to an independent stance of opposition represented the waning fortunes of Resistance aspirations and the decline of the
traditional Midi Socialist block. The PSA defectors saw themselves as the
defenders of the Midi Socialism espoused by Jean Jaurès and Léon Blum. The
PSA attacked the SFIO's timidity in standing up to de Gaulle's authoritarian-
ism, his handling of the Algerian crisis, and the government's inhumane tax
increases. Badiou railed against Poujadism, Pétainism, and the dangers of
the Gaullist constitutional reform.

   However, the demise of the mayor and his municipal agenda was also associated with the disenchantment with pure modernist style and the strict regulation of urban growth and private real-estate interests that both Badiou and Nicod represented. According to Badiou, Toulouse, freed from the Algerian war, should be concentrating on its modernization, on becoming a "prosperous capital, happy and flowering in liberty, within a region inspired toward progress."[63] He continued to argue the merits of limiting the city's growth and emphasizing balanced development throughout the Midi-Pyrénées as by far the most humane and effective form of modernization. He pressed for a modernist renaissance in central Toulouse befitting the regional capital. Badiou garnered substantial support at Toulouse and, with his PSA, was able to maintain a seat on the Municipal Council through the early 1960s. But his vision of Toulouse was increasingly isolated and bypassed by the crescendo of local complaints and by the government's more omnipotent fantasy of a future Toulouse based on industrialization and expansion.

In this regard, Badiou's administration was caught up in the shift from a left-wing progressivist modernism sponsored by the Socialist municipality to a far more relentless version of modernism advocated by the French state. Modernism's initial appeal had been as a revolutionary antidote to reactionary and traditionalist ideology. It was a Socialist revolt against the decay and disorder of the old urban labyrinth that had left working-class families without access to housing or basic public services. The municipality was a theater of operations for social reform. Even the state-sponsored HLM housing projects built on the periphery of the city during the 1950s had some historic legitimacy. Working-class housing in France had traditionally occupied marginal, suburban locations where they would not deflate urban property values. The HLM projects at Toulouse were constructed in traditional working-class strongholds like Saint-Cyprien, Saint-Michel, and Minimes bordering the urban core. They were in areas initially used as sites for the Socialist interwar experiments in public housing and garden cities. They provided affordable modern dwellings for the working classes of Toulouse. Their construction within a strictly controlled perimeter avoided the arbitrary chaos of rampant urban sprawl that seemed to prosper no one but private real-estate interests. In much the same way, the Saint-Georges slum-clearance project was interpreted by Badiou's administration as a continuation of the interwar effort to revitalize the inner city, open it to air and light, and offer modern city conveniences to its deprived citizens.

Over the course of the 1950s this modernist agenda was increasingly paid for and appropriated by state interests. Badiou's Socialist administration had neither the political independence nor the funds to tackle these urban reform programs on its own. Even more compelling was the fact that with the Liberation, the French state reinforced its legitimacy by taking on the modernist program as its own remedy for the decline and social disorder that threatened the country. This absorption of the modernist ethic into official social policy brought with it a far more ominous struggle over social power and cultural imperialism. Clearly the central city was associated with the new forces of the modern economy—finance, banks, commerce, business headquarters, and offices. In the hands of an ascendant state bureaucracy outside the control of democratic municipalism, redevelopment programs such as Saint-Georges could easily be translated as cultural war. The new elites were confiscating central Toulouse as their bastion of social and economic power while the working classes were exiled to peripheral and austere housing estates where they would be less of a social problem. The historic social milieu perceived this as an ideological attack and the imposition of a new modernist mythology about the city, its social makeup, and the built environment.

In truth the appropriation of centrality by the forces of modernism, led by this uneasy mixture of Socialist reformers and state technocrats during the 1950s, was only very partially successful at Toulouse. The city's historic cultural and social groups managed to hang on to the vast majority of the central spaces that were so critically associated with power. Just as remarkable, as well as analogous, was the resilience of the Socialist Party and the left in holding onto political power at Toulouse despite the pressures of Gaullism and the foundation of the Fifth Republic. Although the opposition called for new municipal elections immediately after the national referendum establishing the Fifth Republic in September 1959 and Badiou's sudden departure, the predominantly left-wing city councillors were able to deflect the crisis and refused to resign. They proceeded to elect Socialist Louis Bazerque, Badiou's first adjunct, as mayor. In his first official appearance at the Municipal Council in November 1958, Bazerque gave no testimonial to Badiou's service to the city, made no salutes to his urban policies. Instead, he proclaimed the SFIO's acceptance of the Fifth Republic and of the government's prophecy for Toulouse as, in Bazerque's words, "a regional capital, an administrative, intellectual, commercial—but now also an industrial—city . . ."[64] Bazerque cemented the Socialist Party's alliance with the center-right by appointing his adjuncts from the UNR and the Independent parties. The three parties that remained vehemently anti-Gaullist (the PSA, the Communists, and the Radicals) were increasingly left out in the political cold.

This shifting political configuration at the Capitole was simply a reflection of the *"glissement à droite"* taking place within public opinion. In the December 1958 legislative elections for the Haute-Garonne, both the Communists and Socialists lost seats, while the UNR managed to elect René Cathala from the northern precinct of Toulouse and Jacques Maziol from the southern precinct. Independent(CNI) leader Pierre Baudis won the seat from central Toulouse with the support of the Radicals. The success of Baudis's Union Nationale coalition in the municipal elections of 1959 and his eventual appointment as first adjunct reflected the gradual shift in Toulouse politics toward the centrist and right agenda of the Fifth Republic. Nonetheless, the Socialists remained in control of Toulouse. They were left with the uneasy chore of maintaining their own municipal authority while working within the accepted context of the highly technocratic, right-wing Fifth Republic.

CHAPTER **4**

The City of the Future:
Planning in the 1960s

In February 1959, Charles de Gaulle returned to Toulouse for the first time since his stopover to rein in the insurrectionary city during the Liberation. He toured the aircraft plants at Blagnac, the Faculty of Science, and the optical electronics and toxicity institutes. It was Toulouse's industrial and research potential that interested him. "At this moment of my life, in my last years, I have the sense at the University of Toulouse and at Sud-Aviation of standing on a beach, at the edge of an ocean, the shores of discovery that will carry you the researchers, you the professors, you the students of Toulouse into the unknown land of progress."[1] His speeches were couched in a depoliticized economic discourse on the momentous choice facing the city and France between decline or modernization. Progress was the theme for the city's new economic calling. The tour was meant to open up the possibility of *rapprochement* between de Gaulle's Fifth Republic and Socialist Toulouse, particularly since the General was offering substantial state economic aid as a sign of his largess. Nonetheless, Toulouse was one of the staunchest anti-Gaullist strongholds in the country, and de Gaulle was clearly venturing into enemy territory. Regional IGAME Jean Morin was chosen to act as intermediary between de Gaulle and the city's political and economic notables. In the midst of well-wishing, ceremony, and offers of government funding, de Gaulle made it clear that it was the state that held the purse strings and thus determined the public interest and the objectives of modernization.[2]

French planning entered a new phase with the advent of the Fifth Republic in 1958 and the ascent of Charles de Gaulle to the Presidency. De Gaulle was an avid supporter of the *économie concertée*. Modernization fit into his vision of restoring France to its rightful place as a world power. Economic development became a national duty, and the *dirigiste* efforts of his administration were far more coercive, far more systematized, than the participatory neoliberalism of the 1950s. Nonetheless, the Fifth Republic offered Toulouse an attractive role in the "new France" that de Gaulle invoked. Expansion was now the blueprint for the future. Although many meanings were ascribed to the word, ultimately it was meant to signify a "new attitude." Growth, economic modernization, and industrial development would be constructive aims associated with the appearance of Toulouse as one of the nation's foremost regional capitals. In a 1959 press conference, Mayor Bazerque outlined the new ambitions for the city. "Above all," he said, "we must define the Toulouse of tomorrow, which has completely escaped the sclerosis that quickly awaits a city imprisoned by its traditions."[3] For Toulouse this policy was a drastic turnabout from Badiou's emphasis on the careful balance between a flourishing region and a capital city of manageable size and economic weight. Government emphasis, both on the national and municipal levels, would instead be on the rapid industrial expansion of the provincial capital, which would, by virtue of its economic dominion, jump-start the region around it.

For municipal planners and local developers, the new policy was a bonanza. The continued growth in the population had brought Toulouse up to 330,000 inhabitants by 1962. To this substantial tally was then added yet another stream of immigrants. Young Algerians and Moroccans flooded into the city during 1962 and 1963 with the end of the Algerian war. The nationalization of Algerian agriculture in 1963 brought a wave of European Algerians in 1963 and 1964. In this short three-year period more than 43,000 repatriates appeared in Toulouse. Although many of them were looking for a temporary haven and eventually moved on to other cities or returned to Algeria, over 27,000 *pieds-noirs* settled down in the capital of Languedoc.[4] Given the numbers of people taking up residence plus the rising birthrates, the expectation was that Toulouse's population would swell to 400,000 or 500,000 over the next twenty years, with another 200,000 people living in the suburbs. These population figures and the forecasting of future growth became an obsession with public authorities. They were the basis for claiming Toulouse's power and legitimacy within the "new France" emerging in the late twentieth century.[5] Within the very foreseeable future the city could take its place as one of the singular industrial metropolises of modern Europe. According to the mayor, ". . . no other city in France can play the role of development pole as well as Toulouse." Its peripheral location and the difficulties of communication had, according to Bazerque, made the southwest historically the most independent region of France, with Tou-louse as its central pivot. "Within the Midi-Pyrénées, Toulouse commands all transportation and communication. It is the counterpoint to the central-izing influence of Paris."[6]

There was something suspiciously imperial in this claiming of the Midi-Pyrénées for Toulouse. But hegemony over the new program region did appear more in keeping with the city's historic dominion then had the woefully minuscule department of the Haute-Garonne. Even more impor-tantly, Bazerque's grand eloquence on behalf of the city signaled the under-current of tension that characterized the relations between the Socialist municipality and the technocrats in Paris over the mission to invent the modern city. Louis Bazerque was an avid enthusiast of expansionism. He was without doubt the most visible, the most flamboyant Toulousain of the postwar era. Locally he was known as "the bull." Toulouse experts Chris-tian Beringuier and Guy Jalabert observed of him, with clear cynicism: "The good-natured profile, the corpulent silhouette, the nasal accent, the genuine affection for those close to him still could not hide his dominat-ing personality, the false bonhomie, the loud, gruff speech, his taste for power."[7] British journalist John Ardagh remarked that Bazerque "became a byword in France for a certain kind of old-style Socialist potentate of the Midi."[8]

In any case, Bazerque was painted in local discourse as "quintessenal Toulousain." Born in 1912 to an artisan family that specialized in the remak-ing crafts, he attended Toulouse's law school, played rugby, and eventually practiced law and built up his own local real-estate empire. He was a dyed-in-the-wool advocate of Toulouse. Determined to take every advantage of the government's interest in promoting Toulouse as a growth pole, Bazerque lobbied fiercely for state development subsidies and for the financial favors due its new status. But as a Socialist mayor working within a Gaullist state framework, he wrestled incessantly for some local autonomy in sculpting the city's future. That did not prevent him, however, from instituting a technobureaucratic dominion over the city that drastically undercut the older local practice of democratic municipalism. To say the least, not every-one in the city agreed with Bazerque's vision of the "Toulouse of tomorrow." The opposition to his schemes and to *dirigiste* management, to his perceived willingness to play the irritating sycophant to the technocratic state, was vocal and quite formidable in this struggle to define the meaning of mod-ernism.

The Shift to Expansionism

As soon as Bazerque took over the city offices, his administration launched a planning program fit for "the capital of the southwest." The Plan Directeur d'Urbanisme was initially conceived in 1958, actually approved in 1962, and then underwent a series of modifications to become by 1967 a document known as the Livre Blanc. Supported by the majority of Socialists and their center-right allies on the Municipal Council, the plan was audacious in its approach to city development. But more than simply a reaction to the high-density, controlled-growth policies of the 1950s, its particular design was meant to synchronize with the national government's regional development efforts. The Plan Directeur was an effort at detente, or at least coordination, with the state's own far-flung agenda for Toulouse. The consulting architect with the MRL in Paris, Monsieur Baudouin, traveled down to Toulouse in 1959 to set out, along with Bazerque and his staff, the Plan's main themes. In Baudouin's estimation any urban program had to be boiled down to a simple phrase or a unique concept that would inspire its design and provide it with cohesion. The ideal concept, the poetic vision that Baudoin proposed, was: "Toulouse, on the banks of the Garonne, a happy city, rose amidst the greenery." If there was a way to give the city harmony, it was its color.

Central Toulouse, *la ville rose,* would be a *centre archéologique,* its old buildings with their pink and purple hues preserved through a carefully articulated policy of conservation and renovation. Around it, a first ring of historic faubourgs was distinguished, but little was actually offered by way of a planning strategy for them. Baudouin argued that Toulouse did not take sufficient advantage of its location on the Garonne. The Garonne Valley seemed to him to be excellent for development. With this endorsement, the notorious construction perimeter was extended to 3,500 hectares around the city. The population held prisoner by Nicod's boundary would at last be liberated. But Baudouin did not have some pastoral Occitan reverie in mind for the commune of Toulouse. There, in the suburbs, the whiteness and geometric form of modern architecture might surprise, even shock, but that was a natural reaction to anything new. Regardless, modernism would be the symbol of the new, expanding metropolis. The three development zones comprising greater Toulouse would then be linked through a system of highways and green belts.[9]

The Plan Directeur designated two essential guidelines for growth in these three zones. First, the overdevelopment of the central city on the right bank of the Garonne River would be counterbalanced by directing development toward the left bank. As Jaussely had argued in his city plan of the 1920s, the best opportunity for balanced growth lay in reversing the centuries of urbanization that had favored the Terrefort. Second, rather than suffer the consequences of uncontrolled private development, the territory was further partitioned through the medium of zoning. The strategy was delineated in 1958 by the Ministry of Construction.[10] The commune of Toulouse was penciled into rural zones, industrial zones, residential zones, military zones, and tourist zones. The residential zones were originally drawn around seven peripheral towns which would become suburban axes.

By 1960, however, the government was articulating a more carefully planned network of "satellite cities."[11] Their planning was to be coordinated with that of the municipality of Toulouse and with the communes of the *groupement d'urbanisme* to create a well-harmonized urban region. This kind of all-inclusive design was meant to avoid the suburban ghettos and exiled working-class barracks that already littered Toulouse's outland. The 1958 state zoning decree permitted municipal governments to directly control the construction of housing and infrastructure in specific areas known as *zones à urbaniser par priorité,* or ZUPs. They were meant to extricate suburban space from its mangle of parochial interests so that planned settlements could be launched based on the modern definition of "quality of life." An Atelier Municipal d'Urbanisme was created in 1960 to handle the complicated problems of appropriation, land purchases, and planning. The first project was the ZUP de Mirail, located six kilometers west of central Toulouse. It was planned as a satellite city of 100,000 residents. When it was initially conceived in 1960, Le Mirail was meant to be the main focus for the city's suburban growth. However, no sooner had the Plan Directeur been formulated than it required revision, largely at the behest of state policy makers who foresaw a much more sweeping modernist future for Toulouse.

By the early 1960s regional development was becoming a high-profile policy championed by government modernization enthusiasts. The new program regions had been drawn up, prefects and consultive councils appointed for each region, and development plans sketched out. In this newest guise regionalism was accepted as a trailblazing covenant, a noble guideline for rejuvenating France, and it was applied in a rigorous and ironhanded fashion. In 1963, the Délégation à l'Aménagement du Territoire et à l'Action Régionale (DATAR) was created by the French government to coordinate the campaign for equitably distributing the fruits of economic development throughout the provinces. The agency became the supreme instrument for defining and ordering geographic space as a mechanism for national unity and state control. It centralized and coordinated the investment programs, plans, maps, and formulae that germinated in the virgin field of "regional policy" cultivated by state technocrats. As a framework for regional development, DATAR and the Commissariat du Plan adopted the concept of spatial "growth poles" from geographer Vidal de la Blache and the social scientists working in the prewar years. After boisterous arguments over which and how many cities should be chosen for the honor, eight metropolises were designated in 1964 as growth poles or, as they became popularly known, *métropoles d'équilibres:* the three urban conurbations of Lille-Roubaix-Tourcoing, Lyon-Saint-Etienne-Grenoble, and Marseille-Aix-en-Provence, and the cities of Nancy-Metz, Strasbourg, Nantes-Saint-Nazaire, Bordeaux, and Toulouse.

The whole idea of the *métropoles d'équilibres* sounded, from the start, like slick hyperbole. But there were real benefits to be reaped by the cities chosen as government favorites, since DATAR wielded extraordinary influence in the Gaullist attempt to manage and modernize France. The French high-tech industries chosen for development under the Fourth Plan were each decentralized to a specific *métropole*. As the city's pilot industry it would act as a catalyst for economic modernization. It would stimulate the creation of new business, expand production, and generate real prosperity. Theoretically, this economic alchemy would then trickle down through the *métropole's* regional hinterland.[12] The new pilot industries were always more or less under the control of the state, which used public financing to direct economic growth in each of the chosen cities and ultimately to control the industrial geography of France. In addition, each of the *métropoles* was showered with state revenue to overhaul infrastructure and services. Higher education was deemed essential to the modernization of the new provincial growth centers. Their universities, long ignored and despised as parochial, were suddenly lavished with financial benefits from Paris. Even more sensational was the decision to decentralize many of the prestigious *grandes écoles* and research institutes customarily ensconced in Paris to the new provincial favorites. They were moved to the city where their discipline matched the local pilot industry. The idea was to nurture a high-caliber research environment as the wellspring for advanced technology. The industry itself, the university and the decentralized research centers, the laboratories and technical institutes would form in essence a "scientific complex" on the American model that would be the heart of economic development in each of the select provincial cities.[13] In sum, during the 1960s, the *métropoles d'équilibres* were the set pieces in the government's ambition to remold provincial life according to the dictates of modernization.

The designation as a *métropôle d'équilibre* created a surge of unheard-of excitement and optimism at Toulouse. The local publicity mounted over this government-sponsored campaign to revivify the shabby, impoverished old city as a high-tech capital was extraordinary. The growth of Toulouse would be "spectacular." It was "a *métropole régionale d'équilibre* of over half a million." By the year 2000 it would be "one of the most important centers for scientific research in Europe."[14] Toulouse was finally being accepted into the bosom of French civilization as a measure of its largess and mutability. Aviation was its obvious pilot industry. In 1966 the government announced electronics as a second pilot industry for Toulouse. Massive government funding for research and production in these two industries was coordinated with their decentralization to Toulouse during the course of the Fourth and Fifth Plans of the 1960s. The Plan Directeur was speedily modified to incorporate Toulouse's new vocation as a "scientific and advanced technology" center and the new emphasis on its educational institutions. Based on government subsidization, the ZUP de Mirail project was expanded in 1966 to include a newly built Faculty of Letters for the University of Toulouse and an office complex for the regional prefecture as well as for the regional branch of the state-controlled Office de la Radio et Télévision Française (ORTF). But ultimately the most important change for the city's future was the appearance of the new ZUP de Rangueil-Lespinet, designated as the city's American-style "scientific complex." It was situated along the route de Narbonne in the suburbs southeast of the central city. During the 1960s, the French government poured over 600 million francs into Rangueil-Lespinet to cultivate the kind of scientific atmosphere that would legitimate Toulouse's new role as an aerospace and high-technology capital. The University of Toulouse's expanded and modernized Faculty of Science was the first institution to be moved there, and it was followed throughout the 1960s and early 1970s by a parade of research and educational institutions decentralized from Paris.

As a result of its ceremonial dubbing as a *métropole d'équilibre,* by the mid-1960s the spatial geography of Toulouse was the location for three massive urban-development schemes: the slum-clearance project at Saint-Georges that would turn "downtown" Toulouse into a financial and commercial center, the Le Mirail project that would offer a pristine example of suburban design, and the Rangueil-Lespinet scientific complex. Spreading out from Toulouse across the Garonne Valley was a network of controlled industrial zones, residential zones, and a system of green belts. A vast program for expanding the commune's *équipements généraux* (basic utilities, schools, and sports facilities) was outlined. Five suburban industrial parks were planned that spilled into the communes of Portet-sur-Garonne, Cugnaux, and Villeneuve-Tolosane to the south, Colomiers and Blagnac to the

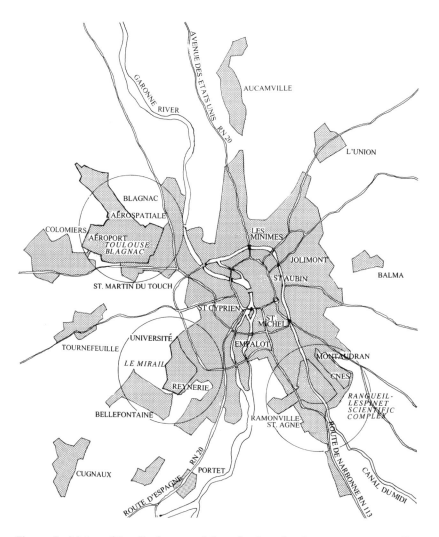

Figure 7. Metropolitan Toulouse and the suburban development programs: Le Mirail, the Rangueil-Lespinet scientific complex, and the Toulouse-Blagnac aeronautic center.

west, and Fenouillet and Aucamville to the north. In 1965 an extensive road system, costing some 660 million francs, was previewed in the Schéma Directeur des Structures by the local Atelier Municipal d'Urbanisme and the departmental Office of Construction, with the blessings of the Ponts et Chaussées. It branched through the Garonne Valley, starring out from Toulouse as the heart, the *métropole,* of the southwest. The blueprint included diverting the old Canal du Midi and using the channel as a roadway. It also designed an extensive system of *rocades* circumventing the city to alleviate, finally, the irresolvable traffic and parking snarls in the central city.

By 1967, this far more extensive and hegemonic *Livre blanc* that had metamorphosed from the original *Plan directeur* was finally approved. Over the course of the 1960s, the plan had evolved in tandem with state regional development policy. It placed increasing emphasis on the two ZUPs of Le Mirail and Rangueil-Lespinet. Perhaps even more significantly, it incrementally interpreted urban planning as transportation and road design. The Schéma Directeur des Structures assumed that a vast spiderweb-like network of roads would provide unity and coherence for the spreading metropolis. By 1968, the combined energies of the state's urban and regional planning agencies and the Ponts et Chaussées, the municipality, the department of the Haute-Garonne, the local commission on the *schéma de structure,* the Atelier d'Urbanisme, Toulouse-Equipement, a Société d'Economie Mixte for construction, and consultants from the university circled over their domain—the vast commune of Toulouse. They designed and redesigned, regulated and reregulated, controlled and administered the powerful magnetic forces of modern urbanization.[15] Their most effective weapons in the battle to command the metropolis were the continuously revised city plan, or Livre blanc, and the development programs assigned for Toulouse in the state's Fourth and Fifth Plans of the 1960s.

The extent and depth of this public regulatory control was dramatic, if not downright sensational. In the space of ten years an extensive web of bureaucratic authority had been spun over an invented set of fields—the city, the suburb, the priority zone, the region. Planning texts were filled with panoramic maps that displayed the new arrangements of space.[16] They imposed a uniform, rational composition upon the whole. Perhaps even more significantly, this vast expansion of planning tipped the scale between municipal and state power conspicuously toward Paris. Although the municipal plans followed the ebb and flow of the state's regional development policy like a shadow, any deviation was treated as a sign of heresy against the efficiency and rationality of modernist doctrine.

This was particularly the case for Bazerque, who was more than capa-

ble of single-handedly fuzzing state policy and antagonizing Parisian officialdom in order to fulfill his own agenda. He was known as an irritating
chief of what could be an irritating city for government planners. In December 1960 Bazerque traveled to Paris to appear before a meeting of the Commission Nationale des Plans d'Urbanisme. He wanted approval for the extension of the city's perimeter around the rapidly growing neighborhood
of Maubec-Purpan, to the west of Toulouse, in order to construct a housing complex there. But state architect Mathieu disagreed, arguing that
"Toulouse was a difficult city for an urbanist to deal with because of its
scattered and diverse nature." He challenged Bazerque over whether the
Plan Directeur "sufficiently ordered" the city's various functions and services. Mathieu and Randet (who represented DATAR) claimed that anyone
working at Purpan would be able to find housing and services at the nearest
satellite city, and the Commission refused to approve Bazerque's Purpan
project.[17] Bazerque complained continuously that the Gaullist administration delayed granting funds to Socialist Toulouse. He was forced to walk a
thin line between adherence to the depoliticized modernization schemes of
Parisian technocrats and defiance of the government's Gaullist political
agenda. When a variety of other cities were chosen as eligible for exceptional state development aid in 1960, Toulouse was passed by. Bazerque
countered with a furious public campaign against these state insults: "We
cannot understand how the Government can neglect the region between
Bordeaux and Montpellier, where Toulouse is the central motor; this is not
only a grave error in the national plan, but an injustice."[18]

The other side of these indignant declarations was the reality that
endorsement as a *métropole d'équilibre* did not always bring with it the
monetary support that the state magisterially divined. Bazerque had to
argue the city's importance among the other provincial urban luminaries. It
was not necessarily an easy task. In confronting the formidable competition
for state patronage from cities like Bordeaux and Montpellier, Bazerque's
most successful strategy was to launch grand-scale prestige development
projects that would increase Toulouse's visibility on the French modernistic
landscape. It was somewhat ironic that Bazerque, a Socialist who found it
difficult to work with de Gaulle's technocrats and his *dirigiste* policies, would
offer the same kind of *grands programs* as the solution to French modernization as did de Gaulle himself.

On the other hand, Bazerque faced substantial local opposition from
both sides of the political spectrum over the metamorphosis of urban planning and the strength of the technocratic manipulation of development. In

the section of the northern suburbs originally declared "rural" by the Plan Directeur, the inhabitants angrily decried their second-class citizenship: "We are forced to drink nonpotable water from our wells, for lighting we have gas lampposts that are maintained by a man carrying a ladder—yet we'll pay taxes to establish, according to those great words, 'Urbanism and Hygiene.' If everyone pays the same taxes, they should receive the same services."[19] In a fury over the indifferent character of the zoning regulations, E. H. Guitard, the director of the Bureau d'Esthetique Urbaine and *La Dépêche du Midi*'s intrepid critic of municipal urban policy, wrote: "according to the logic of urban zones and rural zones, the *dessinateur-classificateur* can take his pen and dig a ditch between two neighbors, two sisters, more profound than a moat around a medieval fortified city—because one will eventually become a poor relative of the other. One zone will be privileged while the other zone will be disgraced."[20] The local property owners' association demanded that the Municipal Council banish any notion of a "rural zone" from the city's plan and that it ease the draconian regulations limiting growth outside the zones designated as proper to development.[21] The Communists, led by Simone Gardès, found themselves defending the proprietary rights of small landowners caught in the "rural zones" against the state's regulatory blitz. The Communists and Badiou's Independent Socialists pushed a vote through the Municipal Council requiring further study of the Plan Directeur and the various *plans de détail* by a committee composed of representatives from the Council and from the public at large as well as of technicians and state administrators.[22] When the plan was approved in July of 1962, the rural zones had disappeared.

When the ZUP du Mirail project was announced, the Syndicat des Propriétaires et des Utilisateurs de Terrains à Batir flew into a vocal defense of proprietary rights, arguing that ZUPs did nothing but accentuate speculation and bureaucratic corruption. When they publicly wrote to the Ministry of Construction to decry the "avalanche of imaginary zones" ruining the countryside around Toulouse, they received little sympathy other than the assurance that everyone would be fairly compensated, that the ZUP was meant to curb speculation, and that state functionaries were not crooked.[23] Nevertheless, the designation of land by the public authorities as a "priority development zone" (where prices were controlled) had the effect of raising real-estate prices all around it. Land sales and suburban construction ventures by property owners and joint investment-building societies profited regally anywhere near a ZUP.

The shift toward an expansionist urban-development policy also opened the way for a virtual rush to the suburbs by real-estate promoters and house-hunters alike. The attractiveness of suburban living, particularly given the lack of suitable housing in the city, even defied the imagination of politicians and planners. The rural beauty of the Garonne Valley attracted ever-increasing numbers of Toulousains to the peripheral areas, in part because so much of the Toulouse commune was dedicated to state-controlled development zones. By the early 1960s some 15,000 to 16,000 people were commuting into Toulouse from the suburbs.[24] Property values in the surrounding communes had risen an average of 800 percent.[25] In addition, the expansion of Toulouse was now the leitmotif of planning, and 200,000 people were expected to take up residence in the suburbs over the next ten to fifteen years.

All of this spontaneous and planned, or *spontanée et dirigée,* expansion made the possibility of conflict between Toulouse and the surrounding communes far more threatening. The expansionist hegemony of the Plan Directeur indeed brought the debate on modernization to one of the most forgotten rural outlands of France. The surrounding communes were quite capable of resisting the regulatory net cast by government planners, regardless of the urban tentacles spreading through the valley. There was already a fair amount of agitation during the 1950s over the fact that anyone living in the neighboring communes could build as they pleased, while the communards of Toulouse were carefully overseen by an army of public agents. It did not help matters that the communes most likely to benefit from the expansion of Toulouse as a *métropole d'équilibre* were expected to chip in part of the financing for the city's pet projects.[26] The garden farmers and greengrocers, the early suburbanites commuting into Toulouse, and the communal authorities that represented them were forced to take a position one way or another on the suburban development that was rapidly overtaking their pastoral existence.

Communal officialdom was normally dominated by a phalanx of traditional notables—landowners, farmers, and businessmen who were often also lawyers and real-estate promoters. They controlled the *mairie* and represented communal interests on the various departmental committees as well as on the General Council of the Haute-Garonne. They were often directly involved in decisions on public utilities, construction permits, and building regulations, as well as in land sales and real-estate speculation. Moreover, the suburban communes were a mix of Socialist, Radical, and conservative fiefdoms. In general, the more populated and more working-class western suburbs veered to the left, while the communes to the east of the city remained more conservative. Depending on the mentality of its local gentry, the commune could support anything from a policy of blocking suburban development to supporting growth to essentially merging communal political power with real-estate promotion. The conservative commune of Labarthe-sur-Lèze refused any compromise with the forces of modernization. The town of Muret, a Radical enclave, constructed some nineteen public-housing projects between 1955 and 1966 besides endorsing a variety of private development projects.[27] The Socialist commune of Ramonville-Saint-Agne negotiated a deal with a private building developer by offering free land for a new school, and its mayor was heavily involved in real-estate speculation. Just adjacent to the planned scientific complex at Rangueil, Ramonville was prime property for the construction of subdivisions. Real-estate promoters bought up large parcels in the hills and constructed luxury homes with attractive patios and swimming pools. By 1975, half of the commune's population was well-to-do middle class. The nearby communes of Vigoulet, Vieille-Toulouse, and Goyrans, with the double advantage of the picturesque *terrefort* hills and the Garonne River within their borders, developed a distinctively elitist aura. Golf courses, equestrian centers, tennis clubs and quaint restaurants filled in the landscape between the private villas. In conservative-minded l'Union, a landowner partitioned 184 hectares, 28 percent of the commune, into nearly 600 *pavillons isolées*.[28]

A number of the outlying communes also made nominal efforts at their own urban plans. The commune of Villeneuve-Tolosane, perhaps hit worst by the uncontrolled construction around ONIA and the Francazal airport, put together a basic agenda in 1958, as did Balma, Blagnac, Colomiers, Cugnaux, Portet, l'Union, and Villeneuve-Tolosane. Some of the suburban communes were dominated by politicians of substantial weight who were able to carry off their own imperial modernization programs. Colomiers, and its powerful Socialist mayor Eugène Montel, was an extraordinary example of Socialist municipalism put to use in a modern development scheme—a "new city," Colomiers-Villeneuve, complete with a Livre Blanc and some 4,000 available dwellings. The municipality began buying up land in the early 1960s, laying out industrial zones and recreational facilities, and competing with Toulouse for businesses and tax revenues. By the end of the 1960s, Colomiers boasted 16,000 inhabitants, 7,000 jobs, and three industrial zones that included the Canon Electric company and Bréguet-Dassault Aviation. Both of these companies had been wrested away from settlement in the Toulouse industrial parks.

It was clear that Toulouse would have to conquer its hinterland in order to control development and initiate a more holistic interpretation of metropolitan space. Throughout the 1960s, however, the city's planning remained within the context of the commune, obsessed with its two icons to modernism, Le Mirail and Rangueil-Lespinet. It naively ignored the rapid sprawl taking place around it. The "vast size" of the Toulouse commune offered plenty of opportunity for city growth without recourse to the harmonization of blueprints with the neighboring communes. In part, this standoff had to do with the political struggles between the various Socialist mayors caught within the spreading Toulouse metropolis. Montel at Colomiers was one, Bernard Audigé at Tournefeuille another, who were capable of standing up to Bazerque's ambitions for Toulouse. Their local influence and political power was linked to the broader issue of communal autonomy. The right of individual communes to steer their own course through the thicket of modern suburbanization became an increasingly thornier issue as the plans for Toulouse grew to imperial proportions. The solution offered by planners to this emerging conundrum was yet another series of invented geographic spaces.

In 1960, a municipal study of "General Planning Principles for the *groupement d'urbanisme* of Toulouse" had called for a "Toulouse urban region" parodying the Schéma Directeur being carried out for the "Paris region." The remolding of growth toward the periphery of Paris was to be used as the model for the provincial cities, which would follow along with their own miniaturized versions of the government's plan for the Seine basin.[29] The land-use reform measures passed by the de Gaulle administration in 1967 called for each major city in France to develop a strategic land-use plan, or Schéma Directeur d'Aménagement et d'Urbanisme (SDAU), for its entire metropolitan area. Its counterpart was to be a *plan d'occupation des sols* (POS) that provided guidelines for building and land-use control. The SDAUs were notorious for their tardy appearance. Toulouse did not begin creating its version until 1969. The document was finally authorized in 1975, but only after another new technocratic entity, the Agence d'Urbanisme de l'Agglomération Toulousaine, had taken over its creation.

This cottage industry in public agencies, policy meetings and planning documents, the drawing and redrawing of maps, depicted the tightening clench of the French planning machine over local urban environments. As attempts to undermine independent local notables and their communal jurisdictions, they generated a lexicon of bureaucratic buzzwords that were progressively used to reinvent geographic space and define the meaning of the modern city. The most frequently used word was *agglomération*, coined in 1954 by the state census office to convey the idea of a multicommunal metropolitan area defined by population density and physical continuity. By 1968, the *agglomération* of Toulouse included twenty-nine contiguous communes around the city. The definition of urban growth was adjusted by INSEE in 1962 to reflect the fashion for functionality and zoning among state planners. The Zone de Peuplement Industriel et Urbain, or ZPIU, was distinguished by daily commuting and employment patterns, as well as the number and size of businesses. Since physical sequentiality was not a factor, the ZPIU came close to sketching an extensive urban region. The ZPIU of Toulouse was formed from a full fifty communes stretching out across the Garonne Valley. By 1975, the SDAU and the Agence d'Urbanisme broadcast its jurisdiction over sixty-one communes sprayed around the city. This progressive conceptualization of France as a series of *métropoles d'équilibres* spreading out into wholly urbanized territories, or ZPIUs and SDAUs, within carefully constructed administrative program regions provided the geographic device for state regulation and control of *aménagement du territoire*. It systematized the conscious policy of urbanization and rigidly set the conceptual and geographic categories for the transformation of France.

The Suburban Dream World: Le Mirail

The grandest development scheme in the planning heyday of the 1960s was the infamous super-suburb of Le Mirail. The Bazerque administration set out to launch one of the largest ZUP operations in France. The size of the project was justified by the economic growth of Toulouse as a *métropole d'équilibre* and by the city's population growth. Bazerque adroitly used the excuse of the North African repatriates arriving after 1962 to convince state authorities that the city's housing supply was strained beyond its limits. Le Mirail would offer "a place of welcome to Algerian immigrants and the opportunity to integrate them into the population."[30] But the most important rationale behind the ZUP du Mirail was that it represented the kind of avant-garde project Bazerque was interested in identifying with a more modern-minded Toulouse. It was a prestigious display of Toulouse's new ambitions as a provincial capital, and one that would attract state interest and funding. The left bank of the Garonne was decided upon as the location for Le Mirail. There it would fit in with the goal of more equitably balancing the city's population on both sides of the river. The ZUP would also be a convenient neighbor to the aircraft factories at Blagnac-Saint-Martin-du-Touch and to the industrial zone of Le Chapitre to the south. The final land purchase was chosen by Bazerque himself, who boarded a helicopter and flew out over the orchards and vineyards to select 800 hectares around the old château of Mirail (used as a Jesuit retreat house), five kilometers from central Toulouse.

To enhance Le Mirail's prestige, Bazerque held an international competition to choose a stellar architect for the design of the project. The winner was Georges Candilis, a disciple and close associate of Le Corbusier. He had studied with the Congrès Internationaux d'Architecture Moderne (CIAM) in Athens before the war, and then moved to Paris in 1945 to work first with André Lurçat and then as Le Corbusier's assistant. As a member of Atelier des Bâtisseurs (ABAT), in Casablanca and in Paris, Candilis focused on the construction of modern low-cost dwellings, an expertise that won him the Opération Million competition to provide generic plans for low-cost reconstruction housing in France. From the 1960s, he turned his attention to town planning and urban theory, designing numerous projects throughout Europe and the Mediterranean. Candilis, then, was a formidable architect in the campaign for architectural modernism and one of the most influential urban practitioners in France's postwar transformation.[31]

Candilis' design innovations for Le Mirail were as bold as the project's scale. Central to his concept of the community's life was the return of the street to its historic function as a place of social activity and personal interchange. The growing despair with sterile life in the *grands ensembles* was a good part of the explanation for this renewed interest in the street. It was also explained by the general frustration with the automobile that disrupted all efforts at planning the model city. In his proposal, Candilis argued that the street, which had always been the primordial root of urbanity and sociability, had been grossly deformed by vehicular traffic. At Le Mirail it would once again become the domain of the people. Surrounded by the rich amenities of urban existence, the street would reconstitute the spontaneous character of daily life that had been shattered by the repetitive uniformity and banality of big cities.[32]

At Le Mirail, Candilis' interpretation of the street was the *rue-dalle*, designed, in the initial plans and models, in the figure of a double-Y shape. It was a pedestrian promenade that threaded through apartment complexes, greenbelts, schools and sports fields and opened up onto a large square that was to be the heart of the new "satellite." There, Le Mirail's central shopping district would tantalize residents into the expansive public space, which would be "the new place du Capitole of the left bank."[33] Unlike the 1950s housing projects, Le Mirail was endowed with exhaustive commercial, educational, and public facilities. Altogether, twenty-three commercial centers, five open-air markets, four hotels, five movie houses, four lycées, fourteen primary schools, four sports stadiums, eight swimming pools, and seven social centers were planned around the *rue-dalle*. The construction of new offices for the regional prefect and a new campus for the University of Toulouse's Faculty of Letters at Le Mirail were to provide the suburb with a certain intellectual presence. With all these institutions gracing the flag-stone promenade and public space, community life would mirror the vibrancy and affability associated with old Toulouse across the river.

Around them would develop a city of 100,000 people living in 23,000 dwellings. A variety of housing options were planned, including family cottages, smaller apartment complexes, and high-rises. All of them were fitted into an alluring residential landscape of parks and greenbelts, the *rue-dalle*, and the artificially constructed Reynerie Lake. A maximum of 75 percent of the construction would be designated public, or HLM, housing, while the remaining 25 percent would be assigned to private developers. The plans for Le Mirail also called for employment for approximately one-third of the resident labor force in light industries developed in the ZUP's industrial zone bordering Le Chapitre. All of this planning and construction was under the authority of Toulouse-Equipement and the Atelier Municipal d'Urbanisme, which would see to the perseverance of the project's design and set down the requirements for public and private involvement.

The publicity for Le Mirail described it as "audacious, avant-garde, a grand vision—a mirror of French urban life in the future." The Livre Blanc pronounced it "the most important urban project in Europe," and Bazerque and his Municipal Council gloated over their daring scheme. Le Mirail was indeed the most well known, and the largest, of the suburban "satellite city" projects launched in France during the 1960s amidst the general economic prosperity and the fervor of regional development. It became a classic urban-design project, studied and discussed by urban planners and architects throughout Europe. Its international notoriety was impressive. Even Soviet Premier Kosygin made the pilgrimage to Le Mirail in 1966 to observe the "ville en marche, ville en liberté, ville en vivre."[34] Two projects at Bordeaux, Hauts-de-Garonne and Bordeaux-Lac, and the satellite city of Grenoble-Echirolles were the only other French projects of this scale attempted. It was difficult to distinguish the notion of a "satellite city" from the "new towns" constructed in the provinces, such as Lille-Est, L'Isle-d'Abeau southwest of Lyon, or Vaudreuil near Rouen. In any case, all of these conceptual and material definitions were inspired by the dominating model of suburban growth adhered to by state planners during the 1960s. All of them were constructed with attention to open air, hygiene, and health and associated the inner city with the congestion and dilapidation that iniquitously led to social and economic debasement. As an alternative, these suburbs were meticulously designed utopias, crafted by architects working from blueprints and scale models. They were carefully zoned so that the various functions of the city were maintained in a rational, ordered context. Human scale and urban culture would, under the direction of state planners, be consciously controlled and cleansed in order to avoid the anarchy of unbridled settlement.

Despite its international reputation, Le Mirail never lived up to the expectations of Candilis, Bazerque, or the French government. It was for all intents and purposes an embarrassing failure. The term "ZUP" stuck to the community like a badge of misfortune, especially when it was cynically besmirched by Toulousains living virtually anywhere else but the *nouvelle*

Figure 8. Le Mirail, view of Reynerie Lake.

Toulouse. The belittling was punctuated by the slender thread, the route de Saint-Simon, that tied Le Mirail to the central city. Very little was accomplished by way of providing an extended road system or basic transportation out to the isolated settlement. Infrequent city buses fought traffic over the Garonne River and through Saint-Cyprien to provide a modicum of public access.

There were few passengers during the 1960s, though, because the actual construction and development of Le Mirail moved at a snail's pace. The broad-sweeping *rue-dalle* and the greenbelts were themselves enormous drains on public investment and slowed down the whole operation. The land purchases were exorbitant, and Bazerque was already pleading in 1965 with the Commission on Urbanism in Paris that either the state land prices should be determined by the real costs of the development project or the plan for Le Mirail should be amended to densify construction.[35] The rigid state regulation of finance and building in the ZUP that was overseen by Toulouse-Equipement choked off private investment rather than stimulating it. It required private real-estate promoters to hack an unknown path through a bureaucratic labyrinth set up by the Ministry of Construction, the departmental HLM offices, the Caisse d'Epargne, and Toulouse-Equipement itself. The financial arrangements were tangled and tedious. On top of this, the state building codes prohibited projects of more than 100 residents outside the satellite city, while those within Le Mirail were based on contracts far too extensive for local construction firms. The linear design of Candilis' housing projects at Le Mirail even further accentuated the necessity for large-scale construction contracts. The fact that investors were obligated to pay for at least part of the installation costs for utilities did not endear them to the project. It was far simpler for Toulouse real-estate investors and construction companies to work in Toulouse where the projects were smaller, regulations less severe, and the infrastructure already in place. Bazerque acidly commented, "This was my first disappointment. Toulouse promoters are curious people. They have no guts; change scares them."[36]

By 1968 construction had only begun on the pilot neighborhood of Bellefontaine bordering the *rue-dalle.* Streets had been laid out, 256 apartments were inhabited, and 400 more were being constructed. The Atelier Municipal d'Urbanisme complained that the ZUP already had a bad reputation. Private construction companies "refused" to work there. There were virtually no services for the first residents of Le Mirail, who were "living in exile." "The dissatisfaction and the growing human and social costs must be taken into account in the long-term plans for Toulouse."[37] By 1973, Tarrius, head of the Agence d'Urbanisme, was forced to face Candilis with the fact that modification of his model new town would be required if there was any hope of saving it from oblivion. Candilis defended the plan's linearity as essential in order to balance the housing volume and harmonize the variety of building styles. But he also compromised with local Toulouse life by admitting that architecture was not "imposed" by the architect and that the blueprints were simply images to show that a neighborhood can be realized without recourse to skyscrapers or housing in horizontal bars. The plan for Le Mirail was "meant to be supple." Candilis argued that the only necessity was the *rue-dalle* or some form of pedestrian walkway. As a result, the *plan masse* was reconfigured with a *"ficelle de dalle"* that could be expanded in the future. The housing projects were cut up into 50- to 100-unit construction programs more in keeping with traditional Toulousain building contracts.[38] The ambitious Candilis plan was simply sidestepped as too difficult and too costly. Although the first two neighborhoods, Bellefontaine and Reynerie, were constructed around the *rue-dalle,* the walkway was greatly attenuated in the third neighborhood, Mirail-Université.

The Faculty of Letters, or the Université de Toulouse–Le Mirail, was actually built on the model of an American university campus, with modern two- and three-story classroom and office buildings, open courtyards, and breezeways. Planners assumed that it would attract the kind of student life enjoyed in the old Latin quarter. To create this kind of animated atmosphere, secondary schools, an educational television center, and a public library were all constructed around the faculty grounds. A few student-housing projects were developed by private promoters.[39] But there was simply no competing with the anarchy of cafes and restaurants, theaters and cheap flats, the municipal library and bookstores that had made the district between the place du Capitole and Saint-Sernin Cathedral the cultural heart of Toulouse. A Latin-quarter atmosphere simply could not be manufactured for Le Mirail. The distinguished Faculty of Letters, once the center of Renaissance learning in the Midi, was isolated in the grassy fields of the "left bank" flood plain. Students daily made the long journey from central Toulouse to the solitary bus stop on the avenue de Tabar and then trekked along a *ficelle de dalle* to the classroom buildings. By all accounts, the Faculty of Letters appeared to have been summarily exiled from Toulouse.

The Regional Complex intended as the heart of Le Mirail suffered from the same deviations and mutations that, step by step, recast the entire project. Candilis' original plan called for a sizable commercial complex carefully balanced and zoned, in the blueprints at least, in line with the town's other functions and activities. But eventually a vast commercial center, dubbed Géant-Epargne, was planned at the heart of the community as the icon of consumption and material abundance that modern suburban living best articulated. In 1966, Bazerque toured the new shopping centers being constructed in Germany and Switzerland and returned to Toulouse intent on a flashier regional commercial center for Le Mirail. After bids from the Carrefour, Monoprix, Mobb, and l'Epargne supermarket and retail franchises, the development contract was awarded to the local Société Epargne chain store conglomerate. In order to extend Candilis' original commercial site, neighboring property set aside for regional administrative offices was appropriated into the new shopping center scheme.[40] It eventually included some 22,000 square meters with forty stores, boutiques, banks, and cafeterias assembled around the Géant-Casino supermarket, opened in 1970, and fortified with about 2,000 parking spaces. Local critics called it Le Mirail's "temple of abundance."

However, since Carrefour had been spurned in the Le Mirail contract, the management decided to take revenge and move forward with plans to erect a new store just outside the ZUP along Highway 20. Carrefour's management baptized it "the biggest supermarket in Europe," with 25,000 square meters of space and seventy-two cash registers, surrounded by forty boutiques. The opening of the new Carrefour in 1972 immediately cut into the revenues at Le Mirail's far more inconveniently located Géant-Epargne. It began a fierce rivalry for clientele at Le Mirail and threatened the viability of the new town's commercial hegemony. The shopping-center war on the left bank heated up further when the Horizon 2000 commercial center, launched by local developer Louis Lemesre, was installed in 1972 along Highway 20 south of Le Mirail. It sported the jumbo-sized Ouragan supermarket and a commercial center packed with snazzy shops. Toulouse's local *TMP Magazine* called it "the battle of the titans" for the 100,000 consumers on the west bank of the Garonne.[41] Géant-Epargne fought back with plans for a major department store and a covered mall. But it was difficult to win against the convenience of Route 20's commercial development as increasing numbers of businesses (Mobb, Crozatier-Meubles, Conforama, Igloosports, and some dozen gas stations) passed up construction at Le Mirail for the consumer traffic along the main road west of Toulouse. Bazerque's ambitious Géant Casino shopping center ended up playing only a minor role in the commercial life of the Le Mirail community.

The difficulty in attracting private investment, as well as the project's outcast reputation, meant that from the first Le Mirail was dominated by

HLM public-housing projects. It seemed more like just another *grand ensemble* than the "city of the future." To make matters worse, public housing at Le Mirail was a bone of contention in the prickly relationship between the municipal government, represented by Bazerque, and the French state, represented by Jacques Maziol. Maziol was a Toulouse municipal councillor, one of the few successful Gaullists in the region, and a pretender to Bazerque's mayoral seat. He was also appointed Minister of Construction in 1962. The Socialist and Communist members of the Municipal Council outdid each other in furious, vitriolic denunciations of Maziol's public-housing policy at Toulouse during the 1960s. They accused him of holding back funding, illegal speculation and graft, and undermining local left-wing political influence. When 100 million francs disappeared in a land sale negotiated by the HLM office, the public-housing program came under direct attack. Maziol was accused of mismanagement. He was charged with unethical behavior in using the scandal to sabotage the 1964 local elections. Even worse, Maziol was condemned as a Gaullist lackey determined to undermine Toulouse's leftist clout by controlling appointments and policy at the departmental HLM office.

In 1963, a state decree increased the number of seats on the local HLM councils appointed directly by the departmental prefect and shrunk the number of elected positions. Maziol explained that the reform was meant to "depoliticize" public-housing policy. But the Toulouse Municipal Council cried foul, accusing Maziol of packing the HLM office with Union pour la Démocratie Française (UDR) militants and centralizing decision making safely in Paris.[42] Communist Georges Ducel produced a "confidential" letter from the Paris UDR committee that endorsed appointment of Gaullist sympathizers to local HLM posts. In any case, Bazerque and the Municipal Council continuously harped on the fact that funding for HLM construction suspiciously declined in the early 1960s, precisely as the planning and land purchases for the Le Mirail project were taking off. Maziol's stalling was interpreted as an all-out Gaullist effort to liquidate Bazerque's pet project. Disputes such as these quickly demolished the fragile alliance between the Socialists and the UDR devised during the inaugural years of the Fifth Republic. By the 1965 municipal elections, Bazerque and his Socialist-centrist coalition shunned any further association with the forces of Gaullism.

By 1975, the city of Toulouse was left with a debt of 531 million francs for the construction of Le Mirail. The ZUP was composed of some 8,000 dwellings in the HLM high-rises and smaller housing complexes lining the *rue-dalle* at Bellefontaine and Reynerie. In them lived about 22,000 people, far less than the 100,000 residents that had originally been expected. The majority of "Miraliens" were young working-class and blue-collar families with children. Some 41 percent of Le Mirail's population was under twenty-one years of age. A good number of the employees at the aircraft factories at Saint-Martin-du-Touch chose to live at Le Mirail. Some of the residents worked at the electronics companies at Le Chapitre or found jobs somewhere on the west bank to make commuting easier. But a fair portion of Le Mirail's residents weathered the daily commute to jobs in central Toulouse. All of the new settlers were forced to trek substantial distances to either the central city or to suburban shopping malls for their daily needs.[43]

In the end living at Le Mirail meant an insular existence in a secluded apartment. The atmosphere was boring and isolating. Despite the theoretical fabrication of a social fabric for Le Mirail, modernism was an aesthetic response removed from and repelled by the spontaneous gestures and necessities of everyday life. It offered only, according to Christine Boyer, "an urbanism of empty scenic spaces and alienating imagery . . ."[44] The *dalle*-promenade that Candilis meant to rejuvenate sociability and community life was often lifeless during the day and completely deserted in the evening. There were few social organizations or places to meet friends and neighbors. The only real community activity took place among the children at the parks and playgrounds. Increasing cases of vandalism and juvenile delinquency attested to the emptiness. The result was a rapid turnover in residences: "For a good number of households moving to Toulouse, Le Mirail is a stage they must pass through; for some it is a stage, for others an impasse."[45]

The Model of Technopolis: Rangueil-Lespinet

The two major flaws in the extravagant plan for Le Mirail were the wildly overestimated population projections and the failure to take into account the suburbanization taking place throughout Toulouse's hinterland. There were a wide range of choices for anyone desirous of the idyllic life of the suburbs. Le Mirail was only one option, and an expensive one at that. The other principal choice was Rangueil-Lespinet.

The suburban development project of Rangueil-Lespinet southeast of Toulouse was ultimately far more successful than the heroic modernism pursued at Le Mirail. The reasons for its triumph over the high modernist suburban utopia on the opposite side of the Garonne are complex.

Rangueil-Lespinet was certainly inculcated with its own modernist agenda. It was conceived as the city's "scientific complex," an American-style research and development park complete with a residential setting deliberately designed for the scientists, engineers, and technicians who would invigorate the new *métropole d'équilibre*. The difference lay in the fact that Rangueil was one of the French government's pet regional development projects and was therefore handsomely funded. It was, as well, perceived within the local community as a representation of Toulouse's past as well as of its future. It was cultivated as an "authentic" manifestation of the city's identity—a historic vision of the direction in which Toulouse ought to be moving in the journey toward the modernist frontier.

The written annals of Toulouse were filled with glowing references to the city's intellectual heritage and the numbers and variety of its educational institutions. It was traditionally a city of students, professors and teachers, libraries, colleges, and institutes. The university, in particular, stood as the symbol of the city's long and once-honorable role as the intellectual capital of southwestern France. The University of Toulouse's academic reputation had been tarnished, along with the rest of the provincial universities, by the exclusive development of Parisian scholarship. But it had continued to diversify and expand its studies throughout the late nineteenth and early twentieth centuries, and it remained the city's most distinguished institution. Its most respected specialty was science. The Faculty of Science had been moved from the Latin Quarter to the stately setting of the allées Jules-Guesde and the Grand Rond in the Saint-Etienne district by the end of the nineteenth century. A medical school was then added. In honor of the arrival of the new university facilities to Saint-Etienne, the city had renovated the Royal Gardens and the Grand Rond that had once been the main attractions of this old aristocratic stronghold. The result had been the turn-of-the-century revival of one of the most beautiful neighborhoods of Toulouse.

Three other research institutes under the jurisdiction of the Faculty of Science further enhanced Toulouse's reputation for scientific research. All three had received status as *écoles supérieures* by the first decade of the twentieth century. First, the Ecole Nationale Supérieure de Chimie was built on the rue Sainte-Catherine close to the new Faculties of Science and Medicine. Paul Sabatier won the 1912 Nobel Prize for chemistry while working in the Institute's laboratories. Then the Ecole Nationale Supérieure d'Electrotechnique et Electronique was constructed on the boulevard Riquet along the Canal du Midi. Finally, the new Ecole Nationale Supérieure d'Agronomie was founded on the avenue de Muret bordering the Garonne River. There was also the Ecole Nationale Vétérinaire that had been constructed in 1829 along the allées Villeneuve (allée Jean-Jaurès) and the canal, and then was moved to the outskirts of the central city just south of Saint-Martin-du-Touch. The addition of these four nationally prominent colleges and the expansion of the science and medical faculties of the University of Toulouse transformed the city's intellectual character.[46] The number of college students enrolled increased by threefold from the beginning of the twentieth century. By 1958, 10,000 students were registered at Toulouse's higher educational institutions. Only five years later, in 1963, that number had doubled to 20,000, making the city the third largest university center in France. The vast majority of the students came from the towns and rural areas of the southwest. Only the engineering *écoles supérieures* and the veterinary college attracted students from all over the country.[47]

The fact that its universities specialized in science meant that Toulouse was an early center for research. Even during the early 1960s, before the decentralization of the Parisian research facilities, about 500 people (over one-third of the work force employed in higher education) were scientists and technicians involved in projects at the laboratories of the Faculties of Science and Medicine and the *écoles supérieures*. The laboratories at the ONIA fertilizer plant and at the aircraft factories added even further to this somewhat unconventional situation. In the late 1950s and early 1960s, the aviation industry employed a higher proportion of researchers than any other industry in France. More than 600 of them worked for the companies at Toulouse. Although they represented only a minute enclave in comparison to Paris, their presence still put the city in the privileged position of being an early beacon for the highly coveted fields of scientific research and technological development.[48] This was perhaps the most distinctive feature of the city's economy throughout the 1950s and early 1960s. It contributed to a vision of Toulouse that contradicted that of the parochial backwater suffering the stain of "underdevelopment." Instead, it accentuated the city's historic intellectual culture, its university life and scientific research. Highbrow and impossibly antiquated: both images carried the weight of the city's perceived history and mirrored the struggle for French identity and custom. In any case, the early preeminence of Toulouse's scientific community is what in many ways distinguished it most among the provincial cities of France.

Nonetheless, the early postwar years were markedly void of investments in scientific education and research. As late as 1958 France still devoted less than 1 percent of its gross national product to science and engineering, far behind the resources allocated by Great Britain, West Germany, the Soviet Union, and the United States.[49] The modernist agenda advocated by government planners slowly forced them to turn their attention to the expensive and high-profile arena of "scientific research and technological development" and to some type of reform of France's retrograde educational institutions. In 1957, Pierre Mendès-France called for a general mobilization of the country's whole research potential. It was a crusade to reestablish the scientific preeminence of France. Politicians as well as scientists from throughout the country lobbied the government to invest in provincial education as part of their patronage of regional development.[50] But, again, it was the spatial mapping of educational reform that was understood as the required underpinning of modernization. For example, in 1957, Hippolyte Ducos, deputy from the Haute-Garonne, took his turn in the National Assembly to call for a complete geographic charting of scientific establishments in France and for increased funding for the science schools of Toulouse.

The result was that the initial 1958 plan for the new Midi-Pyrénées region took up the development of education and scientific research as its essential objective. The expansion of Toulouse's pedagogical institutions was defined as fundamental to its industrialization as a "high-tech" capital and to the economic modernization of its surrounding region. The plan presented a long list of schools to be created at Toulouse. Foremost among them were the *grandes écoles* in aeronautics, which were to be moved from Paris.[51] Since the Faculty of Science buildings on the allées Jules Guesde could not be expanded any further, the city proposed a completely new campus as part of the reinauguration of Midi scholarship. The search for a location suitable for Toulouse's educational renaissance began. It ended outside the central city at the southeast edge of the commune.

East of the city the rural atmosphere lingered far longer than on the flatland of the Garonne plain. The rolling green hills of the Terrefort with their quaint hamlets made it the most aesthetically desirable land around Toulouse. Isolated homes and tiny settlements were snuggled into some of the most superb spots in the Garonne Valley. But development was not easy. Public utilities and even a good network of roads remained scarce. Only a few places had attracted suburban house-hunters. Joliment and the old villages of Soupetard and Juncasse (where Montariol had set one of his housing projects) had been discovered as residential havens. The village of Montaudran, set into a small hollow, was converted into an aircraft center by the arrival of the Latécoère and Bréguet factories and the development of its airport. Just across the Canal du Midi, to the southeast, a Montariol garden-city project and some public-housing units marked what was known as the Rangueil quarter. There, the university purchased 250 inexpensive hectares in 1958 as the site for the new science faculty. The land sale covered the entire area between the route de Narbonne and the Canal du Midi. The decision received unanimous political approval in the Municipal Council, which commented that Rangueil was "destined to become one of the most important districts of Toulouse." Yet despite what appeared to be an auspicious beginning, Rangueil remained essentially untouched in the early 1960s for lack of money.

By then the French government had begun a systematic inventory of the country's scientific potential by the newly organized Délégation Générale à la Recherche Scientifique et Technique (DGRST). A public research fund was created, and the country's preeminent scientific institutions were undergoing thorough reform. In 1962, the massive modernization projects of the Fourth Plan were inaugurated. The nation's scientific priorities were organized into "programs of concerted action" and coordinated with de Gaulle's *grands programmes* for advanced technology industries. At DATAR, Olivier Guichard foresaw the reform and decentralization of some of the most prominent Parisian scientific research institutions as part of the budding policy of *métropoles d'équilibres* and regional development. The creation of scientific complexes in provincial France would, at least in theory, reduce the overwhelming domination of Paris in higher education and add immeasurably to the modernization of economically backward regions.[52]

This, then, was the rationale behind the enormous campaign to create the Rangueil-Lespinet scientific complex at Toulouse. The government's support meant a program of construction and expansion that lasted into the 1970s and dramatically broadened both the size and the scope of the city's education and research facilities. The original property at Rangueil was expanded by the purchase in 1963 of 375 more hectares on the opposite side of the Canal du Midi at Lespinet in preparation for large-scale development. The entire complex was assigned the Fourth Plan "concerted action research programs" in civil aeronautics and fluid mechanics. When a second series of research fields was chosen for "concerted action" during the Fifth Plan, Rangueil-Lespinet received funding for electronics and data processing, research fields corresponding to Toulouse's second pilot industry.

The construction of the new Faculty of Science alone consumed some

235 million francs. Toulouse's two *écoles supérieures* in electrical and chemical engineering were transferred from their old sites in the central city to newly built facilities alongside the Faculty of Science at Rangueil. Two new types of higher educational institutions created during the 1960s were also constructed there. Their foundation was part of the government's attempt to rationalize and modernize France's educational curriculum. The first, established in 1963, was the National Institute for Applied Sciences, which trained engineers in a five-year program of study. The second, opened in 1966 just next door, was the University Institute of Technology (IUT) for engineering technicians. Lastly, a variety of research laboratories funded by the Centre National de la Recherche Scientifique (CNRS) were decentralized from Paris to the emerging Rangueil complex. Their fields of study were chosen to coordinate with the science faculty and institutes already at Rangueil in an effort to encourage the multidisciplinary character of research and to develop common research programs. Probably the most well-known CNRS research program at Rangueil was the electronic optics laboratory that housed the world's largest electron microscope. On the opposite side of the route de Narbonne, the Faculty of Medicine and a modern university teaching hospital were constructed on the high slopes of the Pech-David hills overlooking Toulouse. Joining them was another series of laboratories decentralized from Paris: the National Institute on Health and Medicine (INSERM) facility and two major CNRS laboratories.

The result of all this development was that from the Canal du Midi across the route de Narbonne and up the hills of Bellevue, the architecture and landscape of a modern university and research park took shape. It was in sharp contrast to the densely packed red brick buildings and natural intimacy of the old Latin and Saint-Etienne quarters that had been so much a part of central Toulouse. Instead, the new Université de Toulouse–Paul Sabatier, as it was formally christened in 1970 under the Faure reforms, adopted the airy, spacious appearance of an American university campus. Fountains playing in a stately reflecting pool set off the main entrance to the administration building. The classrooms were surrounded by a grid of orderly breezeways, rectangular lawns, and parking lots. Unlike the University of Toulouse–Le Mirail on the other side of the city, which seemed nonchalantly stuck out in the fields, the Université Paul Sabatier dominated the route de Narbonne into Toulouse and the whole atmosphere at Rangueil. It was the city's, and Languedoc's, new gateway into the future, dramatically staged along the old road south to the Mediterranean. By the early 1970s, the area around it was some of the most expensive real estate at Toulouse.

The development of the new scientific complex continued on the other side of the Canal du Midi at Lespinet. From the mid-1960s, Lespinet quickly filled up with a growing number of aerospace research laboratories and aviation schools decentralized from Paris. By far the most auspicious of the projects were the decentralization of the distinguished Ecole Nationale Supérieure d'Aéronautique (Sup'Aéro or ENSAE) and the Ecole Nationale de l'Aviation Civile (ENAC), the most outstanding university institutions in France for aviation. Their transfer symbolized a formal recognition of Toulouse as the country's preeminent aerospace center and was the occasion for outright glee on the part of Bazerque and the Municipal Council, who were forced to compete for the limited number of prestigious Parisian institutions distributed among the *métropoles d'équilibres*.[53] The price they paid for the government's acknowledgment was quite precise. The city would contribute one million francs each for the decentralization of the two schools—a persuasive example of the bartering required at the coffers of the state planning agencies. But Toulouse was doubly rewarded with state benevolence when the French Space Center (Centre National d'Etudes Spatiales, or CNES) was sent to Lespinet. At a cost of 58 million francs, the open fields sprouted with CNES's research buildings, assembly and testing halls, radar apparatus, and the myriad technostructures associated with a developing space program. All were carefully garnished with pristine lawns, walkways, and access roads, creating an impression of modernization and efficient planning analogous to that of the space agency itself.[54]

A variety of research laboratories were then nestled in around the two schools and the Space Center. Just to the north of Sup'Aéro's sports field was the Aviation Research and Study Center (CERT), the principal research lab for the two aviation schools. On the south side of Sup'Aéro, near the bridge over the Canal du Midi, the Space Radiation Studies Center researched cosmic physics and nuclear particles, while the CNRS-funded Space Applications Laboratory (LAAS) studied space electronics and automation. The total investment at Lespinet reached 100 million francs by the end of the Fifth Plan, most of it funneled through the administrative networks at the Commissariat Général du Plan, its Commission on Research, and DATAR. The decentralizations made Toulouse one of three European centers for space testing and research, along with Noordwijk in the Netherlands and Ottobrun in West Germany. Rangueil-Lespinet became a sacred icon on the altar of successful decentralization projects completed by the French government.[55] It was a fixed feature of state modernist discourse during the 1960s and 1970s. Within the national budgets for research and development in higher education, Toulouse received more funding in the physical sciences, mathematics, chemistry, and medicine than any university city other than Grenoble.[56] The hope was that Rangueil-Lespinet would in fact emulate Grenoble's highly successful nuclear science complex. In a world of its own, rather oblivious to the needs of industry, Rangueil-Lespinet flourished into a multidisciplinary network of renowned research teams studying everything from space biology to groundwater contamination.

Altogether, the Rangueil-Lespinet complex was a massive effort at molding Toulouse's traditional scientific and research predilections into a modern form. It was completely contrived and supported from within the dominion of state planning agencies. The forces of municipal politics played only a whimsical role in the drama of its appearance along the route de Narbonne. They were conspicuous most perhaps by absence. The complex was readily accepted, without choice, by virtually the entire political spectrum as the key to the city's modernization, and a good deal of the local urban planning during the 1960s and 1970s revolved around nurturing it. There was a conscious monumentality, a linear planning to it that was overt and statist. More than anything, the appearance of Rangueil-Lespinet was the epitome of 1960s modernism as it was applied by state bureaucratic and planning elites. The emphasis on zoning and spatial design, the sterile three- and four-story classroom and office buildings, represented a rationalized urban form. It was an up-to-date Toulouse articulated through the medium of a banal, yet domineering, governmental modernist style. In this sense, the entrances to the aerospace institutions along the avenue Edouard Belin at Lespinet were a grand processional not only to aviation but to the power of the French state and its command of a modernist future for Toulouse and for France.

Nonetheless, the development of the complex was imagined to be the project most in line with the city's long-standing image as an intellectual and educational capital. It represented an authentic Toulouse translated into modern norms. Unlike other ostentatious modernist projects, such as Le Mirail or even the redevelopment of Saint-Georges, Rangueil-Lespinet was deliberately represented as the natural progression of the city's own learning and heritage. Even overtly high-tech Lespinet worked as cultural capital, since the old Toulouse-Montaudran airport was situated immediately to the north, its historic Air France runways jutting down parallel to ENAC and to CNES. The meticulously planned appearance of Rangueil-Lespinet was the idiom for a refreshing local optimism about the city's future. It was a statement of the city's science orientation, of its escape from underdevelopment, and of its commitment to efficiency and modernism. More than any other area of the city, Rangueil-Lespinet represented an invented calling in the contemporary, postindustrial world for the constructed entity known as Toulouse.

After the transfers from Paris during the 1960s, Toulouse registered more *grandes écoles* and *écoles supérieures* than any other provincial city.[57] The two aviation *grandes écoles* in particular lent a privileged scientific air to the city's intellectual life, and their students and professors acted as an "academic aristocracy" within Toulouse's elite educational milieu. Altogether, by the early 1970s, over 50,000 students were enrolled within the city's higher education system, and nearly 12,000 people were employed to keep it running. There were 8,600 professors and scientists living at Toulouse, 4,000 engineers, and some 2,000 university administrators. Approximately 4,000 researchers, engineers, and technicians were on staff at the aircraft plants; about 300 to 450 chemists did research at ONIA-APC (Azote et Produits Chimiques) and the Castaigne pharmaceutical company.[58] The long-forgotten diction, "Paris pour voir, Lyon pour avoir, Bordeaux pour dispendre, et Toulouse pour apprendre," began to reappear on public documents and in local magazines and newspapers. Midi scholarship had reemerged at the cutting edge of the scientific future. Learning was once again a Toulouse trademark, and this time it was well in the hands of the French state.

The locals may well have accepted Rangueil into the bosom of their history and imagery, but for the new immigrants settling there, it was a different matter. A large number of the people working in the sparkling classrooms and research labs were untested citizens of the temperamental capital of Languedoc. Only one-fourth of the total staff at the Université Paul Sabatier, for example, were native Toulousain.[59] The prospect of moving to the southwest in the first place was met with trepidation by professionals and scholars. There was considerable reticence about leaving Paris, where most of them originally lived, because they still saw their best career opportunities to be at the capital.[60] In their opinion, Toulouse offered few options for new jobs or promotions outside Rangueil-Lespinet and the aircraft plants. The 1960s was a period of intense competition for positions with the lucrative government research programs. The scientists and engineers "decentralizing" to the city, the graduates of Toulouse's universities and *écoles supérieures,* and those already working at Toulouse before the push of the 1960s produced a glut on the local job market despite the increasing demand for skilled research work. Unemployment among the *cadres tech-*

niques grew by 20 percent each year during the 1960s, one of the highest unemployment increases in the city's labor force.[61] Toulouse simply had an overabundance of "gray matter," as the French called it—highly educated, cutting-edge scientists, computer experts, physicists, and engineers. The aeronautics industry, for example, regularly turned down applications from Toulouse university graduates because they judged the skills received in academia unadaptable to industrial work. The university and CNRS laboratories carried on theoretical research, while industry required the applied version. Of 582 technicians graduated from Toulouse's University Institute of Technology between 1967 and 1970 in the departments of civil engineering, data processing, and electrical engineering, only a little over 200 actually found employment, and of these only half were hired by firms in the southwest.[62] Lacking any job mobility in the city, a shift to a better position required yet another geographic move, probably back to Paris.

Second, the transplanted Parisians considered Toulouse an embarrassing cultural wasteland, lacking not only in the sophisticated amenities of the capital but even in the basic urban services deemed essential for upper-middle-class life. Situated smack in the bosom of backwardness, modern bourgeois living was a dubious affair at Toulouse. Researchers complained that their spouses had difficulty finding good jobs. Housing was an affliction and the suburbs were barren. The city built 1,500 residences in modern, high-rise apartment buildings at Rangueil. But it was precisely families identified as *cadres moyens* who were the most dissatisfied with the arrangements and who complained relentlessly about the lack of services and the isolation.[63]

Government authorities were forced to exert strong pressure on the aviation *grandes écoles* to make the transfer to the Toulouse outback. Both the students and professors feared a deterioration in the quality of their education and their prestige. Construction on the schools proceeded only after the municipal government gave in to the demand for a special Sup'Aéro airplane and a mountain chalet "to compensate in some way for the distance from the capital and the consequent trauma for the students."[64] The two colleges were provided with an enormous physical education and sports facility as well as with parks, language laboratories, and libraries, all in an effort to create the cultural amenities attractive to their faculties and technical staffs. But nonetheless, the schools remained isolated along the road at Lespinet, with a restricted-use bus shuttle the only form of transportation into Toulouse. The greatest conflict over "forced decentralization" came when CNES announced its plan to transfer to Toulouse. A large number of resignations, primarily from engineers and technicians, followed. CNES predicted that some 40 percent of the employees would resign to find jobs in the private sector rather than resettle at Toulouse.[65] Finally, in September 1970, engineers and technicians at CNES staged a strike, demanding higher and more equitable financial compensation for the move to the southwest. The decentralization took place only after they were awarded substantial financial advantages.

In spite of the problems associated with migrating to an infamous "nowheres-ville," many white-collar professionals did settle in the city during the 1960s and early 1970s. But their physical presence did not necessarily mean that they were active in local life. One of the most apparent characteristics about the new elites was that they remained largely detached from old Toulouse and from the cultural localism. In their habits and tastes they were part of a new French middle class, upwardly mobile, affluent, and to a certain extent geographic gypsies, following career opportunities within the magic circle of the *grandes écoles* and the *cadres supérieures*. Henri Sarramon, the president of the Chamber of Commerce and a native Toulousain, called these *arrivistes* "the new economic class with American ideas."[66] Gilles Faÿsse, for example, was in charge of the Université Paul Sabatier's relations with industry and the surrounding community. He was a Parisian journalist who had taken the job at Toulouse to escape the hectic atmosphere of the capital. He worked in the university's administration building and drove the short distance across the Canal du Midi to Lespinet to confer with colleagues at CNES and the space laboratories. Faÿsse and his family purchased an old suburban cottage, Occitan style, in the Rangueil quarter, which they renovated. The family rarely went into the central city, except for an evening's entertainment at a restaurant or film or to stroll around the narrow streets of Saint-Georges or Saint-Etienne in search of antique shops and elegant boutiques. Old Toulouse was an amusing sojourn into local history. Their actual social existence revolved around their friends at Rangueil.[67] They were among the new suburbanites living in large apartments or in single-family homes in the bourgeois enclaves of the city's eastern outskirts.

Once the scientific complex was announced for Rangueil, land prices in the surrounding neighborhood skyrocketed.[68] Upscale housing developments popped up suited to the tastes of the city's new *cadres* of doctors, scientists, and engineers working at the complex. The most prosperous among them purchased elegant villas in rustic areas like Côte Pavée or at Auzeville and Vigoulet-Auzil. They read *Le Monde* rather than *La Dépêche*. They rarely attended traditional social or cultural events at Toulouse but instead took advantage of the region's recreational facilities, particularly skiing in the Pyrénées and boating on the Mediterranean.[69] By Toulouse standards, they lived charmed lives in the hills of the Terrefort. In a sense they existed within the material culture created specifically by the state for Rangueil. It was an exclusive, ultramodern setting of decorous offices, laboratories, modern apartment complexes and suburban *pavillons*—almost hermetically sealed from Toulouse and the Midi. The technicians, engineers, and scientists at CNES ate lunch together in the Agency's modern two-story cafeteria. In the evenings they returned to their homes at Rangueil or the surrounding suburbs. They talked about Toulouse as if it were in another world rather than a few kilometers away. For them, the old Toulousains were an archaic and grizzled breed unable to keep up with the modern age.[70]

Perhaps central Toulouse was indeed another world. Education and scientific research had traditionally been an integral part of the city's history and imagery. But their development during the 1960s and early 1970s brought with it an entirely new professional elite and a new middle class whose tastes and values were radically different from those of the local dwellers. They contributed a wealth of new expertise and brought modern tastes to the well-ingrained customs and habits of Toulouse urban society. In a sense this new bourgeoisie illustrated the broader meaning behind the heroic modernism of the 1960s. The emphasis on functionalism, the rational design and zoning based on health, housing, and standard of living—the stress laid on progressive images of the suburban environment as the alternative to the decrepitude of the inner city—amounted to a program of social and spatial construction. From their drawing boards, Candilis, city architects, and planners could effortlessly arrange and systemize urban space into a coherent and uniform whole. The language of state planning itself delineated the extent of reordering implicit in the program of *aménagement du territoire* and the degree to which social hegemony was its basic subtext. The Livre Blanc and the various national plans of the 1960s based their goals on the project of *les formations des hommes,* the slogan that best articulates the social engineering that lay behind the quest for inventing the modern city. The term was specifically used to describe the well-educated, affluent middle- and upper-middle-class *cadres* for whom the brave new worlds of Rangueil-Lespinet and Le Mirail were created.[71]

Le Mirail represented the future of man as habitant and consumer; Rangueil represented the future of man as technologist and producer. They were essentially dreamworlds, conjured up as spatial imagery and economic strategy in order to forge a new French citizen—committed to progress, committed to the material abundance offered by capitalist production, and committed to the interests of the state. As modernist panoramas, both projects were conceived as part of a calculated reorganization of urban territory into socially ranked geographic spaces, all carefully controlled by public authority. The web of imaginary boundaries that contained these spaces were meant not only to rationalize the landscape but to isolate and protect the social groups who personified the future.

In part, it is clear that the older political and social networks in the city and the surrounding communes were abrogated by the process of suburbanization itself and by the regulatory fiat of state administration. Nonetheless, they still managed to exert substantial influence over the style and pace of modernization taking place in the *pays toulousain*. Louis Bazerque's insistence on the "grand schemes" approach to urban development and his close personal association with high-profile modernization projects were eventually his undoing. Over the course of the 1960s, it became increasingly difficult for him to hold together the fragile Socialist–center-right alliance that was the footing for his municipal administration. Members of his own party questioned whether Bazerque was really following in the footsteps of Toulouse's Socialist municipal tradition or whether his efforts only amounted to political grandstanding vis-à-vis the innumerable Gaullist bureaucrats impatient to expunge his personal fiefdom. Badiou's dissident PSU lambasted Bazerque as a "Socialist-capitalist." In the meantime, the center-right reproached Bazerque for sacrificing everything else at Toulouse for the sake of Le Mirail, which was, at any rate, riddled by financial mismanagement. Pierre Baudis, Bazerque's adjunct mayor and chief rival for political power, called for greater emphasis on private development less hamstrung by public regulation. This would result, according to Baudis, in the restoration of the single-family dwelling to its customary role as a popular alternative for the city's population.[72] At the same time, the communes surrounding Toulouse were notably triumphant in maintaining a safe distance from the imperial plans and regulatory blitz flowing from the public authorities in the city. Communal social and political elites, as well as a myriad of private investors, carved out their own course toward the spreading "Toulouse of tomorrow." The result was a rather serendipitous journey through modernization. It proceeded in part through a massive technocratic campaign to construct Toulouse according to strict state-defined social and material standards and in part through the intercession of indigenous social and political forces, each claiming its own ideas about the future identity of Toulouse.

CHAPTER 5

The City as Bazaar: Tradition, Modernization, and Economic Culture in the 1950s

Central Toulouse was the domain of the *petits patrons,* the artisans, laborers, and shopkeepers, the street merchants who together worked the traditional trades that had supported the city since its earliest history. Their web of tiny workshops, family-run groceries, markets, and construction yards was the filament that held the city's economy together. The longevity and success of this traditional business community was a function of the city's role as the chief market town in the southwest. Toulouse certainly had its "big industries": the state armament factories, a few large foundries, and garment mills. But until the arrival of the ONIA and aircraft plants in the 1920s, there was little evidence of large-scale factory production. This was a city of diminutive regional trade, a fact which determined the historic character of Toulouse as a picturesque, marginally productive microcosm of *jolie petite France,* the nation of small producers, skilled craftsmen, and specialty shops.[1] What particularly distinguished Toulouse, however, was, first, the variety of occupations and trades that made up this traditional economic whirlpool. There was very little tendency toward any predominant type of production.[2] Second, the Toulouse business community had a particular propensity to work within a dense network of lilliputian manufactories.[3] Thousands of independently owned and operated shops fanned out into a wide range of *métiers,* producing an ever-changing assortment of semicustomized products, all catering to local and regional demand.

This traditional Toulouse economy was organized around informal local networks, flexible specialization, and skilled labor. It reached its apogee during the first half of the twentieth century. The First World War and the increased demand for wartime goods, in addition to the city's growing population, expanded the market for custom and ready-made clothes and footwear, machinery and tools, processed foods, and the range of everyday household items. The city's business culture responded by adapting production within the context of its customary local manufacturing system. The neighborhood west of the rue Saint-Rome to the Garonne River (the old medieval Bourse quarter) was filled with the workshops of clothing manufacturers. The heart of the district on the rue de la Bourse and the rue Sainte-Ursule was within easy walking distance to the wholesale houses and department stores along the rue d'Alsace-Lorraine and the place Esquirol. The clothing industry was divided between the traditional tailors producing custom-made clothing and the more important ready-to-wear garment industry (or *confection*) that specialized in shirts and men's apparel. Both relied largely on the domicile system. The vast majority of *travailleuses à domicile* were young women from working-class families in the city or from farming households along the outskirts. They streamed daily through the garment district carrying packs of finished shirts, blouses, and pants back to the shops for payment and to pick up new orders.

Starch works, glass and ceramic manufacturers, and furniture makers were found around the Le Bazacle electrical power station on the Garonne. Over 90 percent of the city's furniture shops were owned by skilled craftsmen working on their own or with a few apprenticed helpers. Mechanics, dye works, tanning and leather, and footwear shops were concentrated in the small industrial sector around the old Saint-Cyprien railroad station on the left bank. There they made use of the abandoned buildings as *ateliers* and warehouses. The city's shoemakers produced children's footwear, moccasins, and slippers with simple machinery in solo shops. Mass production was limited to eleven tiny factories, some at Saint-Cyprien, others near the leather market in the Minimes industrial district. Tiny forges, automobile and moped repair shops, and building construction yards also mingled in old Minimes. It was there that the Bedouce factory produced the perfume made from the Toulouse violets cultivated at the suburban farms just to the north. Boosted by the voracious demand for housing, newly arrived Spanish and Italian construction workers joined with Toulouse builders and bricklayers in a thriving industry supported by a multitude of small-time contractors. Their stockyards and sheds were found everywhere. Ready-to-wear clothing and hosiery manufacturers, paper and carton makers, and skilled mechanics were scattered through the Matabiau and Saint-Aubin districts close to the railroad station. Saint-Aubin was also the location of the city's largest printing factory, the Maison Sirven. Other than the Sirven, Privat, and Fournie companies and the regional printing plant, the majority of the city's printing shops were meager enterprises producing on a small scale.

In general, this cornucopia of shops and *ateliers* was more highly concentrated in the old districts of Toulouse than was the case in most provincial capitals. For example, Toulouse's large number of ready-to-wear businesses exhibited a far greater propensity to cluster in the Cité than was generally the case in France. Even the building and food industries, in which French firms had a far greater inclination to disperse throughout the faubourgs, were more centrally concentrated at Toulouse.[4] Everyday and specialty merchandise *à la toulousaine* was offered within the space and culture of the vernacular. The goods were sold through the city's proud spectacle of daily markets and wholesale and retail shops. The *rez-de-chaussée* of the red brick buildings was a vital mercantile ribbon densely packed with bakeries, groceries, butchers, furniture houses, printing works, plumbers, gift shops, tailors, and apparel manufacturers. These were the businesses that gave the old city its reputation for the sociability and bustle that highlighted its municipal public culture.

Indeed the craftsmen, apprentices, and workers who labored in the city's traditional industries were claimed by regional enthusiasts as one of the last vestiges of Occitan culture. They were portrayed as a true working class of *patrons occitans,* tied to the values and morals of the Midi. Old Toulouse survived, according to local regionalists, chiefly in *"le petit peuple."* Around them was built a wide array of images, at various moments romanticized, irreverent and hostile, defensive or nostalgic. The strenuous efforts at distinguishing their character made these purveyors of the traditional economy a beleaguered component in the tangle of controversies over modernization. The very idea of an artisan, a special class defined by economic culture and practice, was an invention of the twentieth-century debate on French economic development. Defining an artisan class was a matter of deciding what role France's independent craftsmen would play in the process of modernization.[5] The creation of a regional dimension to the petty producers of Toulouse was an integral part of this ongoing debate. They were either steadfast guards over a regional tradition of individualism, alternative production, and humanism or archaic vestiges of the past that needed to be expunged—either victims of, or obstacles to, modernization. In short, the image of Toulouse's independent craftsmen and shopkeepers came to represent the moral and cultural dilemmas involved in the French quest to achieve a modern capitalist ethos.

Historical descriptions of everyday life in Languedoc consistently focused on its sociability, its infectious joie de vivre. Adjectives such as "happy," "joyous," "gay" were frequently used to describe both work and leisure. It was this beguiling vision of conviviality and pleasure that local historians, nostalgic for the city's past, often conjured up in trying to capture what was so special about living in old Toulouse. The venerable Alex Coutet, describing his walks through the city in 1925, was stirred by the aromas of the city's street life: the sweet smell of fennel, the charcoal of the braziers, the fragrance of ripe fruit that swirled around the women's red parasols at the market on the place du Capitole. Strolling to Saint-Sernin on Sunday morning, he threaded his way through the crowds around the junk dealers while the strains of music and the responses of the Mass filtered through the cathedral's stained-glass windows. The old artisan districts were tranquil and serene. The life of the tiny *ateliers* was, according to Coutet, "a happy and simple existence." During the day quietness prevailed, along with a wholesome, calm rivalry between neighboring shops and a dependency on craftsmanship and quality in producing fine goods.[6]

Recounting daily life at Toulouse in the 1920s, Gratien Leblanc noted that "in the morning, everyone goes to the markets." The early birds got the best prices on the boulevard d'Arcole. Later shoppers tried the wagons and stalls set up along the boulevard de Strasbourg or the colorful displays that gave such a picturesque character to the place du Capitole. There were even greater choices under the caste-iron *halle* at the place Victor-Hugo or at the place des Carmes, where the mongers called out their wares in *patois*. Leblanc also described the traditional neighborhood life of the working-class and commercial districts as charming and simple. Their residents often lived in the style of the *campagnards,* in front of their doors and out in the street, with their braziers and chickens.[7]

Northern critics insisted that the real basis for this Languedocean joie de vivre was a general aversion to work. The Toulouse craftsmen and dealers were frequently accused of outright laziness, a disposition associated with life in the Midi. They flaunted the ease, slow pace, and enjoyment of life that were the mark of southern France. They preferred the warmth and neighborliness, the long midafternoon lunches and gay nightlife of their village-districts to the risks and pressures of business expansion and the practice of efficient, hard work. This was a mentality clearly antipathetic to economic growth. The castigations against their irreverence for "sound" business techniques were historic and innumerable. Madame de Rémusat, the wife of the prefect of the Haute-Garonne during the 1830s, wrote that "the basic underlying problem is that no one seriously works at Toulouse. It's southern laziness, a conviction that comes naturally to them. The attitude is universal."[8] Even in the 1930s the admonishments still rang in native ears. Local writer Louis Gratias noted the painful truth: "In the eyes of Parisians, the Toulousain is very often an insignificant braggart singing at the top of his lungs, whiling away the sunny days lounging and chatting."[9] Sun and song, the leisurely pace, easygoing and neighborly—the Toulousains, according to these allegorical inventions, were simply not tuned to the inexorable rhythms of economic efficiency and competitiveness.

Caught somewhere within this amalgam of nostalgic, often bitter, and certainly preachy impressions was the city's vernacular economic community. It is not easy to delineate an accurate social makeup for these petty producers, especially by the mid-twentieth century when the issue of modernization so impinged upon their livelihood and identity. Some were certainly rural migrants getting a start at Toulouse by opening their own shops. Others were former factory or domiciled workers. The term often used to describe them was *petits travailleurs indépendants*. They were skilled in a working craft and owned their own tools. They altered the assortment of goods they produced by relying on the talents of labor, multipurpose equipment, and small-scale production. They labored within a dense network of informal contractual and production arrangements. A business was built around the space and place of community and local connections. Regulations were imposed locally by neighborhood business associations and trade unions, political affiliations, and everyday codes of conduct. Negotiations were largely spontaneous. Family members or a few salaried hands usually made up the only staffs in the shops and work yards that were threaded through the *quartiers populaires*. The owner worked alongside his employees and was barely distinguishable from them.

At the lower boundary of the group were those who shifted back and forth between opening their own rented sheds and finding work in someone else's. Setting up a business was a practical and socially accepted alternative to facing layoffs and unemployment. Business ownership offered the freedom and independence that were traditional aspirations within the working community. It also proffered the possibility of social ascent into the ranks of the petite bourgeoisie. Certainly at the upper boundary, the most successful of the small businessmen would lay claim to *patron* status in the petty bourgeois sense of the word. At Toulouse, this meant real social and political influence. Indeed, within the taxonomy of the state census, all artisans were catalogued as *patrons de l'industrie* (a fact that further muddied the waters around their social identity).

However, to suggest that as a group the petty producers of Toulouse were defined by standards of property ownership, propriety, and savings, as well as paternalism toward their shop hands, would be an inaccuracy. Rather there was a fluidity, an informality about their attributes as a social and economic caste that left small producers in a murky zone between fixed categories. Up to the end of the 1950s the term that petty producers most commonly used to describe their own social consciousness was *artisanat*. It was a term that cast social cohesion upon their identity as skilled craftsmen schooled in specialized methods. Professional status and success was measured not in terms of property nor in managerial acumen but by technical expertise and high-quality production. What counted was their agility with their product lines and their connections and standing within the local economy of Toulouse. It was the inviolability of their independent shops that gave work meaning. These represented their dedication to the tempo and habits of daily life in the Midi. Toulouse was a municipality of grocers and craftsmen in which individualism was the cardinal social virtue. As historian Gérard Cholvy has aptly put it: "Without cease, men and women without great financial reserves but with some resources at their disposal set themselves up and tried their luck."[10]

It is also evident that Toulouse's independent shopowners were as attached to their *quartier* as they were to their *métier* and to the sociability that both offered. Self-image was shaped as much by neighborhood status and local bonds as it was by independent production. The neighborhood *ateliers,* shops, and open markets were communal meeting grounds—places for politicking and debate as well as social gossip. They were the arena of business exchange and negotiations that took place within the larger context of community life. As such, the *atélier* and shop were pivotal symbolic places within the city's culture. They were signifiers of site. The daily world of business was a key component of urban social integrity. Neighborhoods such as Dalbade, Saint-Georges, Saint-Aubin, or des Carmes revolved around the produce market on the main square, the groceries and *ateliers,* and the parish church. This intimate association between economics and culture was evident, for example, during religious holidays, which were celebrated with parades and commercial fairs staged by its businessmen. Even more impressive were the street dances, or *baloches,* sponsored by the neighborhood business associations. There were over sixty district *baloches* in the spring and summer of 1925, including one that filled the entire expanse of the place du Capitole. Usually, four musicians played on a platform set up in the street, which was festooned with Venetian lanterns and with decorated tables offering wine, beer, and lemonade.

The public culture of Toulouse, then, was in good measure nourished by its network of petty producers allied within their neighborhoods, through local business and trade union affiliations, and through political allegiances. The tradition of democratic municipalism was sustained from within this interlocking populist network. Artisans, shopkeepers, and workers ran for the Municipal Council and laid claim to its seats in as many numbers as those in the liberal professions.[11] By commanding the city's economic associations and flexing its formidable muscle in the Chamber of Commerce and the Municipal Council, the small-business community essentially dictated the city's economic policy and its community life. It effectively balanced cooperation and competition between businesses by relying on the historic connection with public community and district interests. It synchronized vernacular economic customs and generated patronage around the emerging images and symbols of modern Toulouse. Local merchant associations, for example, were heavily involved in the sponsorship of air races, rugby matches, and market festivals during the 1920s and 1930s. This kind of entertainment fell well within the tradition of Toulouse street life. It was offered within the context of an exalted form of city and neighborhood boosterism and brought thousands into the central districts where merchandise was conveniently displayed, often at special prices, for easy purchase.

While they were perfectly capable of constructing a modern culture of consumption and entertainment based on these perceptions of neighborhood and municipality, independent shopowners also remained socially conservative and loyal to regional political custom. By the 1920s and 1930s the majority espoused an idiosyncratic mixture of cultural tradition and political consciousness often described as a "reactionary left." Adherence to Radicalism and especially Socialism was by the early twentieth century a privileged component of perceived Occitan identity. This regional "orientation toward the left" functioned as a form of historic cultural practice, an aspect of the region's particularist predilections. It was supported by a burgeoning system of political patronage and a network of unions that incorporated small-business proprietors, artisans, and workers into a coherent political defense of the principles and outlook of *les petits*. The ranks of the left were filled with a mix of artisans and laborers from the traditional small-time trades, the new ONIA and aircraft workers, teachers and professors, engineers and doctors. The badge of Radical-Socialism was a protest against encroachment by northern large-scale capitalism and by the administrative tyranny of the French state. It was a rallying cry in defense of freedom and the dignity of independent labor, a shield against the ignominious slide into proletariat status. According to Cholvy: "The vital role of the *petit atelier,* the *petit patronat,* and the mass of *salariés isolés* gave to this society a unique countenance that well clarifies its behavior and its political and syndical choices."[12] At Toulouse, then, adherence to the left was essentially practiced as a populist culture of opposition. It was braced by a wide and stable foundation from within the labor and business communities that remained largely outside the dynamics of modern capitalist production and regulation.

This culture of opposition was also an indigenously based reaction to the economic grievances and hardships suffered in the Midi. Independent ownership of a shop conferred high social standing and prestige within the community. But the reality was that the world of the petty producer was often unstable and precarious. Respectable skilled craftsmen and property owners could easily find themselves stretched beyond their means. Certainly the marginality of business existence was endemic. Livelihoods were particularly precarious given the difficulty of competition with hundreds of other minuscule shops producing or selling the same goods. Businesses opened and closed down or were sold with distressing regularity. Shops rarely outlived their founders. They were essentially temporary units of production that recombined machines and skills and shifted the variety of available goods in a perpetual municipal cycle.

When the boom in traditional production was cut short by the depression of the 1930s and the Second World War, the difficulties became oppressive. Clothing and hosiery manufacturers, leather workers and metallurgists, among many, survived the lean years by taking refuge in the *micro-atelier.* Costs were cut to a minimum for survival. Many of the shops simply closed in the midst of the economic crisis and wartime scarcity. There was plenty of room for bitter reaction to the reality of Toulouse's economic adversity. The radical left provided the local business community with a political idiom that was accepted as traditional and customary. At the same time, it was overtly modern and progressive in its stance for libertarianism, for improvements in the lot of the working class, and for regional political and economic parity.

In either case, secure with their newly expanded markets in the 1920s or facing the economic uncertainties of the 1930s and 1940s, the city's small businesses actually had little reason to attempt risky changes. The economic and political culture identified with both neighborhood and municipalism guaranteed the underlying pattern of industrial organization. As a result Toulouse's vernacular economy did not participate in the wider evolution toward increasing plant size and mechanization that was affecting the remainder of France during the first half of the twentieth century. Aircraft factories sprouted in the suburbs. The cracking towers of the ONIA chemical plant rose up over the Garonne River. But up to and through the war, artisans, shopkeepers, and *petits patrons* continued to reign over the practices and routines of everyday life in old Toulouse. They were as much a part of what was understood to be the city's authentic culture as the red brick buildings they inhabited. Steeped in local culture and politics, *les petits* were the quintessential Toulousains. By consequence, the city's economic fortunes remained tied to the uncertain fate awaiting its tiny businesses amid the rising tides of mechanization, mass consumption, and corporate command. At the Liberation and "Year Zero," facing the massive campaign to economically modernize France, the Toulouse business community continued to abide by specialized production and small independent shops, with their equally independent owners.

Liberation and Reconstruction

In general, the *patronat* of France, as economic elites, had been left under a cloud of suspicion after the wartime collaboration and Pétainist leanings of some of their most esteemed members. At Toulouse, this hostility would be projected far more at Pierre-Georges Latécoère or Emile Dewoitine than at craftsmen-owners laboring in the old city. Nevertheless, Vichy had paid rather conspicuous lip service to the role of the artisan in modern society. Its Ministry of Production had set up an Artisanal Service under the direction of Jean Bichelonne and Pierre Loyer. It accomplished little other than constructing a romanticized public discourse about the "moral and ethical" character of the *artisanat* as a "natural institution." This traditionalist perception complemented Vichy's project to revive the "innate" provincial regions of France. The folklorist campaigns instituted by the Bureau du Régionalisme for Toulouse during the Vichy years were filled with nostalgic images of authentic regional crafts created by Occitan artisans dressed in native costume. A restoration of provincialist economic culture was viewed by the ultraconservative and ruralist exponents within Vichy as the key to the renewal of France itself. Like so much else during the Vichy years this mythic discourse on regional craft culture had little meaning. Artisans were given only a tenuous role within the government's economic plans. Their trade unions were summarily dissolved in 1941 and heroic craftsmen left to find their way through an ineffectual bureaucratic and regulatory labyrinth controlled by Vichy retainers.

More telling was the role of the petty producers in the fearsome *république rouge* of the Liberation. Certainly, the city's aircraft factories and its public utilities had been the main protagonists in the social experiments attempted at Toulouse. But tradesmen and craft workers had participated in neighborhood and shop yard Committees of Liberation or organized themselves into Comités Patriotiques d'Entreprises. The reconstituted trade unions as well were active leaders of the Liberation turmoil at Toulouse. Bertaux's autonomous Conseil Economique Régional was filled with their local champions: Soubiron of the Groupement Interprofessionnel des Syndicats Patronaux et Artisanaux, as well as members of seven other *patronale* organizations; Fournié of the Union des Syndicats Artisanaux; representatives from the departmental union organization, the garment makers' union, the carpenters' union, the metallurgists' union, and the Chambre des Métiers or Chamber of Trades. Through the preparation of reports on the state of their various crafts as well as their involvement on the short-lived Council, they essentially initiated a locally inspired program of modernization and regional development—one in which traditional industries played a prominent role.

In spite of these ambitions, the material deprivation of the war and Occupation and the stringent rationing into the late 1940s actually made the postwar revival of any normal business activity at Toulouse, as elsewhere in France, virtually impossible. Production and trade muddled along from one day to the next. Transportation was laborious along any of the roads and bridges. Workers themselves had vanished into German factories or into the hills with the Resistance or had evaporated into the general mayhem in and out of the city at the war's end. In the IXth Economic Region surrounding Toulouse, the textile industry lost 42 percent of its workforce, clothing and the leather trades 28 percent of their labor. In 1948, the city's ready-to-wear industry was still only functioning on a thirty-hour work week with a substantially diminished workforce. The most basic of material resources for manufacturing remained rare even at that date.[13] Local Resistance forces beseeched the new government at Toulouse to "feed the people, restart the factories and mines, and produce clothing and shoes." Tempers flared over the assortment of state ordinances promulgated to control allotments and the distribution of goods. Immediately after the Liberation, the Vichy-created Office Central de Répartition des Produits Industriels, as well as its Artisanal Services, continued to control the flow of resources to craft industries. In 1946, allocation was transferred to the Ministry of National Economy. But the defects and abuses within the state system were legion.[14] The annoying regulations, the supply muddles, the skyrocketing inflation on top of perpetual scarcity reaped little but complaints and acrimony.

The growing agitation at the failure of state Reconstruction policy broke out into strikes and protests at Toulouse as well as in the rest of France in April 1947. A strike and mass demonstration organized by the artisans' and shopkeepers' associations brought Toulouse to a standstill. Over 20,000 merchants, artisans, tradesmen, and workers closed their shop doors and marched to the municipal sports park to hear Soubiron and Vergnes, of the Syndicat des Commerçants, rail against the incompetency of state administration: "People don't buy with points, they buy with money!" The protest called for an immediate end to all rationing tickets, points, and regulations inhibiting free trade. The Municipal Council responded by modifying ration regulations in 1947 to make provisioning more efficient and more equitable.[15] In March, 300 members of the furniture-makers' association met to denounce state price controls and production policies. According to Courteau, the general secretary of the Fédération de l'Ameublement, "Primary materials are scarce. A malaise paralyzes the best of the producers. But state policies have simply added to the difficulties, holding down production when we want to increase it to a maximum."[16] In June, workers in the city's banks, gasworks, electrical stations, trucking industry, and railways went out on strike.

It was only in 1948 that the French economy began to revive. The local Chambers of Commerce also took over responsibility for allocating resources to private businesses. As a result, Toulouse's local economy began to show signs of real recovery and a normalizing of trade and industrial production. The most obvious sign of better times was the sudden flowering of the city's expositions, markets, and street fairs. In 1947, Toulouse's most celebrated favorite son, Vincent Auriol, came down from Paris just after his presidential inauguration to officially open the first, if small, postwar Foire de Toulouse. The 1948 fair was a more auspicious undertaking, with pavilions set up throughout the central city. The allées Jules-Guesde was covered with a great tent, the "Blue Pavilion," under which locally made furniture was displayed. The Electricité de France exhibit featured the benefits of hydroelectric power from the Pyrenees. The region's textiles, clothing, and women's fashions were celebrated, as were leather goods and shoes, regional foods and wines. But the fair was more than just a presentation of regional wares. It was also the first postwar display of contemporary materialism for the edification of the Toulousains. The public had its first look at the Renault 2CV and at a whole host of new household appliances and electrical products. The long-unavailable commodities of French North Africa were unveiled in the Pavillons Exotiques along the allées Frédéric Mistral, along with wine, chocolates, and luxury foods from all over France. Toulouse's first Exposition des Arts Ménagers was held in 1948 at the city's sports park. It provided, according to Gabriel Barlangue, president of the Chamber of Commerce, yet another occasion for the artisans and merchants around Toulouse to announce their recovery, "their continuous efforts at production, and the abundancy and wealth of a region that stretched from one sea to the other."[17]

Alongside these formal citywide efforts at reviving the economy, the local businessmen and neighborhood associations sponsored a multitude of street fairs in 1948 and 1949 as a ceremonious reinauguration of the city's commerce and craft production. The variety and originality of these festivities were remarkable. They were led off in July of 1948 by a week-long *grande fête populaire* organized by the 700 members of the Amicales des Commerçants du Quartier du Capitole. The festivities stretched from the place du Capitole down the rue Saint-Rome and the rue des Changes, which were decked out in colorful ribbons and streamers and illuminated late into the night. Musicians roamed the neighborhood; shop windows were stocked with goods at special prices. The city, and for that matter Toulouse's neighbors throughout the region, were invited to a *grand baloche* that went on for three days and three nights on the place du Capitole, which was "positively flooded with light and music." The point of the festival, according to Lapujade, the president of the neighborhood association, was to put Toulouse commerce among the avant-garde in supporting the government's push for price deflations.[18]

In September it was the turn of the Saint-Georges and des Carmes districts. The shops around Saint-Georges set up television cameras so that the crowds could watch themselves during the festivities. Prizes were offered to the most photogenic of the customers. A "Miss Antoine" was crowned on the rue Saint-Antoine-du-T. On the closing day of the fair, a hot-air balloon was launched and a neighborhood dinner organized. The streets around the rue des Filateurs and the place des Carmes organized a competition for the best decorated shops and window displays. Circus performers, mimes, and clowns performed in the streets. A prize was offered for the "most beautiful baby in old Toulouse." And of course an orchestra played for a neighborhood *baloche*. However, des Carmes staged a real advertising coup in closing their fair with a great costume ball with the theme of "Une Soirée 1900." They invited the neighboring commune of Colombette, whose population and officialdom paraded into the city in decorated cars and descended upon the rue des Filatiers in full fin-de-siècle costume. Amidst the party's prizes and contests and lottery, the neighborhood host offered the invitation to "Toulousains throughout the city, of all shapes and sizes—we welcome you! Mask yourselves, change your appearance, chase away your blues and enjoy yourselves in a wild night in old Toulouse!"[19]

In October, the neighborhood around the rue du Taur took its turn at a *"semaine commerciale du coeur de Toulouse."* In keeping with the ambience of the Latin quarter, a solemn parade of politicians and officials, led by Mayor Badiou, walked the neighborhood to open the fair. They ended at "Mon Café" on the place du Capitole, where Xixonet, president of the neighborhood association, spoke of the "desire to bring back to the central city the commercial spirit that it had, to recreate good relations between buyer and seller, to restore normal exchange at a reasonable price and bring a new enthusiasm to negotiations and business."[20]

The Victor-Hugo quarter staged its commercial bazaar in November. Its parade of businessmen and city officials was led by three young girls wearing traditional twilled shawls and ribboned straw hats *à la toulousaine*. They threaded their way through packed streets decked out with garlands and streamers, where shopkeepers dressed in traditional costume displayed their goods. The neighborhood offered prizes, a lottery, and street music as well as a program of music and dancing for children. The halle Victor-Hugo, covered with flowers and Venetian lanterns, was stocked with fresh produce, especially an extraordinary assortment of fish that attracted mobs of people.

In December, the quartier du Capitole offered another commercial extravaganza, this time a Christmas program that included Christmas trees and decorations, the launching of a mammoth hot-air balloon, and a spectacular appearance by Père Noël, who descended by parachute onto the place du Capitole in front of 10,000 people. The scene inaugurated a city-wide "Noël Commercial." Shops and stores both in Toulouse and in the suburban villages were embellished with Christmas decorations, garlands, and flags that greeted the waves of shoppers. The festival was capped with a massive fireworks display put on by the businessmen's associations.[21]

This commercial drama of festivals, entertainment, sales, and street adornment continued into 1949, as did the citywide trade expositions. They were representations of Reconstruction and postwar materialism that eschewed the dark days of war and occupation. The clearest theme articulated in the colorful display of goods and neighborhood joie de vivre was normalcy and abundance. The special "festival prices," the prizes and gifts, were strategies for rekindling the market, for creating new demands, for offering the vision of postwar consumption. In this respect, the Toulouse *petit patronat* organizing these events saw themselves as overtly modern in outlook and in business policy. Their festival speeches consistently reiterated the effort to march in line with government deflationary and production goals. The fairs and festivals were evidence of the willing support of private enterprise and their belief in the efficacy of the unfettered free market to produce the economic revitalization necessary for France's future. The festivals at the rue Saint-Rome were held under the banner of "fidelity, service, and tradition," the keys to good business, and were meant to evoke the vitality and enthusiasm of Toulouse's traditional business community.

Poverty amidst Prosperity: The Depression of the 1950s

This auspicious celebration of postwar good times unfortunately enjoyed the briefest of lives. After the momentary spurt of consumer spending in reaction to the war years died down and the refugees disappeared, both by about 1950–1951, the city's economy fell on hard times. While the Monnet Plan (1947–1952) launched France into the "miracle" of economic growth, Toulouse seemed to be passing through yet another spell of deindustrialization. Some of the city's oldest and largest factories added their names to the obituary list by the end of the war. The hosiery factory of Manuel, which had helped launch the city into the industrial age, closed in 1945, as did the Chelle-Pélissier hosiery company. Two other large hosiery plants, Soulé de Castres and Guichard d'Angoulême, cut their workforces to less than one hundred. The giant iron foundry Ferronneries du Midi closed in 1953. The same fate overtook the Société des Forges et Aciéries de la Chiers, which had begun producing steel in 1940. Even the historic Maison Amouroux with its highly successful agricultural machinery fell into a steep decline and finally closed in 1957.

The economic depression trickled down to the tiny manufactories and shops lining the neighborhood streets, many of which lost their capacity for flexibility and innovation and their ability to compete. In 1950, Toulouse's *maisons de confection,* for example, still represented the fourth-largest ready-to-wear industry in France. Some 7,000 people worked in the clothing industry within the city itself, the majority as domiciled labor, and another 9,000 to 10,000 were employed in the homes of the surrounding countryside.[22] But increasing competition from the garment mills in the northeast that were working with the new synthetic fibers and mass producing stylish, easy-care clothes rapidly reduced the Toulouse garment industry to seventh rank nationally. The city's manufacturers stood in danger of permanently losing even the dependable market of the southwest.

Certainly this propensity to stand by increasingly rigid and antiquated forms of production contributed to the anguish in the traditional industries, particularly in clothing manufacturing. But it was not simply a matter of some type of self-inflicted technological blockage. Instead it is more useful to explain the industrial decline as a crisis in a business culture unable to withstand the mounting economic pressures imposed upon it. Mass production, shifting tastes and markets, the loss of institutional and political support, the breakdown of the traditional urban milieu—all bombarded the world of traditional Toulouse business during the 1950s and the 1960s. These new factors posed severe barriers to small-scale specialization and to the experience of community that supported it. The furniture industry, shoe manufacturers, leather goods, and small metallurgical and woodworking shops all complained vehemently of the catastrophes that had undermined their crafts and severely cut production.

Together with the destruction caused by the wartime aerial bombardment of the aircraft factories and ONIA plant, the closures and cutbacks crimped what little manufacturing existed. The city's industries employed only about 33 percent of the working population in the late 1940s and early 1950s. While the number of people employed in industry throughout France swelled, jobs at Toulouse stagnated in most industries, grew just slightly in others. Production was increasingly dispersed among minuscule craft shops.[23] A local census taken in 1952 revealed that a full 43 percent of the city's specialized shops were owned by craftsmen working without paid help, who relied solely on their own or family labor for production. Another 46 percent of the handicraft businesses employed fewer than ten workers. In all, some 90 percent of the city's industry was composed of more than 5,000 quasi-artisanal *ateliers.* They were joined by another 9,000 commercial and service businesses with fewer than ten employees each that represented 90 percent of the city's service sector.[24] Altogether, by 1954, the intimate atmosphere of daily labor in the old neighborhoods of Toulouse was supported by about 16,000 *patrons.* Alongside workers and employees, they represented the largest single social group in the city. Even a substantial portion of the working class at Toulouse was dispersed throughout these tiny establishments, laboring and selling alongside the owners, all of them surviving on scaled-down ventures. Leather and tanning, textiles and clothing, and furniture making (industries in which minute shops proliferated) employed over 11,000 people, 9,000 of them salaried apprentices and workers laboring in the *ateliers* of the various *vieux quartiers populaires.*[25] This vast foundation of miniature industrial and commercial establishments was more significant to the local economic community than in any other city of the south or in all of France.[26]

The proliferation of *micro-ateliers* was both a traditional and a valid response to the depressed economic conditions in the Toulouse region during the 1950s. The maintenance of a system of marginal shops was a realistic appreciation of the risks involved in expanding during a period of acute difficulties in a traditionally weak market. But the tradition of independent work was also upheld by the city's one prosperous industry. Throughout the 1950s, building construction and public works employed the most people in Toulouse. In 1954, for example, over 10,000 people worked in the building trades. It was the city's, and for that matter the region's, premier industry. The explanation for this bloated good fortune was very simply the housing boom at Toulouse that began in the early 1950s under the auspices of the government's HLM programs. By the end of the decade, with the completion of 5,000 to 6,000 dwellings each year, Toulouse had one of the highest construction rates in France. There was room for everyone in the housing industry. But even with such hearty opportunities for expansion and profits, the local construction craftsmen, as a rule, worked independently. In the mid- to late 1950s, 85 percent of the industry's companies were run by contractors working on their own or with a few laborers.[27] Most of them were masons, painters, carpenters, and plumbers working out of *ateliers* or in small rented construction yards dispersed throughout the *quartiers populaires* of Toulouse. Each day, fully half the construction workforce, some 5,000 to 6,000 people, plied their skills, negotiating work schedules and contracts from within this network of freelance companies.

However, even with this construction boom, which was after all dependent on massive infusions of state funding, the city still withered into a chronic state of economic uncertainty. In France as a whole, the period from 1953 to 1956 was generally characterized by economic stability and expanding productivity and exports; but at Toulouse unemployment jumped to its highest level for the decade. Trade in industrial products slumped back to the dismal levels of the early postwar years. It signaled the economic doldrums that cast a dark shadow over life at Toulouse. The activity that contributed most to industrial sales was building construction. Only minimal exports of shirts, footwear, and processed foods to North Africa, along with the market in the rural southwest, kept Toulouse's small shops alive.[28] The city's business leaders vented the local frustration over "the grave economic paralysis that one can easily see reflected in the acutely miserable conditions of everyday reality."[29]

Information on the income of the *patronat* of Toulouse during the 1950s is sketchy. However, studies done by INSEE in 1956 suggest that the Toulouse *patron* was in about the same income category as the city's employees and workers or in many marginal instances much lower.[30] Government statistics from 1962 corroborate this conjecture. In that year, their income was one of the lowest among the *patronat* of France. It was only slightly above the average income for workers and employees, in contrast to the northeast of France, where the *patronat* often averaged double the income available to the salaried labor force.[31] The wages paid to salaried help in the craft industries, the *salariés isolés,* were even more harrowing. They were among the worst at Toulouse. Workers shifted back and forth between the minuscule shops, attempting to find better earnings and more security. The situation in the clothing and building trades was the most degrading. In 1954, approximately 43 percent of the women employed in the city's industries worked at home, assembling shirts and other apparel, or in small clothing shops. The extent to which women were dependent on this type of low-paid piece-work explains why average salaries for women at Toulouse were below the poverty line.[32] For men dependent on seasonal jobs in construction or on work in small food-processing, machine, furniture, and shoe shops, the menial earnings reduced them to a substandard existence. Despouy, head of the Syndicat des Employés de Commerce, complained that it was impossible to support a family on the meager wages from small shops. "These kinds of pathetic salaries should not exist in a country that prides itself on progress."[33]

The inflationary spirals of the early postwar years had prompted government institution of the minimum wage in 1951, and wage increases continued throughout the 1950s under union pressure to keep worker salaries at least on a par with rising prices. But this did not comparatively improve the possibilities at Toulouse. Altogether, nearly 75 percent of the city's wage earners made less than the national average of 413,000 francs per year. Even in 1956, the city's main distinction among its urban counterparts was still its low salaries.[34]

Mayor Badiou himself was well aware of "the enormous difficulties facing Toulouse: the problem of the artisans, the shopkeepers, the declining economy."[35] Even so, the municipality, mired in financial insolvency, offered few innovative economic programs and certainly no recipe for converting the city into a humming industrial center. The 1928 Jaussely Plan had laid out a set of formal industrial zones along the periphery of the city, but they largely corresponded to already existing manufacturing districts. The Nicod Plan that guided municipal policy during the 1950s pursued the same nonindustrial strategy. It even cut back on the spaces available for new manufacturing under the Jaussely Plan and instead relegated any industrial expansion to one zone north of Toulouse.[36]

A modern industrial orientation was simply not foreseen for the future. If anything, further industrialization risked the kind of unbridled growth Badiou was trying to avoid. He vehemently argued against any further "puffing up" of the city's industrial sector. As the capital city, Toulouse would find its own "modern" way to economic solvency. His outlook for the future was based on Toulouse's heritage as the administrative, intellectual, and commercial heart of the Midi. As the city's most prominent urbanists, Daniel Faucher and Jean Coppolani of the University of Toulouse articulated official perceptions of Toulouse's authenticity and self-image. In their writings from the 1950s and early 1960s, both emphasized the historic grandeur of the city's administrative, educational, and mercantile callings. These were Toulouse's *raison d'être*. They made Toulouse above all a "bourgeois city," despite the fact that workers could easily be found in equal numbers and that it was among the most economically lethargic of any French metropolis.[37]

In the estimation of Toulouse City Hall, new manufacturing should be bestowed upon the other cities of the region that were desperately in need of economic buttressing. In this regard, the profound economic crisis that spread out from the Garonne Valley through Languedoc offered few hopes to its eager capital city. The region proffered little by way of stimulating demand for modern products manufactured at Toulouse. It was the only large city of any size that existed in the southwest in the 1950s.[38] Once more, the surrounding countryside had not shared in the interwar economic boom that had graced the small businesses working away in Toulouse. Languedoc instead continued to deteriorate economically throughout the first half of the twentieth century. Factories closed their doors. The system of rural craft and commercial dealings withered away. Vacant old châteaux were the only evidence of the once-vibrant agricultural life of the Midi. Small towns dissolved into necropoles. Massive medieval fortresses or cathedrals overpowered the few tiny streets and the dilapidated houses that were, by the 1950s, the residue left by centuries of accumulated economic misfortune. With few alternatives, the region's population (especially its young and its skilled) left in droves. By the end of the Second World War, the scarcity of its inhabitants was the most distinctive feature of the southwest. What Toulouse did receive from its rustic hinterland was a continuous stream of peasants and artisans moving to the city in the vain hope of finding work. In any case, it was hardly an atmosphere supportive of brisk manufacturing. Toulouse appeared to be more deeply entrapped in its region's economic coma than it was an integral part of the French system of large cities.

The crisis threatened to derogate the city to a permanent state of depression just as the rest of France was beginning to enjoy renewed prosperity. Without doubt the poverty and distress became shamefully glaring and all the more discouraging in comparison to the expanding abundance in the northern and eastern cities. The material rewards of Reconstruction and modernization did not extend to Toulouse. The early Plans simply had no real effect on its debilitated economic state. The Monnet Plan's only mention of the southwest's participation in the French boom was the natural-gas discoveries at Lacq. In the triumphant national narrative activated by Reconstruction, the energy-rich recesses hidden away in the southwestern wilderness became symbolic proof of French abundance and cause for confidence in its future. Be that as it may, there was little evidence of the growing momentum of French economic expansion at Toulouse. Although the city's population reached 270,000 by 1954, it still remained comparatively old. The city suffered from one of the lowest levels of economic activity and the lowest standard of living of any of the provincial cities. The reality of this poverty explains in good part why the municipal government was continually strapped for funds, spent a comparatively meager amount on its citizens, and was forced to increasingly rely on tax increases and, above all, on state financial patronage.

It was precisely this disparity between the "economic miracle" that so clearly favored northeastern France and the economic deprivation that disgraced the southwest that instigated the postwar calls for *aménagement du territoire,* a balancing of the flagrant territorial inequities. As the government's regional development policy was slowly set into motion from 1955 on, the new officialdom appointed for the Midi-Pyrénées region took over from Vichy's Commission de Propagande de la Région de Toulouse and the Liberation's Conseil Économique Régional the arduous task of cataloguing the vast testimony to the region's unyielding "underdevelopment."[39] It was this collection of socioeconomic statistics, geographic data, and resource potentiality forecasts that essentially recast regionalism in terms of capitalist economic norms.

In 1956, IGAME Louis Périllier defined the Midi-Pyrénées region in terms of the "characteristics of underdevelopment": an imbalance among the various economic sectors, dying production, and a lack of capital, infrastructure, and machinery. This dolorous state of affairs was caused by deep-seated cultural and geographic inadequacies. The region was too far from Paris. It was too far from primary resources and from consumer markets. Archaic cultural attitudes had prevented the rational utilization of the region's best economic attributes. The small scale of manufacture and trade blocked any hope of modern economic practice.[40] In this new definition, the critical parameters for identifying the relationship between region and nation became economic resources, productivity, usable infrastructure, skilled workforce, and technological invention. It created a rigid geographic hierarchy and state classification system based on either the abundance or the lack of appropriate Fordist culture and character—on either a willingness or a refusal to modernize. To a certain degree the heresy of particularism itself was weeded out through the inquisitionary battery of capitalist economic stipulations that had become the sacred text of France's future. The various program regions were prioritized by economic standards that superficially eschewed political convolutions. Nonetheless, they depicted the intent moral zeal behind France's modernist code of conduct.

This aggressive economic dialogue carried on over regionalism was incorporated into the Occitan movement itself. After 1954, two dissident members of the Institut d'Etudes Occitanes, Ismaël Girard from Toulouse and P.-L. Berthaud from Bordeaux, moved away from the conventional cultural and linguistic assessments of Occitan identity and began publishing the review *Occitania*. It systematically linked the fortunes of Languedoc with questions of economic development and specifically pointed to the economic disparities between the southwest and the rest of France.[41] With their own litany of economic measurements, the regionalist rebels substantiated the appalling discrimination that had accompanied French modernization. The three program regions with the highest unemployment rates in France (the Midi-Pyrénées, Languedoc-Roussillon, and Provence-Côte d'Azur) were those historically identified as Occitania. The same three regions lagged far behind the rest of France in industrial development. State planning discourse had deciphered these statistics as evidence of deep-seated cultural and geographic deficiencies, natural phenomena that "resigned" the Midi to the downward spiral of underdevelopment. The Occitanists translated them as the denouement of a state-capitalist ethos sworn to maximizing profits.

The economic breakdown in the Midi was begot by specific choices that revealed the bias implicit in state policy. Time and again the state had chosen to abandon industry in the southwest for easier and more lucrative projects in the developed regions. The hypocrisy was particularly blatant, for example, in gauging natural resources. According to the official explanation for underdevelopment, Languedoc had none. However, the natural-gas reserves at Lacq were integrated into the grand narrative on French wealth and productivity. The riddle of this contradiction was solved simply by divulging that most of the natural gas, as well as the hydroelectric power from the Pyrenees, was exported to the "developed" regions, to Paris and to Spain, where enormous profits could be made.[42]

By the early 1960s, this economic argument initiated by *Occitania* would be parlayed into the theory of internal colonialism by Robert Lafont and the Comité Occitan d'Etudes et d'Action (COEA).[43] For them, *aménagement du territoire* was in essence a conscious policy on the part of the state to destroy the native economy and replace it with tourist, service, and administrative activities controlled by local government minions. Languedoc as a regional entity was simply converted into an economic market by Paris and private monopolies with little interest in the region other than its profitability and the potential of accumulating capital.

The Reaction to Regulation

In the face of depression and these arguments over "underdevelopment," there appeared to be few workable alternatives open to Toulouse's local business community. The petty producers' increasing isolation and their bleak economic circumstance in comparison to the rising fortunes of "the other France" reactivated old fears and defenses over the loss of vernacular culture and the values of *les petits*. They saw themselves as unwilling victims condemned by the evolution of capitalism and by competition from economic forces outside the Midi:

Manual labor has lost its creative spirit, its poetry. We are in an epoch of assembly-line production in virtually all domains. Workers have become "specialized laborers" in the extreme, simply repeating mechanized movements. Under these conditions the skill of the artisan has little dignity because the worker has lost the holistic conception, the harmony and taste of spontaneous invention.[44]

For many petty producers there was apprehension that technical innovations and specialized machinery installed to keep the shop competitive were simply too expensive and too risky. Mass production would undermine traditional methods and workmanship. The clouds on the economic horizon had been evident immediately after the war. From 1949 onward, the various local artisan organizations kept up a steady cry of anguish over what their future would be if something was not done to preserve their role within the modernizing French economy. The relatively high prices for quality goods, the dilemma of preserving traditional techniques, the collapse of customary markets doomed *les petits,* and by extension Toulouse, to economic marginality.

The most broad-ranging protest over their plight was directed toward public powers, both local and national, who were accused of squeezing out small producers with excessive taxes, fees, and regulations. Small handicraft shops and the French *patronat* as a class had been securely protected by French government policy prior to the war. Their production was safeguarded from levies and competition by the "tax on business turnover" *(impôt sur le chiffre d'affaires)* that provided a high proportion of the state's revenues up to 1954. The state also granted a variety of tax exemptions to small enterprises and *artisan-patrons.* However, postwar reconstruction and modernization required expanding public sources of revenue both for local and state government. The advantages of fully incorporating small businesses into the expanding tax structure simply outweighed the dying allegiance to paternalistic state policy. The increasing charges for social-security obligations; rising licensing, patent, and commercial fees; and the ballooning tax structure fell doubly hard on the already depressed traditional sector used to preferential treatment. At a 1949 press conference, for example, Roger Sicre, president of the local furniture-makers' union, pointed to the inflated duties on wood and material, as well as the costs for social benefits, as the source for a 50 percent hike in furniture prices.[45] When the depart-

ment of the Haute-Garonne and the municipality of Toulouse both increased patent fees, commercial taxes, and the gas tax in 1949, merchants
and artisans staged a massive protest and strike that completely closed down
the city on July 6. After a mass meeting at the Halle aux Grains, 500,000
marched through the streets to present their petitions at the prefecture and
at City Hall.[46]

But in the climate of Reconstruction, there was little public patience
for this kind of defiance. Pétainism and the Occupation itself, the contact
they brought with far more advanced German industry, the devastating
economic shortages, and the political upheaval reported from every region
after the war catalyzed a reevaluation of business mentality. One way or
another small-scale production, either as Vichyite fantasy or as seedbed for
the Midi's independent predilections, was left with the stain of regional
particularism. It was associated with the nation's fracturing, with France's
economic decline, and with its military defeat. This crisis of economic
conscience quickly took on the temper of cleansing salient throughout the
Liberation and Reconstruction years. The defeat of the resurgent radical
working-class movements and the attack against craft culture were understood as purgatives necessary to the reconstitution of centralized political
authority and the renewal of France. It was precisely in wayward towns like
Toulouse that the powerful mix of Resistance euphoria and radical working-
class reform (initiated by Communist-led Committees of Liberation both
in the factories and in independent businesses) had proved most threatening to the reemergence of national identity. This emotionally inflamed
struggle over economic culture constituted the drama through which the
state would initiate its heroic drive for national union through modernization. That program had far less to do with regional and democratic
participatory practices than it did with capturing capitalist hegemony over
economic production and establishing a new basis for class relations.

The *Données statistiques sur la situation de la France au début de 1946,*
published by the team of planners assembled under Jean Monnet, specifically identified the constrictive *malthusianisme* that underlay France's
poor economic performance. According to the report, the explanations
behind French backwardness were legion: low productivity of labor, outdated technology, the insistence on protectionism, overcautious entrepreneurs. "We must clear away this fog," stated the Guindey memorandum
given to Robert Schumann in 1947, "and liberate the economy."[47] The
grands commis and *hauts fonctionnaires* who came to power with the war's
end at the Ministry of Finance and Economic Affairs and at the Commissar-

iat Général du Plan had little sympathy for the values and antiquated habits of the French business community. Career civil servants such as François Bloch-Lainé, Paul Delouvrier, and Guy de Carmoy had come to the conclusion that, left on their own, French business elites lacked the dynamism or insight to initiate the economic reforms essential for growth and modernization. The verbal castigations against their ineptitude and obstinacy rolled out of government and planning reports with the intensity and emotion of a moral crusade—a civil war for control over the economy: "French businessmen are generally ignorant of the economic and financial conditions in which they work," "they exhibit a morose fatalism," "Malthusianism was a turning away from life." Their insistence on preserving the rights of small business and their refusal to face the competition of an open market stood in the way of French renewal and European economic integration.

The reaction of the "Fordism à la française"[48] enthusiasts was to declare war on these Malthusian interests who held the French economy hostage for the sake of their own survival. For state technocratic planners, modernization was a canonical faith that required mental and spiritual conversion. The expectations of entrepreneurship were to be built upon technological invention, standardization and mass production, expert evaluation of market signals, and capital investment. The planning corps looked directly to the American model of the company manager bonded to capitalist market dynamics and to competitive organizational structures as a way of supplanting the obsolete image of the French *patron*. The state would take over responsibility for guiding France smoothly toward a modern capitalist conviction and toward a Fordist model of the *économie concertée*.[49] The first step in the campaign was thus a reversal of the public policies sheltering the small shops and inept business practices that were declared to be the root of French economic evil.

The campaign was launched during the Second Plan (1954–1957), which stated that "one of the essential objectives of the new Plan is to restore the free play of competition in the economy." Despite the attempt at a planning consensus achieved through "round-table" discussions and negotiations with a wide spectrum of public and private interests, there was virtually no artisan voice in the government's planning policy. The Plans remained the domain of the experts, who drew out the economic and social lines of modernization without consulting artisan organizations such as the Chambre des Métiers and certainly without reaching down to trade unions and subterranean craft businesses. Only after 1957 were artisans acknowledged with their own modernization commission, but even that was largely a formality. The Second Plan recommended the abolition of protectionist regulations and the reform of taxation in the direction of economic neutrality. The most important turnabout was the replacement of the old "tax on business turnover" with the value-added tax (*taxe sur la value ajoutée* or TVA) in 1954. The remainder of the nation's tax structure was gradually modernized over the course of the Second and Third Plans (1954–1961) into a policy tool that encouraged savings and investments and promoted competition and concentration.

These tax reforms were only one component of the extensive regional development and industrial modernization measures that took shape during the late 1950s. Financial resources available to businesses were expanded and diversified to stimulate investment. The country's largest public credit institution, the Caisse des Dépôts et Consignations, began underwriting industrial investments. Credit became available for companies from the Bank of France. Long-term state treasury loans were granted through the Fonds de Développement Economique et Social (FDES), established in 1954. This last source of public funding was part of a package of state financial incentives for regional development passed in 1954 and 1955 under the sponsorship of Pierre Mendès-France and then expanded in late 1955 under the government of Edgar Faure. The FDES loans were designed specifically to provide low-interest financing for industrial conversion and modernization of private firms, as well as for decentralization projects considered too risky by banks. Despite these opportunities, the major French lending institutions, and for that matter the FDES loans, still concerned themselves primarily with investments in France's larger companies and premier industries. Investment sources for the vast underlayer of family workshops were virtually nonexistent. To rectify this deficiency, Sociétés de Développement Régional were created in 1955 that were essentially small, localized lenders ready to hand down money to modest businesses usually shunned by banks.

Regardless of this campaign to discard the protective umbrella shielding the traditional business community and the measures to stimulate its modernization, critics still contended that the reforms did not risk any ruthless challenge to the vested interests of the *patronat*. The smallest businesses were exempt from the value-added tax. The government preserved the sacrosanct category of *petit artisan fiscal*. An annoying array of registration and notary fees, transfer taxes, and assessments still had to be paid for mergers or for the absorption of one firm by another, making the transactions complicated, expensive, and infrequent.[50] Nonetheless, the reforms did leave independent shops in an unfavorable and more complicated tax situation. In comparison to wage earners, their spectrum of levies were steep and tangled. It was this new tax system, far more than industrial or regional development policies, that squeezed small businesses and incurred their wrath. For the *petit patronat,* the government's ventures into fiscal reform amounted to a vindictive purge against the customary practices that had assured their survival and social standing. The downward economic spiral in places like Toulouse had been publicly laid at the feet of the petty proprietor. The small workshop had selfishly insisted on receiving every advantage in the "cocoon of established rights and privileges for everything that is small, old, traditional, irrational, and stationary"[51] in static France. Toulouse's dependency on its *micro-ateliers* was denounced as one of the principal contributing factors to its ignominious title as one of the poorest cities in France. The abrasive discourse provided an obvious target for accusations of brute *etatisme* hidden behind the economic modernization crippling the craft economy.

The reaction at Toulouse was immediate. In June 1954, 3,000 artisans, shopkeepers, and small industrialists met at Toulouse's municipal stadium to protest against rising surcharges and the "inquisitionary tactics and illegal fiscal policy" used by the state. Among their champions were Gabriel Barlangue from the Chamber of Commerce; mayoral deputies sent from the Capitole; the president of the Union Régionale des Groupements Patronaux; and Léon Gingembre, national leader of the powerful Confédération Général des Petites et Moyennes Entreprises. Antoine Simonian, head of the Comité pour la Défense de l'Artisanat, du Commerce et de l'Industrie gave an impassioned speech denouncing state interference and assessments as the death toll for the small business. "This plot to have hundreds of millions of businesses either paying the same tax or sometimes less than that levied on artisans and shopkeepers is unacceptable." Simonian argued that the obsession with tax policy and regulation as a mechanism for rectifying the economy and making everyone "pay his due" was absurd and inhumane. It was only private initiative freely able to create, manufacture, and export that would produce a true economic renaissance for France. For his part, Gingembre reviled the "administrative dictatorship that creates a climate of terror as it pries and rummages through private life. We must defend ourselves from these continuous injustices, these vexatious and arbitrary state methods." The protest ended with a three-point resolution to be sent to regional Prefect Emile Pelletier: the outlawing of state controls, professional representation on departmental commissions, and immediate fiscal reform.[52]

Throughout the 1950s boundless complaints were lodged against "the aggravating fees, taxes and regulations" that shackled small companies already besieged by competition from factory production and commercial imports into the region. In 1957, Antoine Simonian declared to the Syndicat de l'Alimentation: "We are in an epoch in which statism in a myriad of forms chokes our businesses and deprives business owners of all spirit of initiative. This statism automatically brings with it a cascade of new taxes and ends by stupidly endorsing business insolvencies."[53] Salvan, the president of the Toulouse Chambre des Métiers, lashed out in a 1957 speech at the ignorance of state legislators who simply did not understand the indispensable role of the artisan in the French economy. The result of their tax policies was to quash viable craft production. "We must extricate ourselves from this fiscal iron collar that possesses and shackles us . . . For over a quarter of a century we have benefited from legal and financial regulations appropriate to artisanal activities. We will not cease in bringing the best of our experience and our faith in the service of this cause that we hold most dear to our hearts."[54]

There was an unequivocal defensiveness in this posturing within the context of modernization. The antistatist, antitax stand perpetuated the "culture of opposition" that was the hallmark of Midi political consciousness and had historically nourished the social identity of *les petits*. They remained dissenting and reflexively at odds with Paris. If anything, this confrontational temperament was strengthened by the experience of the Liberation and the city's economic debasement in the face of the French "economic miracle." But individual party allegiance, a commitment either to the political extreme or to moderation, was to a real extent determined by success or failure to achieve economic solvency and some measure of social status within the ongoing "crisis of underdevelopment." As the context for their accustomed political vocabulary and their conditions of production broke down, the notion of a "republic of independent craftsmen" lost cohesiveness. Economic depression, the state assault on small business, and the pressures of modernization ruptured the older Radical-Socialist discourse into a more diverse array of political trajectories. Communist, PSA, SFIO, Radical, as well as Republican advocates vied for endorsement by the city's beleaguered business community. Each party offered a spirited defense of local values and customs within the circumstance of economic modernization. This complex range within local left-wing municipal politics was the counterpart to the social ambiguity and economic instability that characterized vernacular culture during the 1950s. The crisis accentuated the tensions among the social and professional groups that shared the space and culture of the city's customary local economy. It heightened the dissonance within what had been the prevailing oppositional left-wing consensus on behalf of *les petits.* This political dispersion was dramatic enough on its own. But it also disclosed the degree to which the turmoil of the 1950s was generating a broader crisis of identity among the city's petty proprietors.

The more traditional working-class communities to the north around Minimes and Sept-Derniers, and to the west around Saint-Cyprien, heavily favored the Communists. Thousands in these working-class districts (artisans, skilled, and semiskilled workers as well as day-laborers and homeworkers) worked in the tiny shops of Toulouse's indigenous manufacturing trades. Before the war, the French Communist Party shunned any affiliation with the "petty-bourgeois" interests of shopkeepers and craftsmen. But the experience of the Resistance and Reconstruction offered possibilities for a partnership between the two against the belligerent policies initiated by the French government. The Communist Party attempted to organize their own artisan confederation, the Confédération Générale Unifiée de l'Artisanat, in 1945. At a mass meeting held in Paris on "How to rescue petty commerce and the artisanat," André Marty and Jacques Duclos, both from the southwest, were principal speakers.[55] It was local Communist leaders such as Jean Llante and Simone Gardès who defended shopkeeper and property-owner rights against the urban redevelopment programs at Toulouse. Llante chastised Badiou for an urban plan that essentially meant to eliminate small shopkeepers and the totality of artisan production from the central city.[56] This association between the oppositional Communist Party and the defensive interests of petty producers was clearly evidenced in the fact that local Radicals often accused Communist leaders of using shopkeeper protests as a rostrum for their bellicose accusations against the Fourth Republic.

Nonetheless, during the 1950s this alliance between the ill-favored did not extend to the preponderance of small-time producers. Nor did it incorporate any overt notion of Occitan identity in the conventional sense of cultural nationalism and linguistic preservation. Llante himself sometimes referred to Occitanism in terms of an authentic popular culture and a crisis of alienation. A number of prominent leaders of the Occitan movement, most notably Ismaël Girard, were, as well, associated with the Communist Party.[57] But the Communists were, as yet, little interested in vindicating the rights of Occitanism. Nor did the majority of petty producers at Toulouse consciously identify a specifically Occitan agenda within their politics. But the experience of the Resistance and the Liberation, as well as the economic languor of the 1950s, did effectively act to radicalize the political posture of the city's small-time industrialists and artisans. The Communist defense of their interests clearly resonated with a growing sense of estrangement within a modernizing economy. Even though the Communists suffered a stunning defeat in the 1956 legislative election, they still held on to 26 percent of the vote in central Toulouse, while the Socialists and Radicals claimed 22 percent each.[58]

In the late 1940s and early 1950s, the bedrock of petty producers and workers in Toulouse's local industries remained loyal to Socialism. Districts such as the Capitole, the Bourse, and Saint-Auban, for example, voted Socialist. Throughout the neighborhoods, the *petit travailleur indépendant,* the small-time *patron,* the *salarié* represented the core of traditional Midi Socialist support. They remained passionately influenced by the Resistance and the experience of the Liberation. The legacy of Socialist municipalism had been built through the alliances and patronage within this economic community. Even the active members of the Occitan movement identified themselves, in the majority, with Socialism. They all shared an ingrained resentment of the political cadre issuing from the halls of centralism in Paris. The successive stream of Parisian politicos bequeathed little, according to their conviction, but corruption and the eventual ruin of popular democracy. This entrenched network of support allowed Badiou and the Socialist Party to maintain constant control of the Capitole despite substantial pressure from the Radicals and, by 1957, from the forces to the political right. The socialists courted votes from the Union des Syndicats Artisanaux in the controversial 1958 election with measures for "the complete reorganization of the artisanal trades" put forth by the Socialist government of Guy Mollet—before it was "unfortunately crushed" by the arrival of the right wing to power in 1957. However, even among the Socialists, public rifts exposed the underlying tensions pulling at what had been a cohesive political community. By 1958 the appearance of Badiou's renegade PSA muddled the choices within the Socialist block.

The Radical platform offered the most well-established defense of the free market and independent enterprise. Toulouse was a historic Radical-Socialist enclave in which the difference between the two parties was often translated by local supporters simply as a matter of nuance. The Radicals garnered substantial support from the ranks of the *patrons* during the 1950s, despite the fact that the party's influence in national politics was rapidly waning. Their defense of proprietary rights and *les petits* against Badiou's urban policies was a more convincing option than Communism for many small businessmen. Shopkeepers and artisans were prominent on the 1958 Municipal Council candidature list of Pierre Baudis' Independent movement that allied the MRP, Radicals, and Republicans. The political equivocation on the part of independent producers followed the slow drift toward the right that characterized Toulouse politics by the end of the decade. By 1959 central district neighborhoods such as the Capitole, the Bourse, and Saint-Georges were split between electoral support for Bazerque's SFIO and Baudis' Independents. This borderline shift within the local business community was in part the striking catalyst behind the curious Socialist marriage with the Independent bloc and the UNR in 1959.

The extreme right, which did indeed flourish in rural Languedoc and was a vital force in the social upheavals of the 1950s, also had its adherents at Toulouse. The Centre des Indépendants et Paysans, created in 1951 and represented by Jacques Douzans at Toulouse, was a revival of orthodox conservatism in the Midi. Led by local notables untainted by collaboration with Vichy, it was Catholic and staunchly opposed state regulation of any kind. Its list of candidates for the Toulouse Municipal Council was dominated by shopkeepers and local farmers. However, Toulouse was not one of its political bastions.

In the same sense, despite its aggressive stance on behalf of traditional business interests, Poujadism made little headway at Toulouse. Throughout the summer of 1953, Poujade and his fellow tradesmen launched militant protests against the tax inspectors who pillaged *"les petits"* for the benefit of *"les gros."* With assistance from the Communists, they denounced the oppressive, "rotten" regime bent on destroying their interests. In July, protests by the wine growers of Languedoc turned violent, and the region was cut off from the rest of France by CRS riot squads.[59] But at Toulouse, backing for the protest was limited. The Union de Défense des Commerçants et Artisans (UDCA) of Poujade offered a full list of candidates for the Toulouse municipal elections during the 1950s, many of whom designated themselves as *commerçants* or *employé de commerce*. But like the conservative Centre des Indépendants, the party did not receive enough votes to gain any seats on the Municipal Council.[60] In the 1956 legislative elections, the Poujadists claimed about 13 percent of the vote in central Toulouse. Support for Poujade reached close to 20 percent in districts such as des Carmes, Saint-Georges, and Saint-Alban. The city's petty producers could line up at both extremes of the political spectrum.

Toulouse municipal politics, then, from the vantage point of petty producers, was a curious and complex mix of preferences during the 1950s. If political opinion seemed to be shifting subtly to the right by the late 1950s, it was also producing an extensive array of choices on the left. The legacy of the "culture of opposition" continued its compelling influence over the community's political identity. But under pressure from the growing supremacy of modernization policy and mass production, the political consensus built on flexible specialization, skilled, independent work, and a maze of local connections imperceptibly dissolved, destabilizing the political mooring that had been an integral part of the city's business culture. It left an ambiguous mélange of reactive opinion that further tangled the Socialist government's thicket of difficulties in accepting the Fifth Republic and the rule of de Gaulle. The scrambled character of left-wing working-class discourse likewise left open the path for the labor control and compromise necessary for rationalization and capitalist administrative hegemony. Stuck in an economic morass while the rest of France flourished, *les petits* appeared to have been systematically purged from any further role in the modern capitalist economy. Obsolescence was their future. Toulousains on the road to nowhere, living in "nowheres-ville."

The cultural crisis within the traditional business community was perhaps most telling within the old *quartiers populaires*. The population strain of the war years, the physical and economic decay of the central districts in the 1950s, and ultimately mass culture itself were rapidly breaking down the ancient configuration of everyday neighborhood life. The multitude of ebullient commercial festivals held under the banner of Reconstruction and economic recovery in 1948 were essentially the last demonstrations of neighborhood vitality. The enduring, daily world of markets and *ateliers*, local habits, and sociability was passing. Even neighborhood business associations such as the Amicales des Commerçants et Artisanats were of little use in evading the threatening steel trap of state-directed economic modernization. Traditional neighborhood commercial fairs were held only sporadically during the 1950s. The September *baloche* held each year in the Saint-Auban district was perhaps the most notable expression of the continued spirit of neighborhood life in the old quarters. Le Toussaint de Toulouse, when the city traditionally paid respects to its dead, was still celebrated in 1958 with neighborhood street fairs and ceremonies staged by its *patrons*.[61] It was the president of the Amicales des Commerçants who laid the neighborhood wreath at the monument to the dead in Colombette. In 1958 the city and the Chamber of Commerce organized a *"Semaine de la Violette"* in honor of the 100th anniversary of the flower "that had always symbolized the city's friendliness and charm—its violet color mingling with the red of its bricks and its azure sky." The celebration included an exposition of the diverse products made from the flower, an automobile rally through the city streets, and a *grand baloche* at which the "Queen of Violets" was crowned.[62] But these examples stand out as rarities rather than as commonplace events. The significance of traditional festivals and neighborhood display had sadly diminished.

The anxiety over the evaporation of Toulouse's populist neighborhood economy and culture was most prescient in relation to the slum-clearance programs slated for the inner districts. Small producers and shopkeepers around Empalot, in Croix-Daurade, Marengo, and ultimately in Saint-Georges understood full well what "renovation" meant for their social category. Shopowner Besaucèle complained at the July 1959 Saint-Georges protest that the project would essentially ruin all the businesses in the district. He insisted that the municipal councillors he had helped vote into office honorably defend his economic rights.[63] But ultimately, in the words of Jean Llante: "the small boutique simply did not correspond to the shops of tomorrow."[64] Badiou of course denied all this and insisted that the Saint-Georges project was not meant to destroy the *quartier populaire* but to revive its livability and its prosperity. The implications of modernization were obvious enough, however. They opened the floodgates of alarm over the impending doom awaiting those designated as unwilling "to make something of the twentieth century." The creative destruction of modernization was just as capable of annihilating social groups as it was the built environment they inhabited.

The tradition of trade associations, so well embedded within Midi working-class life, underwent, as well, the same crisis of adjustment to the reality of modernization. The friction and apprehension pulling at the city's well-known left-wing political predilections were just as clear in its contiguous culture of syndicalism. Most artisans and shop proprietors still saw their union, as well as the Chambre des Métiers, as the most effective form of professional representation. But the shift in tone and priorities within the associational movement over the course of the 1950s was conspicuous. There was an emphatic militancy to the union protests of the late 1940s and mid-1950s at Toulouse. No doubt the close association of the trade organizations with the impassioned experience of the Liberation years generated this self-confidence and pugnacity. The escalation of state economic control during the 1950s through regulations and tax increases only served to fuel syndical ire and defensiveness. Righteous indignation was the tenet of the antistatist protests at Toulouse. In the 1954 demonstrations, Communist Léon Gingembre of the Confédération Général des Petits et Moyennes Entreprises lashed out at the unjust, arbitrary dictatorship of administrative economic domination. "What we need is another storming of the Bastille— a taxpayer's revolt. It is the unions who should lead it. Today, just as yesterday, the unions should undertake the struggle."[65]

Nonetheless, by the end of the decade, the local business community was beginning to learn the lessons of economic rationality. The belligerent protests and unrest that had marked the 1950s became anachronistic by the end of the decade. Small producers had little choice but to adjust themselves to government policy and to the facts of economic change. Tempers were also cooled by some measure of prosperity and a general rise in the standard of living that finally reached the southwest by the late 1950s—although the degree to which these effectively trickled down to small shops in the traditional trades is open to question.[66] In any case, the idea of an "artisan movement" against the state and against the forces of economic revolution became less persuasive. Instead, petty producers concentrated on preparing themselves for the rigors of open competition. Associational life itself adopted a more realistic, less doctrinaire strategy. In 1958, President Roucolle of the Violet and Onion Producers' Cooperative rather overpolitely described the organization as a "cradle, a solid center, self-conscious, adapted to modern times, certainly struggling for profit, but with integrity and generosity."[67] The Chambre Syndicale de la Nouveauté that represented the city's considerable number of hosiery and shirt makers held its 1959 general assembly at the offices of the Union des Groupements Patronaux. Its vice president defined syndicalism as a noble conception, "particularly in these times when the only effective means of defense is the total union of professionals. The past provides us with valuable lessons for future organization. We will rise to the task with competence and enthusiasm." But rather than organizing street demonstrations, the assembly concerned itself with the lack of union representation on the state board governing unemployment insurance. Most of their members worked in tiny shops with few resources available in times of economic crisis. Their protection necessitated a union voice within the state bureaucracy.[68]

It was also the Chambre des Métiers and the various departmental trade associations that devised a local program of reforms and proposals to "modernize" the local artisan economy. Jacques Fournié, the president of the Toulouse Union des Syndicats Artisanaux, set out the basic agenda in an open letter to the candidates in the 1958 elections. He reminded them that

65,000 people worked in the artisan trades of the Haute-Garonne. This was a substantial weight in the electoral balance. His demands included thorough fiscal reform for the benefit of the artisan class, increasing the availability of credit and loans to small shops, and the regulation of apprenticeship training as essential priorities.[69] Beyond a complete reform of fiscal policy, virtually all of the various unions and cooperatives supported some type of updated Artisanal Statute that codified the sector's protection. Local leaders called for the expansion of apprenticeship programs that offered young artisans some security while learning the trade. Instruction and technical innovation in traditional crafts were consistently offered by the unions as solutions to the malaise. Credits for new equipment and machinery were urgently needed. Lastly among the proposals most frequently recommended by the city's various artisan organizations was an effective retirement system. All of these were attempts to regulate and structurally shape an artisan craft culture that could successfully inhabit a guaranteed niche within the modern French economy.

Although most of the suggestions were made within the older discourse of social justice, protection, and the right of quality craftsmanship, the local trade associations still began incrementally to act as mediators in the process of modernization for their member businesses. They initiated innovations at a level of economic life often completely bypassed by state reforms. Indeed it was the Violet and Onion Producers' Union that organized a Comité de Défense, created a group label for violet merchandise, began to try out advertising campaigns, and sent delegations to various European countries to expand sales. The trade union within the construction industry helped its contractors negotiate loans for new machinery and for the purchase of material and offered training in new construction techniques. The brick and tile layers' cooperative put together a prefabrication facility at Blagnac.[70] The Chamber of Commerce and the trade associations continued to stage "artisan fairs" spotlighting the quality merchandise offered by local producers.

Adapting small shops to economic rationalization meant in part reconfiguring cooperative alliances in a wider and more modern spatial context. Fournié frequently stressed the need for communal or cantonal professional associations and cooperatives. It appeared to be the only effective means of pooling what resources were available to meet the challenge of open competition in the postwar world. In 1961 the Chambre des Métiers from the departments of Ariège, Gers, Hautes-Pyrénées, Haute-Garonne, Tarn-et-Garonne, the Tarn, and the Lot organized themselves into the Fifth

Artisanal Region. It essentially mirrored the Midi-Pyrénées Region, except for the department of the Aveyron, which was oriented from the beginning toward Montpellier rather than toward Toulouse. This regional and spatial shaping of associational perception perhaps best articulated the more temperate approach toward the reality of the state's modernization programs. And it evinces the pattern of co-optation into the capitalist project of spatial construction. At the Fifth Artisanal Region's initial meeting, regional IGAME Roger Moris was invited to speak to the assembled audience of artisans and *patrons*. Salvan, the president of the Haute-Garonne Chambre des Métiers, assured him that the region's craftsmen were ready to work constructively within the government's plans for economic expansion.[71] Essentially the struggle to maintain independence was abandoned for the more pragmatic work of economic survival. Willingly or not, the petty producers and shopkeepers of Toulouse were pushed into the wider realm of regional markets competing with the even more extended forces of the Common Market and Third World production.

But even in the midst of this uneasy turmoil and transition within the traditional trades (or perhaps to be more accurate because of it), the business community still relied on customary economic response. Both in industries reeling under the impact of depression and those in more advantageous circumstances, there was a steady growth in the total number of workshops producing their wares along the streets of Toulouse. This phenomenon can be explained almost entirely by the continued flowering of marginal businesses. Rather than concentrating, the notorious *micro-ateliers* tended to proliferate, dependent for their survival on the energy of a lone "industrialist" and a family. The boom in the building trades in particular added to the wide number of minute shops. The smallest construction firms doubled or even tripled in number. By 1962, the overall number of industrial businesses in the city had grown slightly (from 6,000 to 6,200), and the vast majority of them, approximately 85 percent, employed fewer than five workers or, in many cases, employed only family help.[72] The result was that even in the late 1950s, a city official noted that Toulouse's ". . . industrial motif consists of a very limited number of technically sophisticated large enterprises superimposed over a multiplicity of small businesses with a character more artisanal than industrial, and that have restricted financial abilities."[73]

This trend toward an increasing number of handicraft shops was the reverse of the structural evolution taking place among French businesses throughout the country. At the national level, the total number of industrial establishments had declined substantially between 1945 and 1962, with the disappearance of the smallest artisan *ateliers* the principal cause. In this respect, the evolution of industrial workshops at Toulouse tended to play into the constructed image of the city's business community as unstable and backward. Its *patrons* were opprobrious illustrations of the static French mentality that held back the country's renewal. It also demonstrated that hurling the moral axioms of state modernism into the provinces, that removing all vestiges of government protection, was neither as simple nor as successful at wiping out indigenous business practice as the technocratic corps pretended. By the early 1960s, Toulouse still had a higher proportion of minuscule specialized shops than any other large city in provincial France.[74]

It was rather an incongruous situation given the fact that any hope for an artisan movement in defense of *les petits* had spent itself out by the early 1960s. At the local level, the various trade and business associations had begun adapting themselves to the task of opening the Toulouse craft industries to the stringencies of competition and modernization. But the operation was to be performed on the jumble of independent companies blossoming within the fading traditions of specialized labor and neighborhood space. Most lacked the resources or the disposition to metamorphose into practitioners of modern capitalism. Production for the mass consumer market and modern entrepreneurial methods remained outside their practices. The shift to a modern capitalist ethic would necessitate a mental and cultural conversion—an alteration in the idea of an artisan class and the role they were to play in the future—of the most fundamental kind. It encompassed the broader controversy as to whether Toulouse business proprietors were willing to link arms with their countrymen and march under the banner of "full citizenship through modernization."

In May 1958, Henri Sarramon became president of the Toulouse Chamber of Commerce. Sarramon rose to prominence as the inheritor of his family's wholesale hosiery business and as head of the regional *nouveauté* trade union. His leadership coincided with the creation of a development plan for the Midi-Pyrénées region and with the state decision to "industrialize" Toulouse. But Sarramon's ascendance and his style also paralleled the onset of a heroic struggle to reform and habituate Toulouse business culture to France's new political economy. For Sarramon it was essential that the city's business community "embrace the transformations of modern economic life . . . New times require new methods. Individualism is dead, as is division, ignorance, and ineffectiveness. Unity and a common program of action are called for."[75] This struggle for identity would be carried on within the context of European economic integration and the modernization programs of de Gaulle's Fifth Republic.

CHAPTER 6

Toulouse as Industrial Capital

The Cradle of Aviation

Toulouse, "land of flight," "cradle of French aviation." The old capital of Languedoc was one of the foremost centers of French aviation throughout the twentieth century. Ringed by airports, mesmerized by the exploits of its pilots, the magic of aviation was as much a maxim of collective identity as the older locutions of *la ville rose* or *la cité des violettes*. The paradox was that just beyond the charmed and intimate circle of *micro-ateliers* eternally laboring in the old districts lay the hangars, runways, and assembly halls of one of the most modern and technologically slick businesses any self-respecting city could offer—aeronautics and aerospace. Here was the new Toulouse, fitted out in a veritable symphony of mechanical wizardry, modernistic design, and effortless proficiency. Aeronautics was the most conspicuous expression of the city's aspirations as a modern industrial capital. It was not the only example of big-growth industry at Toulouse. Weapons and chemical production and electronics manufacturing were also carried on over the course of the twentieth century. But aviation was the ideal. The flying machine was the most auspicious symbol, the most visually alluring, of the new technologies that proclaimed modernity. In what had to be one of the great ironies of French regional history, the Garonne River Valley and its boring old city (the ancient land of hayseeds and troglodytes according to northern opinion) was churning out acclaimed marvels of French modernism: elegant, sleek, powerful, mercuric aircraft.

This particular affinity for the skies had a long and proud local history. It was on the grassy meadow known as the Polygone on the left bank of the Garonne just outside Toulouse that Clément Ader began his experiments with kites and gliders that hatched the idea of powered air navigation. In 1890 Ader took his glider *Eole* up to Paris, stuck an extra-light steam engine in it, and took off across the fields of the parc d'Armainvilliers on the first engine-powered flight of an *avion*. Ader's work remained largely unknown to the general public. But at Toulouse the legacy of Ader's *Eole* and his experiments with *Avions* 1, 2, and 3 became the foundation for the city's historic association with flight.

After these initial trials, a few local Toulousain workshops pieced together experimental aircraft powered by automobile engines. They were tested at the Polygone or off the pont des Arts, one of Toulouse's main thoroughfares over the Garonne River. Support for these experiments came from a wide variety of sources within the Toulouse community. The Aéroclub des Pyrénées was organized in May 1908 by Edmond Sirven, head of the city's foremost printing establishment and himself a *globiste* and amateur pilot. It was the Aéroclub and *La Dépêche* that sponsored Toulouse's first air races in 1910 and 1911.[1] The 1910 race became a media event of extraordinary magnitude. Publicized weeks in advance by the newspapers, the *meeting* had all the characteristics of a modern urban *spectacle*. A prerace music festival and fair at the city's new park on Ramier du Château Island inaugurated the festivities. Race tickets of varying prices were sold, tram and train transportation and police security organized, and food concessions set up. The crowds assembled around the Polygone watched six pilots speed their flying machines around a triangular course marked by tall pylons. The display of technological wizardry was an opportunity for a family outing in a festival atmosphere. *La Dépêche* began its full-page race coverage remarking at the number of women and children in the crowd. The city's cafes were filled with families buying maps of the airfield and guides to the pilots' colors from street hawkers: "All morning an enormous crowd assembles throughout Toulouse. Thousands press along the barriers at the Polygone. Spectators fill the place du Capitole and the place Esquirol. Onlookers swarm in the streets. Autos, vehicles of every genre speed toward the race course. Toulouse has never seen such a crowd." The first flight of the day, by a yellow-winged plane dubbed "the butterfly," lasted forty-two seconds and "sent an immediate thrill through the crowd."[2]

The 1911 competition for the "Prix du Voyage" was a race to the neighboring city of Pau. It enthralled about 200,000 spectators crowding the streets of Toulouse, blackening the hills along the city's outskirts to watch "the masters of the air." The organizers were stunned by the enthusiastic reception, and the crowds received nearly as much coverage by the press as did the race itself. Journalists remarked that air races had become the new holiday, *les grands jours de fête,* for the Toulousains. They were public occasions for holiday dress, for promenading the boulevards and streets in anxious anticipation of the aerial passes over the city. "And everywhere the gaiety, the high spirits illuminated in the marvelous charm of the afternoon," wrote reporter Paul Labordère, who was amazed by "the unimaginable sight" of the crowds. The winner, Roger Morin, "flew at such a height and with such grace that the whole city was able to watch the most beautiful spectacle that man has yet contemplated." To accept their awards the following day, market day at Toulouse, Morin and second-place winner Jules Védrines majestically circled the place du Capitole in their Blériot monoplanes as a sea of captivated humanity cheered below. They were formally received in the main hall of the Capitole by the city's Radical mayor Raymond Leygue, the Municipal Council, and nearly every other city notable, who praised them for making Toulouse a center of aviation.[3]

Early contests such as these marked the beginning of a long list of barnstorming pilots traveling the French *meeting* circuit, arriving at Toulouse in their biplanes, hydroplanes, and assorted flying machines for the chance to become the *enfant gâté,* the idol of the Toulousains. The air races rapidly became a modern expression of the city's collective consciousness and its public life. They were a form of mass entertainment in which all of Toulouse could participate. The record-breaking crowds witnessing the novel machines shared a realm of association and experience that molded aeronautical events into the city's tradition of urban ritual and sociability. The festival atmosphere in the streets, the procession of traffic to the airports, the triumphant flyovers by the pilots were all structured into an urban ceremony of flight. Airplanes also dominated the skies over Toulouse's traditional fairs that were held twice each year in May and November along the allée Jean Jaurès, buzzing the fair booths and thrilling the crowds with their acrobatic feats. These spectacles were conceived and promoted with the assistance of the city's vested interest groups: the press, municipal officialdom, merchant associations. They were supported by the city's restaurant, hotel, and café owners, who saw the planes and the crowds they attracted as good for local commerce. The commercial and political value of this type of local cultural production was amplified when linked with an exalted form of city boosterism. Air races were a matter of civic pride, a chance to associate the city with technological progress. The avowed purpose was "to dignify Toulouse and the Midi."

During these early years of experimentation, flight appeared mostly as popular entertainment. But the First World War had proven the airplane had other uses. Not only did the airplane's role as an instrument of war dramatically accelerate the development of the aviation industry, but it significantly modified the early supremacy of Paris as the privileged stronghold of the infant industry. The embryonic factories, each of them increasingly specialized to the demands of war, began to relocate to the safety of the provinces as early as 1914 under the sponsorship of the General Staff and the various governmental ministries. Pierre-Georges Latécoère abandoned the growing dangers of Lille for Toulouse, where state facilities were churning out weapons daily for the Western Front. He used what capital he had to build a small experimental aircraft factory in the suburban quarter of Montaudran, where the city was constructing its first airport. Despite his migration south, Latécoère astutely established his administrative office in Paris. It was from this Paris antenna, close to the ministries and sources of military funding, that he obtained a state contract in 1917 for the construction of a thousand "Salmson" military reconnaissance planes. The zone of Montaudran was quickly developed, and the fully functioning factory started production in 1918—just in time for the armistice.

With the war's end and a new aircraft factory on his hands, Latécoère banked on increased public demand for regular commercial air transportation. Toulouse's moderate climate, its proximity to the Mediterranean and Atlantic Oceans, and its reputation for experimental flight made it an obvious center for the development of commercial aviation. Latécoère's dream turned toward creating a giant airmail circuit connecting Europe with Africa and South America. With the help of Didier Daurat, a veteran French flying ace, his Compagnie Générale Aéropostale used the fields around its Montaudran hangar to open the first regular French air courier service between Toulouse and Rabat, Dakar, and finally Buenos Aires. *La ligne* was born. Toulouse became the French terminus for the only existing transatlantic air lanes. Its pilots, Antoine de Saint-Exupéry and Jean Mermoz, as well as its planes, such as the "White Bird" and the "Rainbow," became legendary. Each stage in the extension of Aéropostale, each maiden flight by pilots temporarily disconnected from earthly existence, searching alone in the sky for some distant locale to set down their flimsy aircraft and deliver the mail, propelled Toulouse out of its isolation and literally connected it, by airplane, with the modern world.

In a 1930 essay assessing *la ligne,* local geographer Daniel Faucher concluded that "the airplane, which leaves Toulouse, will transport mail from Europe to Santiago du Chile in four days, to the benefit of France and of civilization, and realizing the most extraordinary of hopes."[4] That hope was meant largely for Toulouse, because its nascent aircraft factories represented one of the city's only modern industries, and their survival depended on these risky missions. As encouragement, the municipal government and the Chamber of Commerce pursued an aggressive policy of airport construction. By the mid-1930s the city boasted two fully equipped airfields (at Montaudran and at Francazal to the south), and it had begun work on a new facility at Blagnac to the northeast, close to the old Polygone.[5]

An engineer and compatriot of Latécoère, Emile Dewoitine, opened his own small factory in a Francazal hangar in 1921 and began experimenting with gliders and military aircraft. A second workshop (named for Saint-Eloi, the patron saint of metal workers) was added to his newborn company in the Minimes industrial quarter along the Canal du Midi. By 1923, Dewoitine had signed contracts for his new airplanes with Italy, Switzerland, and Japan. But despite its early success, the Dewoitine enterprise experienced the vicissitudes characteristic of all early aircraft firms. In 1927 the Francazal plant closed after financial failure. Undaunted, Dewoitine started a second company, the Société Aéronautique Française, in an old warehouse located near the rural village of Saint-Martin-du-Touch northwest of Toulouse. The advantage of the spot was its proximity to the Polygone and to Blagnac.

Actually, aircraft manufacturing was not the only new form of production to arrive in the shadow of the First World War. The French fertilizer industry was created in 1919, when the patent for the synthetic manufacture of nitric acid was ceded to France by Germany in the Treaty of Versailles. The government chose Toulouse as the location for its new fertilizer plant because, despite the city's distance from both primary materials and the agricultural regions of northern France, sheltering the new industry from possible aerial attacks in the northeast was a more immediate concern. A covey of tiny chemical firms had been members of the city's small-scale manufacturing community since the beginning of the century. In addition, Toulouse had at its disposal the enormous installations of the partially abandoned gunpowder factory bordering the Garonne in Braqueville just south of the central city. It also had an abundant reservoir of cheap labor. With these advantages, the municipality welcomed the newly christened state-run l'Office National Industriel de l'Azote (ONIA) fertilizer plant. The buildings of the gunpowder factory were converted into chemical laboratories and maintenance workshops, while chimneys, furnaces, and cracking towers rose skyward over the Garonne River.

The 1920s then was a decade in which the makings of a new industrial economy was spawned at Toulouse, largely due to what was usually written off as the city's "poor" regional location. The perils of war had transformed the *pays toulousain* into a French economic safe haven. Secure weapons production was the city's contribution to the sacred cause of the Great War. Chemical and aircraft manufacturing followed the trail of safety to the lost outback of southwestern France. This kind of heavy manufacturing could not have been more at odds with the city's traditional industries, but its incorporation into the economy laid the foundation for a shift toward a modern industrial base. By the 1930s, 2,000 or more workers produced 160 tons of fertilizer per day at the ONIA plant.[6] Given the significance of chemical production to twentieth-century industrialization, this was an impressive feat.

Nonetheless, chemical fertilizers do not make for first-rate modernist heroic symbolism—especially for the city producing them. It was instead the airplane that linked the city's historic destiny to modernity. The association of flight with civic promotion and urban festival that had marked the early years of the century provided the groundwork for the representation of aircraft production as a local cultural imperative. It provided Toulouse with a purposefulness, a sense of revived mission, and a powerful productive symbolism generated from its emerging industrial economy. Installed near the hangars and landing strips at Montaudran, the Société Industrielle d'Aviation Latécoère offered new skills and high wages to 900 employees. Dewoitine's company provided jobs for another 400 to 450 of the city's workers. Aéropostale, with an armada of 176 planes by 1929, employed 1,500 people. In total, the city was second only to Paris as a center of aircraft construction and transport. This new "aerial space" over Languedoc reconfigured the regional puzzle and the hierarchy of cities along far more modern industrial lines. Bordeaux and Marseille were historically considered the great southern capitals. Toulouse suddenly leaped ahead as the *tête de la ligne,* nurturing the most sophisticated technological production available. It was Toulouse that appeared to be, according to Emmanuel Chadeau, "the instrument of southern revenge on the north . . . what the railroad did for the dreary nordic regions, the airplane would do for the sun-kissed lands of the south."[7] Aviation represented all that Toulouse could be, all its possibilities in the modern world.

As aircraft manufacturers settled around the airfields, public life in Toulouse was increasingly accompanied by the noise of aircraft engines. Test flights for new models often took place directly over the city. "Sometimes it is only a brief passage in the sky," reported Louis Gratias. "Other times the pilots amuse themselves, rearing up behind Saint-Sernin Cathedral or some other historic monument, saluting them with their roar."[8] The playful escapades were momentarily interrupted in 1920 when a Bréguet XIV crashed into the city streets, terrorizing onlookers. Despite the danger, the aerial experiments became part of the city's daily life. The seaplanes built by the Latécoère Aircraft Company for the transatlantic flights of Aéropostale were tested on the Garonne River just south of the city in the late 1920s. The drone of their engines settling into the water merged into the background of everyday sounds. The small hotel in the center of town that served as the pilots' home, the Grand Balcon, took on the mystique of its famous guests. It was known as *la pépinière de la ligne,* providing a warm and familial environment, baptizing the pilots as the *équipe du Grand Balcon.*[9] In 1930 Jean Mermoz, who had already received a medal from the Chamber of Commerce for his bravery, began the record-breaking flights in the "Comte-de-La-Vaulx" and the "Croix-du-Sud" hydroplanes to South America, cutting the flight time to two days and giving Toulouse proprietorship of the fastest international air courier service available.

Despite these heroic exploits, the world of flight was not without its difficulties. French aeronautics remained a hazardous venture throughout the 1920s and 1930s. Windfall profits could be made on coveted contracts; but the competition and quarrels were fierce, and it was just as easy to fall into the trap of shoestring financing and insolvency. Despite the epic adventures of Toulouse's Aéropostale pilots, French aviation was riddled with trouble by the 1920s and was losing ground to its British and German rivals. Five different private airlines vied for control over commercial traffic in France. Toulouse, Bordeaux, and Marseille battled over command of southern courier and passenger service from Paris to North Africa. By the mid-1930s, Toulouse's upstart status as *la tête de la ligne,* the *cité d'Isaure,* was on shaky ground. Latécoère lost control of Aéropostale to the South American financial interests of Marcel Bouilloux-Laffont. The money-laundering scandals that followed in 1930 left the once-great company bankrupt and purged of its hard-won international corridors.[10]

By 1933 the crisis finally persuaded Pierre Cot at the Ministry of Air to take over Aéropostale and merge it with its French competitors into Air France. It was an essential and long-needed reform that allowed the state to rationalize French commercial aviation and make it more competitive with such formidable foes as Graf Zeppelin and Pan-American. But it critically threatened Toulouse's supremacy as headquarters for the country's most extended system of air lanes. The Chamber of Commerce and Municipal Council, the General Council of the Haute-Garonne, *La Dépêche,* and the city's various air clubs launched a massive lobbying campaign to keep the reconstituted company at Toulouse. In the short term they were successful. Air France took over the South American routes and Aéropostale's hangars and workshops at Montaudran. But in 1936 its main offices were transferred to Paris. In complete defiance of the Air France monopoly, Didier Daurat and Beppo di Massimi of the defunct Aéropostale inaugurated Air Bleu, a courier service between six major cities, but one that was clearly preferential to Toulouse. It was an Air Bleu flight that finally connected Francazal-Toulouse with Le Bourget-Paris in 1935, to the glee of city officials. But the rebel airline quickly collapsed.

Aircraft manufacturing followed the same perilous course as the commercial airline business. Despite the Air Ministry's attempts to rationalize and encourage the industry, the 1930s brought hard times for the small private manufacturers that had been the backbone of Toulouse's aircraft venture.[11] Dewoitine's Société Aéronautique Française, though still operating, slid into bankruptcy. With Toulouse native son Albert Sarraut as French Prime Minister, Latécoère was able to sidestep the Air Ministry's efforts to consolidate independent manufacturers. His plant at Montaudran was, after all, essential to the city's industrializing economy. Nevertheless, financial and contract setbacks, as well as the strikes in June 1936, all but destroyed the Société Industrielle d'Aviation Latécoère. Mayor Ellen-Prévot and his municipal government intervened on the side of the workers in the June 1936 walkout, hoping to end the dispute quickly. But then Latécoère's refusal to comply with the Popular Front's decision to nationalize the aircraft industry provoked yet another crisis.

The *métallos* of the Toulouse aircraft industry were avid crusaders for both the Socialist and Communist causes. Communist militants in the Confédération Générale du Travail led the city's June 1936 strikes, and their fellow workers swelled local union membership. Toulouse, however, was largely a Socialist citadel. The SFIO had organized Amicales Socialistes d'Entreprises in the factories to counteract the growing Communist influence. By 1936 and 1937 large numbers of aircraft workers belonged to Socialist education and youth groups, sports and flying clubs. The Socialist Party claimed a good portion of the city's union leadership. Yet despite the rivalries between Socialists and Communists, there was a local left-wing solidarity among aircraft workers that committed them inexorably to the Popular Front's nationalization program. When Latécoère defied public incorporation, workers occupied the Montaudran plant and staged protests in support of a *sixième groupe*—a sixth public company within the Popular Front's Sociétés Nationales des Constructions Aéronautiques that would be housed at Toulouse. The idea was endorsed by the city's highly visible benefactors within Léon Blum's government. Albert Bedouce as Minister of Public Works and Vincent Auriol as Minister of Finance intervened on behalf of the local union that had written them in Paris that "all the workers, office workers, and technicians in Toulouse aviation are ready to demonstrate that nationalization, under the oversight of the Air Ministry, can put our country at the head of progress in international aviation . . . The working class can show that it can build and erect (airplanes) without the help of swindlers, if it is given the chance."[12]

Theoretically, the southwest had already been awarded a public company, the Société Nationale des Constructions Aéronautiques du Sud-Ouest (SNCASO), that was to be based at Bordeaux. But obviously, Auriol was at pains to avoid stripping Toulouse of its most important industry right in the middle of the depression. Nor had he any intention of betraying working-class support in a town that had voted overwhelmingly for the Popular Front. With pressure from both Auriol and the striking Toulouse workers, Pierre Cot agreed to the sixth company in 1937, the Société Nationale des Constructions Aéronautiques du Midi (Nationale du Midi or SNCAM), with Emile Dewoitine at its head. The new company was initially financed by the city's Chamber of Commerce and local Toulouse banks in what Herrick Chapman describes as an "unusual convergence of labor militancy and local business boosterism."[13] This "convergence" was based on the alliance of interests, the solidarity of municipal politics and culture, that attempted to defend and mobilize the city's economic fortunes. The Nationale du Midi was to make full use of the Blagnac airport, where a new assembly hall would be built by the municipality close by Dewoitine's factory at Saint-Martin-du-Touch.[14]

By the late 1930s Toulouse did seem to be favored by the Ministry of Air's rearmament policies. Spurred into action by Hitler's Anschluss and his annexation of Czechoslovakia, Plan V called for the expeditious construction of advanced aircraft for the French military arsenal. The Nationale du Midi, under Dewoitine's highly regarded management, quickly became one of the workhorses of rearmament, churning out Dewoitine 520s (the only French fighter considered equal to the Messerschmitt) from the Saint-Eloi factory sheds at Minimes. At the same time, the Ministry of Air's decentralization policy was stepped up in an effort to evacuate aircraft production into the provinces, beyond the reach of German bombardment. The flight and testing facilities around Toulouse at Blagnac, Francazal, and Montaudran airports, as well as the existence of the Latécoère and Nationale du Midi plants, made the city an obvious focal point for nervous émigré capital searching for a new site. Louis Bréguet moved his aircraft production to Montaudran following a subcontracting agreement with Latécoère. The old Latécoère factory was purchased and expanded by Bréguet in 1939 for production of the Bréguet 691. Latécoère himself moved what was left of his company to new facilities on the rue de Périole just behind Matabiau railroad station, where he began construction of seaplanes under state contract. The Ministry of Air's research and testing unit (Etablissements de Recherches Aéronautiques) was moved to Toulouse, as was the public-private Groupement de Recherches Aérodynamiques.

The steady flow of contracts for military planes, in preparation for a German attack on France, and the immediate demand for workers of any type, qualified or unqualified, to help build aircraft jetted salaries to extraordinary levels at the factories. In a two-year period, from 1936 to 1938, salaries increased 100 percent at Latécoère's and Dewoitine's plants.[15] Artisans and workers from rural areas surrounding Toulouse streamed into the city to take advantage of the high wages. The draw extended to the *microateliers*, particularly to mechanical and metallurgical workshops, which were stripped of their most skilled laborers. By 1940, 16,500 workers were employed in the construction of military planes at Toulouse. The companies complained continuously about labor shortages and the need to extensively train employees before they could join the production line. The living circumstances for these battalions of tenderfoot airplane makers were just as speedily assembled and ramshackle. For the most part they were housed in temporary barracks alongside the work sheds or simply found rooms wherever they could. Their sheer numbers added to the hopeless congestion of refugees and military reservists overwhelming the city after the German invasion in June 1940.

The June 22 armistice momentarily stopped aircraft production in all of Toulouse's factories. By August 1940, Vichy inaugurated its network of *Comités d'organisation* through the Ministry of Industrial Production, which planned the needs and production goals of each branch of industry. The city's aircraft facilities produced planes, motors, and equipment for the rump army left to Vichy by the terms of the defeat. But in such a critical war industry, German interference was bound to be extensive. In fact, the German Armistice Commission refused recognition of the *Comité d'organisation* for aviation until appropriate arrangements could be made for German supervision. Under the signing in July 1941 of the Programme Aéronautique Commun Franco-Allemand, French manufacturers were to build airplanes for Germany and France at a ratio of one to one, gradually moving to a ratio of five to one. Although the Toulouse factories were under contract with Vichy and the Wehrmacht, their work emphasized research and prototype testing, while actual production was greatly reduced. Dewoitine was evicted from Nationale du Midi by Pierre Laval, and the company merged into the Société Nationale des Construction Aéronautique du Sud-Est (SNCASE).

Once the Wehrmacht occupied southern France in November 1942, any semblance of aeronautical autonomy ended. German administrators appropriated all French aircraft factories for the Luftwaffe. Louis Bréguet and his staff were barred from entering their Toulouse workshop. Machinery and skilled labor were seized from the SNCASE plants and sent off to German Messerschmitt and Junkers plants. The Francazal airport was used as a base for Junkers bombers, while Blagnac became a flight training facility for German pilots. Latécoère continued prototype testing for his hydroplane models under Wehrmacht patronage, arguing that "France could not afford to fall behind the foreigner," until his forlorn, but rather timely, death in August 1943. Emile Dewoitine compromised himself tragically, offering his services to the highest bidder in order to "continue his creative endeavors." He was making prototypes for the German Arado company when the Allied invasion of France began. He discreetly disappeared into the Pyrenees Mountains and then fled to South America. Then the British aerial bombardments of Toulouse in April 1944 destroyed most of the factories at Saint-Martin-du-Touch, Saint-Eloi, and Montaudran. What remained of the SNCASE and Latécoère operations were immediately sequestered and occupied by aircraft workers at the Liberation in August.

Once freed from German control, the aircraft industry momentarily became the heart of Toulouse's brief experiment in *autogestion*. Where management had brazenly collaborated to the extent of repairing and building enemy aircraft, the factory employees burned with the Liberation's patriotic fervor and were determined to restore the French Air Force. Led by Resistance fighters and Communist militants organized into Committees of Liberation, the workers themselves would manage the factories and produce the French-built aircraft needed for the war effort. France, productivity, self-management were their principles. Pierre Bertaux's Accord de Toulouse legitimized the Comités de Libération d'Entreprise and the *Comités Mixtes à la Production* attempting to revive the corpse of Toulouse aviation in the fall of 1944. But there was little left to haggle over, however. Montaudran was in ruins. Less than a quarter of the facilities were left at Blagnac and Saint-Martin-du-Touch. Only the Latécoère factory at Périole was functional. Reconstruction began in August 1944, but it proceeded slowly. The MRU refused to approve factories within 1,500 meters of a city center, which had been the case with the factory sites at Toulouse. Only in 1945 did it finally authorize partial reconstruction of the plants. But it mattered little because the appalling scarcity of labor and material drastically restricted the number of newly minted aircraft rolling out onto the Blagnac runways. In 1946, the city's four companies managed to employ just over 7,000 workers.[16]

Toulouse aviation in general was facing a difficult period of adjustment to postwar realities. The underlying problem was the suspension of state contracts. Although the city's aircraft workers were reconciled to the Fourth Republic by the appointment of Communist Charles Tillon as Air Minister, in general state policy toward the aviation industry was incoherent during the first five years after the war. The blow to the city's economy was severe. The downturn in the city's most modern and productive industry (something that could easily be blamed on wrong-headed Parisian policy) contributed mightily to the oppressive economic adversity that debased Toulouse just as the "French boom" began to shower its bounty on the rest of the country. It was left to city elites to bargain for leverage with Tillon's Air Ministry along with the rest of the aviation enclaves dotting the provincial map. Emile Debard, writing in *La Dépêche,* remarked that the competition had already opened between cities battling for control of commercial air traffic and manufacturing.[17]

Visibility, nurturing the climate of opinion, and city boosterism were the traditional strategies used by the Chamber of Commerce and the municipality to reclaim Toulouse's entitlement as the cradle of French aviation. To begin, air shows were promptly organized almost immediately after the war. Both French and British pilots performed in 1946 in honor of local Resistance parachutists. The twentieth anniversary of *la ligne* was ostentatiously celebrated in March 1948. Officials from Air France and the municipality took part in a solemn ceremony at Saint-Sernin Cathedral, then crossed the city in procession to the Royal Gardens, where Mayor Badiou dedicated a new monument, the delicate figure of Air sculpted by Aristide Maillol, to "the glory of the pioneering teams of the France-South America line."[18] These were the aeronautical counterparts to the street fairs organized by the city's commercial and artisanal interests in an attempt to launch a postwar economic recovery. The inauguration of the refurbished Blagnac airport in 1953 was the occasion for a stunning display of aerial acrobatics by Marcel Doret, the city's favorite stunt pilot and leader of Toulouse's most famous battalion of wartime fighter planes.

The postwar citywide celebrations were clear evidence that despite the shaky fortunes of French aviation, Toulouse continued to look to flight for its identity and its prosperity. By the 1950s, some twenty aviation associations had been founded in the city, many of them with hundreds of members.[19] Beyond the air shows, they offered the opportunity for more formal citizen participation in Toulouse's aviation culture. Organizations such as the Amicales des Aviateurs de Toulouse and the Société de Propogande Aéronautique encouraged civic pride and promotion. The Aéroclub du Languedoc offered "aerial baptisms" as part of local holiday celebrations. Pierre Cot had organized "popular aviation sections" within the factories in the 1930s, in which young workers could learn to fly. The employees at Toulouse's state plant had taken advantage of the program and founded their own flying group[20] that continued after the war. All of these clubs owned a few planes and offered flying lessons, parachuting, or glider rides to anyone anxious to take to the skies. Members were involved in a variety of club social activities, such as regular cafe meetings, annual banquets, and dances that provided the opportunity to socialize with some of Toulouse's most famous pilots. Air France and Sud-Aviation retirement associations and company sponsorship of rugby teams and various sporting events further integrated aeronautics into the larger community. In 1949, for example, Air France sponsored a yacht race on the Garonne with Miss Toulouse as the guest of honor.[21] This mix of associations provided a cultural form to modern industrial production and helped to incorporate the values and language of aviation into daily life. It was a collective induction into aeronautics as a community endeavor.

The city associations and clubs also acted as lobbying agents, pressuring the French government for research and production contracts. The complex array of representatives at a 1948 regional conference on aeronautics illustrates the extent of local involvement. Delegates from the mayor's office, the departmental prefect, and the Chamber of Commerce, as well as the head of Bréguet's research bureau, members of local engineering and aviation associations, faculty from the University of Toulouse, and local "intellectuals" crowded into the Museum of Natural History with hundreds of shopkeepers and aircraft workers to demand that the French government support aviation research and production at Toulouse.[22] This was a rather unorthodox ultimatum considering that most of the public rhetoric coming out of Toulouse was antistatist in the extreme. But it fell within the well-worn argument that the coffers of the state were opened and closed by the slippery hands of political favoritism, and Toulouse was rarely a favorite of the French government. The local aviation disciples understood themselves as simply fighting for what was rightfully theirs in the first place—recognition as the premier center of French aircraft production. Their speeches were the vernacular version of the heroic discourse over that modernist marvel, the airplane. Their defense was rooted in an experience of municipal community that strove to guard the economy as a whole against the consequences of outside exigencies and short-term state calculations.

The production of the medium-size commercial transport called the "Caravelle" rescued the Toulouse aircraft industry from certain oblivion. It was part of the Ministry of Air's more cohesive five-year plan for aviation and the consolidation of the various state-run enterprises into one firm, Sud-Aviation. The reorganization was to make the French aircraft industry more competitive with the large American and British firms. Construction of the new plane was assigned to Toulouse. Local reverence for the Caravelle was particularly ardent because the plane's appearance was accompanied by official French recognition of the city's aircraft tradition.

As part of its new regional development plan for the Midi-Pyrénées, DATAR appointed Toulouse an "official" aviation capital with a particular "vocation" in this field. The designation was simply a recognition of the obvious. But still and all, this state-contrived formal arrangement of the regional cities into an industrial hierarchy with assigned "jobs" rang with the deafening sound of modernist rationalization within capitalist market and geographic dynamics. It also represented the incorporation of popular urban imagery into a mandated public policy created by local and national elites—a facile use of cultural tradition as a transformative mode. It intensified the city's association with the airplane by providing it with a ceremonial baptismal as *le berceau des ailes françaises,* with the Caravelle as *l'enfant de Toulouse.* Under state direction, the country's aircraft companies would be persuaded to "decentralize" to the city, to join up with their cohorts as the invincible *industries de pointe* destined to launch the southwest out of its economic trough.[23] Toulouse was elected, now by state certification, to be the site of an exalted form of modernity. In an article for the Chamber of Commerce's monthly magazine, Georges Héreil, the director of Sud-Aviation, called upon the cultural link between Toulouse and flight. "Toulouse was the birthplace of the Caravelle," he wrote. "The engineers who conceived the plane, the workers who constructed it, the pilots who tested it, are all part of the family that for the past forty years has made this city of Languedoc . . . the premier provincial center for aeronautical construction."[24]

The Caravelle did indeed seem to turn around the city's economic fortunes. Over 275 planes were produced in two series, beginning in 1955 and 1957. Its initial test flight in 1955 was the occasion for a citywide mass celebration, this time attended by film producers, reporters, and photographers from Paris. *La Dépêche* reported:

> As the plane appeared on the runway, one could see that the embankments were covered with tiny silhouettes that rapidly formed a black shadow darkening the white hills. After the takeoff, all the surrounding roads, cars, bicycles, everyone, stopped to follow the bold silhouette of the Caravelle that swept across the Toulouse countryside for the first time.[25]

The Caravelle's debut was accompanied by the first international Salon Aéronautique at Toulouse in 1959. When the first plane was sold to Scandinavian Airlines in April, the city celebrated with a formal ceremony staged by the Chamber of Commerce. Mayor Louis Bazerque, IGAME Roger Morin (president of the city's Small Business Association), artisan activist Antoine Simonian, and a host of city notables stood while Chamber of Commerce President Henri Sarramon paid homage to Georges Héreil and to the "admirable Caravelle that had vanquished economic misfortune."[26] Sud-Aviation blossomed into the city's leviathan company. By 1962, 6,600 people

Figure 9. Production line for the Caravelle at the Sud-Aviation assembly hangar, Toulouse-Blagnac.

worked at its three facilities. Its Saint-Eloi factory in the Minimes industrial district housed engineering facilities for the manufacture of aircraft parts. The largest installation was at Saint-Martin-du-Touch, where the original sheds were expanded with more assembly hangars and flight-testing installations for the construction of the Caravelle. The plant eventually stretched the entire length of the avenue Pierre Latécoère leading into Blagnac Airport. Lastly, research and design offices were built during the Caravelle period along the western extremity of Blagnac Airport near the village of Colomiers.

The two communes of Blagnac and Saint-Martin-du-Touch became the exclusive domain of the aviation industry. The Francazal and Montaudran airports were closed. The Chamber of Commerce focused singlemindedly on cultivating the aircraft enclave northwest of Toulouse. Threequarters of the property at Saint-Martin-du-Touch and a large portion of Blagnac had already been ceded to the airport before the Caravelle period. The city continued its expansion in the early 1960s by purchasing another forty hectares bordering the airport in Saint-Martin-du-Touch. This parcel was reserved as an industrial zone for "decentralizing" aviation companies and was immediately filled up. A second industrial zone of fifty-eight hectares was opened on the other side of the airport in the commune of Colomiers, to which even more aircraft firms migrated. The ten firms identified in 1958 by the census bureau as involved in aeronautical construction jumped to sixteen by 1962. Bréguet inaugurated production of the military transport "B1150 Atlantique" by constructing new assembly sheds at Colomiers that were connected by concrete tracks to the runways at Blagnac Airport. Potez Air Fouga built the military series "Fouga-Magister CM170" at Colomiers next to the research offices of Sud-Aviation.[27]

All in all, by 1962 11,000 people, 30 percent of the industrial labor force, were making a living building airplanes around Blagnac. It represented the largest center for aircraft production outside Paris.[28] The facilities at the airport itself were perpetually expanded and updated as the Chamber of Commerce invested millions in passenger terminals, office buildings, hangars, and services for the aircraft companies. The entire Colomiers–Blagnac–Saint-Martin-du-Touch district became a privileged aeronautics zone, something of an "aviation theme park." It was nurtured by city planners as inviolate territory—a subscribed, rationally articulated vision of Toulouse's technofuture. The principal apprehension was connecting it, both metaphorically and literally—by opening new roads—with the old city.[29]

Nonetheless, not everyone at Toulouse cheerfully embraced the boosterism and obsession with modernist heroic imagery, least of all the crews piecing together the city's latest icon along the assembly line. In 1957 and in 1959, workers interrupted delivery of the first Caravelles with 24-hour work stoppages as protests against the low wages at Toulouse in comparison to salaries at the Parisian aircraft plants. Workers from Sud-Aviation, Bréguet, and Latécoère joined up in demonstration at the Halle aux Grains and then marched to the prefecture on the place Saint-Etienne to present their demand for pay equity.[30] Aggravating the situation even further, Sud-Aviation brought in metallurgists and skilled technicians from its Saint-Nazaire and Marignane plants to work on the Caravelle. They continued to receive higher wages although they worked alongside their lower-paid Toulouse counterparts. Even more irritating to the locals was the fact that the immigrating Sud-Aviation employees were given a monthly indemnity of 70,000 francs to make up for the personal disruption of moving to Toulouse. A "general malaise," resentment, and disquietude filtered through the Blagnac–Saint-Martin-du-Touch factories. Protests and boycotts stalled production. In May 1959 more than 15,000 *métallos* showed up at a public meeting called by the CGT and the CFTC (Confédération Française des Travailleurs Chrétiens) at the Palais des Sports.[31] By June, the Municipal Council frantically passed a resolution calling for an immediate end to the indignities suffered by the Toulouse metallurgists. The grievances were endangering Caravelle deliveries to Air France and Scandinavian Airlines.

The same disgruntled cynicism about the heroic deeds performed inside the Blagnac shrines can be detected among the city's small-scale industrialists who faced the loss of skilled labor to the Sud-Aviation factories. It was more likely, however, that they stood with the local aircraft *métallos,* joining them in their protest marches. *Les petits'* frustrations over oppressive state regulations and taxes squared with aircraft-worker outrage over the state's discriminatory low wages at Toulouse. Both were abundant evidence of the injustices suffered at the hands of Paris. For regionalists, for traditional landed elites, for the Communist opposition, the fanfare over the aviation entitlement could be interpreted as yet another example of central government encroachment into local affairs.

Nevertheless, the city's honor as the country's virtuoso aircraft builder was a largely successful projection precisely because its roots lay within popularly accepted notions of the role of aviation in local culture and history. Just a few weeks after the Palais des Sports protest, 20,000 spectators showed up at Blagnac airport to see the amazing Caravelle, the "Alouette II," the "Bréguet Alizée," the "Mystère IV-A," at the *fête national* air show. One way or another, nothing provoked so much intrigue and public ceremony as Toulouse's airplanes.

The Concorde as Metaphor

The rocky if ostentatious display of aeronautical acumen was in good part the outcome of the tricky relationship between modernist iconographic design, technocratic planning, and the realities of the freewheeling global marketplace. The late 1950s malaise within the Toulouse factories was exacerbated by the lack of any new government-sponsored prototype blueprints. After 1964 Caravelle orders began to decline. The international market was reorienting toward the new demand for increased speed and transport capacity. Essentially the choice for the *Commissariat Général du Plan* was between entirely remodeling the Caravelle to make it competitive with developing American and British aircraft or launching research on a totally new supersonic transport that would require an estimated nine years for completion. The decision was made to finance the research and development of the supersonic Concorde and to produce a simpler, improved version of the Caravelle for a very limited market.[32] It was a risky choice, particularly since the vast majority of French aviation research funds were allocated to this one ambitious project. But the Concorde was typical of the Gaullist attitude toward economic development during the 1960s. Vast sums were funneled into this one project mainly to demonstrate French technological prowess and strengthen the country's claims as a modern industrial power.

The study and production of the Concorde was based on the strategy of producing a revolutionary machine that would still be at the forefront of aerospace technology in the late 1970s. The Sud-Aviation research center at Blagnac quickly doubled its workforce. Studies were carried out on the problems of crossing heat barriers, of creating insulation and refrigeration systems, and of producing a jet engine powerful enough for the speeds anticipated. New computers and electronic simulators were used in the design of the engine and equipment. The Concorde assembly procedure required a full-size layout hall at Blagnac that was equipped with special machines that automatically engraved the plane's pattern on immense tracing plates.[33] Vast sections of its fuselage and wings were trucked through

Toulouse in the middle of the night. To the delight of neighbors willing to sacrifice their sleep, the unearthly forms were trundled across the pont des Catalans and down the allée Jean-Jaurès to the Testing Center at Lespinet.

But while the race to design and test the new airliner continued, any actual construction of planes at the state factory stopped. This meant that Toulouse's exalted role as home of the Concorde actually deflated the city's industry. At Sud-Aviation, the labor force stagnated at around 6,700, with hiring taking place only at the research bureau. Working hours were reduced for employees on the assembly lines. Three hundred of them were temporarily dispatched to state aircraft factories elsewhere in France. The city's private aviation firms suffered from the slump in state production contracts while the Concorde was conjured up inside the Blagnac research sheds. Aviation suddenly shifted in the minds of Toulouse business leaders from luminary to "grave problem." The Chamber of Commerce anxiously opened a public discussion on the dangers of *mono-industrie*, as it began to appear that any decline in aeronautics spelled doom for Toulouse as well: "For the future of the city should we consider unburdening ourselves of the aeronautic industry?"[34] During the May 1968 protests, the workers occupying the Sud-Aviation factory were given special directives from the local union to protect the Concorde and its equipment. The grounds were clear: jobs were riding on the wings of the fabulous machine. Nothing could interrupt its delivery.[35]

What became even more apparent was the city's dependency on the fluctuating decisions of the public powers in Paris and the glaring disadvantages of the promotion of Toulouse as French aviation capital. The solution to Toulouse's troubles, according to DATAR, was to expand the city's "scientific and high-tech" sensibility to include the new French Space Center, or CNES. Its decentralization to Toulouse could help fill the production gap in aviation caused by the long gestation of the Concorde. The new installations would also act as a ballast for the emerging scientific complex at Rangueil-Lespinet. The CNES officially opened in 1968, although the decentralization of operations continued until 1974. It began work on France's second generation of space satellites and the DIAMENT launch vehicles. With the development of bilateral agreements on space research, principally with the United States and the Soviet Union, and the appearance of a spate of European organisms for space exploration, the Toulouse Space Center became an important continental hub for space research. It was an unexpected turn of events in the city's modernist odyssey. Nonetheless, it was clear that planners in Paris were determining Toulouse's economic future. Local posterity was entangled in the erratic currents of the global high-tech market-place and in decisions mysteriously made somewhere else in the board-rooms of corporate and state elites.

In March 1969 the long-awaited Concorde gracefully rolled out of the hangar and down the runway at Toulouse's Blagnac International Airport. The city's Sud-Aviation research facility proudly unveiled prototype 001 of the joint British-French project. In a euphoric holiday atmosphere, thou-sands lined the airport's perimeter, along with television crews and journal-ists, to catch a glimpse of the maiden voyage of the "delicate, slender, supple, majestic, thundering" Concorde. It was a media event of interna-tional importance. In three days' worth of special supplements devoted to the debut of the Concorde, *Le Monde* stressed the massive government investment and the French technological genius that lay behind the plant's avant-garde design.[36] The thirty-minute flight was televised throughout Europe. The prestige of France rode on the wings of the supersonic machine. The Concorde was, by far, the most vociferous metaphor for the French economic miracle, the forced logic of a high-tech national economy built on the prosperity of the 1960s. For Toulouse, it was the culmination of the *fêtes aériennes* that had long been a part of its urban culture, a sign of revived municipalism. The entire city stopped to look toward the skies and the sleek silhouette as it glided through the bright sunshine over Toulouse. It was reported in the press that "Everywhere could be heard the refrain, 'It's flying!'" The day's rugby match was stopped, the horse races were sus-pended, to salute the plane as it passed overhead, with the crowds roaring their approval in the stands. "There is something about the first flight of an airplane, about modern flight," reported local journalist René Mauriès, "there is always an air of mystery, indeed of magic." Every detail of the plane's first flights was reported in the local press. Every local dignitary, every veteran of Toulouse's long aviation history waited to greet the world that appeared at the city's doorstep to admire its creation. According to a local editorial, "A great outpouring of hope and courage carries the Con-corde . . . With its primacy as a European capital of aviation magnificently proven, Toulouse, radiant and with legitimate pride, is ready to assume its mission."[37] It was a historic moment for Toulouse.

More than any other aircraft, the Concorde became the symbol of the new, modern Toulouse. In the words of City Hall, the Concorde was the symbol of "a city turning toward its future."[38] Its first flights elicited an outbreak of Concorde-mania. Elegantly futuristic, of sleek design, enor-mously powerful and fast, the Concorde precisely fit the emerging values of

Figure 10.   Test pilot André Turcat flies the Concorde over Toulouse in tribute to Charles de Gaulle on the night of his death, November 9, 1970.

consumer society.[39] Hotels and cafes were christened La Caravelle, Le Concorde, L'Envol. Glossy color photos of the unmistakable gull-winged SST appeared everywhere, on postcards, tour guides, in bookstores, in restaurants, and on public pamphlets introducing Toulouse. Department stores sold trendy T-shirts embroidered with the design and name of the latest aircraft attractions. The local hairdressers' association dubbed a new coiffure after the Concorde. André Turcat, the test pilot for the Concorde, became the city's new hero. Aerospace brought with it a new glamour, a sense of Toulouse as having arrived at a golden age as the archetype of the technopolis. It was headquarters for the French version of NASA, the birthplace for the swankest, most technologically glamorous flying machine produced anywhere in the world. Public documents and the press hailed the city as an international aerospace capital, the new French "think tank," a center for research and high-tech industries: "Toulouse, the scientific capital of tomorrow."[40]

Alongside all the public posturing over the opening of CNES and the first flights of the Concorde stood the even more persuasive fact that the workforce in aviation ballooned to over 14,000 in 1972. But this auspicious situation did not last long. The main problem was, of course, the Concorde itself. One of the most acclaimed specimens of French technological wizardry though it may have been, the plane nevertheless impressed few commercial airline companies. The Promethean crusade to create the Concorde was undertaken without confirmed orders for the final product, a dangerous commercial risk that amplified as budgetary costs and inflation drove its price tag to exorbitant levels. Controversy over noise pollution and maintenance costs further inhibited sales. By 1976, only sixteen orders had been placed for a plane with a fixed price of 300 million francs. This was far from the eighty Concordes originally slated for production.[41]

The avalanche of rumors about a coming "Concorde crisis" tarnished the lyrical pronouncements on the city's high-tech future. The aviation industry was then badly crippled by the oil crisis and world recession that began in 1973. Panic set in at Toulouse as jobs suddenly disappeared. Sud-Aviation, which had been reorganized yet again and renamed Aérospatiale,[42] laid off 2,000 workers by 1976. The Société Latécoère lost half its workforce. Bréguet Aviation and the city's smaller factories stopped hiring. Local officials pleaded with the government for the development of new aircraft series. But the French government had lost all taste for *grands programmes* in elegant SSTs, particularly after the devastating market performance of the Concorde. The grandiose industrial schemes launched during the 1960s had degenerated into "bottom-line horror stories," as Stephen Cohen has put it.[43]

In the climate of economic crisis faced by the Giscard d'Estaing presidency, investments in civil aviation were scaled down. Toulouse's Space Center was also a victim of the budgetary cuts. By 1976, CNES began laying off its personnel. Toulouse waited in limbo for Paris to make up its mind about the manufacture of the Mercury aircraft series. City officials were then informed that the government's plans for aerospace would not be a part of the economic development programs for Toulouse or the Midi-Pyrénées region.[44] Hopes shifted toward the solution of European cooperation and the development of the French-German Airbus aircraft series.[45]

In 1978, approximately 12,000 men and women worked in Toulouse's aerospace plants. Blagnac–Saint-Martin-du-Touch was unquestionably the country's most important center for aircraft production. Despite its erratic behavior, aeronautics remained the city's premier industry. It paid more in salaries than any other manufacturing or service activity. Aircraft production represented 18 percent of the city's industrial sales volume in 1975, the highest proportion among the city's industries. It was also Toulouse's most important export.[46] Far more than just a "vocation" stamped on the city arbitrarily by DATAR planners anxious to order the provinces and effect modernization, aeronautics was a genuinely home-grown industry at Toulouse. Aircraft manufacturing was, for the Toulousains, deeply rooted in the city's heritage, a natural economic manifestation beyond Parisian politics and planning policy. The Polygone, Blagnac, Rangueil-Lespinet were places of decisive modern experience. The products of that experience (the White Bird, the Caravelle, and then the Concorde) were evidence of local originality and imagination.

The legacy of flight acted as the connecting link between Toulouse's past and its future. In virtually every local history written from the 1950s through the 1970s, the airplane was the agent for Toulouse's modern development. In 1962, Jean Coppolani in his *Toulouse au XXe siècle*, the foremost history of twentieth-century Toulouse, wrote, "The first flight of the Caravelle will remain a historic date for the city. The Toulousains followed the plane's worldwide acceptance with the same interest as that with which their fathers had followed the victories of the Toulouse rugby team in 1925 and their grandfathers had followed the Capitole singers in 1900."[47] Flight was thus the catalyst for a cornucopia of cultural production and historic reference that mobilized community resources in the cause of locally engendered modernization. At times this vernacular version of modernization was co-opted by state and corporate authorities; at times it remained at odds and defensive. Political and class alliances on behalf of Toulouse aviation were molded and modified by the tensions between local community and state power. They were shaped by the competition between rival provincial cities for geographic space and economic mastery. There were a variety of unconventional partnerships and participants in the debate about Toulouse, "land of flight." The screen of images this phrase invoked was created from the special interests, disputes and compromises, the market dynamics surrounding that most dazzling of modernist icons—the airplane.

With so much of its urban economy and culture tied to aerospace, it was with good reason that the Toulousains cringed with every market downturn, eagerly awaited government announcements on aircraft production, and quickly popularized the planes built in its factories. In 1978 a totally refurbished airport was inaugurated at Blagnac. Spacious, built in state-of-the-art design, it represented the city's enduring commitment to its calling as French aviation capital. Thousands visited the construction site, and tours were organized for schoolchildren to explain the significance of the airport to the city's history.[48] A long observation deck was built outside the main terminal. There the citizens of Toulouse could walk out and gaze across the runways to the Aérospatiale assembly hangars in the hopes of catching a glimpse of some spectacular flying machine that would launch the city's industry back on the road to the future.

The Electronic Revolution

By the mid-1960s, a diversification of Toulouse industry was already high on the list of municipal and business elites who lamented the zigzagging fortunes of its prize aeronautical trade. The *Livre Blanc* outlined the dilemma succinctly. Industrial production took place at the extremes: a few giant high-tech aircraft and chemical plants sitting out in the suburbs were juxtaposed against a swarm of lilliputian semiartisanal shops tucked into the old city. This faulty and illogical industrial structure made Toulouse overly dependent on exogenous decisions and vulnerable to every shift in the business climate beyond its borders.[49] The solution was to diversify. A wider mix of modern manufacturing, with companies of varying sizes and capacities interacting through subcontracting agreements and business liaisons, would guarantee a healthier future. These new businesses should, according to the *Livre Blanc,* be welcomed into spacious suburban industrial parks that offered the most up-to-date services available.

On the face of it, this seemed an obvious enough response to the city's problematic role as an industrial capital. But it also illuminated the tangled undercurrents of outlook and opinion concealed just beneath the objectified surface of modernization. Airplanes were certainly Toulouse's most important product and its most breathtaking modernist idol. But the city was hardly suffering from a unidimensional economy. There were more people working in building construction than in the aircraft plants in 1968. Employment in aeronautics represented about 30 percent of the industrial workforce. The rest were divided among the multitude of ingrained manufactories that dotted the urban landscape. In fact, most economists argued that Toulouse was not specialized enough, rather than moaning piteously that the city was tied too heavily to aircraft construction. Local officialdom had wholeheartedly swallowed their own rhetoric about the city as the inner sanctum of aerospace technology. Heroic discourse is, after all, simplistic and naive by design. The reality of the production gyrations that plague all temperamental high-tech industries shocked a municipality used to the protective ambience of its local economic culture and enraptured by the high hopes and passionate elocutions accompanying the birth of its airplanes.

There was plenty of opportunity to upgrade the other industries already well established at Toulouse as a way to offset production lags in aviation. But the elites promulgating French industrial policy during the 1960s took a fundamentalist stand on the virtues of technological innovation and modernist production. The notion of the *industries de pointe* and their supporting *grands programmes* in research and development bloomed into an industrial and regional development philosophy of monumental proportions. High-tech industries like aerospace were destined to transform the economic culture and geography of France. The country was to be shepherded toward the future by the modernist innovations enshrined in nuclear energy, aerospace, and electronics. This articulation of industrial intent—the deliberate and rational invention of a modern industrial genre according to the dictates of modern capitalist norms—monopolized technocratic thinking. It precipitated its own cottage industry in the vast compendium of economic statistics, structural, and sectoral data compiled for every city and town in France. Statistical production was the referential field of DATAR and the growing corpus of regional councils and planning agencies that took up their task in the various *métropoles d'équilibres.*[50]

Their mission was to achieve a utopian industrial structure in each provincial outpost. A transformative public enterprise, supported and controlled by the state, would be surrounded by a covey of research and educational institutions and a mix of attendant companies relying on subcontracts with the mother plant. As a productive ensemble, it would supplant the parochial, particularist interests that had historically laid claim to regional authority. This centralized, rigidly hierarchical industrial structure became the ideal against which all provincial productive patterns were measured. It duplicated the centralized corporate management hierarchies instituted within large companies as the ultimate capitalist ethic of the 1960s and 1970s. The pyramidal fantasy of industrial structure, with power fully in the hands of the state, even more closely paralleled the traditional relationship between Paris and the provincial capitals. The technocratic agenda for economic modernization reiterated endlessly the established pattern of geographic hegemony imparted by national political practice. A fully integrated national economy was simply to follow in step.

Thus, in choosing diversification, the business community at Toulouse was deviating, to a certain degree, from established French planning orthodoxy. An argument can be made that local elites were fulfilling their traditional role in attempting to shelter the indigenous economy from competitive forces and ironhanded decisions outside the city. Their solution was the familiar one. Productive capacity should be spread among a broader range of private proprietors and manufacturing skills. This would enhance economic flexibility and shield the city from the temptations of dependence on aircraft sales. It was the kind of initiative, based on local economic practice and need, that was ignored by state planners as a strategy for regional development.[51] And the local cry for diversified production was well within the modernist paradigm. Electronics and telecommunications seemed a shoe-in. Municipal officials reasoned that the need for electronic equipment in aircraft would produce the kind of subcontracting web between high-tech industries and the kind of informational nexus between manufacturing and the Rangueil-Lespinet scientific complex that would insure a more integrated modern economic base. The attempted installation of an electronics industry in a city that had no previous inclinations toward this highly technical and fiercely competitive field was a clear-cut sign of the modernist logic that *industries de pointe* were capable of conjuring up extraordinary spin-offs in the urban milieu around them. In any case, bringing all its powers of "economic attraction" to bear, the business and municipal elites of Toulouse set out to snag themselves an electronics industry.

The mayor's office and the University of Toulouse organized an electronics exposition in 1965. It opened a freewheeling campaign to "market" liaisons with Rangueil-Lespinet and the aircraft companies to invited electronics manufacturers who were poking around for new locations. Toulouse's new suburban industrial parks were ceremoniously displayed as the most definitive and usable of rationalized manufacturing spaces. Every conceivable financial carrot was publicly dangled to attract private firms to the city. Finally, two American firms succumbed to the campaign. Canon-Electric constructed an assembly plant in 1965 for electric connectors used in aircraft and data processing. It was located in the industrial zone of Colomiers along the northern perimeter of Blagnac Airport. After Motorola CEO Bob Galvin toured the 1965 electronics exposition and received a royal reception led by Mayor Bazerque, the company built a factory for the production of semiconductors in the new industrial quarter of Le Mirail. Foremost in the latter's decision to work in the city was the availability of an abundant female labor force, the large number of engineers and technicians at Toulouse, and the promise of contracts with the aerospace industry. In return for sumptuous financial gratuities, Motorola's management pledged to hire 2,000 employees by 1971.[52]

The capture of a nascent electronics sector for Toulouse was intriguing to state planners if for no other reason than that it synchronized with the Gaullist government's own plan to launch France into the telecommunications industry. A four-year national Computer Plan was established in 1967. An agreement was signed between the government and the joint owners (Thomson CSF and the Compagnie Générale d'Electricité) of the newly created Compagnie Internationale pour l'Informatique (CII). It provided 500 million francs in public aid for the company to research and develop an initial series of medium-powered French computers.[53] The biggest coup for Toulouse in this state-supported bonanza was claimed by Professor Gambou, one of the leading university champions of research links with a new electronics industry. Catching up with personal friend and CII manager Jean Auricoste at the city's electronics exposition, Gambou convinced him to locate the company's ultramodern plant at the Le Mirail industrial park rather than at one of Bordeaux's suburban industrial meccas. With that prize as an endorsement, DATAR formally designated electronics as a new pilot industry for Toulouse. By 1969, the CII plant at Le Mirail was humming into production of the first French computer, baptized IRIS.

The manufacture of electronic and data-processing equipment

opened the possibility of thousands of jobs, particularly for young women left unemployed by the onset of mass production in the city's downsized clothing industry. From its opening in 1967, the workforce at the Motorola plant increased regularly, reaching 1,800 by 1970. The "wrapping" technique perfected during the 1960s for the manufacture of integrated circuits required a low-cost specialized labor force, and the company made easy use of Toulouse's abundant labor, training local men and women in new skills. The CII factory manufactured the entire range of IRIS computers and branched out into production of the highly successful industrial computer MITRA 15, with a workforce that reached 1,600 by 1974.[54]

However, it soon became obvious that, like aeronautics, the nascent electronics industry was subject to yo-yoing boom-and-bust cycles. The market in integrated circuits collapsed at the end of 1970. Oversupplied buyers abruptly canceled orders. The price of circuits fell by half. Then the "hardware crisis" of 1972 undercut the market even further. Motorola cut its workforce to 1,200. Six small local businesses subcontracting to Motorola closed. In 1974, competition from a European joint-venture computer called UNIDATA wiped out sales of CII's IRIS and MITRA series. By 1975, the public discord between the shareholders put the company's survival into question. It was reorganized with Honeywell-Bull purchasing the Thomson CSF shares. With factories in Angers and Belfort, Honeywell-Bull had little interest in the plant at Toulouse and ignored it. Over 550 employees were laid off. Then a long-awaited project for the construction of an electronic components factory by the Electronique Tranchant Company was completely abandoned.[55] The vagaries of the marketplace quickly ended any hopes for an electronics calling for Toulouse.

But there were other threats to the business community's vision of a diversified and interlocking brew of electronics, telecommunications, and aerospace plants. Lille-Roubaix-Tourcoing had its own designs as an enchanted electronics circle, as did Bordeaux and Nantes-Saint-Nazaire. Mayor Bazerque warned that the fierce competition among the *métropoles d'équilibres,* the panoply of obsequious electronics fairs staged by high-tech capitals, posed a grave danger to Toulouse's own business campaign. The city had to upstage its rivals with a commanding *Journées d'électronique* that proved the city's exceptional devotion to the electronics cause. To this end, the 1972 affair opened with an international colloquium where local businessmen, scientists, and engineers could hobnob with the likes of Nobel prize winners, Soviet professors, and European industrialists. The following year's fair was planned around a medical electronics and data-processing theme.[56]

This kind of citywide business development, sponsored independently by the mayor's office and the Chamber of Commerce, authenticated the local shrewdness, the responsiveness to market conditions and competitiveness, that the state planning agencies refused to recognize. In a local interview, Bazerque took the opportunity to jab at the regional bureaucratic apparatus hanging over the Midi-Pyrénées: "In sponsoring the electronics fair we are working for the expansion of the regional economy. We would hope that if this interview falls under the eyes of the region's directors they will find it in their heart to give us their spontaneous support, because we certainly have no taste for begging."[57] Each newcomer settling into one of the sacred suburban *zones d'activités* was construed as an exalted municipal conquest and as testimony to Toulouse's robust economic power—autonomous from the state's image-making and regulatory web.

But despite these local campaigns to compete on the stage of high-tech industries, Toulouse found it a minefield of pitfalls and obstacles. Modernization forced cities to take on corporate attributes. They marketed their virtues, produced space and financing, and competed with an international cast of covetous urban rivals. It was all meant to capture a piece of the action in the global marketplace. The stakes were high and the outcome unpredictable. By 1975, electronics and data processing employed a total of 3,600 people, less than 2 percent of the city's workforce. Innovations in computer production had reduced the role of manual labor to a minimum.[58] Although Toulouse was often considered by private firms as a possible location for their electronic plants, it was always bypassed in favor of another, economically better-situated city. Only a few electronics firms appeared at Toulouse during the 1970s. Thomson CSF finally rescued the CII factory by purchasing it as a subsidiary and then built a second small factory near the Rangueil scientific complex. Collins Radio France moved into the new international business center at Blagnac Airport. The Belgian Logabax, Speri-Rand, and Renix Electronics companies settled in Toulouse and began manufacturing minicomputers and electronic automobile equipment. But the magic of electronics as a mechanism for economic diversification appeared to be more fantasy than reality, or at least that was the judgment of a growing band of critics. The struggle to cash in on the telecommunications revolution did, however, articulate the pious public belief in corporate dynamics and high-tech creativity. It disclosed the tricky interplay between state power and local independence, as well as the uncertain, often rickety, path toward modernization.

In 1976, the urban plan for Toulouse acknowledged the crisis in the city's economy:

> The future looks bad for the businesses that until now had been the motors of growth. A fluctuating aeronautic policy has left Aérospatiale without knowing which civil aircraft will be constructed and assembled at Toulouse . . . APC [formally ONIA] is in the midst of a serious crisis due mainly to the competition of the world fertilizer market. The CII factory that symbolized a new vocation for Toulouse has been pitifully abandoned. The policy followed by the European Space Agency has ended in idle equipment and layoffs at CNES.[59]

After fifteen years of an exalted reign replete with princely ceremony and magisterial elocution, the great *industries de pointe* of Toulouse had fizzled in the face of economic recession and dwindling state interest. The decade of the 1960s was the short golden age of bountifully supported state programs for economic modernization through advanced technology. Nurturing high-tech production was a policy grounded in the technocratic vision of efficiency, productivity, and rational ordering that captured the imagination of planners working under de Gaulle's rule. It was easy to believe in their sorcery and to invest in them when the French economy was in full expansion, as was the case up to 1968 and even afterward, until the world crisis of 1973. But the goals of grandeur and modernization built upon sweeping investments in Concordes and IRIS computers were tenuous, as the 1970s proved.

When the arguments over regional development and provincial particularism are considered, however, a somewhat different picture emerges. Whatever the short-term oscillations in production and market performance, twentieth-century industrialization transformed the provincial landscape in irrevocable ways. Aviation functioned as a cultural catalyst, inculcating the Toulouse community with the ethos and values associated with modern productive capacity. It served as the creative force behind the industrialization of the Toulouse economy. Everyone in Toulouse grew up learning about airplanes. The kind of innate knowledge that percolates through an industrial milieu was acquired almost naturally—through shop-talk and factory training, reading *La Dépêche,* attending air shows and races, belonging to air associations, learning about the city's history. The riveting and lathe-work on vast metal sheets, the aerodynamic tests on fuselages that went on for some sixty years in the weird medley of sheds at Toulouse, radically altered the city's economy and made it, with or without state sanction, an industrial center of substantial repute. Young men in the local area were drawn into the aircraft factories more or less as a rite of passage. Over 70 percent of the workers at the state plant were from the Toulouse region. The recruits were most often local artisans and skilled workers, particularly from the metallurgical and electrical trades. They were enrolled in the factory's Apprenticeship Center for special courses on aircraft construction and then received on-the-job training. The habituation to wage labor and the discipline and practices of large-scale factory production were learned primarily by building aircraft (as well as in the city's weapons foundries and small textile mills). It was this education and tooling that were such a fundamental part of the changing economic and social character of the city.

The plants became an accustomed route to social and economic mobility in the *pays toulousain.* Nearly half of the city's skilled workers held jobs with the aeronautical, chemical, and electronics industries. Jobs in the aircraft plants offered the highest pay and highest status within the Toulouse industrial community. By 1976, salaries in aviation averaged 40,000 francs a year, far above the citywide norm of 27,000 francs. In the chemical industry wages were even higher, averaging 43,000 francs per year. None of the city's other industries paid nearly as much. Nor could the service sector compete with such high earnings.[60] People lucky enough to work for Aérospatiale or Bréguet often stayed in their positions until retirement, content with occupying some of the best jobs in the city. For these reasons, the employees at Aérospatiale and ONIA-APC, for example, increasingly shared the attitudes and values of civil servants rather than those of traditional workers. They tended to live in the *grands ensembles* in the suburbs west of the city and commuted to work by bus or by car. Many of the aircraft employees preferred to live in the communes of Colomiers or Blagnac, where new residential projects, like Colomiers Villeneuve, made working for and living near the aircraft factories even more palatable. Central Toulouse, with all its rebellious left-wing images and contemptuous posturing toward the French state, had been left behind on the road to success.

Unions made less and less headway at the aircraft factories, and strikes became rarer. Existence for modern-minded *métallos* was just too comfortable and their standard of living too high. The few work stoppages that did occur at Toulouse's aircraft plants during the 1960s were essentially over the continued disparities in regional salaries within the aerospace industry. It broke into a serious conflict during an eleven-week strike in the summer of 1963 that closed the Aérospatiale factory. The demand, once again, was parity in salaries with Paris. Although the aircraft plants were hit by the 1968 strikes (as was virtually every other business in the city), their employees were not in the forefront of the May movement. The CGT and CFDT (Confédération Française Démocratique du Travail) laid out a full series of demands and occupied the plant floors. But even with this union presence, the influential and numerous engineers and *cadres* at Sud-Aviation, Bréguet, and Latécoère, as well as at ONIA, voted against all political strikes.[61]

Ultimately, the whole process of twentieth-century industrialization was instrumental to the construction of a national economy in capitalist form and under state regulatory control. The particularist proclivities that had divided France into an unproductive and divisive puzzle of regional economic interests were subjugated to a unified national agenda. It was created partly through two wartime mobilizations that required large-scale planning, decentralizations, and the rationalization of industrial production. The transition to a Fordist regime continued after the war with reconstruction, urban renewal, and regional planning. The shift was stepped up even further by direct state programs in industrial modernization. The unprecedented growth and transformation of the *trentes glorieuses* effectively consolidated this Fordist, corporate-state dynamic in France.[62] It was an extraordinary process of disruption and modernization. The national commitment was to massive capital investment, to technological invention and managerial expertise. Modernization required the mobilization of the country's resources and labor. It necessitated the rational organization of geographic space conducive to state and capitalist control. Large corporate-state power was essentially deployed throughout the country to assure productivity and to guarantee growth, higher living standards, and the national interest. The result was the transformation and discipline of the political economy of France under the aegis of state prescription.

The quandary for provincial cities like Toulouse was how to retain some measure of economic autonomy and flexibility while still reaping the gains of modernization and a higher standard of living. Increasingly over the course of the twentieth century the city's economic lifeline was affixed to Paris. Its most important businesses were nationalized industries under the direct control of state technocrats. Aérospatiale, the ONIA-APC fertilizer plant, Air-France, CNES, and the CII Company were all managed, planned, and financed by the state Planning Commissions, the Ministry of Finance and Economic Affairs, and the Ministry of Industry. Virtually all of the city's private firms in electronics, chemistry, and aeronautics had their head offices in Paris. Toulouse had a reputation for being one of the provincial cities most dependent on the French capital for its economic well-being. It was one image—among the many images of Toulouse—the locals had difficulty swallowing.

On the surface, there is nothing particularly extraordinary about this connection between the national government and the city's high-tech industries. Advanced technology companies, particularly those located in regions considered underdeveloped, are normally dependent on government contracts. Richard Kuisel and others[63] have made the point that, in an economy where a conservative spirit too often crippled entrepreneurial pluck, the nationalized sectors run by the government *grands corps* best expressed the taste for risk, far-reaching endeavors, and dynamism that were the marks of modern business technique. From this point of view, Bernard Dufour, graduate of the Ecole Polytechnique and director of the Aérospatiale plant at Toulouse, and Henri Ziegler, another *polytechnicien* and president of Aérospatiale (who was also instrumental in the creation of Airbus Industries at Toulouse) were considered the city's most important allies and most brilliant capitalists. The nationalized sectors created an environment in which state-controlled creative entrepreneurialism and speculation in technological innovation could flourish and act as models for indigenous business practice.

But there was clearly a detrimental side to this economic dependency. The city's economy was at the caprice of fluctuating government economic strategies and the changing political climate in Paris. On top of that, the "spin-off" phenomenon associated with the industrial production ensembles devised by state planners in the *métropoles d'équilibres* did not materialize. For small subcontracting firms, the cost disadvantages of Toulouse were often too high despite the presence of potential clients. True subcontracting firms at Toulouse, such as Auriol, Ruggieri, and Badin, committed only a modest portion of their production to the high-tech idols. The vacuity of the promises of the imperial policy of *industries de pointe* was such that an Airbus Industries official pronounced the Midi-Pyrénées and Toulouse to be "technological deserts." DATAR's representative at Toulouse asserted he had "no idea why electronic companies would move to Toulouse. There is nothing for them here."[64]

Toulouse was instead linked to an extended network of national production, market, and labor systems, essentially as one among many geographically dispersed research and production units. The 14,000 aerospace employees working at Toulouse in 1971 represented 15 percent of the industry's national workforce. The cities of Nantes, Bordeaux, Marseille, and most of all Paris possessed aircraft manufacturers that provided the parts and services required by the factories at Toulouse. Subassemblies for the Caravelle aircraft, for example, were manufactured at the state factory at Saint-Nazaire and then shipped to Toulouse by truck convoy. Sections of the Concorde's famous wings were manufactured at the Aérospatiale plant in Paris. Its engine was made in Britain. In 1967, Aérospatiale purchased 23 percent of its subcontracted equipment in Paris, while only 7 percent was purchased from firms in the Toulouse region.[65] The same situation existed in electronics. Inexorably tied to its Parisian management office, CII did not bother much with local subcontractors, nor did Motorola or Thomson CSF. In 1970, only 7 percent of total purchases by the CII plant were from Toulouse.[66]

In assessing all the various aspects of modernization, the new industries of Toulouse were clearly where corporate-state elites gained a real mastery over the city's future. And it is here where it was easiest to raise the specter of internal colonialism. The regional development and industrial-planning schemes under the Fourth and Fifth Republics offered prosperity and national recognition. But they were also perceived as technocratic tools for state manipulation and influence, a mutilation of the city's defined and independent disposition and its economic culture. The Toulouse economy had been recast in the image of "high-tech" Fordism, its pugnacious workforce "conquered" by the routines of large-scale capitalist production and by the sweet sound of high wages and social mobility. The city's productive spaces had been standardized and regulated. Modern Toulouse, the "scientific and high-tech capital," could now be manipulated within a national, and global, context. All of this had been accomplished by the hand of the French state. Local business leaders became increasingly skeptical about DATAR and the Ministry of Industry's talents for regional development and called instead for "a demystification of the regional 'vocations' proclaimed by official discourse that have produced nothing over the last ten years." A battery of local Toulouse economists reproached the government for its illogical industrial policies: first massive support for prestigious industrial projects like the National Computer Plan and CII, then their abandonment for investments in nuclear energy. By the early 1970s, deputy mayor Pierre Baudis was accusing the government of abandoning Toulouse for President Georges Pompidou's pet project, the industrial expansion of the Gulf of Fos.[67] Major asymmetries of economic power were created as the French state and single multinational firms negotiated with competing towns and local political actors. It was clear where the advantage lay.

But the capacity to intercede in the realms of cutting-edge industries was tricky and oscillatory. *Aménagement du territoire* as a system of state power was forced to wrestle with local claims to economic legitimacy and local perceptions about the cultural and historic form of industrial development. Industrial production of this stature also became the fixation against which historic regional enmities were played out. The civic battles between Toulouse, Bordeaux, and Marseille over commercial aviation, or for that matter over electronic and computer jockeys, revealed the interplay between shifting notions of regional hierarchy and economic geography. The competition for high-growth industries forced cities to become more "entrepreneurial," obsessed with nurturing a favorable business climate. Local elites clashed economic swords with rival claimants over coveted state contracts and over official validation as high-tech capitals.

These duels over urban image and economic control produced, in modern form, the antagonisms that defined notions of space, geography, and national identity in France. They molded the tensions between centralization and decentralization—between Paris and the provinces—according to modern capitalist values. The meaning of Languedoc, Provence, or Aquitaine became increasingly associated with the ability of each to attract technological pioneers to its industrial zones and with the role each would play in a modernized global economy. It was vivid testimony to the fractious construction of a national industrial motif as the deferential route to modernization. The boundaries circumscribing modernization remained fluid. Recessions interceded. Local alliances vied with each other to define the frame of reference that constituted national economic unity. Far from simply state fiat, inventing industrial capitals for France was a muddled and complicated task.

CHAPTER 7

Gentrification and the
Capitalist Landscape

The transformation of the industrial sector was a vital ingredient in the city's arrival as a respectable *métropole d'équilibre*. But in a larger sense, it was the transformation of *mentalité*, the *formation des hommes*, within Toulouse's economic culture that was cardinal. The fabrication of a capitalist personality for the city's businessmen (still defensively clutching their regional heritage in the bygone capital of Languedoc) was presumed essential to rejuvenating French prosperity and identity. This ideal of the new entrepreneur, of a psychic "transformation," meant the construction of a broad-ranging societal and spatial dynamic. It reconceptualized the city as a whole around the values, landscape, and culture of modernism and market capitalism. Particularly during the 1960s and early 1970s, the "golden age" of French prosperity and economic planning, the city and the region became the canvas upon which a new capitalist topography was constituted. Yet despite heroic exertions on its behalf, modernization was fragmented and only partially effective at Toulouse. What may be more to the point, the alchemy of modernization produced all variety of results when applied to the city's colloquial economic culture. This chapter looks at three elements in this struggle to reconfigure Toulouse and its hinterland around a coherent set of modernist norms: the dramatic attempts to find a niche for Languedoc within the European community and the global export market; the public campaign to convert the city's petty producers into "gentrified" entrepreneurs; and the reconfiguration of medieval Toulouse into a "downtown" landscape.

Exporting to Survive

In 1958 the Violet and Onion Producers' Cooperative bemoaned its catastrophes: "frost in 1956, hail in 1957, frost and hail in 1958, and now the opening of the Common Market."[1] French entry into the European Economic Community (EEC) at the beginning of 1958 profoundly changed the economic climate for the traditional industries of France. With their tariff protection removed, the country's handicrafts were forced into competition with larger European, especially German, businesses that were mass-producing goods for the growing consumer markets. Purchasing choices were moving away from basic foodstuffs and everyday domestic goods (both usually produced locally) toward leisure and luxury items such as television sets, sports equipment, appliances, and fashionable clothing. The allure of the new consumer culture offered throughout Europe threatened to destroy the conventional small producers of France. The reaction of the *patronat* was suspicion and defensiveness. Their national leaders warned of "the catastrophic consequences and the eventual defeat of French industry" and demanded safeguards against the threat of open competition.[2] Business opinion at Toulouse was divided as to what policy to pursue. The opening of the Common Market actually had less of an immediate impact on Toulouse than on the rest of France, if for no other reason than the city's distance from France's original five partners (Belgium, Italy, Luxembourg, the Netherlands, and West Germany). Toulouse businesses were traditionally oriented toward the colonial market of the "franc zone" in North Africa for their few exports. If nothing else, the city's geographic exile was made even more conspicuous by the economic union between the European Six. Many saw little hope in counteracting the currents of "European-wide consumerism" that left Toulouse even more peripheralized than it had been before. The new topography of the Common Market simply dramatized its historic isolation.

Toulouse was not so far removed, however, that it could hope to dodge the flood of cheap, appealing imports that began to appear at its portals. The fear of foreign goods undermining the local market was often the first reflex reaction to the reality of European economic integration. As if to underscore the cultural threat foreign competition posed to local community, the brick and tile workers' union warned of a possible inundation of the "second-rate" Italian version of these sacred building materials. The imports, according to union officials, were made by low-paid laborers unskilled in the time-honored techniques that had given Toulouse its unique color and visual presence.[3] The *micro-ateliers* that lined the city's streets were accustomed to relying on regional demands for their orders. For them, meeting the challenge of open competition by stepping into the export market was daunting. The opinion of one Toulousain artisan-patron was symptomatic of attitudes: "Me, I haven't a chance. My prices aren't competitive, I can't equip my shop for work like that. I don't want to take the risk of investing in the fluctuating export market because no one can help me, while my foreign competition is supported by their governments."[4] The members of the *violette toulousaine* cooperative fretted as well over how to participate in the emerging world of global exports. Doubting any prospect of sales within the Common Market, they decided to look instead to the United States. Even the president of the cooperative questioned whether the industry's small family firms, with their limited commercial experience, could compete without government aid.[5]

The problem of expanding the market for locally made goods was certainly not a new one for the Toulouse business community. Efforts had been made throughout the twentieth century to promote trade with North Africa. The Colonial Exposition held in 1931 represented the apogee of these early attempts at solidifying the city's traditional export market. After the war, Gabriel Barlangue, head of Toulouse's Chamber of Commerce and the IXth Economic Region, regularly traveled to Tunisia to reopen trade between Toulouse and its North Africa partners. What was so different about the issue of exporting in the late 1950s was the sense of urgency and the fact that reliance on France's wayward "colonial zone" was suddenly a short-sighted maneuver. It was both the Algerian Crisis and the Common Market that imparted this tone of apprehension about export markets. To protect the traditional sectors from the initial shock of European-wide competition, the French government carried out devaluations in 1957 and 1958, with the result that French exports remained high despite the opening of the Common Market. But the writing was on the wall. North Africa was no longer a privileged, secure trading enclave. The public had been won over by American-style patterns of consumption. The government was committed to economic modernization. France's traditional industries appeared to be at a critical juncture. Exporting was no longer a luxury. It was now essential for survival.

This question of *"exporter pour survivre"* encapsulated the collective neurosis over business mentality at Toulouse. During the 1960s and 1970s it was the controversy around which the very identity and culture of the petty proprietor—and by extension Toulouse itself—were most at stake. Exporting was understood to be the chrysalis through which local businessmen would emerge from their cocoon of traditionalism as modern entrepreneurs practicing sharp-edged capitalist strategies. Offering updated consumer goods to the outside world was essentially synonymous with embracing modern market culture. It was a ceremonial rite of passage to modernist maturity. As such, foreign trade unceasingly tormented the city government, as well as the community's business leaders, perhaps because Toulouse was held up as such a glaring example of passé economic Malthusianism. Toulouse would "survive" (and the public discourse mirrored the sense of urgency and peril that modernism imposed) only by transforming its ingrained economic culture into something more suitable to contemporary realities. To a real degree, the choice seemed suddenly to be between extinction or a willingness to experiment with more modern forms of business practice and managerial rationalization. Even IGAME Louis Périllier commented that the whole population was conscious of the economic drama being played out over the construction of a modern mentality for the city's petty producers.[6] The future was at stake. In this sense of a cultural crisis, the "drama" at Toulouse was a refraction of the struggle to modernize *mentalité* that was taking place throughout France.

During 1958 and 1959, dramatic attempts were made at Toulouse to prepare for the onslaught of open competition within the European Economic Community. A Committee of Exporters was organized so that "ALL manufacturers, artisans and food producers could find markets outside the regional frontiers." A nonprofit association, Sud-Export France, was created to coordinate export ventures and exchange commercial savvy.[7] The Toulouse Chamber of Commerce held special meetings on exporting that had almost a revivalist tone. Progressive-minded entrepreneurs stood and testified to the efficacy of the modernist creed before assembled audiences of craftsmen: "I have gone all over the world looking for new markets. I quickly discovered that foreign competition was no more or less dangerous to my products than competition within my own country, my own city, or on my own street—in a word, the competitive character of my products was the same everywhere."[8] The Union Régionale des Groupements Patronaux (URGP) opened a new branch for the "exporters of Toulouse Midi-Pyrénées," which immediately held a local conference on "Export Trade" in May 1959. The URGP argued that the flexibility and adaptability of the small shop was precisely what was needed to weather the inevitable hazards of the international market. The *chefs d'enterprise* had the obligation not just to survive but to thrive under the new conditions of open competition—if for no other reason than to maintain their independence and the integrity of France.[9] Local unions quickly marshaled "export programs" of one kind or another. The Violet Producers' Cooperative created a union label for their perfume and sent delegations throughout Europe to promote sales. Hosiery producers from Toulouse joined with their counterparts at Castres to coordinate efforts at introducing their products on the export market.

The main event, however, in the local preparations for brandishing Toulouse products on the global marketplace was the city's annual trade show. It was held at the exposition park on the Ile de Tounis just south of the central district. During the 1950s it was a modest affair, attended mainly by a few North African companies. But by the early 1960s, the Chamber of Commerce officially reoriented the show around an international theme. Chamber officials explained that ". . . an international outlook is a vital necessity if one hopes to promote our regional economy in the perspective of the new European commercial currents in which we will be participating."[10] The fairground was renovated, and a modern circular pavilion, christened the "Palace of Nations," was constructed to accommodate foreign visitors. In 1964, 1,800 firms attended the trade show, 200 of them from foreign countries. Following along with the international theme, the city organized a series of cultural introductions to various European countries. Representatives from Germany, for example, descended on the city in 1959 to instruct the community on contemporary German society. They were followed by Dutch, Belgian, and Luxembourgian delegates, as well as the American Ambassador, who were all given baronial tours of the city and its highest quality goods, including garments and shoes, furniture, metalwork, and edible delicacies.[11]

These exertions by civic elites to proselytize the doctrine of adaptation to commodity production for the global marketplace gave rise to a zealous public discourse. It was aimed at overturning the ingrained habits and values of the city's producers. Even so, it was quite often articulated as a resurrected cultural crisis of looming proportions over French identity and regionalism. In a 1968 conference on "Toulouse and the Midi-Pyrénées," Louis Armand of the Académie Française summarized Toulouse's difficulties in the modern age:

> Our country is like a cell with an overpowering nucleus (Paris) and an air-tight membrane that seals out any contact with neighboring markets. The whole country has been focused on Paris, from which everything springs. Now we need to turn our backs on the real enemy and look outward. If we want to develop our foreign markets we can no longer be restricted by a linear Napoleonic hierarchy

that refuses to acknowledge the diversity and the complexity of the provinces. Accepting European union requires the sanctioning of a genuine life for the regions.[12]

It was in pursuit of an "independent economic personality" that the city's business vanguard launched a campaign to unlock Spain as a viable export market for Toulouse. International, or at least European, commerce remained fantastic and unfeasible for many of the proprietors laboring in the old city. A more realistic possibility, at least according to the locals, was to simply open trade relations with Toulouse's closest neighbor.

Barlangue and the Chamber of Commerce had attempted commercial ties with Spain as early as 1948, as soon as France officially reopened trade negotiations after the war. By the end of the 1950s, the strategy had evolved into a down-to-earth acceptance on the part of local business elites of Toulouse's peripheral location in relation to the five member countries of the Common Market. Spain was just across the Pyrenees Mountains and seemed to lie open as an economic frontier. The strategy could also build on a reinvented past of cultural and economic ties between the Midi and Catalonia. In 1954, Professor Jean Sermet of the Faculty of Letters delivered a public lecture at the Académie des Jeux Floraux entitled "Toulouse and Spain." It was commissioned by regional Prefect Emile Pelletier and was bountifully illustrated with historic proof of their close association: "What is the Place du Capitole but a typical Spanish plaza mayor!" But more precisely, Sermet historically defined the economic territory Toulouse now sought to control:

> Toulouse is one of the strongest urban personalities in France because it naturally dominates the land between the Massif Central and the Pyrenees, between the Mediterranean and the Atlantic. The city is thus the Pyrenean capital and has been since the Middle Ages. If the southwest, designated by Paris as "the French desert," can hope to find its redemption, it will be with Toulouse as its heart.[13]

Chamber of Commerce President Henri Sarramon reached into the depths of historical memory as well to find: "There is, for Toulouse, a kind of predestination not just to contemplate Spain from afar, but to rekindle the mutual friendship that is dear to all." Sarramon talked of rediscovering the "road to Compostella," the "promised land" of Spain.[14] A historic pattern of cultural and economic geography was exploited by government and business gentry to invent the idea of a modern "Mediterranean market." It would be a new constellation adjacent to the distant and elusive Common Market. Spain appeared to be a magic formula for Toulouse.

The campaign began in earnest in 1959 when the Chamber of Commerce sent an initial delegation to the trade shows of Spain and began promoting Toulouse as the "gateway to the Iberian Peninsula." But the dream of a Mediterranean economic empire was frustrated by long-standing bilateral agreements that kept tariffs high and exchanges between France and Spain limited. It was also well understood that Toulouse would benefit from commerce with Spain only if its products were complementary rather than competitive. It was not clear to everyone that complementarity would necessarily be the case. Brickmakers complained bitterly that cheap Spanish labor produced the same building materials at half the price and could easily flood the regional market. The textile, garment, and leather and shoe industries faced the same threat. Thus the early sallies across the frontier during the 1960s were meant to ease commercial tensions and reassure local manufacturers that trade with Spain would indeed be profitable.

The first serious discussions between Toulouse businessmen and their Spanish counterparts took place at the annual Toulouse trade show and at the great international trade fairs at Valencia, Barcelona, Lérida, and Saragossa. Economic cooperation was given formal investiture in 1965 with the establishment of La Conférence Permanente des Chambres de Commerce Françaises et Espagnoles (COPEF). The council included thirty-nine French Chambers of Commerce from the Midi and twenty-three Spanish Chambers from Catalonia and eastern Spain. Its French office was opened at Toulouse, where it worked under the patronage of Henri Sarramon and Roger Moris, who had become regional prefect for the Midi-Pyrénées. Much of its work during the 1960s was simply a matter of public relations and promoting cross-Pyrenean investments by private companies.[15] But its purpose as an administrative instrument was essentially to normalize market relations and to stabilize a trading frontier that had every likelihood of stirring up hostility and xenophobia.

The most formidable obstacle of all, however, was the Pyrenees Mountains themselves. "Pyrenean capital" it may have been, but Toulouse was not in the most favorable position to conduct trade with Spain. The two main passes over the mountains were at Hendaye-Béhobie on the Atlantic coast and at Perthus on the Mediterranean coast. In the middle between them, there was no easy crossing over the Pyrenees directly from Toulouse. On the other hand Bordeaux and the Aquitaine region fabricated their own "Spanish destiny" by envisioning a major route from the heart of the Common Market at Brussels and Amsterdam down through Paris, Bordeaux, across the mountains at Hendaye to Madrid, Portugal, and North Africa. Toulouse and the Midi-Pyrénées championed a Mediterranean network against this threat to its own Spanish ambitions. Henri Sarramon reminded his public that the ancient road to Compostella forked at Bordeaux and went down to Toulouse, the route de Narbonne and across Perthus to Barcelona.[16]

This Mediterranean alternative was pressed even further when Toulouse public authorities began envisioning a water channel that extended from the Ruhr in Germany to the Rhône River Valley and then through a system of canals down to Sète that linked up with the Canal du Midi. Highway systems were drawn up that began at Hamburg and Geneva, passed through Clermont Ferrand and down the Midi-Pyrénées to Rodez, Toulouse, Tarbes, and Gibraltar. Imaginary lines crisscrossed planning maps with increasing fury as local and state elites attempted to remold regional geography into modern capitalist form. Toulouse's main concern, however, remained improving its highway connections with Spain, since most wares traveled by truck over the Pyrenees Mountains. The largest projects envisioned were two three-mile tunnels through the mountains at Puymorens and Salau in the department of the Ariège just south of Toulouse.[17] In one imperial engineering feat, 2,000 kilos of dynamite were used to blast a road through the mountains at Gavarine. Opening up the trans-Pyrenean routes was reckoned essential to any hope of industrializing Toulouse or renovating local handicrafts. Nothing would stand in the way of expanding markets.

Finally, in October 1970, a commercial agreement was signed between Spain and the European Economic Community that inaugurated commercial relations between them. The accord set up preferential high tariffs on all goods entering Spain from the European Economic Community in order to protect Spanish industry and agriculture from a flood of Community products. But despite this obstacle, the possibility opened for Toulouse to realize, finally, the dream of becoming Spain's main trading partner within the Common Market. Between 1968 and 1975, trade between the Midi-Pyrénées region and Spain quadrupled in value. But the Spanish market did not precipitate the economic prosperity that had so long captured the hopes of the Toulouse business community. Initially, Spanish imports into the Toulouse region during this period jumped by 400 percent. They consisted mostly of machine tools, hosiery, home appliances, motorbikes, furniture, shoes, and agricultural products. These were precisely the same commodities Toulouse hoped to offer. In contrast, the growth in exports to Spain was far less spectacular, around 80 percent.

The balance of trade was still positive for the Midi-Pyrénées, but sales to Spain were initially about the same as they were in all the French regions.[18] Most of the exports were agricultural products and raw materials, as well as semifinished goods that were then finished in Spain and sold back to the Toulouse region, often in direct competition with local industries. This situation prevailed in the leather and shoe industries, textiles and clothing, and the paper and carton industries. It was the case regardless of the fact that the customs duties for each of these sectors varied, and in the case of leather and shoes were actually quite low.[19] Rather than achieving some harmony and coordination of specialized production with Spanish industry, the handicrafts of the Toulouse region found themselves undercut in their own local market by rival industries just across the border. The sweat shops of Barcelona and Madrid proved to be stiff competition.

The most important exports to Spain from the city of Toulouse were from the two leading export industries, aircraft and chemical fertilizers. The other industries that benefited most from Spanish trade were the city's paper and carton manufacturers and especially the milk-processing plants that provided fresh milk daily to Catalonia and the Basque country. Henri Sarramon acidly remarked that "the only things the Midi-Pyrénées and Spain exchange are oranges and milk."[20] On the other hand, to everyone's surprise, by 1967 the southwest was selling more to the European Community than it was buying, due largely to the demand for the region's agricultural and processed food products, its textiles, and its footwear. At Toulouse itself, shops fabricating small machine and mechanical apparatus and those specializing in food products chalked up 14 percent of the city's European export sales.[21] But the profits from this traffic with the EEC were hardly enough to ignite the city's economy. The *pays toulousain* represented only 2 percent of French exports.

Business and public officialdom launched exhaustive campaigns during the 1970s to persuade small producers to enter the export market. The Nationale Compagnie Française d'Assurance pour le Commerce Extérieur (COFACE), the Ministry of Commerce, the local customs office, the Chambre des Métiers and trade unions, and the local banks all established extensive informational programs, services for contacts in foreign countries, and aid in the administration of foreign accounts. All of it was directed specifically at the *patronat*. The Chamber of Commerce evolved in tandem with the shift toward European-wide trade and capitalist logistics. As a local institution, it adjusted and framed modernization within the context of the vernacular setting. The Chamber offered a complete package of foreign-trade assistance to the small proprietors of Toulouse. It offered help with contract negotiations, setting up financing, and contracting transit agents. In 1970 the Chamber organized its first annual conference on exporting and even established prizes for *les meilleurs exportateurs*. Finally, through the Chamber's efforts, exporter "clubs" were created that organized field trips to foreign countries to establish business contacts. By 1976, foreign trade had become such a local fixation that it was included as one of the primary goals of the Seventh Regional Plan for the Midi-Pyrénées. The plan instituted a series of export incentives for small businesses that included financial aid, tax credits, and subsidies. It organized a program for "new exporters" that included contacts with the French Center for Foreign Commerce and other national organizations for foreign trade.[22]

But to the dismay of the business community, despite all these administrative exertions, sales to Spain began to decline during the 1970s, and by 1976 the Midi-Pyrénées was buying more from Spain then it was selling.[23] The deficit in the trade balance and the fact that Spain represented so little of the region's foreign commerce destroyed any further ambitions for Toulouse as a Mediterranean commercial capital and the EEC's gateway to the Iberian peninsula. There appeared to be little advantage in the city's location along the Spanish border. Six other regions of France, among them Aquitaine and Bretagne, exported more to Spain than did the Midi-Pyrénées. Bordeaux's route to Compostella was simply more profitable than the road through Toulouse.

The problem was not limited to the collapse of the Spanish export market, however. By 1976 exports in general from the Midi-Pyrénées began to deteriorate due in part to an abnormal drought in the region and to the depreciation of the franc during the recession. But public officialdom suspected that it was more a matter of habitual, narrow-minded provincialism. The city's small producers were simply unable to keep up with cheap textiles, clothing, and shoes produced not only in Spain, but in Italy, Greece, Eastern Europe, and South America. The language used by petty producers themselves was imbued with an apprehensive, battle-like quality. Textile manufacturers complained of cheap Italian wool fabrics and the "brutal import" of cotton jean material from the Third World. Hosiery and shoe manufacturers were "menaced" by six million pairs of footwear imported from Israel. Imported Polish socks sold at just over a franc a pair while the region's homemade variety cost over six francs a pair. Under these conditions it was difficult for small-time manufacturers to hold on to their own tried-and-true local market, much less export to foreign countries. The leather industry, for example, lost its crucial trade with West Germany to factory-produced leather goods from the Third World.[24]

All of the various local trade syndicates sent out a unified hue and cry for protection against cheap imports by the application of Article 107 of the Treaty of Rome. They demanded an end to French price controls. They called for state measures to preserve traditional French production. They generally saw their difficulties provoked by the decline of the franc on the international market, high salaries and heavy tax obligations, and severe competition from aggressive foreign governments willing to support traditional industries while the Fifth Republic of de Gaulle did everything to undermine them. By 1978, the majority (65 percent) of Toulouse's total export market involved products produced by its three modern industries: aviation, chemical fertilizers, and electronics. The city's customary specializations played only a minor role in foreign trade. Approximately 600 businesses at Toulouse were involved in the export market, and for most of them sales were extremely limited. An even more frustrating side to this feverish attempt at global capitalism was that over 70 percent of the trade was done with only five countries, with West Germany and Italy the largest markets for local goods.[25]

In assessing the causes behind the debilitation of foreign trade, members of the Toulouse Chamber of Commerce concluded: "The struggle against this 'savage' competition seems impossible . . . due to the fact that our businesses are oriented around quality production, a wide range of goods, and regional specialties." The difficulties were cast in terms of the gulf between the traditional weight of skilled production within business culture and the growing supremacy of skilled managerial expertise within the modern economy.

> The problem is not about producing excellent *confits* or exceptional *foies gras:* it is about familiarity with foreign sales. Knowing how to export is not an easy thing. To small businessmen exporting still appears dangerous and too complicated; their lack of information, the complexities of representation, and the formalities of filing orders add to financial problems of all types and to the fear of change.[26]

The apprehension in these public pronouncements soared because the drop in foreign trade and the failure of the Spanish export market made the commercial failings of the city's industry agonizingly apparent just as

Spain requested entry into the Common Market in June 1977. The specter of Toulouse flooded with Spanish goods and Spanish labor once tariff and immigration barriers disappeared was enough to reverse the general disposition toward cooperation and congeniality. Staunch opposition to Spanish inclusion in the EEC was suddenly the conviction of the Toulousains. The entire business community suffered from a severe form of collective neurosis over this highly volatile issue. The Pyrenees Mountains were visually transformed into a "great wall" protecting Toulouse from the Spanish peril that would mean the city's doom. At the very least, if the Toulousains could not stop the entry of Spain into the European Economic Community, they demanded protective tariffs to ensure their economic security. Even regional Prefect Tony Roche admitted that while it was difficult to refuse association with Spain, "What other choices have we besides closing up, withdrawing into ourselves to meet the assault of this new competition . . . We certainly feel the necessity of preserving the soul and personality of our country and the interests of our citizens."[27]

In 1978, the French government stepped into the crisis and, in typical form, offered spatial planning as a way to extricate Toulouse and its region from impending commercial oblivion. President Giscard d'Estaing announced the creation of yet another regional development plan for "the Great Southwest"—an invented geographic unit comprising the three regions bordering Spain: Aquitaine, Languedoc-Roussillon, and the Midi-Pyrénées. Its purpose was to force economic adjustments to Spanish competition through state planning and subsidization. The first page of the plan bluntly stated: "What the southwest lacks is a tissue of dynamic business. In their place, the state is ready to take on responsibility for the future of the southwest."[28]

The Conversion of Mentality

The rather contemptuous paternalism of this rescue operation disclosed the friction between perceived notions of provincial temperament and the idea of a national culture in France. Collective French identity was to be forged out of the dynamic of modernization and the virtues of adaptability and competitiveness. The pettyfogging attachment to outdated regional economic customs threatened the viability of the nation. France would find itself by expunging these passé traits and embracing the great currents of progress and modernization that animated the postwar world. Even regionalism itself was to be appropriated as rationalized economic space within a universe defined by commodity production, accumulation, and market control. A cartography of modernization was to supplant the older forms of particularism. If the small producers of Toulouse would not adhere to the new faith, they were simply to be abrogated as obsolete to the renewed sense of French cultural integrity.

The greatest assault against traditional economic culture was led by Charles de Gaulle and the *dirigiste* state of the 1960s—just as France joined the no-holds-barred competition of the Common Market. The family-owned *atelier* and boutique certainly did not conform to de Gaulle's vision of a dynamic, modern France capable of taking up its proper role as a global economic power. In 1960 de Gaulle appointed a special commission of experts to study the obstacles to economic expansion and to recommend proposals for a complete liberalization of the economy. The Armand-Rueff Committee produced a catalogue of the debilitating rigidities and regulations that obstructed market mechanisms, artificially held up prices and held down productivity, and clogged the distribution system. The Committee recommended a complete dismantling of the trade protectionism that had, as de Gaulle put it, "isolated and lulled (France) while vast currents of trade energized the world market." The Toulouse Chambre Syndicale de la Nouveauté immediately condemned the Armand-Rueff report as a menace—for good reason, according to local opinion. Its judgment inaugurated the government's program for a massive purge of the country's industrial and commercial structure. Simply put, the Gaullist state directed all of its planning efforts during the 1960s toward big business, toward advanced technology, and toward promoting mergers. Stripped of their protective cover, specialized local shops were left to the perils of the open market and their collective angst over exporting. The pressures of competition would complete the dirty work of elimination. The *grands commis* anticipated that the old mentalities would simply disappear along with them.

To carry out the state's modernization program, the Third and, particularly, the Fourth and Fifth Plans (1958–1970) that covered the period of de Gaulle's presidency were vastly expanded in both their methods and scope. Highly technical, increasingly oriented toward rationalized targets and projections for every sector of economic life, they were an ongoing epistle of progress and economic change. One can hear the battle over the decline or rejuvenation of France, the victory of progress, in a grand state narrative replete with its own signs and signature jargon: *planification, l'impératif industriel, l'aménagement du territoire, grands projets,* to give but a few examples.[29] As such, the plans were highly political documents in that, under de Gaulle's charge, planning became not just a technical operation managed by civil servants but a mechanism for carrying out the government's modernist economic and social mandates.

Much of the real work of the Commissariat Général du Plan was accomplished by a series of "modernization commissions" for various sectors of the economy. In 1961, the commission on the artisanat recommended vigilant attention to adapting French artisans to the rigors of the free market. Second, it endorsed collective action on the part of the Chambre des Métiers and the unions, as well as by the government, to resolve the impediments to apprenticeship training and to technical innovations.[30] The report essentially augured compliance with the state's program of economic modernization. This was made even more obvious in the comprehensive reform of the artisan trades issued by the government in March 1962. The artisan movement had demanded an update of the Statute of the Artisanat throughout the 1950s, largely as a form of protection against the winds of modernization that were eroding their influence. When the state finally consented, however, artisan crafts were effectively reshaped to fit technocratic norms. The 1962 decree shifted the definition of the artisan from the individual to the enterprise. Businesses employing fewer than five salaried workers and manufacturing certain products within the state's nomenclature of economic activities were designated as a *secteur des métiers*.[31] In other words, the social category of artisan was replaced by the rationalized economic category of production. The decree essentially removed any further question as to where the petty producers fit into the fabric of French society as a social class. Instead, it submerged the issue in the depoliticized economic discourse of modernism. The objectivity conferred upon the technical categories of economic planning replaced the process of sociopolitical negotiation. At the same time, the 1962 reform answered the overtures for protection with an unequivocal stance for the free exercise of the various *métiers* within an open market economy.

Mayor Bazerque's municipal economic programs followed along in step with the French government's guidelines for social removal and *aménagement du territoire*. Toulouse was to be remolded into a *métropole d'équilibre*, a research and development factory of scientists, researchers, and engineers churning out trailblazing technological marvels. The orientation of public policy was toward welcoming decentralized businesses that would reenergize the economy and spawn the great industrialization of Toulouse. DATAR "missionaries" were sent down from Paris to oversee the conversion of the city. They were installed at the prefecture on the place Saint-Etienne under the title of "Regional Economic Mission." There they coordinated the central administration's plans and "facilitated innovations." In 1967 DATAR chief Jérôme Monod himself arrived at Toulouse to preach the government's gospel of industrialization and the need to create a lush manufacturing environment out of an underdeveloped wasteland. His "four essential conditions" for the transformation of Toulouse would be reincarnated as the bedrock for the city's Livre Blanc: the creation of industrial zones, the building of infrastructure, the conversion of local mentality, and *formation des hommes*.[32] Planning sights were set over the utopian horizon in the suburbs. It was there that industrial parks would welcome pioneering entrepreneurs up to date on the newest production and sales strategies.

By the early 1970s, four industrial zones comprising roughly eighty-seven hectares had been laid out by the Livre Blanc along the periphery of the city. Toulouse's one original industrial zone, Le Chapitre just across from the ONIA plant, was expanded southward during the 1960s with two further land purchases along the route d'Espagne. These were developed as the industrial precincts of Thibaud and Bois Vert that would welcome chemical manufacturers. The Montaudran industrial park to the east was reserved for attendants to the Rangueil-Lespinet complex. Near the airport, Saint-Martin-du-Touch was set aside for aircraft construction. The Le Mirail industrial zone was scheduled for *arriviste* electronic companies. This spatial coding was meant to introduce a new business *cadre* into the community, one that was consciously disassociated and segregated from the disappointing influences of the *petits patrons* of the central districts. The traditional small shops stubbornly embedded in the interior of derisive old Toulouse were essentially blackballed. While petty producers listened to endless state sermons on the efficacy of unfettered competition, firms courageously undertaking decentralization to the "underdeveloped southwest" were awarded generous state development grants that subsidized 25 percent of their investment.

The impact of the strident new public policy on the Toulouse business community was tangled and in a certain sense ambiguous. Once the institutional moorings preserving their status were removed, Toulouse's smallest and most vulnerable manufactories fizzled against the cheap, trendy merchandise offered by the European Community and the Third World. During the ten-year period between 1962 and 1972, *micro-ateliers* that depended solely on family labor decreased, both in number and in their influence within the city's business community. From a high of nearly half of the city's industrial ventures, they represented only about 40 percent by 1972.

Shops employing one to five salaried workers closed their doors as well. On balance, Toulouse lost nearly 1,000 small businesses on the fringe of production.[33]

From the point of view of the modernizers, Toulouse had been freed from the grip of the *artisans-patrons* least willing and least able to tackle the rigors of a modern consumer economy. Nonetheless, there remained an underlying strata of *micro-ateliers* in all the local industries that seemingly weathered any storm and belied all efforts to expunge them. Metallurgical, carpentry and furniture-making, clothing and textile shops continued to produce for a limited market, with more or less marginal businesses blended with legitimate companies. Their tenacity and adaptability underscored the simplistic, largely condemnatory quality of the technocratic verbal assault on "Malthusianism." About 4,300 of these shops still found shelter in the red brick buildings of central Toulouse during the late 1960s and early 1970s. Virtually all of the smallest textile, garment, shoe, and hosiery manufacturers, all of the furniture makers, and the small producers in the food industry continued to practice their *métiers* along the city's ancient arteries.[34] Those without financial reserves or those unable to ferret out a niche in the global marketplace eventually disappeared. Other companies battened down against the market fluctuations or modernized their production. Machine-shop operators and metallurgists with their own equipment did particularly well servicing transport vehicles. Skilled electricians and mechanics opened appliance, television, and automobile repair shops. Even small producers in the food-processing and garment industries hung on in the old neighborhoods despite the vast forces of suburbanization transforming the fabric of the city.

The most important representatives of this world of *petits travailleurs indépendants* were in the building construction trade. By their number and by their influence they embodied what remained of the work and values of the traditional Occitan petty-producer class. Or, perhaps more appropriately, the builders of Toulouse became distinguished, somewhere in the collective imagination, as the figures most associated with *la ville rose*. Well over a third of the businesses with a handful of employees on the payroll were in this field of work, over 1,600 shops.[35] As a perpetually shifting undercurrent of independent specialists, they fashioned the tile, brick, and plaster that historically distinguished the city's built environment and endowed it with such an intense visual imagery. They worked it with their trowels and levels and an experienced eye for line and curve. For many, and certainly for themselves, small building contractors represented the spirit of enterprise, the Proudhonian pride of independent labor, that were core elements of regional legacy: "In response to those who accuse the artisanat of a shortsighted corporatism, the builders of Toulouse offer a solid professional organization, free and independent labor, and a sincere willingness to adapt themselves to modern economic life."[36] Perhaps more than in any other of the city's diverse assortment of trades, builders understood their craft and their own identity within the mix of cultural and visual impressions invented for traditional Toulouse.

While the construction frenzy at Toulouse lasted, that is, until the late 1960s, these denizens of local construction dogma fared well, as did everyone in the building industry. There were more people busily constructing the new Toulouse than was the case for any other urban building program in France. The local bonanza was so robust that no matter what their size, all companies and all fashions of work profited. But the stumbling block for local craftsmen, as in all of the local trades, still lay in adapting to new techniques and styles. The generously endowed public-housing projects sprouting up around Toulouse favored large-scale contracts for the massive prefabricated structures in cement and plaster that symbolized the state's vision of modernity. They were, in truth, far cheaper than hand-worked brick and tile. There were efforts among local contractors to respond to modern building form by retooling and purchasing new equipment. These exertions were encouraged, and in part subsidized, by regional officials, the Fédération Nationale des Artisans du Batiment, as well as by the local union and the Chambre des Métiers. Marcel Dauriac, for instance, whose carpenter grandfather had been prominent in the *compagnonnage* of Toulouse during the nineteenth century, revitalized the family's carpentry business by introducing the new technique of lamellation and specializing in the construction of public sports arenas and sports equipment. In 1965 the business was producing 30 million dollars' worth of sales with a workforce of thirty.[37] Nonetheless, lucrative government contracts were often simply beyond the capacity of the city's independent freelancers. Despite the panoply of opportunities, they still dealt with the same predicament over modernization that plagued the more depressed crafts. Over 200 small contracting businesses failed between 1966 and 1972.

Needless to say, the windfall opportunities enticed outside contractors who had little trouble making peace with modern building design. Four large construction companies had already moved to Toulouse during the 1930s. Then, after 1954, Italian and Spanish contractors moved into the city in the hopes of landing work on an HLM project or on the new universities. By investing in general contracting, rather than in specialized tasks, they quickly established sizable companies with crews manned by unskilled North African immigrants and Italian or Spanish laborers paid paltry wages.[38] The Deromedi Brothers, who built the notorious eighteen-story high-rise on the Allée Charles-de-Fitte, were the most successful example. About twelve local companies, including Charles André and Malpel, were involved in the construction of the apartment towers for the Saint-Georges redevelopment project. But large French companies from outside the region, cashing in on urban renewal programs, were prominent. Nationwide general contractors, such as Balancy, Bouygues, or SPIE Batignolles, which opened a sprawling workyard in the new suburban industrial park of Bois Vert, quickly absorbed a substantial part of the construction workforce. Particularly by 1967, when construction work began to level off, many of the local craftsmen were simply absorbed into their work crews or made money subcontracting with them for temporary jobs. The end result was that by the early 1970s the seven largest companies at Toulouse employed over half the industry. Six of these well-financed giants were owned by investors from outside the southwest. Only one of the firms was actually Toulousain in origin.

The reaction to this crisis was one of the most emotionally charged controversies at Toulouse, precisely because it represented the visceral struggle between vernacular business culture, local images of urban place and economic life, and modernization. For public elites bent on progress, the small-time carpenters, tilers, and plasterers of Toulouse were glaring specimens of the lame-duck economy that held back the city's claim as a modern industrial capital. They were little more than haughty craft drones squabbling over the right to keep themselves poor and backward. They were the last relics of a way of life condemned to death by its own obstinacy. Whether they were willing to accept it or not, construction in brick and tile was prohibitively overpriced, an extravagance for public building. Their presence was even more annoying to modernist sensibilities because it was precisely these small building contractors who were the most vocal in justifying indigenous business practices and local economic rights. Skilled craftsmen in the building trades steadfastly defended their construction methods, arguing the importance of quality housing and insisting that building was an art. Vernacular styles in brick and tile personified local heritage and independent labor. They proclaimed mass-produced prefabricated structures as "popular housing," poor in quality and hideous in appearance—at once threatening their own and the city's historic identity. The conclusion was that the "prefab" substitutes for tasteful Toulouse building were triumphant only because they were foolishly blessed with bounteous government solicitation. The dispute over building techniques and architectural style thus embodied the apprehension over the forces of monopoly capitalism and state regulation meant to annihilate the *petits peuples* and the economic customs they practiced.

A variety of government measures were promulgated during the 1960s that offered, at least in theory, a life raft to any craftsman ready to skirt the reefs of disaster by taking up the challenge of modernization. The qualifications for the title of *maître-artisan* were tightened up by the 1962 artisanal reform. Apprenticeship training was expanded. At Toulouse, the Chamber of Métiers worked in conjunction with the Chamber of Commerce to improve educational resources, widen access to the *brevet professionnel* and the *brevet de maîtrise,* and facilitate technical and business management training. However, small producers themselves did not necessarily conceptualize their economic misfortune in terms of inadequate skills. Many refused to undertake the master or apprenticeship license programs because of the cost and because they deemed the training inappropriate to their daily working needs. Cloaked in the stature of shop savvy and experience, workers avoided association with the "student residue" of the technical schools. They learned their trade in the *atelier* and hired workers directly through their neighborhood and business networks. Public authorities, and the city plan for Toulouse for that matter, continued to harp on *formation professionnelle* and adjustments in mentality and attitudes. On the other hand, small producers pointed to economic policy as the culprit in their demise. Competition from foreign imports, the lack of available capital, and the constraints of government price controls were the essential preoccupations of the *patrons,* according to the local hosiery union. As well as decrying the "dumping" of foreign products onto the domestic market and the tightening bind of price regulations and high social welfare payments, small businessmen demanded state aid for machinery and new technology in order to compete.[39]

In truth, funding for the *micro-atelier* was not easy to obtain. The main public and private credit institutions in Toulouse were merely branches of large Parisian financial houses. Few Parisian bankers were amenable to subsidizing a marginal business in the remote southwest that could not even match part of the loan with its own resources. Sociétes de Développement Régional set up by the government in 1955 were intended to alleviate the problem of financial discrimination against small shops. Toulouse's version, the Société Toulousaine Financière et Industrielle du Sud-Ouest, or TOFINSO, loaned millions of francs in credit each year. But from its inception, TOFINSO invested in larger companies on sound financial footing, firms that would generally be acceptable credit risks at any bank. These were the businesses chosen as exemplars of a modernized France. TOFINSO rarely descended into the firmament of borderline small ventures.[40] The point was not to shore this residue up but to get rid of it.

TOFINSO also exemplified the implicit political tensions bubbling just beneath the veneer of modernization during the 1960s. The technocratic narrative on business *mentalité* and the conversion to contemporary Fordist practices was reproduced in an endless stream of state documents and public homilies. But it barely cloaked the authority of de Gaulle and the Fifth Republic that lay just beneath the discourse. This gave it an abrasive edge bound to incense local political sentiment. Whatever fracturing may have occurred within the "reactionary left" expression of local politics during the 1950s and 1960s, Toulouse remained steadfastly anti-Gaullist, so much so that local political analysts referred to the "allergic response to Gaullism" as a "syndrome peculiar to the *midi toulousain."*[41] Among the many images of Toulouse was that of *le capitale antigaulliste*. By 1965 Bazerque's shaky Socialist-center coalition had broken off all relations with the likes of Jacques Maziol and Charles de Gaulle. Every national referendum offered to the electorate under the Fifth Republic went down to defeat at Toulouse. Within the vernacular setting, the imperial crusade to modernize and control urban life could easily appear to be a Gaullist political strategy for conquering a contemptuous left-wing city. The repudiation of any role for small independent producers in France's future and the government campaign against customary business practices smacked of an assault against his old adversaries by the General himself. Indeed Peter Gourevitch has argued that state regulatory and administrative centralization under the Fifth Republic was in large part provoked by a "fear of the left"—particularly the kind of leftist politics practiced by local elites.[42]

By the end of the 1960s of course, the *dirigisme* and rigid modernist stipulations of the planned economy provoked reaction from a wide variety of bitterly alienated French. Centralization and regulatory heavy-handedness were the maxims of Gaullism's triumphant ten years between 1958 and 1968. The exaggerated "statism" of French Fordism was bound eventually to have repercussions. Particularly in places like Toulouse, where state modernization represented such an inversion of local culture, the drama of the *grands commis* forcing modernization on a cantankerous *France profonde* left plenty of room for angry reprisals.

Nineteen sixty-eight at Toulouse materialized much as it did in Paris and the other large cities of the provinces. There were, however, a few distinctive features of the Toulouse revolt. First, the protests at the University of Toulouse were among the first to occur, just on the heels of the far more renowned struggle at Nanterre. The student movement began on April 23 with a protest march at the Faculty of Letters in the old medieval Bourg against the Vietnam War and against the attempted assassination of German student leader Rudi Dutschke. By the 25th, a student "general assembly" at the University's amphitheatre ended in violence and the evacuation of the Faculty of Letters by the CRS riot squads. It was a replication of the events at Nanterre just a few days before. Second, from the onset, the student protests at Toulouse received the support of the city's working classes. Among the first to come out publicly in support of the student movement in the early days of May was the Union Syndicale CGT du Bâtiment. The leading protagonists in the allegory of *la ville rose,* the builders of Toulouse who had, perhaps, been most caught up in the dispute over modernizing the city, descended into the streets first against de Gaulle's regime. "Indignant and angry" over the police brutality and repression used to mask the failure of the regime, the local Builders' Union called for a total worker mobilization against Gaullist policy.[43]

On May 13 over 40,000 workers and students marched from the Place Jeanne d'Arc to the Place du Capitole, calling for the resignation of de Gaulle. At the head of the massive procession, linked arm and arm, were Mayor Louis Bazerque girded in tricolor sash, and leaders of the CGT, the CFDT, and the Fédération de l'Education Nationale (FEN). Alongside were members of the Municipal Council and the Communist and Socialist parties, Jean Llante foremost among them, as well as deputies and senators from the Haute-Garonne. Against the celebrated pink and white facade of the Hôtel de Ville, the speakers reminisced about the last time such a tremendous crowd had gathered at the Capitole roaring the name of de Gaulle: "Ironically, in August 1944, Toulouse, resistant and courageous, had descended into the streets to salute de Gaulle as the head of liberated France. Much water has passed under the bridges of the Garonne since then. Our hopes have been dashed. Today, Toulouse cries out in fury!" Baghi of the CGT thundered out to the crowd that "In 1958 the forces of Gaullism reduced the unions and the parties of the left to silence. Today, ten years later almost to the day, we are clearly confirmed in our belief that the government has unilaterally stood against us."[44] The 13th also marked the beginning of the workers' boycott at Toulouse. For France as a whole, the improvised general strike brought the political crisis to a head. At Toulouse, the vast majority of construction workers walked off their jobs to join the protest at the place du Capitole. Public utilities and transportation were completely closed. Virtually all hourly wage earners in the aircraft factories walked out.

The strike rapidly closed the city and began the long month of paralysis that brought France to a virtual standstill. By May 23, some 27,000 construction workers were out on strike, the largest and most influential of the worker-solidarity movements. The Builders' Union sanctioned all protest and strike initiatives. Construction workers staged a protest motorcade of about 200 cars and 300 mopeds that jammed the narrow streets around Saint-Sernin Cathedral amidst total confusion and wound its way to the rue Deville and the offices of the Chambre Patronale. There, union leader Rocchia demanded the convocation of a bipartisan commission to resolve the grievances and low pay endured by the city's construction crews. Work on Le Mirail ceased. Toulouse truckers blocked the main roads into the city. SNCF was completely shut down. Sud-Aviation, Bréguet Aviation, and ONIA were all occupied. At the peak of the protest in Toulouse against the Gaullist regime, approximately 100,000 workers walked out. Their demands consisted of a characteristic list of grievances to be rectified by higher salaries and full employment.

The most prominent of the mandates, however, was the guarantee and extension of union liberties and the CFDT's insistence on some measure of *autogestion* within the workplace. On May 24, 8,000 protesters marched through Toulouse shouting "Power to the workers!" "de Gaulle to the factory!" The Hôtel de Ville was hung in red and black flags. Mayor Bazerque announced his support for the Municipal Council's formal condemnation of the government's brutality against the students in Paris. Led by Jean Llante and Jean Doumeng of the Communist Party, as well as Baghi and Duthil of the CGT, 4,000 workers marched down the boulevards to the Bourse du Travail the following day, demanding a guarantee of union rights and the vindication of the working class by progressive social-reform programs. In a charged atmosphere, another 50,000 workers and students paraded down the rue de Metz and the rue d'Alsace-Lorraine with a host of local political luminaries and municipal councillors, shouting "de Gaulle to the museum!" as they passed near the Musée des Augustins. At the place du Capitole, Georges Gorsse, general secretary of the FEN, called for the union of all workers, peasants, educators, and students against the hostility of Gaullist power and capitalism: "We are here to create a new society— democratic and socialist. This is the end of capitalist exploitation and oppression."[45]

The Municipal Council's motion of censure against the government had triggered a further breach within the jittery centrist alliance constructed around Louis Bazerque. Since 1967, the main parties of the left had been affiliated in the *Fédération Départmentale de la Gauche Démocrate et Socialiste de la Haute-Garonne* (FGDS), which gave its full endorsement to the student and worker agitation. Its tongue-lashing of Gaullism underscored the crisis of modernism: "the regime has, during ten years of power, remained mindless to popular aspirations and revealed itself definitively incapable of solving the disorders created by modern transformation." The FGDS pledged itself to regional liberty as the key to economic revival. The splinter Parti Socialiste Unifié (PSU) advocated "profound structural modifications in French society," including *autogestion* and local control over economic growth and the resolution of regional underdevelopment. Calling for a common left-wing program, Jean Llante and the Communists augured the democratization of planning and the economy. Bazerque himself pronounced the street protests to be "a prerevolutionary, if not revolutionary, situation."

This mix of left-wing parties, momentarily aligned in the revolt, offered the motion to the Municipal Council denouncing the government's odious police repression and its refusal to repent in the face of popular indignation. It called for a complete vindication of the rights of the laboring classes as the only way to social peace. It berated the "false regionalization, pretending to be democratic, that held the local collectivities in the tightening noose of centralized control." The Independents, however, led by mayoral adjunct Pierre Baudis, presented their own text, calling, more conservatively, for social peace and new elections. The Socialist initiative carried the day, although it severed the affiliation between Bazerque and Baudis. Nevertheless, Bazerque and the Socialists remained diffident and approved an aid package of 300,000 francs for striking workers in the "Municipal Council's ancient tradition of sympathy for the cause of working-class struggle."[46]

While Georges Pompidou, Georges Séguy of the CGT, and representatives of the *patronat* sweated out negotiations in Paris to end the general strike sweeping France, the local unions at Toulouse refused to accept the compromises offered by the government. By May 31, however, the CGT announced its decision to retreat in the face of de Gaulle's offer of immediate elections. The unions at Toulouse followed along, little by little, with the CGT's settlement, convinced by further pay concessions within the Grenelle Accords and by police raids against factory occupations. By early June, railroads and bus service, gas and electricity, and mail delivery had all been restored in the city. Building construction projects were moving forward. The city's metallurgists and aircraft workers held out the longest. But by June 8, the "social crisis" at Toulouse was over. The "cultural crisis," however, continued unabated. About 4,000 students, workers, and journalists demonstrated outside the ORTF offices on the allée Jean-Jaurès in support of its staff boycott. On the 12th, Toulouse experienced its own "night of the barricades" when a student march at the place du Capitole ended in violent clashes with the CRS. The students at the University of Toulouse held out until mid-June, when the police finally raided the faculties and ceremoniously dismantled the red banners hanging from the buildings. By the June 23 legislative elections, order had essentially been restored at Toulouse.

The elections themselves came as a painful shock to a city government that had allied itself with the "revolutionary forces" marching through the streets and to workers who had only slowly accepted the compromises offered by union leaders. Two Gaullist deputies were elected from Toulouse from the northern and southern precincts, while Independent Pierre Baudis defeated Socialist André Rousselet in the central city. Only the western districts, including Saint-Cyprien and Saint-Gaudens, remained faithful to the Socialist cause (electing Jean Dardé and Hippolyte Ducos). This transitory Gaullist triumph in an anti-Gaullist stronghold decidedly thickened the drama of Toulouse municipal politics. It forced a solemn scrutiny of the policies and leadership within the local left-wing camp. More immediately, however, Louis Bazerque, the flamboyant commander who had led his local Socialist forces through the thicket of Gaullist management during the 1960s, found himself increasingly isolated. The 1968 revolt had further dulled his pivotal alliance with the political center and their new champion Pierre Baudis. On the other hand, his Socialist pedigree had been badly tarnished by too-close association with precisely those Gaullist modernization schemes that had proved his own constituency's undoing. The vision of a renewed left-wing municipal coalition under his leadership rapidly began to evaporate.

After the events of May 1968 and the departure of de Gaulle, the Pompidou (1969–1974) and Giscard d'Estaing (1974–1981) administrations shifted the tone of the French government's approach to economic modernization. Georges Pompidou certainly abided by the ongoing technocratic epistle to national union through economic renewal. But there were subtle adjustments in method. First, the new president of the Republic abandoned de Gaulle's visionary slant on modernization and the deference to national prestige. He chose, instead, more practical goals of profits, competitiveness, and genuine prosperity. The reality of Pompidou's economic policy was bound to continue the squeeze on small businesses. But the contradiction between the government's desire for modernization by expunging "Malthusian" business interests and its need for the political support of precisely those social groups that composed those interests was, after the crisis of 1968, far more apparent. The protests of 1968 had marked a crisis in state-managed Fordism. It represented a rejection of the excessively imperial modernization programs carried out by Gaullist technocrats. It was a social movement against a "new France" that lacked any semblance of democratic participation by the young or by traditional social groups.[47] As a result, Pompidou was less anxious to modernize at the expense of French shop-keepers, craftsmen, and small businessmen. He struggled instead to steer a more balanced course, paraded under the banner of "The New Society," between economic restructuring and concessions to declining industries and social categories. Artisans and shopkeepers were granted improved access to social-security benefits and retirement systems. FDES loans were set aside for *petits travailleurs indépendants* in the underdeveloped regions. The Royer Law of 1973 specifically shielded the tiny workshops and groceries of France from the competition of supermarkets and big companies. In an effort to appease the clamor against regulatory centralization, the 1972 regional reform created elected regional Conseil Économiques et Sociaux, although their actual installation was slow and their powers limited.

Second, the oil crisis of 1973–74 vastly reduced the possibility of massive investments in modernization programs and regional development. The absorption with grand-scale planning during the 1960s had been built on an expanding economy. In the far more depressed economic atmosphere of the oil crisis, the government's policies were adapted to a stringent climate of recession, unemployment, and budget cuts. Under the Giscard d'Estaing administration that followed Pompidou's, the promotional buildup of provincial *métropoles d'équilibres* was tempered and the policy of state-assigned preferential *industries de pointe* forsaken. The high-tech juggernaut simply ran out of steam. Giscard expressed the view that modernization need not be at the expense of further social and economic dislocation. The *grands commis* continued its championship of economic modernization and the conversion of business mentality. Nevertheless, it was cultivated with moderation rather than with the smug dogmatism of the 1960s. The point was to avoid social conflict and to reconcile as many traditional social groups as possible to the winds of the future. The strategy for "underdeveloped regions" was shifted to saving jobs, cushioning declining economic sectors from the troubled international market, and promoting a dense network of small and medium-sized businesses. A recession-weary workforce redeployed through a system of small producers could sidestep the onerous stigma of high unemployment. It was clearly a step back from the state *dirigiste* practices of the "golden age" of capitalism.[48]

Government planners began offering a whole new policy agenda to the traditional industries. It was intentionally directed toward what was called the *petite et moyenne entreprise,* or the PME in the shorthand of public documents of the mid-1970s. The definition of the PME was notably fuzzy. It usually referred to companies employing a staff of at least ten, but the cutoff was precisely in the gray area of semiartisanal production. Hence, the PME often encompassed *"artisans dynamiques"* among its numbers. The more mundane term *artisanat* was generally conferred upon any business with fewer than ten employees. In any case, according to the reevaluated official dogma, small business need not be doomed by the forces of modern consumption patterns and the free market. There had been, according to the National Council on Regional Economies' report to the Midi-Pyrénées, too much hostility and suspicion between French small producers and the state planning agencies. A fresh sensitivity to their livelihood and to the role they played in regional and communal life was in order.[49] The PME could be resurrected within a diversified business web of reciprocating exchanges and subcontracting arrangements. This sudden attention given to small scale was a new concession to realities. In part it was a response to the passing of de Gaulle and his patronage of the dazzling creations of France's high-tech industries. They had fallen, like inflexible Goliaths, to the recessionary crisis. It was also a measure of the political settlement after the 1968 crisis, when the limits to modernist coercion became abundantly clear. Public documents were suddenly filled with glowing descriptions of the PME as the backbone of the French economy, capable of renovating and expanding the country's traditional industrial tissue.

What appeared to be only a matter of semantics was far more a question of social engineering. The term that dominated public discourse about France's forever problematic traditional economy remained the "metamorphosis of mentality." The most flaccid artisans and *patronat* had been removed from their entrenched positions by the pressures of international competition, the European Economic Community, and the recession. The survivors were hailed as modern company managers, offering the rewards of their creative individualism and the dexterity of small-scale specialized production to an inimical global marketplace. Public elites saw the question of the PME in terms of entrepreneurial attitudes and management strategies.

The social consciousness of the *artisanat* had been invented out of craft skills and a certain kind of populist independent-mindedness in daily work patterns. The modern small businessman was a new cultural identity that subsumed France's independent producers into a *cadre* wedded to contemporary capitalist ethics and regulation. It was an economic form of gentrification or, in the French, *embourgeoisement*. In the new myth created by public policy, the small proprietor was smart, naturally competitive, imbued with *élan vital*. Organizing production was to become the essential practice of this new man—the business virtuoso. The creed was labeled *direction participative aux objectifs,* or DPO, an ersatz version of American management practices that was exhaustively debated, between 1973 and 1975, in reference to the work of the Sudreau Commission on business reform. Time and skills were to be invested in the supervision of output, budgetary and accounting controls, market analysis, information gathering, and the adaptation of innovative techniques. It was defined in essence as an emerging French spirit, a "technology of excellence" not simply in terms of hardware but in realization, production, and business organization.

An arsenal of services flourished in support of the commercial know-how and financial savvy now deemed essential to business identity and achievement: advertising and marketing specialists, public relations and financial consultants, resources on commercial strategies and computer and telecommunication hookups. It was not simply the economic meaning behind these new categories of understanding that held sway but the vast range of psychological and sociocultural virtues conveyed in this search for a modern French identity. The small producer, who had hung on and remained largely outside the capitalist dynamic, was to be reeducated and linked up to a spreading web of overseers under the auspices of corporate-state control.

At Toulouse, a good share of this capitalist ethic was mediated through the Chamber of Commerce and business associations that struggled to convert the city's business culture. If nothing else they launched a bona fide anagrammatic binge. DPO teams such as APROMIP, ARIST, ADERMIP, and DRI introduced the pioneering doctrine among the PME.[50] APROMIP inaugurated "Marketing Industrie," a consortium of seventy local garment, textile, food-processing, and furniture companies that were introduced to the latest marketing and advertising strategies. ADERMIP undertook the daunting task of acquainting small businessmen with the applied research bonanza at the Rangueil-Lespinet scientific complex. The *Animateurs Industriels* were originally ten DPO sharpshooters at Toulouse responsible for detecting and analyzing the viability of local company projects and seeing them through as the equivalent of management gurus.

The most illustrious local practitioner of the "technology of excellence" was Claude Duffour, who became president of the Toulouse Chamber of Commerce in 1971. Duffour was the leading member of the city's one outstanding industrial bourgeois dynasty. His family's company, Duffour et Igon, had launched the city's chemical-pharmaceutical industry in 1900. He not only managed the historic firm but had also invested his inheritance in a computer company, Duffour Informatique, based in the Le Chapitre industrial park. Once empowered as commander of the city's business community, he immediately began preaching the gospel of modernization to the local fold. Under his leadership, the Chamber dramatically expanded its role in shaking up the local *patronat*. During a 1978 convention on subcontracting at Toulouse, Duffour lectured local firms:

> The economic future of France in large part depends on its small and medium-sized enterprises. I do not believe in a lack of creative spirit despite the difficulties facing small businesses. New generations abound with men of new ideas and action. The new spirit may not have infected more than a handful of firms, but it is spreading fast—you will see. A new, very different generation is emerging.[51]

Nonetheless, the chasm between this modernist discourse and the actuality of local business routines was often dramatic and irrefutable. The 1973–74 economic crash did indeed accelerate the demise of those small producers unable, due largely to ruthless market conditions, to weather the storm. The state seized the opportunity of the crisis to force the rationalization of the most traditional sectors of industry by severely restricting credit to marginal industries. Despite the symbolic offer of FDES loans, it became far more difficult to obtain credit in underdeveloped regions such as the Midi-Pyrénées, where small shops in traditional sectors prevailed. Liquidations at Toulouse multiplied sharply. The leather, clothing, and building industries were shaken not only by the crisis itself but by continued competition from the Third World and from French firms expanding their markets into the southwest as a way to counteract the constriction in demand. By 1975, roughly 2,000 to 2,300 shops that employed less than five workers remained, less than half the number that had been in business during the early 1960s. Local economists concluded that the effect of the recession was a selective and cruel purge of the weakest firms. The disappearance of the family-owned *micro-ateliers* hit the most vulnerable part of the economy:

artisans and workers in the habitual local industries whose income was meager and who had the most difficulty adapting their skills to modern needs.[52]

Building construction was one of the principal victims. Local contractors reprimanded the government for attempting to fight a recession without "building." They challenged conservative cutbacks with the city's effective Socialist remedy: Toulouse's mammoth public swimming pool, its library, and Jean Montariol's first public-housing projects were all constructed in the midst of the depression of the 1930s and had helped to absorb unemployment. They accused state administrators of placating them with a "parsimonious sprinkling" of development aid that produced nothing.[53] By the mid-1970s small contractors had formed alliances dubbed *"les compagnons"* as a shield against the crisis. They demanded that the government set aside a certain percentage of its construction contracts for the local building trade, which could then create the time-honored vision of *la ville rose* free from competition. At a local colloquium held in 1980 on the state of the Toulouse economy, *les compagnons* disrupted the orderly sessions arranged by public officials, leaping out of the audience, bellowing that bureaucrats could take a few pointers from the real decision makers in the economy, owners of local construction businesses. What was needed was a more dynamic *esprit d'entreprise* and less concern with the grandiose economic designs conjured up by high-minded technocrats.[54]

The passions of modernizers could be just as melodramatic. Regional subprefect Blanc stormed into the offices of the shocked Union Départmentale des Syndicats d'Entrepreneurs et d'Artisans du Bâtiment in 1975 and demanded that they change their attitudes immediately so they could reequip and respond to modern demands.[55] There was still work available in construction during the late 1960s and 1970s. But according to technocrats defending the future of France, the city was saturated with passé craftsmen technically unable, or worse, unwilling, to take on state construction projects. Local builders complained about unemployment, but there was constant demand for workers skilled in new techniques. Many of the state contracts were left open each year. It was hardly surprising that outside companies would fill the void left by the local *patronat's* obstinacy and their attachment to expensive local construction styles. Their craving for work was just a cry for sanctuary from the modernism that had long ago proved successful.

Yet hard as they tried to inculcate Toulouse business with the spirit and strategies needed to compete in the hardball global marketplace, the crusade was only partially effective. Whether French modernist values were coherently advanced through the city's subterranean network of artisanal and petit-bourgeois economic agents is very much open to question. Conclusions about any real structural change in Toulouse industry can only be made with careful restraint. Although some consolidation did take place, it was not of magisterial proportions—particularly considering the Promethean modernist drive exerted on behalf of industrial reordering. The industrial structure "modernized" only moderately.[56] A shift took place away from the independent proprietor toward what would essentially be considered small and medium-scale companies. The smallest categories of production, that is, artisan shops in the old districts of Toulouse, represented 43 percent of the city's industry in 1952. They continued to increase up to 1962, when they represented 47 percent of local industry, and then slid in number over the next ten years to 40 percent. These figures are dramatic as much for their stability as for any radical rupture in the local business culture. Public policy and market forces had clearly jolted the regional productive structure. But the customary image of the *petit travailleur indépendant* working out of a home or small rented *atelier* still remained, despite all efforts to efface it, an influential cultural and economic force in Toulouse. There was a fluid foundation of marginal producers that persisted intact throughout the *trentes glorieuses*. It was the 1973 recession that did them in. By the end of the crisis, they controlled only 25 percent of Toulouse manufacturing.

The traditional response to economic depression (which was, after all, not a new phenomenon to Toulouse) had been to seek refuge in the *micro-atelier*. But without institutional and political support, the economic pressures of the 1973 crisis proved pernicious to the loose federation of autonomous specialists that had always been the bedrock of the city's economy. Instead, they were incrementally merged into the salaried labor force and into the structure of a modern capitalist economy. Finding a job with one of the big construction companies or garment mills was a smarter choice than facing the hardships of surviving alone. Those *ateliers* that were left were far less influential in hiring new labor. In 1962, jobs were about equally divided among small, medium, and large businesses. By 1975 only 18 percent of the city's labor force found work within the shrunken network of small producers, while 50 percent were working in the aircraft, chemical, and garment plants.[57] Even more significantly, the traditional industries, in which small shops abounded, contributed far less to the city's economic productivity. In 1952 they were responsible for over 70 percent of the city's industrial sales. By 1975 they produced only 50 percent of sales. Small producers generated less than 1.5 percent of the city's industrial revenue.[58] In sum, even though the number of *patrons* and artisans remained almost constant between 1954 and 1975, their economic and social influence over urban life had dwindled. Toulouse had become a world of salaried employees and middle-class professionals.

Just the same, the city's vernacular economic community did not simply wither away under the competitive pressures of modernization and cyclical economic crises. What is perhaps most interesting was its ability to survive and adapt in the midst of what was plainly a hostile environment. The clothing industry, for example, underwent a clear process of rationalization and consolidation. Many of the ready-to-wear firms invested in new machinery, revamped their product lines, and began selling on the mass consumer market. The largest of them were the Etablissements Ramonéde, which increased its sales twelvefold during the 1960s and built new factories in the suburban industrial zones of Colomiers-en-Jacca and Muret-Marclan, and Vêtements MAS, with its factory in the industrial zone of Thibaud. There were also nearly 100 medium-sized firms (Sarfati, Carcel, Guichard, Tricotage Toulousain among them) that represented the modernized *confection* industry. The success of Tricotage Toulousain was particularly noteworthy because it was right out of the annals of local history. The company was the original Maison Etcheparé established at Toulouse in the late nineteenth century. By the 1960s it was still owned and managed by the sons of the original founder. The family had completely retooled the firm into a showcase of modern hosiery production.

Examples of the local capacity to "modernize" could be found in shoe manufacturing, furniture making, the mechanical trades, and food processing. Even the notoriously sour building contractors, who were always on the front lines in the crusade against urban planning, hung on to a sizable share of construction, especially in the suburban housing market. They whetted their local networks, tailored their skills to contemporary demand, and signed on for public loans. Those with regular crews set up partnerships with real-estate promoters and architects, such as Maisons UNIC or Maisons PERRET, each of which built 100 suburban homes every year around Toulouse. Joseph Bixio, a North African who arrived in the city in 1963, opened his own plasterer's shop, producing custom-made items for a limited clientele. By the late 1960s, it was completely mechanized with a crew of thirty-five.

Amoung Bixio's masterpieces were a unique strip of molded plaster set into the flight simulator for the Concorde and custom-designed ceiling arches for the amphitheater of the Faculty of Science at Rangueil. But even those contractors with less distinguished records could still rely on a well-honed local web of real-estate backers, draftsmen, notaries, and licensing and permit bureaus that allowed them to stay in on the local construction market. In the food-processing industry, a Toulouse entrepreneur invented a new type of quick-cooking granulated rice, opened the firm SOCOPAN, and began selling the product throughout the European Community. These examples translate into an undistinguished, disregarded, but unmistakable shift in vernacular economic culture toward more stable small and medium-sized businesses with salaried workforces. It coincided with a fresh image of the artisan-proprietor as the manager of a firm with responsibility for positioning a product within the modern local, as well as global, marketplace. Fantasies of PMEs run by razor-sharp CEOs were given celebrity status in state parlance during the 1970s. But the shift in *mentalité*, the modernization of French identity, often took place in conventional, familiar ways within the context of vernacular culture.

Petty producers, whether dubbed *artisanat, petits patrons,* or PME—and the flux reveals the ongoing ambiguity in their social categorization—were never, of course, a homogeneous group in the first place. There were definitive internal cleavages. Unquestionably, part of the local business community at Toulouse exhibited a real resiliency and adaptability even without institutional support, tax exemptions, and protectionism. Some *artisans-patrons* paid the price of modernization with shop failures. But the marginality of business existence was, after all, an acknowledged component of the temporary production clusters upon which the municipal economy had historically been built. Others, however, defined and executed modernization as modest change designed not to overstep the bounds of customary doctrine. Some industrial restructuring did indeed take place. Isolated work became less realistic at Toulouse. More labor was drawn into the mass-production nexus. But a 1984 census report found that the Midi-Pyrénées was the French region least affected by industrial consolidation and most affected by local culture and values.[59] The *petite entreprise* still wielded considerable clout within the local economy. It consumed less capital than the large companies. It was capable of responding to market variations rapidly, if on a small scale. Small shops mobilized labor through informal local networks. They taught skills, leveraged professional standing in the community, and often furnished a jump into Toulouse's high-tech suburban plants. It was hardly the stuff of modernist mythology—at least as it was woven by state technocrats in their quest for the new France. But at this rather conventional level, local businesses formed an indispensable undercurrent of diversified, malleable production units that gave balance and depth to the urban economy.

All of this points to the conclusion that flexible, small-scale specialization was not simply a residual left over from the socioeconomic battles with modernization. Nor was it archaic. It embodied, instead, an alternative model of economic negotiation associated with perceived notions of regional culture and with a sense of habitability and urban space. Economic entitlement was distributed differently from that of the Fordist or Marxist model. Production and accumulation relied on economies of scale, modest machinery, and fluid social arrangements. Work habits were integrated into the wider routines of community and urban life rather than into the strict discipline of the factory setting. Production was absorbed into the vernacular setting rather than being divorced from it. The persistence of this alternative pattern of production demonstrates the heterogeneous nature of modernization and the variety of images and conceptual arrangements operating within it.

By 1978, with the worst of the recession over, the *artisanat* and the *petite entreprise* enjoyed something of a comeback at Toulouse, a clear indication of the sector's capacity to preserve itself, although not in some antiquated, passé form. Small firms were both transformed by and themselves acted upon the dominant model of state-capitalist economic restructuring. As a whole, vernacular business culture was simultaneously displaced by and preserved within modern capitalist forms.[60] Although the city's export market bumped along rather feebly, proprietors adapted to seeing themselves and the economy of Toulouse within a national and international context. Business elites took up the cause of modernization and, within the boundaries of local experience, shifted vernacular traditions toward capitalist norms. At the same time, modernization standards themselves were made more elastic by the process of ideological and political bargaining carried on with local culture. The most successful small businesses at Toulouse made the necessary changes within their means and found a niche for themselves within the modern economy. After all, the firm that won second prize in the Chamber of Commerce's 1970 contest for "the best exporter of the year" was the small Etablissement Dedieu that produced the cherished crystallized candy made from Toulouse violets.

Downtown Toulouse

Although *les petites entreprises* may have remained an aphorism on the Toulouse urban landscape, there was no denying they had lost their customary influence over the city's culture and its economy. The cohesiveness and habitability of the neighborhood system that nurtured the *petits travailleurs indépendants* had long since atrophied. By the early 1970s, its vitality had been drained by endless neglect. The vision of modern France held little but contempt for the archaic setting and social frictions of "bygone" urban places. Petit-bourgeois and working-class families spurned the dilapidated buildings and congestion that had become bywords for old Toulouse. Instead, they headed for the public-housing projects and tract homes blooming in the suburbs. The population of the historic districts fell from 41,000 in 1962 (when the effects of depopulation were just beginning) to 30,600 in 1975. By then central-city residents represented less than a quarter of the commune and only 6 percent of the metropolitan area.

Those steadfast city dwellers who persevered made their homes, as always, in the forsaken relics of Toulouse's noble past. The worst cases of building decay awaited the wrecking ball of a promoter anxious to get at the costly property under their foundation. In some cases, this *déracinement* extended, of course, to the whole physical fabric of the old neighborhoods as the vociferous plans for slum renewal and modernization were unveiled. But there was still a multitude of vintage *oustals toulousaines* that were reasonably habitable and that still marked the vivid image of a city dressed in vermilion. They remained the domain of the *travailleurs indépendants* and *petits commerçants* who had always lived in them. Large sections of the city, even in 1975, abided under the authority of the traditional Toulousain working classes. Their enduring presence and their influence over everyday urban life cannot be overlooked. But it was unequivocal testimony to the social alterations that had taken place that many of them were older people who simply clung to their neighborhoods and parishes. Elderly couples lived alone in the flats above the street, their grown children having long since fled to the suburbs. Their neighbors were immigrant workers. As always, Spanish, Algerian, Portuguese, and Italian settlers relied on the cheap rooms in the century-old buildings for a place to live. They became, along with the aging population of small producers and shopkeepers, the main occupants of old Toulouse.

Added to the general diaspora was the commercial revolution that swept away many a city grocery, bakery, and butcher. The historic image of the Cité was that of a teeming nerve center filled with a cornucopia of open-air markets, specialty shops, and neighborhood purveyors. Initially this image was enhanced by the thriving consumer culture that engrossed French tastes after the long dearth of the Second World War. *Succursales,* or retail chain stores, were introduced by the locally owned Epargne food market. Epargne also initiated the "American technique" of self-service in the euphoria of the commercial celebrations in the late 1940s. A *flâneur du marché* stopped in front of the new Epargne on the rue d'Asterlitz in the spring of 1949 to be greeted by a large *"Entrée Libre"* sign hung over the door: "Everything, all the domestic goods, the food products, the daily necessities, were right under your eyes, neatly arranged, from jam to fresh meat and fish. 'Help yourself to what you need,' I was told, 'take it to the cash register and pay the marked price.'"[61]

The availability and open display of abundant goods for the convenience of the customer shifted selling toward variety merchandising. The most striking outcome was the appearance of Epargne's first bona fide supermarket, an event that harvested a medley of chain-store "superettes" for the Cité and surrounding neighborhoods during the 1950s. Ghislain Thiéry, who had started as a tailor and then progressively moved into ready-to-wear sales, renovated his shop on the rue d'Alsace-Lorraine in 1961. After months under an enormous cover marked *"Transformations,"* Vêtements Thiéry reappeared as a modern emporium complete with neon lights, enormous pane-glass windows, and a full selection of clothing goods. At the grand opening the store was infused with the essence of violets, while sales clerks handed out violet bouquets to the customers. It was this kind of commercial drama that kept the old city a vibrant and eclectic place despite the changes wearing away at the urban fabric.

The spatial compactness of its trade distinguished Toulouse from the other provincial capitals. Even in 1967, three-quarters of the most important commercial thoroughfares in Toulouse were found between the boulevards and the Garonne River. Forty-five streets in central Toulouse employed nearly half the city's commercial workforce.[62] The rue d'Alsace-Lorraine and the rue de Metz formed the great mercantile cross garnished with the luxury department stores Le Capitole and Nouvelles Galeries and the more "popular" Monoprix and Printafix national chains. The boulevard Strasbourg and the boulevard Carnot stretched out in a commercial ribbon from the place Wilson. Hundreds of neighborhood shops congregated in a tight corona around them. What commerce was not in the Cité was usually just across the river in Saint-Cyprien.

All this may have been gladdening reassurance that Toulouse was still the commercial heart of Languedoc, but for the locals it spelled unending frustration. Despite the fact that suburban living had become the norm for tens of thousands of Toulousains, there were few services available anywhere except in central Toulouse. Epargne had early followed the flight to the suburbs with some twenty-five *succursales* located along the main roads out of town where they joined up with a sprinkling of overpriced boutiques. But the suburbs were long a commercial wasteland. The nine communes around Toulouse had access to only 240 retail traders for their 37,000 inhabitants, and most of those were the outdated shops in the old villages. Even the *grands ensembles* were deprived of basic mercantile services until the mid-1960s. There was one food store for every 300 residents at Empalot.[63] Shopping meant a time-consuming campaign against notorious traffic snarls to get into the Cité. The charms of old Toulouse rarely impressed customers suffering daily aggravation over the debasement of urban existence.

Thus the supermarkets and commercial malls that sprang up at suburban locales from the late 1960s were celebrated as authentic respites from the nuisances of Toulouse life. A cabal of Carrefour, LeClerc, and Casino *hypermarchés* rapidly materialized along the highways out into the valley. By 1973, as if they were magically grown, the Haute-Garonne had one of the thickest supermarket networks in France.[64] Toulouse's three original commercial complexes—"Supersuma Grammont (Mammouth)" to the northeast, "Géant Epargne" at Le Mirail, and "L'Escale" at Purpan—offered a plethora of food and household items, bakeries and butchers, dry cleaning and cafeterias to elated local suburbanites. Coveys of new retail emporia, often branches of central city luxury shops, fluttered around them. Adjacent to their parking lots were gas stations, garden centers, hardware stores, and the inevitable do-it-yourself *bricolage* outlets.

The malls were to act as the social and recreational frame for modern suburban existence. The original plan for Supersuma Grammont encompassed a bowling alley, tennis courts, and a swimming pool. The Horizon 2000 mall designed for the route d'Espagne to Muret (still under construction in 1971–72) was to include movie theaters, nightclubs, and a conference center, as well as a children's playground and zoo. In its conception it far surpassed the simple notion of commercial services. Instead, private investors attempted to profitably fund the transference of traditional urban functions into a suburban setting. The metamorphosis accented consumerism and recreation as the community ideals. Although the suburban consumer utopia of Horizon 2000 fell short, the southwestern highway to Muret and the Pyrenees Mountains was, by the late 1970s, still the most heavily concentrated commercial corridor around Toulouse. Its Carrefour supermarket, in the commune of Portet, was hailed as the largest in

Europe—seventy-two cash registers and 25,000 square meters, surrounded by forty boutiques. In 1972, yet another commercial complex was planned along the old route de Narbonne at Ramonville-Saint-Agne. With the sumptuous consumer choices materializing at the suburban commercial malls, there was little need to fight traffic into old Toulouse.

For the stunned proprietors of the central city, the competition from the suburban *grandes surfaces* was devastating. Well over a thousand retail and wholesale traders along the streets of Toulouse had already joined the list of *ateliers* closing their doors by the end of the 1960s. From 8,500, the number of shops dropped to 7,300. But it was the appearance of the suburban malls in the late 1960s and the 1970s, on top of the ruthless 1973 recession, that made practicing a mercantile living in the city a speculative venture only the dauntless dared to invest in. By 1975 only about 3,000 commercial shops remained.[65] Most of the victims were neighborhood affairs selling food and everyday needs. Their local clientele simply disappeared into the suburbs as did the once-dependable metropolitan traffic. The number of greengrocers plummeted from 1,200 in 1962 to 259 tenacious stalwarts. The number of butchers and delicatessens dropped from 1,200 to 165 gallant suppliers. Pinned to the wall by the *grandes surfaces,* shopkeepers and artisans broke out in protests in France and at Toulouse from 1969 to 1973. They were organized by a new coalition for shopkeeper defense, CID-UNITA. Michel Martucci, the delegate from the Haute-Garonne to CID-UNITA, predicted:

> If small shops disappear, France, a country with so much choice in food, will end up eating whatever is in the supermarket. They will determine what's in our bellies. The malls are a world of cement, kilometers of cement wall without life. In twenty years we will see five levels of underground parking, a supermarket on the street level, a dispensary for nervous disorders on the mezzanine, and fifteen floors of HLM above.[66]

The Royer Law of 1973 promised to humanize the modernization process by protecting *les petits* from the competitive advantage of large stores. But it was little compensation to the inner city. Central Toulouse had passed through a socioeconomic transformation that had ravaged the traditional habits of sociability and public culture so closely associated with its identity.

The Livre Blanc cautioned against the aging of the inner city's commercial web and the disappearance of its urban vitality: "The narrow lots, the incapacity of the streets to support automobile traffic reveals the contradictions between modernism and the traditional sector. The degradation is symptomatic of a process of impoverishment that is bound to be dangerous."[67] Even in the neighborhoods left unscathed by modernist slum clearance, the public spaces and streets that had once constituted the spatial fabric of everyday life were still under assault. Their confiscation by the automobile, by parking, and by leviathan traffic jams was the most overt sign of the vulnerability and deterioration of the inner districts. Workdays in the *micro-ateliers* and stores of Matabiau, des Carmes, and the Capitole were accompanied by the din and pollution of the cars, taxis, buses, and trucks choking the streets. The districts had been conquered by the imperialism of the gasoline engine. The "rights of pedestrians" were often called upon to express the general indignation with the deteriorating quality of life in central Toulouse. Anonymous letters arrived at the city planning offices:

> As Toulousains, we would like to stroll along the place du Capitole, the place Wilson, and the rue d'Alsace, making purchases or sitting outdoors at the cafes or in the squares. But the exhaust fumes from the cars are filthy and noxious. The bells of Saint-Sernin can't be heard over the car horns. Even the narrow sidewalks have been taken over by cars, so that it's impossible for a woman with a baby carriage to pass along the streets. No wonder families are fleeing from the central city to the safety and tranquility of the suburban supermarkets and parks. A policy must be found to prevent these displacements of people and businesses and restore the life of the city.[68]

Local activists decried the social agenda implicit in the neglect of the central city's economy and its physical structure. Modernist planning had precipitated ". . . a collapse in the public sociability—the life of the cafes, the tradition of promenading the streets and squares—intrinsic to Toulouse. The city has dissolved into a series of functional compartments devoid of any social role, suffering under continuous displacements to the residential zones, the work zones of the suburbs."[69] The economic vulnerability of small businesses, the constant commotion on the streets, the destruction of Saint-Georges, the abandoned buildings and aesthetics—all seemed to doom historic Toulouse to a modernist void. The traditional economy and the mellowed red neighborhoods it had imbued with community integrity were relegated to the fringe of the modernist project for the city's future.

There were protests against these malignancies eating away at neighborhood culture during the 1968 uprising. The student "mouvement du 25 Avril" occupied the state-endorsed Municipal Cultural Center, "the temple and symbol of bourgeois culture," and demanded its immediate closure as a defilement against "popular culture." The CGT organized worker strikes by neighborhood in an attempt to ventilate the indignation over the ruination of old Toulouse at the hands of de Gaulle's modernist minions. A hundred men and women "intent on breaking the banality and monotony of evenings spent in isolation in front of the TV" met in the salle du Sénéchal to debate cultural decentralization and the reanimation of their neighborhoods. Local architect Lefèbre divulged to the irate audience that construction regulations and real-estate deals added up to a "secret urbanism" devoid of any popular participation. Modernism had essentially ended any likelihood of creating a true city in the sense of habitat, sociability, and cultural expression.[70]

The retort to this tyranny was the organization of neighborhood "committees of defense" that would snatch control away from feebleminded state planners and renovate urban life from the bottom up. In one of many promises made amidst the euphoria of the 1968 revolt, Mayor Bazerque promised neighborhood participation in solving the inveterate problems of public transportation. He pledged his troth to the new Léo-Lagrange sports complex and swimming pool to be built on the place Riquet. These were symbols taken directly from the annals of the public-works programs offered by Socialist municipalism.

Indeed, the municipality went the limit in celebrating July 1968's Bastille Day in the populist tradition of Toulouse. In an intriguing exposé on cultural perceptions, the head of the city's "festivals committee" sketched out the "two different publics" to which celebrations were targeted: "If you want to play to the tourists, then you highlight regional folkloric spectacles. If you want to please the locals, well then you hire every music group you can find, including the Grand Orchestre du Capitole, and stage open-air concerts and dancing in the streets."[71] Accordingly, the place du Capitole was once again the scene of a *grand baloche*, replete with fireworks, neon lights, and decorations. Saint-Cyprien and Minimes staged singing competitions. At the place du Salin, sixty-five *boules* teams competed for the city's grand prize. A number of the *grands ensembles,* Empalot for example, organized children's festivals. But whether any of this constituted an "authentic" revival of neighborhood life is shaky. The socioeconomic foundation upon which neighborhood culture had historically rested had slipped too far to support celebrations for blatantly political purposes. Bazerque's attempt to indulge in nostalgic images of a culture that had been undermined by his own modernist handiwork would, in the end, backfire.

There was, in reality, little evidence of neighborhood renewal even after the 1968 uprising and the regulatory protection offered by the Royer Law. Certainly, adjustments were made by the traditional community. A number of the local shops took up the commercial tactics of the splashy suburban marts and converted groceries into supermarkets or opened branches in outlying districts. Some converted their stocks and services to the specialized daytime needs of commuters working in the city. The most acclaimed sign of this kind of commercial resourcefulness was the Garrigou-Medica store on the rue de Metz, a vast household-goods emporium owned and operated by a local retailer. Saint-Aubin, a *petit patron* stronghold, was one of the few districts that underwent actual building restoration during the 1970s. There were also signs of a revived political consciousness. A Union of Neighborhood Committees was created in 1970 and became a minor protagonist in local political debate. At the same time, the number of left-wing neighborhood political associations began to rise in number and prestige. The popularity of neighborhood Communist cells was expedited by their revival of Occitanism as an adversarial stance against modernization.[72]

Nonetheless, traditional neighborhood culture had, for the most part, vanished. Only vestiges were left in districts such as Saint-Cyprien, around Saint-Sernin Cathedral in the Bourg, or Saint-Aubin. As its actual daily practice faded, the mythical portrayal of popular culture crystallized around nostalgic and reverent yearnings for the *grand village*. It was a collective narrative uttered mainly by those disenfranchised by the process of modernization—the elderly, petty proprietors, paraindustrial and independent workers, those engaged in banal daily services, the urban poor—and by the radical left that often represented their interests. They recounted a "good life," a conviviality, in which the rhythm of daily work, the simplicity of life, the friendly neighborhood gatherings at the cafes and in the streets personified a tranquil world that was uniquely Toulousain. These were the charms of old Toulouse, the rich mosaic of its indigenous public culture. Its narration formed the oral tradition that matched the vivid imagery of *la ville rose*. This melancholic representation of traditional urban culture and habitat flourished (as did the spirited defense of Toulouse's vernacular architecture) largely as a foil to the modernist visions offered as the city's future. It was, of course, devoid of any memory of the poverty and vulnerability that historically stalked the parishes and districts. Nonetheless, the intimacy and joviality of the *ville bonne enfant* was an attractive and powerful motif. It redeemed both the discarded, who understood it as synonymous with the humanity modernist officialdom lacked, and the officialdom, who eventually embraced it as a form of modernism itself.

When the city plan for Toulouse finally began tackling the deterioration of the inner districts, the image of the *grand village* appeared as the subtext, or anachronic theme, for its conversion into a culture and entertainment precinct for the city's new social elites. Localism was appropriated as an enhancement of modernist values. Or, as sociologist Sharon Zukin has put it, the vernacular was both destroyed and restored in a new landscape of power.[73] The urban plan for Toulouse that appeared in the mid-1970s, known as the Schéma Directeur d'Aménagement et d'Urbanisme or SDAU, set out the agenda for a central city "in grave difficulty." Like its predecessors, the SDAU was largely a product of the compromises made between state technocrats, local notables, and their various constituencies. The SDAU itself and its adjoining Plan d'Occupation des Sols (POS) were worked out within a knotted ball of administrative committees and special commissions. As a result, the document was caught up in the machinations and surreptitious bargaining between state and local officialdom—a routine that included hidden collusions, out-and-out conflict, and the resort to bribes when necessary. It as much depicted political and financial wrangling as it did any sound planning agenda. The labyrinthine procedure gave prodigious power over the city's future to the mayor of Toulouse and to the senior representative for the Ministry of Equipment in the Haute-Garonne, who essentially controlled the purse strings.[74] The ambitions of the mayor were particularly illuminating, however, since any work on Toulouse's SDAU was actually held off until after the mayoral elections of 1971.

In what is considered a watershed political event by local analysts of every stripe, Louis Bazerque and the Socialists were soundly defeated by the centrist alliance of first mayoral adjunct Pierre Baudis. It was the first time the Socialists handed over the keys to the Hôtel de Ville since 1925. In good measure, the defeat of Bazerque expressed the bitter displeasure toward the hypermodernist projects that had transformed the city over the previous decade. Pierre Baudis clearly made his political stand on a revisionist approach to modernization. His campaign manifesto articulated a modernization in which habitat, work, and leisure would be balanced within a "profoundly human" urban environment: "We should, above all, fashion a city for the people who live here, for their tranquility, their comfort and happiness. I am a believer in Toulouse's tradition of humanism. We must modernize with our eyes open, guarding our serenity from excessive turbulence, protecting the poor and unfortunate from isolation." It was a motif that reflected Baudis' allegiance to the Giscardian philosophy that modernization need not proceed at the sacrifice of social harmony. But it also sounded vaguely like the ghost of 1950s mayor Raymond Badiou.

Baudis' middle-class, centrist pedigree also opened the possibility for more harmonious relations with the state elites installed at the prefecture on the place Saint-Etienne. Thus the SDAU that was fashioned in concert with state planners was acutely concerned with "quality of life" and "habitat." Suburban development at Toulouse was wrapped in an environmentalist cloak, so that the residents "had the pleasure of living in contact with nature, water, and trees."[75] Central Toulouse was to be restored to its heritage as the regional capital of the Midi. It would yet again be reincarnated as a cultural, commercial, and business center worthy of its long history, but this time with less brutality and more sensitivity. On the surface, this was the same tried-and-true depiction sketched out by Jaussely's and Nicod's dreams for Toulouse. But the substantive meaning behind the planning discourse was unmistakable. The revitalization of the central city would proceed as a cosmetic and functional shift to the modern downtown motifs considered appropriate by the city's new middle classes. It was this new bourgeoisie, the city's *cadres,* who had cast their votes for Baudis in the 1971 election and who, through the *literae scriptae* of planning text, wrestled for control of central-city space. In a word, old Toulouse was finally being gentrified as part of the struggle over social power and cultural dominance that had marked the city since the war's end.

The new elites understood the notion of downtown Toulouse partly as a quaint playground or leisure park. The preservation-based revitalization called for in the SDAU amounted to zoning the inner districts as an archaic attraction and as an entertainment and tourist precinct. The city as historic curio had, of course, required a cleansing out, a removal of the bothersome working classes deemed responsible for social dissension and retrograde urban habits. Only after it was rubbed out as a volatile political space was the built environment of old Toulouse painted as charming, quaint, and worthy of saving. The vernacular "habitat" of the inner districts was to be reclaimed for the new middle classes.

The formula for revitalization remained a mystery. But the red-brick aesthetics that had once been such an embarrassment to modernist zealots was now complimented by planners as "the spirit of the Cité." The "foamy pink of the Roman tile roofs, the sea of ocher, violet, and crimson" finally made it out of the refuse of architectural whimsy and into officially sanctioned urban design. The narrow alleyways were no longer simply public nuisances; they were prized as excursion trails into the city's intimate past. Promenading on a summer evening through medieval Toulouse, sitting at its cafes on the place du Capitole or at Saint-Georges, superficially restored the communal tradition of *le grand village*. The drama was heightened when the city installed arty floodlighting to illuminate the city's churches, museums, and aristocratic townhouses. The new *boulevardiers* could enjoy the spectacle of Toulouse's lived history from the tourist's perspective—detached and culturally inquisitive—but only after *la ville rouge* had been cleansed of any perceived social and political threat. The public rhetoric on urban tranquility and the "quality of life" was meant as a form of class distinction. The revival of the historic city simply reproduced the social and spatial hierarchies that were the leitmotif of rationally crafted modernist urban visions.

From the mid-1970s a variety of historic cultural institutions were renovated and blessed with substantial state and municipal support.[76] The Théâtre du Capitole, the *grande dame* of Toulousain cultural establishments, was updated and its programs expanded to include the full range of operatic and *bel canto* performances. The city's orchestra benefited from sumptuous sponsorship by the Municipal Council and various state cultural agencies. It was awarded regional status in 1974 and the old Halle aux Grains refurbished as its new symphony hall. It was one of the more explicit instances of the appropriation of traditional infrastructure as cultural capital. An annual summer music festival, *"Musique dans la Ville,"* was organized for Toulouse. The state donated over five million francs for the renovation of Saint-Sernin Cathedral and for the Jacobins monastery and church. The Musée des Augustins was restored with a combination of state and municipal funds. Baudis' critics argued that the *patrimoine toulousain* had become a form of cultural consumption for his middle-class boosters.[77] Indeed the purchasing power required to enjoy the city's transmuted cultural amenities became a fixed feature of emerging class distinctions. This process of gentrification, in which the vernacular landscape and culture of Toulouse were appropriated as didactic entertainment, was particularly conspicuous in relation to Occitanism. The renaissance of Occitan cultural forms was a convoluted and, in some ways, impenetrable affair. But it deserves consideration, if only in passing, because it so cogently illustrates the manipulation of cultural tradition within the tangled nexus of modernization.

As both cultural conception and modern phenomenon, Occitanism followed two disparate trajectories. The radical left retained the image of *occitanisme* as a populist culture of opposition. In this orbit it was a political idiom associated with an embattled regional identity struggling against Parisian-state imperialism. By the early 1970s, the older COEA gave way to movements such as the Parti Nationaliste Occitan, La Fédération Anarchiste Communiste d'Occitanie, and "Lutte Occitane," which led the defense of Larzac in the department of Aveyron. "Volèm Viure al Païs" (VVAP) was a more urban band of workers, artisans, women, and students. All of them were self-described as revolutionary and populist. VVAP styled itself a Socialist political-cultural movement with a platform of five demands: removal of the prefects, the election through universal suffrage of a regional assembly, the collection and administration of taxes by region, the creation of an independent regional investment bank, and the priority of available jobs to those living in the region. The list is a germane indication of the degree to which "decolonization" had become the leitmotif of the radicalized Occitan movement by the 1970s and early 1980s. But it remained largely peripheralized outside the mainstream of French politics.

Far more accessible was Occitan culture itself. The aftermath of the 1968 revolt brought an abatement of the cultural centralism emanating from Paris. In its place, Occitanism, as an erudite cultural form, enjoyed a lavish renaissance sponsored largely by the new middle classes, who seized it as a discovery of regional identity. Books and journals devoted to Occitan language and literature flowered. The Conservatoire Occitan and the Institut d'Etudes Occitanes at Toulouse attracted increasing numbers of researchers and students each year who wrestled with questions of "authenticity" and then went off to establish Occitan dance companies, music groups, and local theater colonies. These activities were supported by the consumption and recreational habits of the city's new elites. Living the vernacular became a matter of purchasing record albums of "modern" Occitan folk singers, such as Maria Roanet, or watching television documentaries on Occitan folklore. Attending performances of *les ballets occitans* or seventeenth-century *école toulousaine* art exhibits or searching through the Saint-Raymond and Paul-Dupuy museums for vestiges of old Toulouse were now associated with a sense of intellectual prestige and urbane status. Local culture was essentially appropriated, within the modernist paradigm of image, intellectual cultivation, and leisure entertainment, to become a consumer market. But it was only open to the new bourgeoisie, who were thought capable of appreciating the value of historic authenticity and aesthetic quality.

While the regionally dispossessed continued their rebukes of internal colonialism and laid plans for the revival of an autonomous Occitania, the very culture they defended was merged into a system of cultural production defined by the region's new elites. It was valorized simply as cultural capital. Folkloric spectacles "played to the tourist." Any political overtones were resolutely neutralized by the detached gaze, the tasteful pursuit of pleasure by the modern bourgeois *flâneur.*

The SDAU's emphasis on the central city's commercial revitalization as well played off this historicist version of commodification, entertainment, and an amenity economy. Within the mended *oustals,* luxury shops and department stores were to revive old Toulouse as a regional center for high-end retail consumerism. The rising affluence of the city's new social elites was reflected in the contrived desires and captivating images of commodity culture that materialized on the inner-city landscape. The most symbolic gesture was the resurrection of the city's ancient commercial heart, the Grand rue (or the rue Saint-Rome, des Changes, and des Filateurs), into a pedestrian promenade. Spared of the lunatic automobile traffic, by 1975 the historic Grand rue was an extravaganza of trendy boutiques flashing the latest American and European fashions at young consumers. Then, of course, there was the Saint-Georges district. The shopping arcade beneath the place Occitan filled up with showy fashion outlets and canned music whirling around the sumptuous supermarket. High-fashion couture and hair salons, trendy cafes, posh "artisanal" boutiques, and gourmet food stores glamorized the refurbished pedestrian paths and car-choked alleys fanning out from the place Saint-Georges.

The rue Croix-Baragnon in the Saint-Etienne district became a ribbon of art vogue. Its wine-red walls opened onto chic galleries filled with antiques, paintings, elegant furniture, and home decorations. Picturesque little bistros found niches in the inner courtyards off the street. Finding the newest restaurants hidden in the maze of medieval streets, the one that served the most authentic cassoulet or paella, the best nouvelle cuisine, became an entertaining game of cultural consumption among the affluent. With the strict emphasis on cuisine and culinary "authenticity" as a metaphor for cultural values, Toulouse's outdoor markets prevailed as one of the city's most attractive entertainments. The Halle Victor-Hugo, surrounded by gourmet stores and antique shops, and the massive market along the boulevard de Strasbourg were popular sites for the central-city experience. They provided the occasion for a "mingling" of the social classes.

There were, nonetheless, other downtown functions. The centrality of *la ville rouge* marked it as a symbolic landscape, one which, despite the encumbrances and traffic jams, still attracted powerful corporate and state interests attempting to control the city. The Jaussely and Nicod Plans, as well as the SDAU, all accented the central district as the administrative and business center mandatory for a regional capital. The city's historic function as the administrative heart of Languedoc was easily harmonized with the vast extension of public and corporate "tertiary" services that marked the postwar managerial explosion.

Although virtually the whole service sector swelled at Toulouse, public services essentially dominated the city. The workforce employed by the government increased from around 20,000 in 1954 to nearly 70,000 in 1975.[78] A veritable army of bureaucrats administered and maintained the growing number of collective responsibilities that fell under the government's jurisdiction: education, transportation, health and medical services, telephone and television, plus the growing number of economic and social services such as housing administration, unemployment and social benefits, economic planning and development, and so on. The old courthouse on the place du Salin, the prefectural offices on the place Saint-Etienne, and the Capitole remained the summits of public administration. But a new *cité administrative* of modern office buildings was constructed during the 1960s along the boulevard Armand Duportal just beyond the Latin Quarter to house the growing number of government agencies. Civil-service departments were squeezed into available *oustals* throughout the Bourg and Cité. The "housing crisis" in *la ville rose* was bequeathed to its new daytime residents—thousands of public officials and civil servants who commuted into the conquered city each day.

A small covey of corporate services (management services, public relations and advertising, brokerage and marketing consultants) also materialized within the city's modern production environment. City planners and municipal officials specifically spotlighted its crucial urban role during the late 1970s. By then, the effort to diversify and enrich the city's economic palate was associated with the sensitive issue of making Toulouse a true regional capital, a real "decision-making center" rather than merely an economic appendage of Paris. The sharp and somewhat startling emphasis on services after years of fixation on Toulouse's industrial might was a reflection of the whole iconographic extravaganza around corporate and entrepreneurial market strategies that took hold after the recession. The great concern became more office space. New office buildings sprouted up along the edge of the medieval core as enticing carrots to attract management and marketing gurus: the Occitan and Le Sully office complexes in the renovated Saint-Georges quarter; Les Américains on the place Wilson; and the imposing Belvédère, whose step-pyramid design was vaguely reminiscent of the Occitan belltowers of the city's cathedrals.

It was, however, the corridor that stretched from the place Wilson down the allée Jean-Jaurès that was chosen within the SDAU as Toulouse's slickest locale for "financial and corporate headquarters." The grand promenade of Jean-Jaurès was touted by municipal officials as the Champs-Elysées of Toulouse, which would open onto a *centre d'affaires* for the *"activités nobles de gestion"* on the summit of Jolimont-Marengo. The brick facades along the boulevard were replaced by high walls of tinted glass. Fifteen insurance companies, a dozen loan and credit organizations, twenty real-estate agencies, the headquarters of TOFINSO, the Credit Agricole, the offices of Air-Inter and Air France, and the headquarters of the French–United States Association all settled into two lines of office high-rises that together formed the only skyscraper canyon at Toulouse.

By the mid-1970s, the great intersection of the place Wilson, boulevard de Strasbourg, allée Jean-Jaurès had become the most animated spot in the city. Each night the movie theater and cafe marquees created a whimsical light show for the throngs of people out communing in *la ville rose.* A downtown commercial mall aptly called the *"complexe immobilier des Américains"* packed fifty luxury shops, fast-food restaurants, a "drugstore," and a theater into a monument of modernist glitz and consumer entertainment. In the upstairs corner eatery, diners could peer out at the urban spectacle below while they ordered from an electronic menu fastened onto the table. The place Wilson and its ring thoroughfare were jammed in daylight with streams of pedestrians, cars, taxis, and buses. At dusk it transformed into an urban festival of *boulevardiers,* lively outdoor cafes, street performers, and musicians.

Modernism had come to Toulouse. Indeed, the "downtown," the suburbs, and the expanding urban region around it had all been transformed by the pressures and tensions inherent in the construction of a capitalist landscape. Local geography, the city, and sociocultural identity were all synchronized into a discrete environment conducive to Fordist production and modern norms. The economic activities essential to state-corporate power were designated as the determining factors for any status in the hierarchy of cities. The region itself was appropriated as an esteemed space for the infrastructure and networks essential to commodity and labor markets. Business practices, class consciousness, and cultural identity had been transmuted through a process of gentrification. It imbued them with a modern middle-class outlook. Irascible petty producers were rehabilitated as sagacious capitalist entrepreneurs. Modern urban aesthetics were redefined by the "quality of life," the leisure and "habitat" of the city's new *cadres.* Regional authenticity itself was subsumed and commodified within an ever-expanding market for culture and lifestyle that became the reference point for modern living.

But the destruction and staged reincarnation of vernacular Toulouse was not complete. *Les petits peuples* were a tense mix of shopkeepers and petty producers, immigrants and guest workers, the elderly and the poor. They still challenged the new elites for territorial claim over old Toulouse and managed to control and define its sense of place in many a neighborhood. Each segment of the city yielded profoundly different images of "modern" Toulouse, be it the historic neighborhood realms of the *grand village,* the slums and ethnic ghettos, the financial district at Jean-Jaurès, or upscale Saint-Georges. Added to them were the visual impressions created from suburban expansion: the lines of bungalows *à la toulousain,* the rationality of Le Mirail, the Concorde sitting on the tarmac at Blagnac, the run-down *grands ensembles.* Each acted as a symbolic reference, a discrete spatial component in the struggle over modernization. The region and its local culture remained an enigmatic force that impeded the full mobilization and coherent structuring of cultural geography for capitalist processes and for state administration. These exertions over the city and the region, the diverse uses of community culture and space by both vernacular and state-corporate interests, yielded an urban environment that was essentially the fruit of compromise and conflict. Toulouse was neither a modern utopia nor a Languedocian municipal reverie. It was the product of a long process of historic development and sociocultural struggle into which modernization was blended. The result was that the vernacular, and the capitalist landscape imposed upon it, were both modulated and altered.

Conclusion: Constructing the New Toulouse

Cities are complex entities. They are a maelstrom of turbulent forces, ambiguities, and irreconcilable currents and countercurrents in which whole sets of prejudices and concepts overlap and compete. It is far more than one history of one city can capture. This risk of opening a Pandora's box of urban tribulations is made even more perilous by the fierce scrutiny under which the city, and the region, were held during France's passage through the *trentes glorieuses*. An even more formidable challenge is the theoretical corpus created to provide cognitive maps for threading one's way through the urban environment. By the mid-1970s, the French themselves had become exhausted by these urban endeavors and threw them aside in an *anti-cité* reaction. In 1981 François Bedarida concluded that "the first error has been to see urbanism as a solution to all the problems of society."[1] But by that time, urbanists and planners used to worrying about the city could afford to breathe easier. The momentum of urbanization had begun to slow. The "second French Revolution" was winding down.

My purpose in studying Toulouse has been to examine this modern "French Revolution" as it took place within a local urban community. The revolution was definitively about how France intended to lead a modern urban existence. The task of chronicling how one city was transformed by this was complicated by my own set of overlapping and competing agendas. In part, I conceived the account of Toulouse's contemporary experiences as a reflection of the modernizing processes reshaping France as a whole. And indeed the capacity of the *grands commis* to institute a regime of modernist regulation that included explicit norms, institutions, and mechanisms for adapting and controlling behavior extended fairly evenly throughout France. It was the unabashed intent of state-corporate interests to purge the provincial particularisms that had effaced France and replace them with a uniform territory molded by modernist values and a regime of Fordist accumulation. Localism was trivialized. It was through the chrysalis of modernization that true French identity and nationhood would be achieved. It was an overtly autocratic combination of progressivism and nationalism.

True to the power and coercive capacity of this restructuring, the pattern of urban settlement and spatiality at Toulouse was much the same as in any other city of France. Modernization under state auspices created a rationalized geographic landscape devised as capitalist markets and their corresponding administrative matrixes. A coherent hierarchy of national, regional, and urban realms was produced. As a result, there was an unmistakable pattern to the urban revolution taking place throughout provincial France. Examining Toulouse uncovers the spectrum of changes reshaping all French cities. Just on the face of it, the searing image of a 1960s housing project like Empalot or Charles-de-Fitte is lamentably easy to find in any good-sized French town, along with all the psychic alienation and ethnic and social problems that have grown up with them. Sarcelles outside Paris is perhaps the most infamous. Le Haut du Lièvre at Nancy, Le Quartier des Fontaines at Tours, Duchère at Lyon—the list is endless. Each city had its suburban ZUP programs akin to Le Mirail. Toulouse's archrival Bordeaux sported two major ZUP projects, Hauts de Garonne and Bordeaux-Lac. Grenoble had the "new city" of Grenoble-Echirolles, Dijon the ZUP de la Fontaine-d'Ouche. Slum-clearance projects along the lines of Saint-Georges went on in a variety of towns. The fracas over Les Halles at Paris is notorious. Lyon's La Part-Dieu renovation is among the most illustrious in France. Bordeaux revamped its Mériadeck district. Each *métropole d'équilibre* had its *industries de pointe* with their suburban research and industrial parks. Each region transmuted into a nascent economic market, nurturing its "business climate" vying for privileged infrastructure and public investment and searching for new technologies and a niche in the global marketplace.

Even more, the transformation of Toulousain culture and society mirrored that taking place throughout France. The city went through a major population explosion. By 1975, the residents of Toulouse were more diverse in origin, and they were much younger. Over 75 percent of them were living in the suburbs. The social classes that had traditionally dominated Toulouse, and French, society dwindled in number and in their influence over everyday life. Old Toulouse was dominated by a petite bourgeoisie of lawyers and public officials and by the *travailleurs indépendants* who ran the shops and groceries that gave the city its street-corner community atmosphere. Just after the war, in 1945, the heads of almost half of French households were still independent workers who lived by running a small business or farm. In Toulouse, the proportion would be closer to three-quarters.

Over the course of the *trentes glorieuses,* there was an increasing monopolization of the Toulouse economy by large-scale capitalist interests. It succeeded in containing and controlling both the urban region and the labor force within it. Toulouse left behind isolation and "underdevelopment" and was integrated into a systematized productive nexus. The older social groups were relegated to a mere shadow of their former selves. Those unable to adjust were left behind as "the new poor." By the mid-1970s, the vast bulk of the city's, and the country's, working population were wage earners in the employ of someone else—most often large public or private conglomerates with tentacles spread across the country. High-tech industries, research and education, corporate and public administration revived the Toulouse labor market with a whole new range of skills that integrated it into the national competitive network. Salaries and incomes shot upward. Toulouse became more modern, more affluent, and more "middle class" in tone.

Henri Mendras has dubbed this social process "the triumph of the central constellation."[2] The second French Revolution was a decidedly modern, middle genre affair. The state-directed plans for aesthetic modernism and for economic modernization constructed an urban landscape suitable for a new society and a new French citizen: a neobourgeois fully embracing contemporary existence. This vast new social category, wedded to the virtues of progress and the new ideal of Frenchness, exercised hegemonic influence. Their identity was built on mass cultural values and the practice of consumption. Community and space were woven into "habitat" and "lifestyle" rather than into older notions of class, populist culture, and sociability associated with, in this case, *la ville rose.* Certainly the displacement of the urban working classes to the suburbs, where they were offered home ownership and a "quality" living environment, manifested the fruition of modern norms as the new pivot for urban life. Modern middle-class values and tastes, the new set of rituals created by cultural and material consumption, became the obligatory model that all social groups ascribed to, with varying degrees of gusto.

Access to this new social constellation, and the materialism it espoused, was found by enrolling as a Fordist employee. In this sphere, *les cadres* exercised particular magnetism. In 1945 the idea of the *cadres* did not even exist as a recognizable social and occupational category in France. By 1975 they composed one-fifth of the workforce. The second French Revolution was, first and foremost, the *cadres'* saga. They were the shock troops, the vanguard of material accumulation, the high-priestly class sanctioning the rationalization of France and the technological paradigm. At Toulouse, they formed well over one-quarter of the city's working population. Scientists, engineers, business administrators, and computer jockeys were the city's neobourgeoisie. The Blagnac aeronautic compound, the Rangueil-Lespinet scientific complex, and the swank office buildings along the allée Jean-Jaurès were their domain. This was the new Toulouse—the new France. It was unhampered by urban decay and social conflict. Poverty and backwardness had been left behind, the chaos of an unbridled, disputatious history rejected. Modernism was about social and economic power and the structuring of people's lives. It touched institutions, the forms of urban culture, as well as everyday interactions and individual self-definition. It was about the formation of a coherent culture and landscape that triumphed over the historic dissonance that threatened French nationhood.

This coherence recast local political leverage in ways that harmonized with the modernist agenda. The central figure in French local politics was the mayor. His prestige was connected to the vitality of municipalism and local civic participation in France. They were traditions that expressed local community and the capacity for autonomous decision making. At Toulouse, the "orientation to the left" was built on a stable coalition of labor and business interests that guaranteed Socialist municipal dominion for the majority of the twentieth century. It reflected a place-bound sense of political community. An aggrieved sense of regionalism, populist sentiment on behalf of *les petits,* and a strong syndical tradition held sway. Socialist mayors Raymond Badiou and Louis Bazerque allied with business elites, the Chamber of Commerce, and labor and trade organizations to defend local interests and engage in active civic boosterism. But it was hard to hold the coalition together in the face of the state-powered modernist machine. Municipalism gave way to technocratic managerialism. By the 1960s, Louis Bazerque's mayoral charisma represented a threat to the Fifth Republic's struggle to rid itself of the traditional bastions of municipal power. That Bazerque would base his local dominion on an ambitious local version of urban modernism and procapitalism made the political squabble all the more heated. By 1971 the tide had turned against the "culture of political opposition" hanging on in the capital of Languedoc.

Much has been made at Toulouse about the defeat of Bazerque and his modernist pomposity at the hands of "Giscardian" Pierre Baudis. The *"saga des Baudis,"* of both Pierre and his son Dominique, who succeeded him at the Capitole, was the political corollary to thirty years of modernization. The old left-wing alliance staggered because the interests it represented—the network of small producers working within the local economy and workers in the city's big industries—were either antipathetic to state-capitalist designs or were incorporated into it. In either case, modernization ripped apart the older collaboration between classes nourished from a particularist style of political culture. The cleansing of the inner-city neighborhoods was simply the spatial expression of modernist social and political alteration. The Pierre Baudis administrations heavily accented technocratic management of the city and the reliance on experts. The *cadres* who supported his regime were not embued with the traditional left-wing esprit. They were moderates and conservatives in their political allegiances, and their interests lay with national politics. They lived out at Ramonville or Vieille-Toulouse in luxury homes and spacious apartments. And Pierre Baudis and the SDAU offered an *idéologie pavillonnaire,* the dream of greenbelts and sports and recreational facilities that would enhance the quality of their suburban lifestyles. The mayoral seat at Toulouse had moved in line with the state apparatus and with national objectives.

Modernism thus represented a complete rejection of the city's history, a refusal to acknowledge social conflict. It was the celebration of bureaucratic power and rationality over localism and urban chaos, over the threat of parochial political loyalties. The veil of objectivity and detachment behind which urban planning by the technocratic corps took place, the sense that their work rose above the vagaries of politics, produced a language and a web of regulatory control that permitted extraordinary freedom for centralization and the coherent rationalization of the provincial landscape. Modernism simply monumentalized the new social constellation and corporate-state power as self-referential myths.

Nevertheless, both modernism and modernization are, like all historic processes, unevenly developed across time and space and thus inscribe quite different images across the regional map. They certainly exhibit a synchronic and systematic character, but even here, the regional reactions to modernism's pulse-like crises and restructuring differ. The actual depth of its socioeconomic power and cultural imperialism is a thorny issue, as is the notion of a spatial character to capitalism. Without doubt, the institutions of state administration and Fordist capitalism utilized the modernization of the city and the region as a mechanism for economic control and social engineering. The appropriation of old Toulouse, for example, into the narrative of material consumption and social distinction leaves real questions about the capacity of a community to maintain any degree of autonomy. The city's culture, symbolic language, and historic identity could all be easily reproduced by state and corporate entities eager to provide the city's economy with a competitive advantage and its society with cohesiveness. The grand narrative about the city's historic talents in aircraft construction and the play off Toulouse's intellectual history as the prologue for Rangueil-Lespinet are striking illustrations. Yet given this overt capacity for reproduction, it is still worth considering the divergences and alterations that appear within the modernist landscape. The application of the state-capitalist framework was filled with contradictions brought on by the encounter with local culture and territory. Exploring these intricacies and variations and the degree to which they were generated by local forms of power was my second motive in studying Toulouse.

The issue of local power received a great deal of attention in France during the Mitterand government and the Socialist measures for regional reform. After decades of centralized planning, the question was often as rudimentary as, "Does local power really exist?" It was certainly the subtext of state-driven modernization programs to effectively finish off any last vestiges of particularist influence. As a Parisian state planner flatly told me, "The Midi doesn't exist." Under these conditions, is there a social and economic collectivity that can be deemed "local"? Is it recognizable in a system of known practices, a landscape determined by vernacular culture and environment? Is there a "sense of place," a "critical regionalism," that people associate themselves with in their everyday lives? The notion of "local" has become as much an object of debate as the "region" or the "city" or modernization itself. It is further complicated by incertitude over definition and over postmodern, tourist images of authenticity.

What this book argues is that a process of negotiation took place between the institutions and forms of modernization and those of the vernacular. Both the city and the region in France were the handiwork woven from sociocultural and economic conflict and compromise. They were the fruit of an ongoing and highly contentious debate about the nature of modernization and the construction of modern urban life. The actual potency of modernism was deflated by a host of particularist ambiguities and contradictions. Cities and regions are living communities endowed with certain physical and social assets that are the product of a long history. Urban identities emerge out of particular structures of experience that bind together space, time, and memory. There is a complex range of cultural practices, social values, and visual images that defy easy categorization but that nonetheless conjure up a unique urban identity—in this case, Toulousain. Local power appeared in a variety of twisted forms, depending on the situation. It reinvented itself in enigmatic guises in response to the pressures acting upon it. The local urban community was just as capable of utilizing and manipulating historical references as was modern material culture. It was just as able to envision its own version of modernization and the future. Traditions and an identifiable vernacular agenda and discourse were often formulated as a play off the dominant modernist ideology. Political and economic interests allied in curious "local" coalitions that are not easily understood within accepted models of class and social relations. Jean Llante's and the Communists' defense of petit bourgeois shopowners and Occitanism is one example. The alliance between business elites and workers in defense of Toulouse aviation is another. In the process, what appears is the suppleness and adaptivity, the active manipulation and wily strategies of "local power and culture." Its ability to mediate the terms by which modernism would be applied created acceptable boundaries for transformation and change.

There is no doubt that local elites often implanted themselves within the landscape drawn by technocratic interests, even, as in the case of Bazerque or the petty producers, when they appeared to be a threat to it. The point was rarely to struggle for a return to some nostalgic past. That dream was relegated to the most extreme supporters of the *passéiste* and ancient power of the village. Nor was it to create islands of ancient production sealed off from the evils of modernization. Instead, the vernacular persisted through collective resistance, through accepted alterations, and by refocusing and shifting the notion of modernization itself. There were limits to the administrative and market coherence that could be achieved by coercive state power. And for all its hegemonic symbolism, modernist aesthetic design can seem, from one point of view, ironically wimpish. The vitality of modern building as a synonym for progress and the future was actually short-lived. This was particularly the case for the "middling modernist" variety of construction that went up in provincial places like Toulouse. This kind of modern form has spent far longer as a passé spectacle of visionary illusion. Le Mirail represented an exhaustion of utopia. The capacity of state-corporate interests to rationally order and control the city and the individuals within it was partially derailed by local allegiances and community capital. Authority over the economy and over the built environment and the uses of space had to be negotiated among a wide variety of participants.

What is particularly striking is the vernacular environment's capacity to absorb modernism into the multilayered texture and fabric of urban life. It precipitates a distinctive kind of cosmopolitanism that is often ironic, sometimes playful. In unanticipated ways, it deflects the banality of technocratic planning and modernist imperialism.

On a trip to Toulouse in November 1995, I stood, once again, on the place du Capitole. The red brick of its loggia is resplendent after a recent renovation. The pink marble facade of the city's most celebrated monument, the Palais du Capitole, gleams in audacious testimony to the endurance of Toulouse culture. But the building is now flanked by the two most celebrated icons of advanced capitalism—McDonald's and Burger King. Yet they are themselves outflanked by one of the most elegant recreations of a fin-de-siècle grand cafe you could find in France. And they all pay homage to the outdoor market, with its colorful awnings and booths, that has taken over the square each week since the dawn of time.

The place du Capitole has become something of a celebration of the city's porous quality, its capacity to soak up the historic processes that act upon it. There are few *baloches* in the old districts. But during the summer months, the place du Capitole and the place Saint-Georges are jammed with young people listening to rock and jazz concerts, including a "battle of the bands" between Toulouse and Bordeaux. That unfortunate "exhaustion of utopia," Le Mirail, can now be reached by a flashy metro system installed under the city's great linear artery: from Joliment, down the allée Jean-Jaurès, out through Saint-Cyprien to Le Mirail. The shades of Jaussely and Nicod linger still. And in what has to be one of the greatest ironies, the Belle-Fontaine district of Le Mirail, the original settlement pushed through entirely by public fiat, has been successfully renovated through a process of local community-based planning. This wily resiliency of the vernacular (and its own imperialist proclivities) is perhaps articulated best in the 1995 celebratory inauguration of the Cathedral of Evry outside Paris, the first cathedral built in France since the beginning of the twentieth century. Designed by the Swiss architect Mario Botta, it is made of over one million *briques rouges de Toulouse.* Toulouse culture has slyly managed to win over even Parisian design elite—a sweet revenge.

Small business remains a potent force on the Toulouse urban landscape. A medley of boutiques, *atéliers,* groceries, bakeries, and self-service cafeterias preside over many a *petit quartier* in old Toulouse. Both the Chambre de Commerce and the Chambre des Métiers are now installed in swank new headquarters, offering an extraordinary array of services to Toulouse's small-time entrepreneurs. The Chambre des Métiers' new offices are part of the redevelopment of the nineteenth-century boulevard de Strasbourg that encompasses a myriad of flashy hotels, meeting suites, and advertising and marketing services suited to the late twentieth century. They shoulder the Toulouse-Technopole-Sud business park that continues to expand the city's economic boundaries into the suburbs and out into the global marketplace. The Airbus now reigns supreme as the city's idol. The image of an Airbus A340 flying majestically over the place du Capitole graces Toulouse's home page on the World Wide Web—the city's two great symbolic references merged in cyberspace. But then again, the products of the "city of Isaure" can also be found at its new nine-acre theme park, the Cité de l'Espace, where tourists can climb aboard an Ariane rocket, simulate space flight, and visit a new planetarium. Despite the defection of the Hôtel de Ville to the enemy, Socialism has persisted as a dynamic force in the *pays toulousain,* especially in the suburban communes. By the elections of the late 1970s (in which "political heritage" weighed heavily), the Socialists reigned supreme throughout the vast expanse of metropolitan Toulouse. While the Baudis dynasty governs from the Capitole, the electorate continues to vote Socialist in legislative and presidential elections—the newest *paradoxe toulousain.*

These kinds of incongruencies exemplify precisely the bumptious, disputatious nature of the modernization process. The dialectical tension between the modernizing tendency toward homogenization and the local tendency toward differentiation underlie the whole operative dynamic. Toulouse was in part pressed into a modern matrix. Urban modernism and economic modernization in part conformed to the particularist landscape and were merged into the layers of the city's history.

Notes

Introduction

1. See *GEO,* Spring 1989, as well as *Le Monde,* 16 October 1987, and *Architecture méditerranéenne* 36(April 1991). The most recent and best introductions to Toulouse are Marie-Louise Roubaud, ed., *Toulouse,* France Series, no. 4 (Paris: Autrement, 1991); Jean Coppolani, Guy Jalabert, and Jean-Paul Lévy, *Toulouse et son agglomération* (Paris: La Documentation Française, 1984); François Taillefer, *Atlas et géographie du Midi toulousain,* Atlas et géographie de la France moderne (Paris: Flammarion, 1978). In English, see John Ardagh's *France Today* (New York: Penguin, 1988).

2. See Jean Fourastié's classic *Les Trentes Glorieuses ou la Révolution Invisible de 1946 à 1975* (Paris: Fayard, 1979).

3. On the relationship between modernism and modernization see David Harvey, *The Condition of Postmodernity* (Cambridge, Mass.: Basil Blackwell, 1989), chapter 2, as well as Paul Rabinow, *French Modern, Norms and Forms of the Social Environment* (Cambridge, Mass.: MIT Press, 1989).

4. Michel de Certeau, *The Practice of Everyday Life,* trans. Steven Rendall (Berkeley, Calif.: University of California Press, 1984), 95.

5. Commissariat général du Plan, *Rapport de la commission villes,* Préparation du sixième plan de développement économique et social, 1971–1975 (Paris: La Documentation Française, 1971), 18–19.

6. See Henri Lefebvre, *La Révolution urbaine* (Paris: Gallimard, 1970).

7. Kenneth Frampton, "Towards a Critical Regionalism: Six Points for an Architecture of Resistance," in *The Anti-Aesthetic, Essays on Postmodern Culture,* ed. Hal Foster (Seattle, Wash.: Bay Press, 1983), 16–30. See also John B. Jackson, *Discovering the Vernacular Landscape* (New Haven, Conn.: Yale University Press, 1984), 13–41.

8. Italo Calvino, *Invisible Cities,* trans. William Weaver (New York: Harcourt Brace, 1974).

9. Fernand Braudel, *The Identity of France,* trans. Siâm Reynolds, 2 vols. (New York: Harper and Row, 1988), 1:250.

1. Red Flower of Summer: Toulouse before 1945

1. On the early history of Toulouse see Daniel Faucher, "Réflections sur le destin de Toulouse," *Revue géographique des Pyrénées et du Sud-Ouest* (RGPSO) 30 (June

1959): 102–104; Michel Labrousse, *Toulouse antique, des origines à l'établissement des wisigoths* (Paris: Boccard, 1968), chapters 8–10; John Drinkwater and Hugh Elton, eds., *Fifth-Century Gaul: A Crisis of Identity* (Cambridge: Cambridge University Press, 1992).

2. Emmanuel Le Roy Ladurie, "Occitania in Historical Perspective," *Review* 1(Summer 1977): 23.

3. The history of Toulouse and Occitania during the Middle Ages is well documented. The best general sources are Philippe Wolff, *Regards sur le midi médiéval* (Toulouse: Privat, 1978), as well as his *Histoire de Toulouse* (Toulouse: Privat, 1974), and his edited collection *Histoire de Languedoc* (Toulouse: Privat, 1967). Also excellent are Gérard Cholvy, ed., *Le Languedoc et le Roussillon* (Roanne, France: Horvath, 1992); Archibald R. Lewis, *The Development of Southern French and Catalan Society, 718–1050* (Austin, Tex.: University of Texas Press, 1965). On Occitania, the best introductions are André Armengaud and Robert Lafont, eds., *Histoire d'Occitanie* (Paris: Hachette, 1979); Robert Lafont, *La Revendication occitane* (Paris: Flammarion, 1974); Gérard de Sède, *700 ans de révoltes occitanes* (Paris: Plon, 1982). See also the Exposition catalog, *Huit centième anniversaire de l'indépendance municipale. De Toulouse à Tripoli: la puissance toulousaine au XIIe siècle, 1080–1208* (Toulouse: Musée des Augustins, 1989).

4. Wolff, *Histoire de Toulouse*, 107.

5. For the history of Toulouse under the Old Regime see Giles Castor, *Le Commerce du pastel et de l'épicerie à Toulouse de 1450 à 1561* (Toulouse: Privat, 1962); Georges Frêche, *Toulouse et la région Midi-Pyrénées au siècle des lumières vers 1670–1789* (Paris: Cujas, 1974). In English, see Robert Schneider, *The Ceremonial City: Toulouse Observed, 1738–1780* (Princeton, N.J.: Princeton University Press, 1995) as well as his *Public Life in Toulouse, 1463–1789: From Municipal Republic to Cosmopolitan City* (Ithaca, N.Y.: Cornell University Press, 1989) and Robert Forster, *The Nobility of Toulouse in the Eighteenth Century* (Baltimore: Johns Hopkins University Press, 1960).

6. Occitan was subdivided into four major dialects: central Occitan, which was chiefly the language of Languedoc; northern Occitan, spoken in Limousin and Auvergnat; Provençal; and Gascon. The Toulousains spoke a subdialect of central Occitan called "langue mondine." For an excellent philological discussion, see René Nelli, *Mais enfin, qu'est-ce que l'occitanie?* (Toulouse: Privat, 1978), chapter 1, as well as Robert Lafont and Christian Anatole, *Nouvelle histoire de la littérature occitane*, 2 vols. (Paris: Presses Universitaires de France, 1971). See also Fausta Garavini and Philippe Gardy, "Une littérature en situation de diglossie: la littérature occitane," in *Popular Traditions and Learned Culture in France, from the Sixteenth to the Twentieth Century*, ed. Marc Bertrand (Saratoga, Calif.: Anma Labri, 1985), 255–74.

7. P. Jousset, *La France géographie illustrée*, vol. 1 (Paris: Librairie Larousse, 1918), 307.

8. *Oustal* is the Occitan word for *maison* or house. Thus, *oustal toulousaine* is the traditional name for an urban dwelling at Toulouse, and distinguishes it from *l'hôtel* and *la maison suburbaine*.

9. Stendahl, *Travels in the South of France* (New York: The Orion Press, 1970), 60–68.

10. Henry James, *A Little Tour of France* (New York: AMS Press, 1975), 125–33.

11. Edith Wharton, *A Motor-Flight through France* (New York: Charles Scribner's Sons, 1908), 117.

12. The terms "everywhere" and "nowhere" to describe the differences between the north and south were used by Jean Antoine Claude Chaptal in 1819 in his work *De l'Industrie française*. For the development of the "two Frances," see Roger Chartier, "The Two Frances, the History of a Geographical Idea," in *Cultural History between Practices and Representations*, ed. Roger Chartier (Oxford, England: Polity Press, 1988), 172–200, as well as Edward Whiting Fox, *History in Geographic Perspective, The Other France* (New York: Norton, 1971); Charles Anatole et al., eds., *Le Sud et le nord, dialectique de la France* (Toulouse: Privat, 1971); Hervé Le Bras and Emmanuel Todd, *L'Invention de la France* (Paris: Pluriel, 1981); and Eugen Weber, *Peasants into Frenchmen: The Modernization of Rural France* (Stanford, Calif.: Stanford University Press, 1976).

13. Pierre Bonnaud, *Terres et langues. peuples et régions*, 2 vols. (Clermont-Ferrand, France: Auvernha Tara d'Oc, 1981), 2:362.

14. See Martyn Lyons, *Révolution et terreur à Toulouse* (Toulouse: Privàt, 1980) and Jean Sentou, *Révolution et contre-révolution dans la France du midi: 1789–1799* (Toulouse: Presses Universitaires du Mirail, 1991). See also Jacques Arlet, *Le Vie à Toulouse sous Louis-Philippe (1830–1848)* (Portet-sur-Garonne: Loubatières, 1994). The three institutions that had controlled Toulouse since the Middle Ages, the Parlement, the Capitoul, and the University, were all dissolved. The University of Toulouse reemerged under the educational reforms of Napoleon. But it was made part of the rigid, centralized educational system that was strictly controlled by the national government in Paris. As a result it lost its independence and its prestige and faded into the background of "provincialism."

15. François Crouzet argues that "the decisive turn in the industrial history of the southwest took place during the period of the Revolution and the Continental blockade" and that by the period of the July Monarchy (1830–1848) the retardation of the Midi in comparison to the north and east of France was clearly evident. François Crouzet, "Les Origines du sous-développement économique du sud-ouest," *Annales du Midi* 71(1959): 75. See also André Armengaud, "À propos des origines du sous-développement industriel dans le Sud-Ouest," *Annales du Midi* 72(1960): 75–81; and Roger Brunet, "Mutations du XIXe et problèmes du XXe siècle," in *Histoire de Languedoc*. Ronald Aminzade gives a more optimistic portrayal of Toulouse's nineteenth-century economic fortunes, as well as an excellent survey of industrial development, in *Class, Politics, and Early Industrial Capitalism, A Study of Mid-Nineteenth Century Toulouse, France* (Albany, N.Y.: State University of New York Press, 1981), chapter 2. See, more recently, Christopher Johnson, *The Life and Death of Industrial Languedoc, 1700–1920* (New York: Oxford University Press, 1995).

16. The depression reached famine proportions in the Pyrenees Mountains. The phylloxera plant louse destroyed the vineyards of lower Languedoc, and a series of diseases infected the silkworms cultivated along the Mediterranean. See *Histoire de la France rurale*, ed. Georges Duby, vol. 3, *Apogée et crise de la civilisation paysanne*, ed.

Maurice Agulhon (Paris: Seuil, 1976), 388–94. See also Roger Brunet, *Les Compagnes Toulousaines, étude géographique* (Toulouse: Faculté des Lettres et Sciences Humaines, 1965), 383.

17. Louis Vigé, *Toulouse et le département de la Haute-Garonne, population de 1801 à 1943* (Toulouse: R. Lion, 1945), 23; Région Midi-Pyrénées, *Programme d'action régionale 1958* (Paris: Imprimerie des Journaux Officels, 1959), 21.

18. The *Réseau du Midi,* owned by the northern banking empire of the Péreire Brothers, inaugurated its first line between Toulouse and Bordeaux in 1856. Between 1863 and 1884 lines were constructed that linked Toulouse with the Pyrenees Mountains, with Marseille, Carmaux, and with Paris. See Aminzade, *Early Industrial Capitalism,* 42–43, as well as Geneviève Bavignaud, "L'époque contemporaine: Fondements et aspects matériels," in *Le Languedoc et le Roussillon,* 368–70.

19. For the history of Toulouse's commercial thoroughfares and medieval streets, see J. Chalande, *Histoire des rues de Toulouse* (Paris: Montpensier, 1973), as well as Pierre Salies, *Dictionnaire des rues de Toulouse: Voies publiques, quartiers, lieux-dits, enseignes, organisation urbaine* (Toulouse: Milan, 1989). On the city's fairs and markets see Jack Thomas, *Le Temps des foires: Foires et marchés dans le midi toulousain de la fin de l'Ancien Régime à 1914* (Toulouse: Presses Universitaires du Mirail, 1993).

20. On the evolution of popular culture and everyday life, see Robert Mesuret, *Evocation du vieux Toulouse* (Paris: Minuit, 1960), quote from 18; Gérard Cholvy, "L'epoque contemporaine: Mentalités et croyances," in *Le Languedoc et le Roussillon,* 403–521; Gérard Cholvy, *Histoire de Languedoc de 1900 à nos jours* (Toulouse: Privat, 1980). For visual impressions of Toulouse, see Pierre Salies, *La Vie quotidienne à Toulouse en cartes postales anciennes* (Paris: SFL, 1976). General studies for France include *Histoire de la France urbaine,* ed. Georges Duby, vol. 4, *La ville de l'âge industriel,* ed. Maurice Agulhon (Paris, Seuil, 1983) and John M. Merriman, ed., *French Cities in the Nineteenth Century* (New York: Holmes and Meier, 1981).

21. Gérard Cholvy, "L'époque contemporaine: Mentalités et croyances," in *Le Languedoc et le Roussillon,* 449. See also Jean Sentou, *Fortunes et groupes sociaux à Toulouse sous la révolution (1789–1799), Essai d'histoire statistique* (Toulouse: Privat, 1969).

22. The most important insurrections in the south were the strikes at Decazeville in 1886, the strikes at Carmaux in 1892, and the revolt of the winegrowers in 1907. For turn-of-the-century politics at Toulouse see A. Dijonnet, *Le Socialism à Toulouse de 1908 à 1932* (Toulouse: 1974) as well as G. Bechtel, *1907: La grande révolte du midi* (Paris: Laffont, 1976).

23. For the history of *La Dépêche,* see Henri Lerner, *La Dépêche, journal de la démocratie,* 2 vols. (Toulouse: Privat, 1978) and Ch. Bellanger et al., eds., *Histoire générale de la presse française,* 3 vols. (Paris: PUF, 1969–1972).

24. Alfred Girard, "L'industrie et le commerce du pays toulousain," in *Documents sur Toulouse et sa région,* ed. La Ville de Toulouse, 2 vols. (Toulouse: Privat, 1910), 1:314, and Louis Ariste, "Le Prolétariat toulousain," 2:355–64. For working-class politics in nineteenth-century Toulouse, see Ronald Aminzade, *Ballots and Barri-*

cades: Class Formation and Republican Politics in France, 1830–1871 (Princeton, N.J.: Princeton University Press, 1993).

25. The few sources on Toulouse popular culture during the interwar years, other than the city's newspapers, remain Gratien Leblanc, *La Vie à Toulouse il y a cinquante ans* (Toulouse: Privat, 1978) and Pierre Gaches (Galan), *Toulouse les jours heureux, 1919–1936* (Toulouse: F. Boisseau, 1975). See also Henri Delpech, *Recherches sur la niveau de vie et les habitudes du consommation, Toulouse 1936–1938* (Paris: Recueil Sirey, 1938). On France see Olivier Barrot and Pascal Ory, eds., *Entre-deux guerres, La Création française, 1919–1939* (Paris: François Bourin, 1990) and Henri Noguères, *La vie quotidienne en France au temps du Front Populaire (1935–1938)* (Paris: Hachette, 1977).

26. On politics at Toulouse during the interwar years, see A. Vie, *Histoire politique de la municipalité Toulousaine de 1929 à 1939* (Toulouse: Privat, 1961); A. Clauzet and B. Daguerre, *Contribution à l'histoire du front populaire à Toulouse* (Toulouse: Privat, 1971). On France, see Pascal Ory, *La Belle illusion: Culture et politique sous le signe du Front Populaire* (Paris: Plon, 1994).

27. Louis Gratias, *Le Nouveau visage de Toulouse* (Paris: José Corti, 1934), 21.

28. These various refugee groups were instrumental in the organization of the Resistance in the southwest. Silvio Tentin was involved in the development of the *Libérer et Fédérer* movement at Toulouse. The first maquis unit in the south was formed in 1940 by a French reserve officer, Pierre Degon; fifteen German anti-Nazis including the former Prussian minister Otto Kleper; and some former members of the International Brigade who had fought in Spain. The Spanish refugees from the Civil War played a prominent role in all of the various Resistance units founded in the Toulouse region. They were commanded first by Jesus Rios and, after his death in 1944, by Luis Fernandez. Over 12,000 Spanish Republicans fought in the Resistance in the Languedoc area. They were eventually involved in the liberation of Toulouse, although most of their action took place in the countryside around the Pyrenees. See the articles by Emile Temime, "Les Espagnols dans la Résistance. Revenir aux réalités?" and Geneviève Dreyfus-Armand, "Les Espagnols dans la Résistance: Incertitudes et spécificités," in *Mémoire et Histoire: La Résistance*, ed. Jean-Marie Guillon and Pierre Laborie (Toulouse: Privat, 1995).

29. Wolff, *Histoire de Toulouse*, 507–8.

30. Cholvy, *Histoire de Languedoc de 1900 à nos jours*, 229. See also the excellent collection of articles on Vichy, the Occupation, and the Resistance in "Les années quarante dans le Midi," *Annales du Midi* 104(July-December 1992). On Toulouse, see Jean Estèbe, *Toulouse 1940–1944* (Paris: Perrin, 1996).

31. Quoted from *La Dépêche de Toulouse* in Eric Malo, "Le Camp de Noé (Haute-Garonne) de 1941 à 1944," *Annales du Midi* 100(July-September 1988): 338–46. See also Gret Arnoldson et al., *Les Camps du sud-ouest de la France. Exclusion, internement et déportation, 1939–1944* (Toulouse: Privat, 1994) and Jean Estèbe, "Les Juifs en midi toulousain pendant la seconde guerre mondiale: Etat de la question," *Annales du Midi* 104(July-December 1992): 461–75.

32. Cited in German military papers in Robert O. Paxton, *Vichy France, Old Guard and New Order, 1940–1944* (New York: Columbia University Press, 1972), 240. See also Jean-Pierre Azèma and François Bèdarida, eds., *La France des années noires,* 2 vols. (Paris: Seuil, 1993).

33. G. Bixel, "Carte de la souffrance de la Haute-Garonne," quoted in Michel Goubet and Paul Debauges, *Histoire de la Résistance* (Toulouse: Milan, 1986), 60–61. During the summer of 1943, the Milice denounced both Maurice and Albert Sarraut for using Communists in their newspaper's organization. In response, a number of Milice were beaten or killed. Sarraut's assassination in December was retaliation for the attacks, but it led to the arrest of Frossard and his agents by prefect Chesneaux de Leyritz, who was then himself denounced by Milice units. During the summer of 1944 about 100 men, women, and children were massacred by SS units in the villages of Marsoulas, Mazères, Buzet-sur-Tarn, Castelmaurou, and Villaudric.

34. For an extensive description and photographs of the Allied bombing of Toulouse, see Ville de Toulouse, "Numéro spécial consacré à la Libération," *Bulletin Municipal* (October 1944), as well as United States Strategic Bombing Survey, Physical Damage Division, "AIA aircraft plant, Toulouse, France," Report no. 19C, 1947.

35. On June 9, 1944, the Gestapo arrested seventeen of the city's most prominent leaders, among them Albert Sarraut and Jean Baylet of *La Dépêche* and André Haon, mayor of Toulouse. They were incarcerated at Saint-Michel prison and then sent to Compiègne, where a number of them were deported to the concentration camp of Neuengamme. Toulouse was thus left entirely without official public control amidst the confusion of the Allied invasion and German retreat.

36. See the Socialist underground Resistance paper *Le Populaire du Midi,* July 1943. On the emergence of the Resistance movement in the southwest, see Jean-Louis Cuvelliez, "Les débuts de la Résistance dans la région de Toulouse," in *Mémoire et Histoire: La Résistance.*

37. Pierre Laborie, "Opinion et répresentation: La Libération et l'image de la résistance," *Revue d'histoire de la deuxième guerre mondiale et des conflits contemporains* 33(July 1983): 65–91. See also Serge Ravanel, *L'Esprit de Résistance* (Paris: Seuil, 1995).

38. See the Communist Resistance newspaper *Front National,* 1 May 1943.

39. The fighting in Toulouse was carried out by sections of the Franc-Tireur et Partisans Français (FTPF) from the Haute-Garonne and the Lot (under Robert Noireau, known as Colonel George); the Comité Français de Libération guerrilla brigades from the Haute-Garonne and the Tarn as well as the demibrigade d'Armagnac (Groupe Parisot); maquis units of the Main-d'oeuvre Immigrée; the Corps Franc Pommiés (Groupe Chiron); and the Force Françaises de l'Intérieur (FFI) of the Haute-Garonne—all of them unified, momentarily at least, under the command of Colonel Berthier, Ravanel's adjunct and chief of the FFI forces of the Haute-Garonne. For a full description of the liberation of Toulouse and the Resistance forces involved see Pierre Bertaux, *Libération de Toulouse et de sa région* (Paris: Hachette, 1973) and Michel Goubet, "Une 'république rouge' à Toulouse à la Liberation: Mythe ou réalité?" *Revue d'histoire de la deuxième guerre mondiale et des conflits contemporains* 33(July 1983): 25–30. See also Roland Trempé, *La Libération dans le midi de la France,* Actes du Colloque, 7–8

Juin 1985 (Toulouse: Presses universitaires du Mirail, 1986) and H. R. Kedward, *The Liberation of France, Image and Event* (Oxford, England: Berg, 1995).

40. Bertaux, *Libération de Toulouse,* 35.

41. For the emotional intensity of the first days of the Liberation, see "Numéro Spécial Consacrée à la Liberation," *Bulletin Municipal,* 65–83.

2. Regionalism, Municipalism, and Modernization

1. See Henry Rousso, *The Vichy Syndrome, History and Memory in France since 1944,* Arthur Goldhammer, trans. (Cambridge, Mass.: Harvard University Press, 1991).

2. On the practice of geography and social theory in France and elsewhere, see Edward Soja, *Postmodern Geographies, The Reassertion of Space in Critical Social Theory* (London: Verso, 1989).

3. For an excellent analysis of regionalist theories and the search for France, see Herman Lebovics, *True France, the Wars over Cultural Identity, 1900–1945* (Ithaca, N.Y.: Cornell University Press, 1992); Daniel Nordman and Jacques Revel, "La formation de l'espace français," in *L'espace français,* ed. Louis Bergeron et al., vol. 5 of *Histoire de la France,* ed. André Burguière and Jacques Revel (Paris: Seuil, 1989). See also Maurice Agulhon, "Conscience nationale et conscience régionale en France de 1815 à nos jours," in *Histoire vagabonde: Idéologies et politique dans la France du XIXᵉ siècle,* 2 vols. (Paris: Gallimard, 1988), 2:144–74.

4. R. Andréant, "Le Languedoc et la France (1905–1914)," *Annales du Midi* (1977): 53–65.

5. As quoted in Cholvy, "L'époque contemporaine: Mentalités et croyances," in *Le Languedoc et le Roussillon,* 507.

6. See Bechtel, *1907: La grande révolte du midi,* and Robert Lafont, *Mistral ou l'illusion* (Paris: Vent Terral, 1980).

7. Andréant, "Le Languedoc et la France," 54. The Radicals governed the municipality from 1888 to 1906, then from 1908 to 1912 and after the First World War from 1919 to 1925.

8. See Lafont, *La Revendication occitane,* chapter 4, 242–48, and Gérard de Sède, *700 ans de révoltes occitanes,* chapter 10.

9. See Madeleine Rébérioux, "Jaurès à Toulouse (1890–1892)," *Annales du Midi* 75(1963): 295–310.

10. See Le Roy Ladurie, "Occitania in Historical Perspective," *Review,* 21–30, and Cholvy, *Histoire de Languedoc,* chapter 6. On the broader perspective of early Midi socialism, see Tony Judt, *Socialism in Provence, 1871–1914: A Study in the Origins of the Modern French Left* (Cambridge: Cambridge University Press, 1979). See also Antonio Gramsci, *The Southern Question,* Pasquale Vericchio, trans. (West Lafayette, Ind.: Bordighera, 1995).

11. The city had been declared an independent republic in 1189 and enjoyed twenty short years of self-rule under a constitution. According to the ordinances of 1687 under the Old Regime, the city was governed by the Capitoul, composed of twelve appointed "consuls" chosen from lists of candidates who represented the various districts, or *partidas,* of the city. The districts were then subdivided into *melos,* groups of neighboring houses, each governed by a *dixainier.* Under the French Revolution, a "General Council of the Commune" was elected by all citizens who could prove they had worked for ten days. A "Municipal Council" was elected by universal manhood suffrage during the 1848 Revolution. It was summarily repressed in 1852, and power over the city was largely delegated to the departmental prefect. For a full examination of the various interpretations of Occitan *mentalité,* see Gérard Cholvy, "Histoire contemporaines en pays d'oc," *Annales* 33(July-August 1978): 863–79.

12. See in particular Jean-Yves Nevers, "Du clientélisme à la technocratie: Cent ans de démocratie communale dans une grande ville, Toulouse," *Revue française de science politique* 33(June 1983): 440.

13. Marcel Roncayolo makes this point about the public figure of the town mayor as portrayed in vaudeville and the comedies of Labiche, as well as in the novels of Flaubert, in *Histoire de la France urbaine,* ed. Georges Duby, vol. 5, *La Ville aujourd'hui,* ed. Marcel Roncayolo (Paris: Seuil, 1985), 577.

14. Jean Coppolani, "Esquisse géographique de la banlieue de Toulouse," Part II: "Les paysages et les subdivisions de la banlieue," *RGPSO* 34(December 1963): 352–53.

15. For a description of suburban architectural styles and suburban districts around Toulouse, see Wanda Rewienska, "Quelques remarques sur la physionomie de la ville de Toulouse," *RGPSO* 8(1937): 73–88. On working-class suburbs in Paris during the interwar years, see Tyler Stovall, *The Rise of the Paris Red Belt* (Berkeley, Calif.: University of California Press, 1990).

16. *Atelier pour service de nettoiement, Régie des abattoirs, Régie de l'usine d'incinération, des ordures ménagères, Régie des pompes funèbres,* and so forth. See Nevers, "Cent ans de démocratie communale," 447.

17. For an excellent analysis of interwar architecture and urban design at Toulouse, see "Conseil d'architecture, d'urbanisme et de l'environnement de la Haute-Garonne and Ecole d'Architecture de Toulouse," *Toulouse 1920–1940: La ville et ses architectes* (Toulouse: OMBRES, 1991). Gwendolyn Wright, *The Politics of Design in French Colonial Urbanism* (Chicago: University of Chicago Press, 1991), provides an outstanding discussion of housing and municipal reform efforts and the appeal of regional styles and scientific management. See also Jean-Claude Vigato, *L'Architecture régionaliste, France 1890–1940* (Paris: Norma/IFA, 1994).

18. Montariol worked as the head architect for the Office Public d'HBM at Toulouse from 1925 to 1939 as the Socialist government's chief propagandist for modern style. Yet his use of decoration remained Classical in character. The Toulouse Municipal Library is perhaps the best example of his mixed style. Conseil d'architecture, *Toulouse 1920–1940,* chapters 3 and 4. On housing reform, see Nicholas Bullock and James Read, *The Movement for Housing Reform in Germany and France* (Cambridge: Cambridge University Press, 1985); R. Quilliot and R. Guerrand, *Cent ans d'habitat social, une utopie réaliste* (Paris: Albin Michel, 1989); J. P. Flamond, *Loger les peuples,*

essai sur l'histoire du logement social en France (Paris: La Découverte, 1989); and Mari-Jeanne Dumont, *Le Logement social à Paris 1850–1930, Les habitations à bon marché* (Liège, France: Mardaga, 1991).

19. See for example Yves Cohen and Rémi Baudoui, *Les Chantiers de la paix sociale (1900–1940)* (Fontenay, France: ENS, 1995) and Jean-Pierre Gaudin, *L'Avenir en plan: technique et politique dans la prévision urbaine, 1900–1930* (Seyssel, France: Champ Vallon, 1985). Both provide excellent overviews of interwar efforts at urbanism by Henri Sellier and a host of social reformers, as does Jean-Louis Cohen, *Architecture et politiques sociales, 1900–1940* (Paris: Parentheses, 1985).

20. Jaussely's classes at the Institut d'Urbanisme included master plans, open-space allocations, garden cities, and civic centers. In conjunction with his work on the Cornudet Law, he designed city plans for Paris, Grenoble, Briançon, Carcassone, Tarbes, and Pau. He also designed, in collaboration with Charles Nicod, an award-winning urban plan for Berlin. For further information on Jaussely, see Jean-Pierre Gaudin, *Desseins des villes: "art urbain" et urbanisme* (Paris: L'Harmattan, 1991), 31–33, and Capell Torres, "Planning Problems and Practices in the Jaussely Era," *Planning Perspectives* 7(1992).

21. Jean Coppolani, chief urbanist at Toulouse during the 1970s and 1980s, called the Jaussely plan a "brilliant exercise in the tradition of Haussmann. It carved up the city with avenues twenty-five to seventy-five meters wide without any consideration for neighborhood or the historic urban structure." Although historic monuments were preserved, in Coppolani's estimation, they were treated as isolated cases, divorced from the neighborhood context. Coppolani, *Toulouse aux XXe siècle* (Toulouse: Privat, 1963), 400–1.

22. For the various intellectual currents behind the regionalist movement at the turn of the century, see Paul Rabinow, *French Modern: Norms and Forms of the Social Environment* (Cambridge, Mass.: MIT Press, 1989), chapter 6, as well as Nordman and Revel, "La formation de l'espace français," *L'espace français*, 142–49.

23. See Pierre Doueil, *L'Administration locale à l'épreuve de la guerre (1939–1949)* (Paris: Receuil Sirey, 1950) for a detailed account of early efforts at regional administration.

24. Paul Vidal de la Blache, "Régions françaises," *La Revue de Paris* 17(December 1910): 821–49. See also Henri Hauser, *Le Problème du régionalisme* (Paris: Presses Universitaires de France, 1924).

25. Quoted in Emmanuel Chadeau, *Latécoère* (Paris: Olivier Orban, 1990), 160. See also Georges Baccrabère and Georges Jorré, *Toulouse, terre d'envol* (Toulouse: Privat, 1966), 87–91.

26. *La Dépêche,* 21 August 1941.

27. See Charles-Louis Foulon, *Le Pouvoir en province à la Libération* (Paris: Armond Colin, 1975), 14–15, as well as Philippe Buton and Jean-Marie Guillon, eds., *Les Pouvoirs en France à la Libération* (Paris: Belin, 1994).

28. The DGEN was initially led by François Lehideux. Between 1942 and 1944 the agency drafted two plans: the ten-year plan, or *Plan d'Equipement National,* produced in 1942, and a shorter version called the *Tranche de Démarrage,* completed in

1944 after the DGEN fell under the authority of the Ministry of Finance. See in particular Henri Rousso, "Vichy et la 'modernisation,'" in *Reconstructions et modernisation, la France aprés les ruines 1918 . . . 1945. . .* , ed. Direction des Archives de France (Paris: Archives Nationales, 1991), 76–81, and Richard Kuisel, *Capitalism and the State in Modern France* (Cambridge: Cambridge University Press, 1981), chapter 5.

29. The construction of regional "satellite cities" would provide workers with a "healthier climate" and avoid the risks of tuberculosis. As specialized corporative towns, they would also permit the worker to have access to the ownership of his or her property. The models for these new regional centers were Pau, Tarbes, Bagnères, Figeac, and Soucy in the southwest, which all specialized in aircraft production. DGEN, *Rapports et études sur la décongestion des centres industriels,* vol. 3, *Résultat des expériences de décentralisation de la période d'avant-guerre, 1930–1939* (Paris, 1944).

30. *La Dépêche,* 29 June 1941.

31. Roland Trempé, "La région économique de Toulouse aux lendemains de la Libération," *Annales du Midi* 94(January-March 1982): 79.

32. On Toulouse, see Robert Condat, "Une revue toulousaine au temps de Vichy: Pyrénées," *Annales du Midi* 104(July-December 1992): 391–412. For general studies of France, see Christian Faure, *Le Projet culturel de Vichy* (Lyon: Presses Universitaires de Lyon and CNRS, 1989), 54–58, and Jean-Pierre Rioux, *La Vie culturelle sous Vichy* (Paris: Complex, 1990).

33. See in particular Rose-Anne Couedelo, "Aménagement et urbanisme, l'insertion des pouvoirs publics 1919–1950," in *Reconstructions et modernisation,* 214–15, and Doueil, *L'Administration locale,* 176–77.

34. *Bulletin municipal de Toulouse,* 48(June 1944).

35. Guy Labédan, "La Répression à la libération dans la région de Toulouse," *Revue d'histoire de la deuxième guerre mondiale et des conflits contemporains* 33(July 1983): 105–12, and the articles on the Liberation and the purges in "Les Années quarante dans le Midi," *Annales du Midi* 104(July-December 1992).

36. Emmanuel Le Roy Ladurie, *Histoire de Languedoc* (Paris: PUF, 1974), 125.

37. Quoted in M. Goubet, "Une 'République rouge' à Toulouse: Mythe ou réalité?" *Revue d'histoire de la deuxième guerre mondiale et des conflits contemporains* 33(July 1983): 25–40.

38. See Pierre Laborie, "Opinions et représentations: La Libération et l'image de la Résistance," *Revue d'histoire de la deuxième guerre mondiale et des conflits contemporains* 33(July 1983): 65–91.

39. See Roland Trempé, "Aux origines des comités mixtes à la production: Les comités de libération d'entreprise dans la région Toulousaine," *Revue d'histoire de la deuxième guerre mondiale et des conflits contemporains* 33(July 1983): 41–64.

40. *Bulletin municipal* 48(July-August 1944). See also Goubet, "Une 'République rouge' à Toulouse," 37.

41. *Bulletin municipal* 49(July 1945).

42. Trempé, "La région économique de Toulouse," 61–90.

43. Bertaux, *Libération de Toulouse,* 260.

44. Ibid., 261–62.

45. Ibid., chapter xix.

46. Quoted in Trempé, "La région économique de Toulouse," 88.

47. M. Goubet, "Un exemple de 'pouvoir régional' dans la Clandestinité: Le C.D.L. de la Haute-Garonne," *Résistance R4,* no. 16 (1970) and Foulon, *Le Pouvoir en province,* chapter 6.

48. See Laborie, "L'image de la Résistance," 76–86, as well as Jean-Pierre Rioux, *The Fourth Republic, 1944–1958,* vol. 7, *The Cambridge History of Modern France* (Cambridge: Cambridge University Press, 1987), chapter 4, and G. Madjarian, *Conflit, pouvoir et société à la Libération* (Paris: Union générale d'édition, 1980).

3. Constructing Modernism in the 1950s

1. *La République du sud-ouest,* 6 January 1947.

2. Institut National de la Statistique et des Etudes Economiques (INSEE), Direction régionale de Toulouse, *Annuaire statistique régional retrospectif,* part 3 (Toulouse: Direction régionale, 1951), 214–15. See also S. P. Kramer, "La Crise économique de la Libération," *Revue d'histoire de la deuxième guerre mondiale* 111(July 1978): 25–44.

3. The average salary at Toulouse was 4,000 francs a year. INSEE, "Les Salaires en France en Octobre 1946," *Bulletin de la statistique générale de la France* 2(April 1947): 287–88.

4. INSEE, Direction régionale de Toulouse, *Etude statistique de l'agglomération de Toulouse* (Toulouse: Direction régionale, 1952), 279–301. See also Bernard Kayser, "Le nouveau visage de Toulouse," *RGPSO* 32(September 1961): 225–35.

5. *La République du sud-ouest,* 10 September 1946.

6. For population and housing figures in the communes surrounding Toulouse, the best sources are INSEE, *Dénombrement de la population* for 1936 and 1946, Département de la Haute-Garonne, Toulouse (Paris: Presses Universitaires de France, 1937 and 1947), as well as INSEE, *Résultats statistiques du recensement général de la population,* effectué le 10 Mars 1946, vol. 3, Département de la Haute-Garonne (Paris: Imprimerie nationale, 1947) and INSEE, *Recensement général de la population de Mai 1954,* Résultats statistiques, Population-Ménages-Logements-Maisons, Département de la Haute-Garonne (Paris: Imprimerie nationale, 1960).

7. Jean Coppolani, "Esquisse géographique de la banlieue de Toulouse," Part II, "Les paysages et les subdivisions de la banlieue," *RGPSO* 34(December 1963): 352–54. The highest population increases in the suburbs of Toulouse were in the commune of Portet-sur-Garonne. Only 1,000 inhabitants lived in the commune in 1936, but by 1954 their numbers had swollen to 4,000.

8. On French reconstruction and urban policy, see Danièle Voldman, *La Reconstruction des villes françaises de 1940 à 1954, Histoire d'une politique* (Paris: L'Harmattan, 1997); Patrick Dieudonné, *Villes reconstruites, du dessin au destin,* 2 vols. (Paris: L'Harmattan, 1994); Bruno Vayssière, *Reconstruction-Déconstruction. Le hard french ou l'architecture française des trente glorieuses* (Paris: Picard, 1988); as well as Anatole Kopp,

Frédérique Boucher, and Danièle Pauly, *L'Architecture de la reconstruction en France 1945–1953* (Paris: Moniteur, 1982).

9. For a condensed version of Badiou's opinions on urban planning and the regional role of Toulouse, see *La Dépêche du Midi*, 19 March 1957. See also Jean Coppolani, "Une politique d'isolement communal: Toulouse," RGPSO 42(October 1971): 391–409.

10. Ch. Nicod, "Plan Nicod, Rapport succinct" (December 1948), Plans d'aménagement de Toulouse, Dossier Administratif, Archives municipales de Toulouse (AM) 5S576. On the Nicod Plan see also Jean Coppolani, "Le nouveau plan d'urbanisme de Toulouse," *La Vie urbaine* (1956); Marie-Françoise Manolesco, "La municipalité de Toulouse, 1940–1944, Plan Nicod 1942," Mémoire de maîtrise, Université de Toulouse-Le Mirail, 1987.

11. L'Ordre Régional des Architectes de la Circonscription de Toulouse, Syndicat des Entrepreneurs du Batiment et des Travaux Publiques, Letter to the Mayor of Toulouse (14 September 1946), Comité Consultif du Bureau d'Esthetique Urbaine, AM 24/163.

12. On the MRU, architecture, and public-housing policy see Olivier Piron, ed., *Une Politique du logement, Ministère de la Reconstruction et de l'Urbanism* (Paris: Institut Français d'Architecture, Plan Construction et Architecture, 1995). See the excellent summary of the modernist ideal at the war's end in "La Ville selon Le Corbusier," *Urbanisme* 282(May-June 1995) as well as Manfredo Tafuri, "Machine et mémoire: The City in the Work of Le Corbusier," in H. Allen Brooks, ed., *Le Corbusier* (Princeton, N.J.: Princeton University Press, 1987).

13. *La République du sud-ouest*, 10 and 20 March 1947.

14. *La Dépêche du Midi*, 2 April 1949.

15. *La Dépêche du Midi*, 19 April 1949.

16. *La Dépêche du Midi*, 21 July 1949. See also Coppolani, "Une politique d'isolement communal," 400–1.

17. On Joliment, Empalot, and the many other modern construction projects at Toulouse, see Bernard Kayser, "Le nouveau visage de Toulouse," RGPSO 22(September 1961): 229, as well as Daniel Faucher, "Du nouveau sur Toulouse," RGPSO 32(September 1961): 201–5. See also "L'equipement des grands ensembles," *Urbanisme* 28(1959): 1–120. Two of the projects, Lazaret-de-Lalande in the northern farming area and Chateau de l'Hers along the Rouge de Castres east of the city, were built on a more modest scale, with smaller apartment buildings, single dwellings, and individual gardens.

18. See the abundant building statistics in the 1962 departmental census published by INSEE, *Recensement général de la population de 1962*, as well as Ministère de L'équipement et du Logement, *Agglomération toulousaine, Project de livre blanc* (Toulouse: 30 November 1967), 102–7; Bernard Kayser, "Le nouveau visage de Toulouse," 232.

19. *La Dépêche du Midi*, 26 April 1957.

20. For an extraordinary portrait of life at Empalot, see Philippe Berthaut, ed., *L'Empal'Odyssée, traversée dans la mémoire d'Empalot, quartier de Toulouse* (Toulouse, le

Lézard, 1993). Monsieur Calas' descriptions are taken from "enfin locataire," 28. See also René Kaës, *Vivre dans les grandes ensembles* (Paris: Editions Ouvrières, 1963). *A History of Private Life,* ed. Philippe Ariès and George Duby, vol. 5, *Riddles of Identity in Modern Times,* ed. Antoine Prost and Gérard Vincent, trans. Arthur Goldhammer (Cambridge, Mass.: Harvard University Press, 1991) offers an excellent analysis of the shift to modern apartment living.

21. *Bulletin municipal* 59(April-May 1955): 256–61.

22. "L'Enquête sur le logement à Toulouse," *La Dépêche du Midi,* 8 June 1954.

23. *La Dépêche du Midi,* 2 March 1953.

24. Georges Lacroix, "Rapport du commissaire enquêter," January 1957, 150–51, 172, Plans d'urbanisme directeur 1955–1962, AM 64/81.

25. "Une importante conférence sur la politique du logement," *La Dépêche du Midi,* 18 May 1954.

26. Lucien Babonneau, "Nouveau visage de Toulouse," and "Urbanisme et harmonie," *La Dépêche du Midi,* 12 May and 1 June 1954.

27. *La Dépêche du Midi,* 24 July 1960.

28. Babonneau, "Defense de Toulouse contre le désordre anarchique de la construction," Dossier Administratif, AM 5S576.

29. Pierre de Gorsse, "Nouveau visage de Toulouse," *Auta* (August 1956).

30. Ch. Nicod, "Rapport et conclusion de l'enquête documentaire," January 1957, 56, Plans d'urbanisme directeur 1955–1962, AM 64/81.

31. Commission départmentale de l'urbanisme, séance du Octobre 1955, Plans d'urbanisme directeur 1955–1962, AM 64/81.

32. INSEE, *Recensement 1954,* Population, ménages, 31.

33. See Jean Coppolani, "La population de Toulouse depuis 1954" (Toulouse: L'institut de Géographie, Université de Toulouse–Le Mirail, 1978) and his "La population de Toulouse en 1975," *RGPSO* 48(1977): 9–31.

34. INSEE, *Recensement 1954,* Population, ménages, 64–65; *Livre blanc,* 102–4.

35. Engénieur en Chef des Ponts et Chaussées pour la Haute-Garonne, "Voitures en circulation," as quoted in *La Dépêche du Midi,* 21 January 1961.

36. Nicod, "Rapport et conclusion de l'enquête documentaire," 52.

37. *La République du sud-ouest,* 10 May 1947.

38. Alex Coutet, *Toulouse ville artistique, plaisante et curieuse* (Toulouse: Richard, 1926), 22.

39. Jean Coppolani, "L'Évolution des paysages urbains de Toulouse depuis 1945," *RGPSO* 49(September 1978): 348.

40. Anne-Marie Arnauné-Clamens, "L'operation de rénovation urbaine du quartier Saint-Georges à Toulouse," *RGPSO* 48(February 1977): 90–91. See also "Toulouse: rénovation urbaine quartier Saint-Georges," *Urbanisme* 183(1981).

41. Lacroix, "Rapport du Commissaire Enquêter," 171. On the drama of the renovation of Les Halles in Paris, see Jacques Herbert, *Sauver Les Halles: Coeur de Paris* (Paris: Denöel, 1971). Norma Evenson, *Paris: A Century of Change, 1878–1978* (New Haven, Conn.: Yale University Press, 1979), also describes the impact of postwar slum clearance in the capital.

42. *Sociétés d'économie mixte* were set up by the government in 1951, and then improved in 1957, to coordinate and finance the development of specific urban and rural zones throughout France. The Toulouse-Equipement version included the city of Toulouse, the department of the Haute-Garonne, the departmental HLM offices, the Chamber of Commerce, the Caisse d'Epargne de Toulouse, the Caisse Nationale de Dépôts et Consignations, and the Société Centrale pour L'équipement du Territoire. It was initially responsible for the Saint-Georges project, as well as new construction at Empalot, the development of the Rangueil quarter, and the city's three industrial zones. See J.-E. Godchot, *Les Sociétés d'économie mixte et l'aménagement du territoire* (Paris: Berger-Levrault, 1966).

43. This description of the Municipal Council debates on Saint-Georges is taken from the *Bulletin municipal* 63(June-July 1959): 263–76.

44. Series of articles by E. H. Guitard in *La Dépêche du Midi* entitled "Où en sont les taudis," August 1957; "L'aménagement de Toulouse, exposé et commentaire," 2 February 1957, and "Le plan projeté par 'Toulouse-Equipement,'" 13 June 1959.

45. *Bulletin municipal* 63(June-July 1959): 263–76.

46. *Bulletin municipal* 63(June-July 1959): 264.

47. *L'Avenir,* 1 September 1957.

48. *La Dépêche du Midi,* 14 January 1959.

49. *La Dépêche du Midi,* 6 July 1959.

50. Ville de Toulouse and SETOMIP, *Rénovation Saint-Georges* (January 1977), 5–7.

51. SETOMIP, *Rénovation Saint-Georges,* 11. After the initial sales and building demolitions, the whole construction project sank into an impasse between 1963 and 1965.

52. Guy Jalabert, "Vieilles pierres et société urbaine," RGPSO 49(1978): 358. See also Manuel Castells et al., *La Rénovation urbaine à Paris, Structure urbaine et logique de classe* (Paris: L'Ecole Pratiques des Hautes Etudes, 1973) and his *The Urban Question* (London: Edward Arnold, 1977).

53. The term "jacobinism" is used consistently by historians describing the shift in economic policy making from the Commissars of the Republic to the central state bureaucratic machinery in 1946 and 1947. It clearly connotes "robbery" and the loss of independent initiation on the part of the provincial capitals in the effort to reestablish central state power. See, for example, the discussion in Foulon, *Pouvoir en province,* 269–74.

54. These twelve included the departments of Ariège, Haute-Garonne, Lot, Hautes-Pyrénées, Tarn, Tarn-et-Garonne, Gers, Basses-Pyrénées, Aude, Aveyron, and Pyréndes-Orientales. The twelfth, Landes, was transferred to the Fourth Administrative Region around Bordeaux in March 1958.

55. Jean Gravier, *Paris et le désert français* (Paris: Flammarion, 1947).

56. Communication du Ministre de Reconstruction et de l'Urbanisme au Conseil des Ministres, *Pour un plan national d'aménagement du territoire* (Paris, February 1950).

57. Sources on the French government's regional development policy and *aménagement du territoire* are numerous. A good starting place is Marcel Roncayolo, "L'aménagement du territoire (XVIIIe-XXe siècle)" in *Histoire de la France,* vol. 1, *L'Espace français,* 604–28. See also Pierre Bauchet, *L'Expérience française de planification* (Paris: Seuil, 1958); Olivier Guichard, *Aménager la France* (Paris: Laffont-Gonthier, 1965); J. F. Gravier, *L'aménagement du territoire et l'avenir des régions françaises* (Paris: Flammarion, 1964); Priscilla DeRoo, Jean-Paul Laborie, and Jean-François Langumier, *La Politique française d'aménagement du territoire de 1950 à 1985* (Paris: La Documentation Française, 1985); and Pierre Randet, *L'Aménagement du territoire, Genèse et étapes d'un grand dessein* (Paris: La Documentation Française, 1994).

58. See, for example, Bonnaud, *Terres et langues,* II:363, and Rémy Pech et al. (Pambenel), *Politique en Midi-Pyrénées* (Paris: Editions Eché, 1987), 16–17. A local article on "Le programme d'expansion régionale" in *La Dépêche,* 19 November 1958, outlines the immediate concerns over the viability of the Midi-Pyrénées. For a more general description of these regional efforts, see Pierre Grémion and Jean-Pierre Worms, *Les Institutions régionales et la société locale* (Paris: Copédith, 1968).

59. F. Cousteaux, "L'Industrialisation de Toulouse," *Les nouvelles industrielles et commerciales* (NIC), mensuel de la Chambre de Commerce et d'Industrie de Toulouse, 44(15 November 1959): 20.

60. Région Midi-Pyrénées, *Programme d'action régionale 1958,* 42–43 and 80, as well as Louis Périllier, Préfet de la Haute-Garonne, *L'Expansion économique dans la Haute-Garonne* (Toulouse: Imprimerie préfectorale, November 1956), 12–13.

61. INSEE, "Les salaires dans l'industrie et le commerce en 1954, d'après les déclarations de salaires 1024," *Etudes statistiques* 3(July-September 1956) and INSEE, "Les salaires dans l'industrie, le commerce et les services en 1956, d'après les déclarations de salaires 1024," *Etudes statistiques* 4(October-December 1958): 85–86.

62. *La Dépêche du Midi,* 20 November 1958. See also "Journées économique et sociales de la région de Toulouse," *Exposées de MM. les préfets de la région de Toulouse sur la situation économique de leur départements 1955* (Toulouse: Imprimerie préfectorale, 1955).

63. See *La Dépêche du Midi,* 7 March 1959 and 12 May 1959.

64. *La Dépêche du Midi,* 19 November 1958.

4. The City of the Future: Planning in the 1960s

1. Charles de Gaulle, *Discours et messages,* vol. 1, *Avec le renouveau, 1958–1962* (Paris: Plon, 1970), 80.

2. *La Dépêche du Midi,* 15 February 1959. On the role of the French state, see Pierre Birnbaum, *Les Sommets de l'état* (Paris: Seuil, 1977); Ezra N. Suleiman, *Private Power and Centralization in France* (Princeton, N.J.: Princeton University Press, 1987); and André Gueslin, *L'Etat, l'économie et la société française, XIXe-XXe siècle* (Paris: Hachette, 1991).

3. "L'Industrialisation de Toulouse," NIC 44(15 November 1959): 19. See also Ville de Toulouse, *Destin d'une grande ville* (January 1959). On the Gaullist version of

modernization, see André Gauron, *Histoire économique et sociale de la cinquième Republique,* vol. 1, *Les temps des modernistes* (Paris: La Découverte, 1988).

4. Christiane Toujas-Pinède, "Les rapatriés d'Algérie dans la région Midi-Pyrénées," *RGPSO* 36(December 1965): 321–72.

5. It would be impossible to catalogue the enormous compendium of population studies and reports issued by the government during the 1960s. They evidence, however, the ongoing stress laid on the relationship between demographics and national power in France and the tribulations over the French birthrate, mobility, and identity. See, for example, the reports issued by INSEE under *Etudes et statistiques* for the 1960s.

6. "La promotion économique de Toulouse et sa région," *NIC* 51(June-July 1960): 3.

7. Christian Beringuier, André Boudou, and Guy Jalabert, *Toulouse Midi-Pyrénées, la transition* (Paris: Stock, 1972), 284.

8. John Ardagh, *France Today,* 159.

9. Réunion du conseil d'administration, 19 December 1959, Plans d'urbanisme directeur, 1955–1962, AM 64/81.

10. See IFA-PCA, *Une Politique du logement,* 43–50, and Roncayolo, *La Ville aujourd'hui,* 101–4; Réunion du conseil d'administration, 19 Decembre 1959, Plans d'urbanisme directeur, 1955–1962, AM 64/81; as well as Ville de Toulouse, *Destin d'une grande ville.*

11. *Livre blanc,* 21–22.

12. See Région Midi-Pyrénées, Conférence interdépartmentale, *Programme d'urgence de développement économique et social de la région Midi-Pyrénées* (Toulouse: IGAME, 1962).

13. This policy was initially articulated in the 1957 Surleau Report. See, for example, Jean Gottmann, "Pour une géographie des centres transactionnels," *Bulletin de l'association de géographes français* 385–86(January-February 1971): 41–49, as well as Pierre George, "Les villes-métropoles," in *Aménagement du territoire et développement régional,* no. 1 (Grenoble: Institut d'études politiques, 1968), 140–45, and Edmond Lisle, *Recherche scientifique et aménagement du territoire* (Paris: La Documentation Française, 1973).

14. See, for a few examples amoung many, Daniel Faucher, *Toulouse* (Paris: La Documentation Française, 1961); Comité industriel d'action économique de la région de Toulouse, *Richesses et esperances du Midi-Pyrénées,* ed. J. D. Vervo (Toulouse: Larrieu-Bonnel, 1962); and Louis Bazerque, *La Mutation de Toulouse,* rapport synthèse devant l'assemblée municipale, 11 July 1969, reprinted by *Les Documents de La Dépêche* (Toulouse, 1969).

15. *Livre blanc,* 22–30. For a summary version of the planning scheme, see Louis Bazerque, "La mutation d'une ville, Toulouse," *Le Moniteur des travaux publics et du batiment* 12(March 1967). On the theoretical motifs behind the imperial engineering and urban designs of 1960s modernism, see Peter Hall, *Cities of Tomorrow, An Intellectual History of Urban Planning and Design in the Twentieth Century* (Oxford, England: Basil Blackwell, 1988). On the power of the French bureaucracy, see Michel Crozier's

classic critique, *The Bureaucratic Phenomenon* (Chicago: University of Chicago Press, 1964).

16. One good example, among many, of these visual panaromic references is Mairie de Toulouse, *Toulouse dans sa région à la veille du VIe Plan*, text by Louis Bazerque (12 November 1970).

17. Commission nationale des plans d'urbanisme, Réunion du 16 Decembre 1960, AM 64/81.

18. "La promotion économique de Toulouse et sa région," NIC 51(June-July 1960): 3.

19. *La Dépêche du Midi*, 12 May 1959.

20. *La Dépêche du Midi*, 17 April 1957.

21. *La Dépêche du Midi*, 4 August 1960.

22. *Bulletin municipal* 64(June-July 1960): 352–65. The 1958 state decrees required *plans directeur d'urbanisme* for each city as well as *plans de détail* for each sector of the *agglomération*.

23. *La Dépêche du Midi*, 23 January and 2 February 1961.

24. Jean Coppolani, "Les migrations quotidiennes vers Toulouse en 1954 et 1962," RGPSO 38(1967): 165–73. See also Robert Marconis, *Midi-Pyrénées, XIXe-XXe siècles. Transports, espace, sociétés*, vol. 2, *Croissance et crise de l'agglomération toulousaine* (Toulouse: Milan, 1986). On France, see Nicole Haumont, *Les pavillonnaires* (Paris: Centre de recherches d'urbanisme, 1975).

25. On land speculation in the suburbs of Toulouse, see the research reports published by the Centre Interdisciplinaire d'Etudes Urbaines at the Université de Toulouse–Le-Mirail, such as Marie-Christine Jaillet and Guy Jalabert, "La Société des lotis, les propriétaires pavillonnaires autour de Toulouse," published in "Les Périphéries urbaines," Actes du Colloque, Angers, 6 et 7 Décembre 1984, *Géographie sociale* 2(September 1985): 183–89. See also Guy Jalabert, "Spéculation foncière et urbanisation dans la banlieue Toulousaine," RGPSO 42(December 1971): 431–53. Jalabert argued that suburban land values did not jump as high as in some cities, such as Nice. Nor did they reach the prices in some of the neighborhoods in central Toulouse. Nonetheless, the incessant demand for housing made suburban land sales and construction projects a lucrative business.

26. *Livre blanc*, 114–16.

27. Coppolani, "Une politique d'isolement communal," 403.

28. Guy Jalabert, "Spéculation foncière," 434–35, 448. On the various attitudes toward development and the relationship between the suburban communes, see Michel Idrac, "Le Fonctionnement de l'agglomération Toulousaine," *Géographie sociale* 2(September 1985): 247–52.

29. M. le Juillou, "Principles généraux d'un plan directeur du groupement d'urbanisme de Toulouse," 1960, Etudes Urbaines, 1960–1966, AM 64/83.

30. Commission nationale des plans d'urbanisme, Réunion du 16 Decembre 1960, Plans d'urbanisme directeur 1955–1962, AM 64/81.

31. See Georges Candilis, *Bâtir la vie, un architecte témoin de son temps* (Paris: Stock, 1977). Both CIAM and ABAT were founded by Le Corbusier as think tanks for modern architecture and urban theory. Candilis teamed with architects Shadrach Woods and Alexis Josic for the 1960s town planning and new systems projects. He was also appointed by the French government as lead architect for the regional development–tourist resort program built along the Languedoc-Mediterranean coast-line during the late 1960s and 1970s.

32. Ville de Toulouse, Concours Toulouse Le Mirail, Equipe Candilis, Dony, Josic, Woods, "First Prize Presentation," 1966, and Equipe Candilis, Dony, Josic, Woods, "Concours ZUP Le Mirail Toulouse," 1966, AM 72/1. On the other French suburban programs, see Roncayolo, *La Ville aujourd'hui,* chapter 8. For the role of architectural design in the conception of culture and society under the Fifth Republic, see Eric Lengereau, "L'architecture entre culture et développement (1965–1995)," *Vingtième Siècle* 53 (January–March 1997).

33. For descriptions of the plans for Le Mirail, see Ville de Toulouse, Concours Toulouse Le Mirail, "First Prize Presentation," as well as the Société d'Equipement de Toulouse Midi-Pyrénées extract "Un pari tenu: Le Mirail" from *Entreprise* 744(13 December 1969) and Jean-Paul Lévy, "Le Mirail en 1977," *RGPSO* 48(1977): 103–14.

34. Advertising slogan for Le Mirail during the 1960s quoted in Levy, "Le Mirail en 1977," 103.

35. Commission nationale des plans d'urbanisme, Réunion du 2 April 1965, AM 72/3.

36. Louis Bazerque, quoted in Béringuier et al., *Toulouse Midi-Pyrénées, La transition,* 260–61.

37. Réunion d'atelier municipal d'urbanisme, 7 November 1968, AM 72/1.

38. Réunion d'agence d'urbanisme, 9 April 1973, AM 72/2.

39. Lévy, "Le Mirail en 1977," 111.

40. Ministère de l'Equipement, Direction de l'aménagement foncier et de l'urbanisme, Groupe d'etudes et de recherches, *Grands surfaces commerciales périphériques,* Eléments d'information pour les responsables de l'aménagement urbaine (Paris: La Documentation Française, September 1974), 119.

41. *TMP Magazine,* January 1972, 9.

42. *Bulletin municipal,* 68(March-April 1964):113–16.

43. Agence d'urbanisme, "Etudes préalables à la programmation de la deuxième tranche du Mirail, opinions et attitudes face au Mirail, enquêtes et observations sociologiques," Annexe 1, June 1973, AM 72/2.

44. M. Christine Boyer, *The City of Collective Memory, Its Historical Imagery and Architectural Entertainments* (Cambridge, Mass.: MIT Press, 1994), 61.

45. G. Dompnier, "Cadre de vie et évolution sociale de l'ensemble d'habitations des Muriers/Toulouse-Le Mirail," quoted in Notes et études documentaires, *Toulouse et son agglomération,* no. 4762 (Paris: La Documentation Française, 1984), 103. On life at Le Mirail, see also G. Dompnier, "Toulouse Le Mirail et Colomiers Villeneuve, vingt ans après (1960–1982)," *RGPSO* 54(1983):34–50. See also Raymond Ledrut and C. Androy, "Toulouse, sociologie et planification urbaine," *Urbanisme* 93(1966). For general studies on France, see Raymond Ledrut, *L'espace social de la ville, problèmes de sociologie appliquée à l'aménagement urbain* (Paris: Anthropos, 1968). For a more recent study of the Paris suburbs, see François Maspero, *Roissy-Express, A Journey through the Paris Suburbs* (London: Verso, 1994).

46. See the series of articles on Toulouse's various educational institutions in Ville de Toulouse, *Documents sur Toulouse et sa région*, 2 vols. (Toulouse: Privat, 1910), vol. 1, as well as R. Deltheil, *L'Université de Toulouse et son rôle régionale* (Toulouse: Privat, 1941), and Coutet, *Toulouse ville artistique*, 262–66. For the role of the city's research institutions in French scientific endeavors as a whole, see Mary Jo Nye, *Science in the Provinces, Scientific Communities and Provincial Leadership In France, 1860–1930* (Berkeley, Calif.: University of California Press, 1986), as well as Harry M. Paul, *From Knowledge to Power: The Rise of the Science Empire in France, 1860–1939* (Cambridge: Cambridge University Press, 1985).

47. INSEE, Direction régionale de Toulouse, *Etude statistique de l'agglomération de Toulouse*, 111. See also Commissariat du plan, DATAR, and INSEE, Projet de loi des finances pour 1969, *Rapport sur l'éxécution de plan et sur la régionalisation du budget d'équipement et aménagement du territoire*, vol. 3, *Statistiques et indicateurs des régions françaises* (Paris: Imprimerie nationale, 1969), 140; Marie-Claude Berthe, "L'aire d'influence de Toulouse," *RGPSO* 32(September 1961): 251–52.

48. Délégation Générale à la Recherche Scientifique et Technique (DGRST), *Contributions de l'état à la recherche et au développement en 1963*, résultats de l'enquête menée en 1964 et 1965 dans le secteur publique, *Le Progrés scientifique* (Paris: La Documentation Française, 1966), 176. The 3.4 percent of researchers employed at Toulouse was above that of any of the other regions except the Rhône-Alpes with Lyon and Grenoble and Provence Côte-d'Azur with Marseille and Montpellier.

49. DGRST, *France Science Research and Development* (Paris: Eurofab Engineering, 1972), 12.

50. See, for example, protests by the CNRS staff and by the Syndicat National des Chercheurs Scientifique in 1957. On the change in attitude toward education, science, and engineering research, see Robert Gilpin, *France in the Age of the Scientific State* (Princeton, N.J.: Princeton University Press, 1968); Charles P. Kindleberger, *Economic Growth in France and Britain 1851–1950* (New York: Simon and Schuster, 1964), 159–60; also Jean-Marc Sylvestre, *La France bancale* (Paris: Laffont, 1980), 174–76, and Organization for Economic Cooperation and Development (OECD), *Reviews of National Science Policy, France* (Paris: OECD Publications, 1964).

51. See Région Midi-Pyrénées, *Programme d'action régionale*, 96–98 (1959), as well as *Programme d'urgence de développement économique* (1962).

52. Ten provincial university communities were chosen for development: Bordeaux, Grenoble, Lille, Lyon, Marseille, Montpellier, Nancy, Strasbourg, Rennes, and Toulouse. There is a large body of literature on the state conceptualization of the relationship between pilot industries, scientific complexes, and urban development. For the French government's analysis, see, for example, Commissariat général du plan, Quatrième plan de développement économique et social, 1962–1965, *La Recherche scientifique et technique* (Paris: La Documentation Française, 1961); DATAR, *Documents relatifs à la décentralisation des activités "tertiaires"* (Paris: La Documentation Française, 1968); and Commissariat général du plan, Cinquième plan de

développement économique et social, 1966–1970, *Rapport sur les industries de pointe* (Paris: La Documentation Française, 1969). See also the more general discussion in Pierre Durand of DATAR, *Industrie et régions,* 2nd ed. (Paris: La Documentation Française, 1974). Also Edmond Lisle, *Recherche scientifique et aménagement du territoire* (Paris: La Documentation Française, 1973), 39–40, and Yan de Kerorguen, "The Technopolis: Gray Matter and Bright Lights," in *France High Tech,* ed. Thierry Grillet and Daniel Le Conte des Floris (Paris: Autrement, 1985): 208–12.

53. Louis Bazerque, Maire de Toulouse, "La Promotion économique de Toulouse et sa région doit être comprise de tous et puissamment aidée," NIC 51(June-July 1960): 3.

54. For the history of CNES and the development of the Toulouse facilities, see "1962–1972: Les Dix ans du CNES," *La recherche spatiale,* CNES, Revue bimestrielle d'information 11(January-February 1972): 1–40.

55. DATAR, *Documents relatif à la décentralisation des activités "tertiaires,"* 19.

56. This included CNRS, the universities, the *écoles supérieures,* and the technical institutes. Commissariat général du Plan, Quatrième plan 1962–1965, *La Recherche scientifique et technique,* 350–56; Commissariat général du Plan, Cinquième plan de développement économique et social, 1966–1970, Rapport particulier, *La Recherche scientifique et technique,* 2 vols. (Paris: La Documentation Française, 1965) 2: chapters 1 through 3. In 1966 and 1968, Toulouse received 10 percent of all research funds allocated to the provincial capitals while Grenoble received 62 percent. Commissariat général du Plan, DATAR, and INSEE, Projet de loi des finances pour 1968, *Rapport sur l'exécution de plan et sur la régionalisation du budget d'équipement et aménagement du territoire,* 3 vols. (Paris: Imprimerie nationale, 1967) 2: 380–97.

57. The complete list of Toulouse's national colleges includes the Ecole Nationale Supérieure d'Aéronautique, the Ecole Nationale de l'Aviation Civile, and the Ecole Nationale d'Ingénieurs de Constructions Aéronautiques; the Ecole Nationale Supérieure d'Electronique, Electrotechnique, Informatique et Hydraulique; the Ecole Nationale Supérieure de Chimie; the Ecole Nationale Supérieure d'Agronomie; and lastly the Ecole Nationale Vétérinaire.

58. INSEE, *Recensement général de la population de 1975,* Résultats au sondage au 1/5, Population, ménages, logements, immeubles, Département de la Haute-Garonne (Paris: Imprimerie nationale, 1976), 57. For detailed studies of the workforce in higher education and research at Toulouse, see Vannina Audibert, *L'Evolution de l'emploi dans le secteur tertiaire public et parapublic de l'agglomération toulousaine,* 2 vols. (Toulouse: Institut d'études de l'emploi, July 1973), 1: 167–75 and 2: Enseignement et recherche. See also Francine Teyssier, *L'Emploi public dans l'agglomération toulousaine,* 2 vols. (Toulouse: Institut d'études de l'emploi, November 1970), 1: 34–41 and 2: Education Nationale.

59. Monsieur Gilles Faÿsse, Chargé des rélations extérieures, Université Paul Sabatier, interview by author, Toulouse, 8 June 1979.

60. Marseille, Lyon, Grenoble, and Lille also provided important contingencies of the research labor force. For issues of professionalism and geographic mobility, see Michel Piquard, *Les Activités tertiaires dans l'aménagement du territoire* (Paris: La Documentation Française, 1971), 13–14.

61. INSEE, Direction régionale de Toulouse, "Statistiques mensuelles, I. B. Emploi," *Bulletin régional de statistique* 4me trimestre (1960–1968): 3.

62. Monsieur P. Beulin, DATAR, Bureau régional d'industrialisation, interview by author, Toulouse, 12 June 1979. Béringuier et al., *Toulouse Midi-Pyrénées,* 79.

63. Ville de Toulouse, Atelier municipal d'urbanisme, "Quelques problèmes posés par le lancement et la réalisation des ZUP, l'enquête a porté sur les ZUP de Toulouse Rangueil. . ." 7 November 1968, AM 72/1. See also the descriptions and oral histories of Rangueil presented in Minelle Verdié, *Ces gens là, histoires du logement ordinaire* (Paris: Syros, 1995), 51–68.

64. *TMP Magazine,* May 1976, 20–21.

65. CNES, *Rapport d'activité,* July 1973-July 1974, 171.

66. Beringuier et al., *Toulouse Midi-Pyrénées,* 324.

67. Monsieur Gilles Faÿsse and the Faÿsse family, interview by author, Rangueil, 8 June 1979.

68. When the decision was announced to move the Faculty of Science out to Rangueil, land prices in the nearby neighborhood of Bellevue jumped from 8 francs to 80 francs a square meter even before the school was actually built. See Jalabert, "Speculation foncière," 446–47.

69. On the changing tastes and lifestyles of the French middle classes, see Pierre Bourdieu, *Distinction, A Social Critique of the Judgement of Taste,* trans. Richard Nice (Cambridge, Mass.: Harvard University Press, 1984), as well as Luc Boltanski, *The Making of a Class: Cadres in French Society* (New York: Cambridge University Press, 1987).

70. Monsieur Didier Bernadet, President-Directeur Général, Compagnie pour L'Electronique, L'Informatique et les Systems, and engineers employed at the CNES, interview by author, Lespinet, 9 June 1979.

71. See, for one example among many, the speech by Jérôme Monod, the regional delegate from DATAR to the Comité Régionale d'Expansion Economique Midi-Pyrénées, reprinted in *NIC* 122(September 1967): 3–5, as well as the report on the Sixth Plan for the Midi-Pyrénées by Pierre-Alain Maurech, "Colloque 68, Toulouse et la Région Midi-Pyrénées dans le VIe Plan," *NIC* 135(December 1968): 29. Kristin Ross discusses "New Men" in *Fast Cars, Clean Bodies: Decolonization and the Reordering of French Culture* (Cambridge, Mass.: MIT Press, 1995), chapter 4. For a broader examination of the social and cultural shifts during the 1960s, see Henri Mendras, *Social Change in Modern France: Toward a Cultural Anthropology of the Fifth Republic* (New York: Cambridge University Press, 1991) and Michel Forse et al., eds., *Recent Social Trends in France, 1960–1990* (Montreal: McGill-Queen's University Press, 1993).

72. Pierre Baudis, "Le Problème des grandes villes françaises," 9 October 1971, 5.

5. The City as Bazaar: Tradition, Modernization, and Economic Culture in the 1950s

1. On the character of the traditional French economy, see the path-breaking work of Charles Kindleberger, *Economic Growth in France and Britain, 1851–1950* (New

York: Simon and Schuster, 1964) as well as Fernand Braudel and Ernst Labrousse, eds., *Histoire économique et sociale de la France,* vol. 4, *Des Années 1880 à nos jours. L'Ere industielle à la société aujourd'hui (siècle 1880–1980),* part 2: *1914–1950* and part 3: *De 1950 à nos jours* (Paris: Presses Universitaires de France, 1980 and 1982). See also the series of articles on the traditional economic classes in Jean-Daniel Reynaud and Yves Grafmeyer, eds., *Français, qui êtes-vous?* (Paris: La Documentation Française, 1981). More recent theoretical work on the French economy includes Patrick Fidenson and André Strauss, eds., *Le Capitalisme français: Blocages et dynamismes d'une croissance* (Paris: Fayard, 1987) and André Gauron, *Histoire économique et social de la Ve République,* 2 vols. (Paris: La Découverte, 1988).

2. On the early analyses of Toulouse in comparison to other French cities see, for example, Jean Hautreux et al., *Le Niveau supérieur de l'armature urbaine française* (Paris: Construction, 1963), and François Carrière and Philippe Pinchemel, *Le Fait urbain en France* (Paris: Armand Colin, 1963). Most of the statistical studies done in the early 1960s argued that the excessive industrial variety of Toulouse was far removed from the healthy diversity found in other large French cities. Instead, it suggested a kind of directionless industrial malaise that precluded the type of manufacturing specialization essential for the development of a successful export market.

3. The data for this chapter is taken in part from the information on Toulouse in the *Fichiers des établissements industriels, et commerciaux* (Toulouse INSEE, microfilm) which classifies industrial plants by their size according to the number of salaried workers they employ and by their industrial activity. Focusing on traditional industry provides the best opportunity for understanding the transformation of Toulouse's business classes, their mode of production, and their culture amid the rising tide of modernization.

Within the analysis of industry, the entire spectrum of size categories is considered under the *Fichiers* label of "industrial establishment." This includes handicraft shops with producers working alone, with family help, or with one or two apprentices. It is certainly problematic whether artisanal trades of this type and size can be justifiably included within a technical definition of "industrial" or "manufacturing establishment." However, the importance of the petty producer to traditional industry and to the entire economy of Toulouse makes their inclusion in any type of structural analysis a necessity. For an in-depth analysis of France's industrial structure during the 1950s and 1960s, see Michel Didier and Edmond Malinvaud, "La Concentration de l'industrie s'est elle accentuée depuis le début du siècle?" *Economie et statistique* 2(June 1969): 3–10.

4. Institut d'aménagement et d'urbanisme de la région parisienne (IAURP), *Cahiers de l'IAURP,* vol. 7, *Activités caractéristiques du centre-ville à Grenoble, Nancy, Rennes, Strasbourg, Toulouse* (Paris: IAURP, March 1967), 33–44.

5. On the invention of the *artisanat* see the excellent discussion in Steven M. Zdatney, *The Politics of Survival, Artisans in Twentieth Century France* (New York: Oxford University Press, 1990), chapter 1. See as well Jean Robert, *L'Artisanat et le secteur des métiers dans la France contemporaine* (Paris: Armand Colin, 1966); Marc Durand and Jean-Paul Frémont, *L'Artisanat en France* (Paris: Presses Universitaires de France,

1979); and B. Lambert, *Les Syndicats, les patrons, et l'état* (Paris: Editions Ouvrières, 1978).

6. Coutet, *Toulouse, ville artistique,* xi, 287–88.

7. Leblanc, *La Vie à Toulouse,* 76–77, 118–20.

8. Quoted in Philippe Wolff and Jean Dieuzaide, *Voix et images de Toulouse* (Toulouse: Privat, 1962), 254.

9. Gratias, *Le Nouveau visage de Toulouse,* 11–12.

10. Cholvy, *Histoire du Languedoc,* 115. See also the work of Lila Leontidou, *The Mediterranean City in Transition: Social Change and Urban Development* (Cambridge: Cambridge University Press, 1990), and her "Postmodernism and the City: Mediterranean Versions," *Urban Studies* 30(1993): 949–65. Leontidou argues that informality in the economy and housing sector, and piecemeal urban development, were characteristics ingrained in Mediterranean urban culture and form.

11. For example, see the election results in *La Dépêche du Midi,* 9 March 1959.

12. Cholvy, *Histoire du Languedoc,* 120.

13. Roland Trempé, "La Région économique de Toulouse aux lendemains de la libération," RGPSO 94(January–March 1982): 24–26. See also *Monographies d'industries de la région Toulouse, 1945–1946* (Toulouse: Fournié, 1946). See also Alain Beltran, Robert Frank, and Henri Rousso, *La Vie des entreprises françaises sous l'occupation. Une enquête à l'échelle locale* (Paris: Belin, 1994).

14. See, in particular, Zdatney, *The Politics of Survival,* 162–64, and Kuisel, *Capitalism and the State,* 214–18.

15. *La République du Sud-Ouest,* 26 and 28 August 1946, 11 April 1947, 2 and 10 June 1947. On the strikes and malaise of the late 1940s, see Hubert Bonin, *Histoire économique de la IVe république* (Paris: Economica, 1987), chapter 4.

16. *La République du Sud-Ouest,* 28 March 1947.

17. *La Dépêche du Midi,* 29 November and 1 December 1948.

18. *La Dépêche du Midi,* 3 and 4 July 1948.

19. *La Dépêche du Midi,* 30 September 1948.

20. *La Dépêche du Midi,* 1 October 1948.

21. *La Dépêche du Midi,* 22 November and 8 December 1948.

22. Only four substantially sized garment factories existed at Toulouse: Saler-Puig, Etchepare, Guichard, and Soulé. See Jean Bastie, "L'Industrie de la confection à Toulouse," RGPSO 25(September 1954): 313–24.

23. INSEE, Direction régionale de Toulouse, "Statistiques mensuelles, I. B. Emploi de la main-d'oeuvre," *Bulletin régional de statistique,* 4e trimestre (1952–1958): 3. See also INSEE, Direction régionale de Toulouse, *Recensement général de la population de 1962,* Population active ayant un emploi selon l'activité économique detaillée, le sexe, et le statut à trois chiffre, Département de la Haute-Garonne, agglomération de Toulouse (Toulouse: INSEE, microfilm).

24. INSEE, Direction régionale de Toulouse, *Etude statistique de l'agglomération de Toulouse,* 173–95.

25. INSEE, *Recensement général de la population de Mai 1954,* Résultats statistiques,

Population-Ménages-Logements-Maisons, Département de la Haute-Garonne (Paris: Imprimerie Nationale, 1960), 34.

26. *Recensement 1954,* F. Doubin, Mémoire de Stage, *De la Capitale provinciale à la métropole régionale, Toulouse* (Toulouse: Ecole Nationale d'Administration, 1961).

27. INSEE, Direction régionale de Toulouse, "Les établissements industriels et commerciaux en 1958," 14–16.

28. INSEE, Direction régionale de Toulouse, "Note sur l'indice du chiffre d'affaires déclaré à Toulouse," *Bulletin régional de statistique,* 4e trimestre(1954): 15–16; INSEE, Direction régionale de Toulouse, "Statistiques mensuelles, IV. Commerce intérieur," *Bulletin régional de statistique,* 4e trimestre(1956): 6. Traditional trades as a whole were responsible for over 70 percent of the city's industrial sales, which gives perhaps the best indication of Toulouse's heavy dependence on them. Only when Sud-Aviation began construction and sale of the Caravelle in 1956 and revitalized the city's aircraft industry did industrial sales begin to expand.

29. *La Dépêche du Midi,* 9 June 1954.

30. It is extremely difficult to measure the available income of French *patrons* (particularly that of *petits commerçants* and artisans) in the underdeveloped regions where income reporting was easily dodged. Studies by INSEE reveal that in 1956 the income of the country's *patrons* was about at the same level as the *cadres moyens,* around 25,000 francs. This figure must be adjusted to the economic decline that characterized Toulouse during the 1950s and to the competition between the city's thousands of small shops. We can surmise from this that the Toulouse *patron* was in about the same income category as the city's *employés* and *ouvriers.*

31. Commissariat Général du plan, DATAR, and INSEE, Projet de loi de finances pour 1966, Annexe, *Rapport sur l'éxécution du plan en 1964 et 1965 et sur la régionalisation du budget d'équipement de 1966,* 2 vols. (Paris: Imprimerie nationale, 1965), 2: 184.

32. INSEE, Direction régionale de Toulouse, "Les Salaires et effectifs dans l'industrie et le commerce en 1953," *Bulletin mensuel de statistique,* nouvelle série, supplément (July–September 1955): 41.

33. *La Dépêche du Midi,* 7 March 1961. For a general analysis of the conditions of the French working class, see Gérard Noiriel, *Ouvriers dans la société française, XIVe-XXe siècles* (Paris: Seuil, 1986).

34. INSEE, "Les Salaires dans l'industrie et le commerce en 1954, d'après les déclarations de salaires 1024," *Etudes statistiques* 3(July-September 1956). INSEE, "Les Salaires dans l'industrie, le commerce et les services en 1956, d'après les déclarations de salaires 1024," *Etudes statistiques* 4(October-December 1958): 85–86.

35. *Bulletin municipal,* 63(June-July 1959): 271.

36. Plan d'aménagement de Toulouse, Rapport succinct, December 1948, Plans d'aménagement, Dossier administratif, AM 5S576.

37. See Daniel Faucher, *Toulouse* (Paris: La Documentation Française, 1961), 16–19; Jean Coppolani, *Toulouse, étude de géographie urbaine* (Toulouse: Privat, 1954) and his "Le Type urbain de Toulouse," RGPSO 34(March 1963): 33–47.

38. The next largest neighboring town was Perpignan with 75,000 inhabitants along the Mediterranean coast. The medium-sized towns of the southwest, Pau and

Tarbes to the west, Montauban to the north, each with only 40,000 citizens, functioned as the seats of their departments and suffered the same economic stagnation as the region. Région Midi-Pyrénées, *Programme d'action régionale 1958* (Paris: Imprimerie des journaux officiels, 1959), 137. See also Jean Coppolani, "Les Sociétés urbaines de Midi-Pyrénées depuis 1954," *RGPSO* 56(July-September 1985): 339–51.

39. See, for example, Comité industriel d'action économique de la région de Toulouse, "L'Industrie dans la région Midi-Pyrénées" (November 1958).

40. Louis Périllier, *L'Expansion économique dans la Haute-Garonne* (Toulouse: Imprimerie préfectorale, November 1956), 12–13, 46.

41. Berthaud in particular revived Comproux's vision of a regional capitalist class oriented toward Occitan culture. See Lafont, *La Revendication occitan,* 258–66.

42. Gérard de Sède cites the statistic that Occitania produced 60 percent of French hydroelectric power, but consumed only 20 percent of it. Both the bauxite of Provence and the uranium of Limousin were in the majority exported (*700 ans de révoltes occitanes,* 266). Gérard Cholvy also discusses the specific state decisions to support industrial ventures in the developed regions that immediately undermined the fragile economy of Languedoc, *Histoire du Languedoc,* 180.

43. See Robert Lafont, *La Révolution régionaliste* (Paris: Gallimard, 1967).

44. *La Dépêche du Midi,* 16 January 1953.

45. *La Dépêche du Midi,* 7 April 1949.

46. *La Dépêche du Midi,* 7 July 1949.

47. As quoted in Bonin, *Histoire économique de la IVe République,* 166.

48. This phrase is used by Alain Lipietz in his superb analysis of French national developmentalism in "Governing the Economy in the Face of International Challenge: From National Developmentalism to National Crisis," in *Searching for the New France,* James F. Hollifield and George Ross, eds. (New York: Routledge, 1991), 21. Richard Kuisel initially called state management of the French economy "neo-liberalism," in his *Capitalism and the State,* 248–49, while Peter Gourevitch preferred the term "neo-mercantilism," in "Making Choices in France: Industrial Structure and the Politics of Economic Polity," in *France in the Troubled World Economy,* ed. Stephen S. Cohen and Peter A. Gourevitch (London: Butterworth Scientific, 1982), 1–20.

49. There are numerous good sources on the ideology and policies cultivated under the auspices of French state planning during the 1950s and 1960s. The best sources are probably François Bloch-Lainé himself in *A la Recherche d'une économie concertée* (Paris: Epargne, 1962), Pierre Massé, *Le Plan ou l'anti-hasard* (Paris: Gallimard, 1965), and Jean Fourastié and Jean-Pierre Courthéoux, *La Planification économique en France* (Paris: Presses Universitaire de France, 1968).

50. Among many studies of French industrial and tax policies, see Jean-Jacques Carré, Paul Dubois, and Edmond Malinvaud, *French Economic Growth,* trans. John P. Hatfield (Stanford, Calif.: Stanford University Press, 1975); Peter Hall, *Governing the Economy, The Politics of State Intervention in Britain and France* (New York: Oxford University Press, 1986); and Robert Delorme and Charles André, *L'Etat et l'économie* (Paris: Seuil, 1983).

51. Herbert Luethy, *France Against Herself* (New York: Meridian Books, 1957),

287. For a revealing portrait of *"la microphile"* and the regional dimension of the small enterprise, see Georges Cazes and Alain Reynaud, *Les mutations récentes de l'économie française* (Paris: Doin, 1973), 35–40.

52. *La Dépêche du Midi,* 9 June 1954.

53. *La Dépêche du Midi,* 13 February 1957.

54. *La Dépêche du Midi,* 31 January 1957.

55. Zdatney, *The Politics of Survival,* 165. See also Martin Schain, *French Communism and Local Power* (New York: St. Martins Press, 1985).

56. *Bulletin municipal* 63(June–July 1959): 265.

57. Comproux defended this association between members of the Institut d'Etudes Occitanes and the Communist Party in the review *Oc* 14(October 1951).

58. *La Dépêche du Midi,* 28 November 1958.

59. On the Poujadist movement see Jean-Pierre Rioux, "La Révolte de Pierre Poujade," *L'Histoire, études sur la France de 1939 à nos jours* (Paris: Seuil, 1985); Sean Fitzgerald, "The Anti-Modern Rhetoric of Le Mouvement Poujade," *Review of Politics* 32(April 1970): 167–90; and Stanley Hoffmann, ed., *Le Mouvement poujade* (Paris: Armand Colin, 1956).

60. See, for example, *Bulletin municipal* 63(March-April 1959): 83–90.

61. See the descriptions in *La Dépêche du Midi,* 2 November 1958. For the demographic viability of the artisanal neighborhoods, see Jean Coppolani, *La Population de Toulouse depuis 1954,* Documents scientifiques des centres de recherche de l'Institut de Géographie Daniel Faucher, Université de Toulouse Le Mirail, no. 9 (1978), 25–27.

62. See *La Dépêche du Midi,* 28 June 1958.

63. *La Dépêche du Midi,* 6 July 1959.

64. *Bulletin municipal,* 63(June-July 1959): 265.

65. *La Dépêche du Midi,* 9 June 1954. See also G. Lefranc, *Le mouvement syndicale de la libération aux événements de mai-juin 1968* (Paris: Payot, 1969).

66. The mean hourly salary for men increased 33 percent between 1958 and 1962 in the Midi-Pyrénées against a rise of 44 percent for France. The buying power in the southwest also began to rise after 1958 at an annual rate of 3.58 percent (3.72 percent for France). At Toulouse, the improvement in economic circumstance is generally attributed to increased production in the aircraft industry. No doubt there was a general spin-off effect from aircraft production. The metallurgical trades, for example, were bound to benefit. But the degree to which craftsmen and workers in the traditional industries experienced an improvement in their lot is far cloudier; Région Midi-Pyrénées, *Du IVe au Ve plan 1962–1965–1970* (Toulouse: La Préfecture, 1963), 12.

67. *La Dépêche du Midi,* 23 June 1958.

68. *La Dépêche du Midi,* 14 March 1959.

69. *La Dépêche du Midi,* 28 November 1958.

70. *La Dépêche du Midi,* 26 February 1953, 15 November 1959.

71. *La Dépêche du Midi,* 28 March 1961.

72. INSEE, Direction régionale de Toulouse, *Etude statistique de Toulouse,* 173–95; INSEE, Direction régionale de Toulouse, "Les etablissements industriels et commerci-

aux en 1958," *Bulletin régional de statistique,* 3e trimestre (1959): 14–16; INSEE, Direction régionale de Toulouse, *Exploitation du fichier des établissements industriels et commerciaux,* 1962 (Toulouse: INSEE, microfilm).

73. F. Doubin, *De la Capitole provinciale à la métropole régionale,* 4–5.

74. INSEE, *Les Etablissements industriels, artisanaux et commerciaux en France en 1958* (Paris: Imprimerie nationale, 1959); Doubin, *De la Capitole provinciale à la métropole régionale,* 10.

75. "La Chambre de Commerce et d'Industrie de Toulouse a confirmé sa vocation industrielle," *NIC* 53(October 1960): 7.

6. Toulouse as Industrial Capital

1. The first great flying competitions in France were held in 1909 at Reims-Béthany (which attracted half a million spectators), Port-Aviation (30,000 spectators), and Douai and Vichy (10,000–15,000 spectators). Toulouse, Bayonne, and Biarritz organized their own initial *meetings* in 1910. See Edmond Petit, *La Vie quotidienne dans l'aviation en France au début du XXe siècle (1900–1935)* (Paris: Hachette, 1977), chapter 4.

2. *La Dépêche,* 1 August 1910.

3. *La Dépêche,* 1 and 7 March 1911.

4. Daniel Faucher, "Toulouse, tête de lignes aériennes," *RGPSO* 1(15 July 1930): 256.

5. Even more important than climate or geography, the availability of airport facilities was the critical factor determining the location of aircraft manufacturing companies throughout France. See Guy Jalabert, *Les industries aéronautiques et spatiales en France* (Toulouse: Privat, 1974).

6. A. Taillefer, "L'Office national industriel de l'azote," *RGPSO* 28(1957): 20, 31.

7. Emmanuel Chadeau, *Latécoère* (Paris: Olivier Orban, 1990), 92–93.

8. Gratias, *Le Nouveau visage de Toulouse,* 99.

9. See, for example, the descriptions of the Grand Balcon in Georges Baccrabère and Georges Jorré, *Toulouse, terre d'envol* (Toulouse: Privat, 1966), 61; Pierre Lagarde, *Histoires et mémoire de Toulouse* (Marseille: Jeanne Laffitte, 1981), 139–41; Pierre de Gorsse, *Les Grandes heures de Toulouse* (Paris: Perrin, 1978), 356.

10. See Nicolas Neiertz, "Argent, politique et aviation, l'affaire de l'Aéropostale (1931–1932)," *Vingtième siècle* 24(October–December 1989): 29–40.

11. See the excellent analysis of French politics and government aircraft construction policy in Emmanuel Chadeau, *L'Industrie aéronautique en France* (Paris: Fayard, 1987), chapter 7.

12. A. Nicolas, Secrétaire du syndicat des métaux, Section Aviation, à M. le Ministre de Finances, 1 June 1937, as quoted in Herrick Chapman, *State Capitalism and Working Class Radicalism in the French Aircraft Industry* (Berkeley, Calif.: University of California Press, 1991), 132–33.

13. Ibid., 133.

14. Latécoère's company remained private. The workers from his plant were given the right to transfer to Nationale du Midi, and the majority of them did. The upshot was that in reaction Latécoère abandoned Toulouse for the town of Anglet, near Bayonne, where a new prefabricated aircraft plant was built. Only the Latécoère research and prototype division remained at Montaudran, with a much reduced workforce. On the complex and contorted process of nationalization in the aircraft industry, see Chadeau, *Histoire de l'industrie aéronautique en France,* as well as his *De Blériot à Dessault: Histoire de l'industrie aéronautique en France, 1900–1950* (Paris: Fayard, 1987), and Georges Lefranc, *Histoire du front populaire* (Paris: Payot, 1965).

15. Jalabert, *Les Industries aéronautiques,* 248–49.

16. INSEE, Direction régionale de Toulouse, *Structures des principales industries, Année 1946* (Toulouse, 1946), 7.

17. *La Dépêche du Midi,* 17 December 1948.

18. *La République du Sud-Ouest,* 26 August 1946; *La Dépêche du Midi,* 5 March 1948.

19. I am indebted here to the work of Georges Baccrabère and Georges Jorré, *Toulouse, terre d'envol,* for their excellent chapter on aviation associations at Toulouse.

20. Chapman, *State Capitalism and Working-Class Radicalism,* 129.

21. *La Dépêche du Midi,* 18 and 19 June 1949.

22. *La Dépêche du Midi,* 15 February 1948.

23. See Commissariat Général du Plan, Cinquième plan de développement économique et social, 1966–1970, *Rapport sur les industries de pointe,* March 1969 (Paris: La Documentation Française, 1969).

24. "Dans le sillage de la 'Caravelle' près de 20,000 familles vivant de l'aviation," *NIC* 41(June-July 1959): 6–8.

25. *La Dépêche du Midi,* 28 May 1955.

26. *La Dépêche du Midi,* 11 April 1959.

27. Bréguet Aviation and the Société Latécoère benefited in particular from subcontracting work on the Caravelle. The workforce of the latter doubled between 1954 and 1962 during the manufacture of the plane's fuselage. Aircraft contracts attracted two new manufacturers (SEMCA and Microturbo) to the suburbs north of the city near Aucamville. INSEE, Direction régionale de Toulouse, "Les Établissements industriels et commerciaux en 1958," *Bulletin régional de statistique* 3(1959):14; INSEE, Direction régionale de Toulouse, *Exploitation du fichier,* 1962.

28. Altogether, by 1962 Toulouse aircraft companies employed 12 percent of the workforce in the French aeronautics industry—the largest concentration in the provinces. The other provincial aviation centers were Bordeaux, Nantes-St. Nazaire, Marseille, and the region of the Centre just south of Paris. Paris itself continued to dominate aircraft production with about 40 percent of the workforce. Michel Hannoun and Philippe Templé, *Les Implantations industrielles et l'emploi régional en France,* Les Collections de l'INSEE E40 (Paris, July 1976), 86–89.

29. Conseil régional de Midi-Pyrénées, Elaboration du plan de développement régional, *Maîtrise de l'urbanisation de l'agglomération toulousaine,* Rapports des groupes de travail (Toulouse: Conseil régional, September 1976), 26–31.

30. *La Dépêche du Midi,* 22 March 1957.

31. See the reports in *La Dépêche du Midi,* 21 May, 28 May, 8 June, 12 June 1959.

32. Commissariat Général du Plan, Quatrième plan de développement économique et social, 1962–1965, Commission des transports, Rapport particulier, *Aviation civile et construction aéronautique,* Part IV (Paris: La Documentation Française, 1961), 120–22.

33. Notes et études documentaires, *L'Industrie aéronautique et spatiale française,* no. 3764 (Paris: La Documentation Française, 16 February 1971), 15.

34. "Le Grave problème de l'industrie aéronautique," *NIC* 104(November 1965): 13. With 12,000 employed in 1968, the aeronautics industry remained in what aggravated local economists called a state of "semiunderemployment."

35. *La Dépêche du Midi,* 20 May 1968.

36. *Le Monde,* 4,5,6 March 1969.

37. *La Dépêche du Midi,* 3 March 1969.

38. Ville de Toulouse, *Toulouse* (Toulouse, 1971), 16.

39. Maurice Crubellier, *Histoire culturelle de la France, XIX-XXe siècle* (Paris: Armand Colin, 1974), 288, and Henri Mendras, *La Seconde révolution française, 1965–1984* (Paris: Gallimard, 1988), 272–87. See also Ross, *Fast Cars, Clean Bodies,* Introduction.

40. Examples of this public rhetoric abound. See, for example, publications by the City of Toulouse such as *Toulouse* (1971), *Toulouse-Information* (1965), Les Documents de *La Dépêche, La Mutation de Toulouse* (1970), Région Midi-Pyrénées, "Eléments pour une politique régionale," *Les Dossiers de Midi-Pyrénées* 2(November 1973): 93–95, 197–202, and Jacques Bonnaud, *Panorama et structures économiques de la région Midi-Pyrénées* (Toulouse: Direction régionale de la main d'oeuvre, October 1976), 61.

41. Commissariat Général du Plan, Préparation du VIe Plan, Commission de l'Industrie, Commission des Transports, *Rapport du comité industrie aéronautique et spatiale* (Paris: La Documentation Française, 1971), 8–19. See also the local report in *TMP Magazine,* July-August 1973, 8.

42. In January 1970, the nationalized firms of Sud-Aviation, Nord-Aviation, and the Société d'Etudes pour la Propulsion à Reaction (SEREB) were reorganized into one company, the Société Nationale Industrielle Aéronautique et Spatiale, or SNIAS. The name was later changed to Société Nationale Industrielle Aérospatiale, or Aérospatiale.

43. Stephen S. Cohen, "Informed Bewilderment: French Economic Strategy and the Crisis," in *France in the Troubled World Economy,* 23–24.

44. Comité économique et social Midi-Pyrénées, *Rapports sur le programme de développement de Midi-Pyrénées* (Toulouse: Commission du développement régional, October 1976), 3. See as well the reports by the Commissariat Général du Plan and DGRST, Préparation du 6e Plan, Rapports des Commissions du 6e Plan (1971–1975), 2 vols., *Recherche* (Paris: La Documentation Française, 1971), 1: 32; Préparation du 6e Plan, Commission de l'Industrie, *Rapport du comité industrie aéronautique et spatiale* (Paris: La Documentation Française, 1971), 10–20; Préparation du septième plan de développement économique et social, 1976–1980, *Rapport de la commission industrie* (Paris: La Documentation Française, 1976), 227–28.

45. Airbus Industrie was a European joint venture between Aérospatiale and aircraft manufacturers within the German Federal Republic (Dornier, Messerschmitt, and VFW-Hokker), Spain (CASA), and England (Hawker Siddeley, British Aerospace). The company was (and continues to be) based in Toulouse. In the 1970s, it controlled a workforce of 17,000 throughout the various participating countries in Europe. "Economie Midi-Pyrénées, Aéronautique—Les conditions du rétablissement," *TMP Magazine,* 26(July-August 1973): 7–8, outlines the company's role in reviving aeronautics at Toulouse.

46. INSEE, Direction régionale de Toulouse, *Compte régionale des industries,* enquête annuelle 1975, Département de la Haute-Garonne (Toulouse: INSEE, microfilm); Guy Isaac, ed., *Midi-Pyrénées et le marché commun* (Toulouse: Université des Sciences Sociales de Toulouse, 1978), 25.

47. Coppolani, *Toulouse au XXe siècle,* 228.

48. "Les Nouvelles installations," NIC 215(Spécial Aéroport): 11.

49. *Livre Blanc,* 82.

50. The examples here are exorbitant in number. DATAR's chief annual publication was *Statistiques et indicateurs des régions françaises,* which gives a breakdown of the industrial and economic parameters used by state planners to define the quality of the provincial regions. A typical illustration of the cottage industry in statistical research during the 1960s and 1970s is Michel Noël (a CNRS researcher), "Mobilité spatiale des industries, croissance et urbanisation," *L'Espace géographique* (1974): 48–56. For the state planning corps' theoretical and policy statements on the *industries de pointe* and *aménagement du territoire,* see Commissariat Général du Plan, Cinquième plan de développement économique et sociale, 1966–1970, *Rapport sur les industries de pointe,* and Pierre Durand's report for DATAR, *Industrie et régions* (Paris: La Documentation Française, 1974). An excellent analysis of French economic policy can be found in Alain Lipietz, "Governing the Economy in the Face of International Challenge: From National Developmentalism to National Crisis," 17–29.

51. On the theoretical failures of the policy of *aménagement du territoire,* see Xavier Greffe, *Territoires en France, Les Enjeux économiques de la décentralisation* (Paris: Economica, 1984), 34–41, as well as Philippe Aydalot, *Dynamique spatiale et développement inégal,* 2nd ed. (Paris: Economica, 1980). See also Patrick Fridenson, "Atouts en limites de la modernisation par en haut: Les Entreprises publiques face à leurs critiques (1944–1986)," in *Le Capitalisme français 19e–20e siècle, Blockages et dynamismes d'une croissance,* 175–95.

52. *TMP Magazine,* April 1975, 11; "Motorola géant des semi-conductors," NIC 130(May 1968): 17.

53. See Commissariat Général du Plan, Commission permanente de l'électronique, Premier rapport de la Commission, *Situation de l'électronique en France* (Paris: Imprimerie nationale, March 1962); Commissariat Général du Plan, Préparation du 6e plan (1971–1975); Commission de l'industrie et Commission permanente de l'électronique, *Rapport du comité électronique, informatique et industrie des télécommuni-*

cations (Paris: La Documentation Française, 1971). On the effectiveness of state interventionism in electronics, see John Zysman, *Political Strategies for Industrial Order: Market, State, and Industry in France* (Berkeley, Calif.: University of California Press, 1977).

54. Association pour l'emploi des cadres (APEC), *L'Emploi des cadres, Midi-Pyrénées* (September 1977), 11; Ville de Toulouse, *Toulouse* (1971), 16; *TMP Magazine,* December 1974, 12.

55. Pierre Mazataud, "Deux greffons fragiles sur l'industrie de Toulouse: Motorola et la Compagnie internationale pour l'informatique," *RGPSO* 46(April 1975): 142. Direction régionale du travail et de la main-d'oeuvre de la région Midi-Pyrénées, Echelon régional de l'emploi de Toulouse, *Les Emplois de l'électronique,* E. Redon, chargé d'études (Toulouse: Echelon régional de l'emploi de Toulouse, June 1969), 4–5.

56. *TMP Magazine* 18(April 1972): 10–11.

57. Ibid.

58. Electronics did employ more women than any other Toulouse industry except for textile manufacturing, so even this fairly negligible opportunity represented a real gain in women's employment status.

59. Conseil régional de Midi-Pyrénées, *Maîtrise de l'urbanisation,* Rapports, 12.

60. François Pradel de Lamaze, "Les Salaires en Midi-Pyrénées," *Statistiques et études Midi-Pyrénées,* Revue trimestrielle de la direction régionale de l'INSEE à Toulouse 1(1977): 3–6; "Les Salaires dans l'industrie, le commerce et les services en 1974," *Les Collections de l'INSEE,* no. 304, série M 76(May 1979): 110–15. See as well the article by George Ross, "Destroyed by the Dialectic: Politics, the Decline of Marxism, and the New Middle Strata in France," *Theory and Society* 16(1987).

61. *La Dépêche du Midi,* 20 and 21 May 1968. See also Serge Mallet, *Essays on the New Working Class* (St. Louis, Mo.: Telos Press, 1975).

62. On this issue, see André Gauron, *Histoire économique de la cinquième république,* 2 vols. (Paris: La Découverte, 1988). See also David Harvey, *The Condition of Postmodernity,* as well as A. J. Scott and M. Storper, eds., *Production, Work, Territory: The Geographical Anatomy of Industrial Capitalism* (Boston: Allen & Unwin, 1986) and Michael Dunford, *Capital, the State, and Regional Development* (London: Plon, 1990).

63. Kuisel, *Capitalism and the State in Modern France,* 260–67; Ezra N. Suleiman, *Elites in French Society, the Politics of Survival* (Princeton, N.J.: Princeton University Press, 1978), 223–44.

64. Monsieur M. Darnaud, Airbus Industries, and Monsieur Beulin, DATAR, interview by author, Toulouse, 19 and 20 June 1979.

65. Notes et études documentaires, *L'Industrie aéronautique et spatiale,* 8.

66. Small electronics producers at Toulouse faced rugged competition. Their prices remained as much as six times higher than those of firms outside the region. Mazataud, "Motorola et CII," 144–46.

67. Pierre Baudis, Député-Maire de Toulouse, "Le Problème des grandes villes françaises," Ville de Toulouse, 9 October 1971; Michel Idrac and Jean-Paul Laborie, "L'économie de Midi-Pyrénées en crise," *RGPSO* 47(1976): 21; Conseil régional de

Midi-Pyrénees, Elaboration du plan de développement régional, *Développement des activités industrielles,* Rapports des Groupes de Travail (September 1976), 17.

7. Gentrification and the Capitalist Landscape

1. *La Dépêche du Midi,* 23 June 1958.

2. *Bulletin du conseil national de patronat français,* no. 124(September 1954), quoted in Bela Balassa, "The French Economy under the Fifth Republic, 1958–1978," in *The Impact of the Fifth Republic on France,* ed. William G. Andrews and Stanley Hoffmann (Albany, N.Y.: State University of New York Press, 1981), 121. According to Balassa, the safeguards were to include harmonizing social charges, equalizing social benefits (the length of vacations, male and female wages, and the length of the workweek), extending the transition period into the Common Market, increasing the common external tariff, and avoiding limitations on cartels.

3. "Briquetiers et tuiliers de notre région souhaitent une normalisation du marché a fin de poursuivre leur expansion," NIC 44(15 November 1959): 6–7. See Alain Duhamel, *Les Peurs françaises* (Paris: Flammarion, 1993).

4. "Exportateurs passez à l'action," NIC 39(April 1959): 9.

5. *La Dépêche du Midi,* 4 July 1960.

6. Louis Périllier, *L'expansion économique dans la Haute-Garonne* (Toulouse: Imprimerie préfectorale, November 1956), 12.

7. *La Dépêche du Midi,* 29 November 1958 and 13 February 1959.

8. "Exportateurs passez à l'action," 9. See also Chambre de commerce et d'industrie Midi-Pyrénées, *Pourquoi j'exporte* (Toulouse: Chambre régionale de commerce, 1974).

9. The *Union Régionale des Groupements Patronaux* was the leading professional organization for the *patronat.* See the two articles: "Le Groupement des exporteurs de Toulouse Midi-Pyrénées crée sous l'égide de l'Union Régionale des Groupements Patronaux," NIC (May 1959): 18; "Notre pays doit prendre conscience des possibilitiés et des conditions de progrès d'une économie moderne," La vie de l'URGP, NIC 64(November 1961): 19.

10. "La Foire de Toulouse," NIC 99(April 1965): 7–8.

11. See the series of articles on the Toulouse Fair in *La Dépêche du Midi,* April 1959.

12. Pierre-Alain Maurech, "Colloque 68, Toulouse et la région Midi-Pyrénées dans le VIe plan," NIC 135(December 1968): 31.

13. Jean Sermet, "Toulouse et l'Espagne," Académie des Jeux Floraux, 17 December 1954 (Toulouse, 1955).

14. Henri Sarramon, "Sur les chemins de Compostelle," NIC 50(November 1961): 3–4.

15. Henri Sarramon, "La Conférence permanente des Chambres de Commerce françaises et espagnoles," NIC 100(Espagne 1965): 27–29, as well as Jacques Bonnaud, *Panorama et structures économiques de la région Midi-Pyrénées,* 116–17.

16. Henri Sarramon, "Sur les chemins de Compostelle," 10. See also the description of the Toulouse-Bordeaux competition in Beringuier et al., *Toulouse Midi-Pyrénées,* 23–29.

17. See Conseil régional de Midi-Pyrénées, Elaboration du plan de développement régional, *Désenclavement de la région,* Rapports des groupes de travail, 24–26, and Annexes au rapport du groupe de travail, Annexe 5, "Toulouse, porte de l'Espagne?" (Toulouse: Conseil régional, September 1976), 110–12.

18. Bonnaud, *Panorama et structures économiques de la région Midi-Pyrénées,* 122; Guy Isaac, ed., *Midi-Pyrénées et le marché commun,* 107–8. By the 1970s, the import of Spanish goods had stabilized at around 5 percent of the region's total foreign purchases.

19. Isaac, *Midi-Pyrénées et le marché commun,* 118–23.

20. Quoted in Béringuier et al., *Toulouse Midi-Pyrénées,* 29.

21. INSEE, Direction régionale de Toulouse, "Tableaux statistiques de Midi-Pyrénées—1978," *Statistiques et études Midi-Pyrénées* (1978): 173. In France as a whole the export/import ratio rose in machinery and equipment, the chemical industries, and in textiles, clothing, and shoes. Trade at Toulouse thus generally reflected French commercial patterns. For a full history of French foreign trade, see INSEE, *La Mutation industrielle de la France, du traité de Rome à la crise pétrolière,* 2 vols., Collections E31–32 (Paris: INSEE, November 1975), 1: 51–67.

22. Mission régionale Midi-Pyrénées, "Opération pilote petites et moyennes industries dans Midi-Pyrénées," *Bulletin régional d'informations économiques* 1(1979); Le Préfet de la région Midi-Pyrénées, Préfet de la Haute-Garonne, "Letter to the Mayor of Toulouse from Tony Roche, Prefect for the Midi-Pyrénées" (Toulouse, 1 December 1977, mimeographed), 7.

23. Chambre régionale de commerce et d'industrie Midi-Pyrénées, *Présent et avenir de Midi-Pyrénées* (Toulouse: Chambre régionale, September 1970), 46; 2nd ed. (September 1977), 48.

24. Conseil régional de Midi-Pyrénées, Elaboration du plan de développement régional, *Développement des activités industrielles,* Annexes au rapport du groupe de travail, Annexe 3, Rapports sectoriels (Toulouse: Conseil régional, September 1976), 111–25, 165–71.

25. INSEE, Direction régionale de Toulouse, "Tableaux statistiques de Midi-Pyrénées—1978," 173.

26. *TMP Magazine,* April 1977, 14.

27. Préfet de la région Midi-Pyrénées, "Letter to the Mayor of Toulouse from Tony Roche" (Toulouse, 1 February 1979, mimeographed), 3.

28. Ibid., 4.

29. See Lionel Stoléru, *L'Impératif industriel* (Paris: Seuil, 1969), which quasi-officially set out the new economic orthodoxy. For summaries of de Gaulle's modernization and planning policy, see Alain Prate, *Les Batailles économiques du Général de Gaulle* (Paris: Plon, 1978), as well as the series of essays in *The Fifth Republic at Twenty,* ed. William Andrews and Stanley Hoffmann (Albany, N.Y.: State University of New York Press, 1981), and Peter Hall, *Governing the Economy, The Politics of State Interven-*

tion in Britain and France (New York: Oxford University Press, 1986). For a broader picture of the French state's role in the economy, see Maurice Lévy-Leboyer and Jean-Claude Casanova, eds., *Entre l'état et le marché: L'Economie française des années 1880 à nos jours* (Paris: Gallimard, 1991).

30. Commissariat Général du Plan, Quatrième plan de modernisation et d'équipement, *Rapport de la commission de l'artisanat* (Paris: Imprimerie nationale, 1961), 28–29.

31. On the 1962 decree, see Zdatney, *The Politics of Survival,* 179–80, as well as Durand and Frémont, *L'Artisanat en France,* 21.

32. Monod spoke to the general assembly of the CODER (Commission on Regional Economic Development), a consultive body chosen from among local and regional elites. Monod, "Les Conditions d'un bon aménagement du territoire," NIC 122(September 1967): 3–5. See also Monod's *La Transformation d'un pays. Pour un géographie de la liberté* (Paris: Fayard, 1974).

33. INSEE, Direction régionale de Toulouse, *Exploitation du fichier des établissements industriels et commerciaux,* 1962 and 1972 (Toulouse: INSEE, microfilm). See also Bonnaud, *Panorama et structures économiques de la région Midi-Pyrénées,* 72–82.

34. ASSEDIC Toulouse Midi-Pyrénées, *L'Emploi évolution 1969–1970* (Toulouse ASSEDIC: Imprimerie CLEDER, 1971), 45–47, 56–63.

35. Marcel Barreau, "L'industrie du batiment dans la région Midi-Pyrénées," RGPSO 41(1970): 264–68.

36. *La Dépêche du Midi,* 10 August 1958.

37. "L'Entreprise dauriac," *TMP Magazine* 76(July–August 1978), 12.

38. Marie-Paul Cabé, "Les Entreprises du batiment et leur main-d'oeuvre à Toulouse," RGPSO 32(September 1961): 239–42.

39. See the *Rapports sectoriels* in textiles, hosiery, metallurgy, food processing, leather, and building construction in Conseil régional de Midi-Pyrénées, *Développement des activités industrielles,* Annexe 3, 109–81.

40. Conseil régional de Midi-Pyrénées, Elaboration du plan de développement régional, *Maîtrise du financement au service du développement régional,* Rapports des groupes de travail, 12–16; Annexes au rapport du groupe de travail, Annexe 3, "Annexes concernant les circuits de financement," 107–26; and "Propositions pour une place de la S.D.R. dans la vie économique régionale" (Toulouse: Conseil régional, 1976), 135–41.

41. See, in particular, Pambenel, *Politique en Midi-Pyrénées,* 37–39.

42. Peter A. Gourevitch, *Paris and the Provinces: The Politics of Local Government Reform in France* (Berkeley, Calif.: University of California Press, 1980), 228.

43. *La Dépêche du Midi,* 8 and 13 May 1968. On the events of May in Toulouse, see Jacques Godechot, "1968 à la Faculté des Lettres de Toulouse," *Annales du Midi* 90(July-December 1978): 473–96.

44. *La Dépêche du Midi,* 14 and 15 May 1968. On the crisis of 1968 in France, see Keith Reader, *The May 1968 Events in France: Reproductions and Interpretations* (New York: St. Martin's Press, 1993).

45. *La Dépêche du Midi,* 17–19 May 1968.

46. *Bulletin municipal,* 22 and 29 May 1968.

47. See Birnbaum, *Les Sommets de l'état,* 126, and Lipietz, "Governing the Economy in the Face of International Challenge," 28–31.

48. On the end of the "golden age" of capitalism and French planning, see Henri Rousso, ed., *La Planification en crises (1965–1985)* (Paris: Editions du CNRS, 1987). See also Alain Lipietz, *Mirages and Miracles* (London: Verso, 1986), and Andrew Glyn, "The Rise and Fall of the Golden Age: An Historical Analysis of Post-War Capitalism in the Developed Market Economies," in *The Golden Age of Capitalism: Lessons for the 1990s,* ed. Steven Marglin (Oxford, England: Oxford University Press, 1990).

49. Conseil national des économies régionales et de la productivité, "Réflexions et suggestions quant aux aides à apporter aux petites et moyennes entreprises," in Conseil régional de Midi-Pyrénées, *Développement des activités industrielles,* Annexe 6, 217.

50. The Association pour la Promotion de la Moyenne et Petite Industrie dans Midi-Pyrénées (APROMIP) was the chief organization charged with promoting small business in the region. The Agence Régionale d'Information Scientifique et Techniques (ARIST) researched new processes and products for small business as well as tackling their economic feasibility. The Association pour le Développement de l'Enseignement et des Recherches de Midi-Pyrénées (ADERMIP) acted as chief broker between small business and the applied research laboratories at Rangueil-Lespinet. The Délégues aux Rélations Industrielles (DRI) were essentially industrial management consultants. The pamphlet by the Ministère de l'Industrie, du Commerce et de l'Artisanat, *Les Délégues aux rélations industrielles,* no. 2649 (Paris: DRI, 1977) is an excellent summary of the DPO system. See also Préfecture régional de Midi-Pyrénées, *Elements pour une politique régionale,* 122–25, and Mission régionale Midi-Pyrénées, "Opération pilote petites et moyennes industries dans Midi-Pyrénées," *Bulletin régional d'informations économiques* (First trimester, 1979).

51. Claude Duffour, "Toulouse capitale de la sous-traitance," editorial, NIC 216(1978): 2.

52. Idrac and Laborie, "L'Economie de Midi-Pyrénées en crise," 21–22; Jean-Pierre Puig, "L'Economie régionale au cours du VI Plan," *Statistiques et études Midi-Pyrénées* 1(1977): 9–10.

53. Conseil régional de Midi-Pyrénées, *Maîtrise de l'urbanisation de l'agglomération toulousaine,* Rapports des groupes de travail, 13.

54. Speeches and discussion, "Le Batiment et T. P. dans l'économie locale," Colloquium on the Economy of Toulouse, The Belvedere, Toulouse, 28 June 1980. On the practices of local building contractors, see also Marie-Christine Jaillet, *Les Pavillonneurs: La production de la maison individuelle dans la région toulousaine* (Paris: CNRS, 1982), the concluding chapters.

55. Conseil régional de Midi-Pyrénées, *Développement des activités industrielles,* Annexes au rapport du groupe de travail, Annexe 3, "Rapports Sectoriels," 172.

56. Studies done on the industrial structure of twentieth-century France disclose the same ambiguity. According to Edmond Didier and Edmond Malinvaud, "La

Concentration de l'industrie s'est-elle accentuée depuis le debut du siècle?" in *La Concentration des établissements industriels françaises en 1962 et 1972*, ed. INSEE, Collections E43 (Paris: INSEE, 1976), the clearest change in the structure of French industry was the erosion of the smallest shops and their artisan-proprietors and the increasing shift to a salaried workforce. Nonetheless, there remained a dense industrial tissue of small companies that formed the bedrock of the French economy. After 1962, there was a moderate increase in the average size of industrial plants that chiefly benefited medium-sized companies. Malinvaud concluded that these late trends did not critically affect the situation. Postwar French economic growth took place without a radical turnabout in its industrial structure. Nonetheless, the issue is a complex one caught in a labyrinth of technical definitions of the *établissement*, the *entreprise*, and *le groupe*. Maurice Parodi, *L'Economie et la société française depuis 1945* (Paris: Armand Colin, 1981), 118–21, and Patrick Roux-Vaillard, "L'industrie," in *Profil économique de la France au seuil des années 80*, ed. Jean-Pierre Pagé (Paris: La Documentation Française, 1981), 197–99 argue that although the French economy continued to be made up of a large number of modest companies, a clear process of consolidation took place. The largest companies absorbed increasing numbers of the workforce and vastly consolidated their financial power, particularly as a result of the 1973 oil crisis. France, then, had a dual structure composed of an extensive network of small-time PMEs (1.4 million companies employed an 11-million-strong workforce) and, at the other extreme, gigantic companies of global dimension. It followed, in many ways, the same description as that used for Toulouse: "a few giant companies in the suburbs superimposed over a multitude of small workshops in the old city." See also François Jenny and A. P. Weber, *Concentration et politique des structures industrielles* (Paris: La Documentation Française, 1974); Jean-Pierre Gilly and François Morin, *Les Groupes industriels en France. Concentration du système productif depuis 1945*, Notes et études documentaires, no. 4605–4606 (Paris: La Documentation Française, 1981).

57. IAURP, *Activités caractéristiques du centre-ville à Grenoble, Nancy, Rennes, Strasbourg, Toulouse*, Annexe 5, 52; Direction régionale du travail et de la main d'oeuvre de la région Midi-Pyrénées, Echelon régional de l'emploi de Toulouse, *Structure des emplois, région Midi-Pyrénées* (Toulouse: Echelon régional de l'emploi de Toulouse, March 1975).

58. Here, the term "small producers" refers to businesses with fewer than ten employees. INSEE, Direction régionale de Toulouse, *Compte régional des industries*, Enquête annuelle 1975, Département de la Haute-Garonne (Toulouse: INSEE, microfilm).

59. These were dubbed *"effet régional."* INSEE, *Disparités et diversité des régions françaises à la vielle du IXe plan*, Archives et documents no. 109 (Paris: INSEE, July 1984), 30–31.

60. See Gérard Adam, "Les petites entreprises: Un monde contrasté," in *Français, qui êtes-vous?* ed. Jean-Daniel Reynaud and Yves Grafmeyer, 181–90. For the theoretical arguments on capitalism and geographically uneven development, see Edward W. Soja, *Postmodern Geographies*, chapter 4, as well as Alain Lipietz, "The Structuration of Space, the Problem of Land, and Spatial Policy," in *Regions in Crisis*, ed. J. Carney, R. Hudson, and J. Lewis (London: Croom Helm, 1980), 60–75.

61. *La Dépêche du Midi,* 22 April 1949. See also "Enquête: Le Libre service," in NIC 123(October 1967): 36–38.

62. Ministère de l'Equipement, "Etude des fonctions tertiaires de l'agglomération et problèmes d'aménagement" (Toulouse: May 1967, mimeographed), 16–18. See also IAURP, "Activités caractéristiques du centre-ville," 24–33.

63. Michel Idrac, "La Mutation de l'appareil commercial à Toulouse," RGPSO 42(December 1971): 465–66.

64. Ministère de l'équipement, Direction de l'aménagement foncier et de l'urbanisme, *Grandes surfaces commerciales péripheriques* (Paris: La Documentation Française, 1974), 104–5. Idrac, "La Mutation de l'appareil commercial à Toulouse," 455–76.

65. Région Midi-Pyrénées, Préparation du VIe Plan, Rapport d'orientations régionales, *Le Commerce* 4(June 1969): 23–24; ASSEDIC Toulouse Midi-Pyrénées, Région Midi-Pyrénées, *L'Emploi, évolution 1974–1975* (Toulouse: ASSEDIC, 1976), 44–45; Chambre de Commerce et d'Industrie Midi-Pyrénées, "Tableau de bord du commerce. Structure de l'appareil commercial. Synthèse régionale" (Toulouse, 1976).

66. CID–UNITA was a group of organizations merged into a national Comité d'Information et de Défense-Union Nationale des Travailleurs Indépendants; "Commerce, la guerre des grandes surfaces," *TMP Magazine,* 15 January 1972; "La Loi Royer," *TMP Magazine,* 29 December 1973. See also Daniel Bertaux and Isabelle Bertaux-Viame, "Artisanal Bakery in France: How It Lives and Why It Survives," in *The Petite Bourgeoisie: Comparative Studies of the Uneasy Stratum,* ed. Frank Bechofer and Bryan Elliot (London: MacMillan, 1981), 155–81.

67. *Livre Blanc,* 92–93.

68. "La Ballade du Pieton" (1972), Etudes urbaines, AM 64/83.

69. Pierre-Yves Péchoux and Marc Saint-Saëns, "Commentaries," RGPSO 49(September 1978): 359–60.

70. *La Dépêche du Midi,* 6 July 1968.

71. *La Dépêche du Midi,* 10 July 1968.

72. See Nevers, "Du Clientélisme à la technocratie," 453–54, as well as Comité de ville du PCF, ed., *Toulouse, les communistes et le changement* (Toulouse: PCF, 1977).

73. Sharon Zukin, *Landscapes of Power, From Detroit to Disney World* (Berkeley, Calif.: University of California Press, 1991), 195. See also Henri Lefebvre, *The Production of Space,* trans. Donald Nicholson-Smith (Oxford, England: Basil Blackwell, 1991).

74. Irene B. Wilson, "Decentralizing or Recentralizing the State? Urban Planning and Center-Periphery Relations," in *Socialism, the State and Public Policy in France,* ed. Philip G. Cerny and Martin A. Schain (New York: Methuen, 1985), 188–92; Guy Jalabert, "La planification urbaine dans l'agglomération," RGPSO 48(January 1977): 49–67.

75. Pierre Baudis, quoted in *La Dépêche du Midi,* 24 April 1971.

76. On the cultural renaissance of the 1970s and 1980s, see Ateliers Jean Jaurès, *Livre Blanc, la culture à Toulouse et la région* (Toulouse: Privat, 1983) and "La Vie culturelle," *Les Dossiers de Midi-Pyrénées,* 4(May 1976).

77. See the interview with Alain Savary in *TMP Magazine,* March 1977, and

312 Notes to Pages 262–267

Conseil régional de Midi-Pyrénées, *Maîtrise de l'urbanisation de l'agglomération toulousaine,* Rapports des groupes de travail, 25. For a general critique of culture and the new middle classes in France, see Bourdieu, *Distinction,* 267–74.

78. INSEE, *Recensement général 1954,* Population, ménages, 36; Vannina Audibert et al., *L'Evolution de l'emploi dans le secteur tertiaire public et parapublic de l'agglomération toulousaine,* 2 vols. (Toulouse: Institut d'études de l'emploi, July 1973), 1: 167–69.

Conclusion

1. François Bedarida of the Institut d'Etudes Politiques de Paris in "Un lieu de conflits," *Cahiers français* 203(October-December 1981): 87.

2. Henri Mendras, *La Seconde révolution française, 1965–1984* (Paris: Gallimard, 1988), chapter 2. For the most recent analysis of this process of social transformation, see the excellent article by Richard Kuisel, "The France We Have Lost: Social, Economic, and Cultural Discontinuities," in *Remaking the Hexagon: The New France in the New Europe,* ed. Gregory Flynn (Boulder, Colo.: Westview Press, 1995).

Bibliography

Archives, Libraries, Public Documentation

Agence d'Urbanisme de l'Agglomération Toulousaine
Archives Départementales de la Haute-Garonne
Archives Municipales de Toulouse (AM)
Atelier Municipal d'Urbanisme, Toulouse
Bibliothèque Municipale de Toulouse
Bibliothèque Nationale
Centre National d'Études Spatiales (CNES)
Chambre de Commerce et d'Industrie Midi-Pyrénées
Commissariat Général du Plan
Commission Départementale de l'Urbanisme, Haute-Garonne
Commission Nationale des Plans d'Urbanisme
Conseil Régional de Midi-Pyrénées
Délégation à l'Aménagement du Territoire et à l'Action Régionale (DATAR)
Délégation Générale à la Recherche Scientifique et Technique (DGRST)
Direction Départementale de l'Équipement, Haute-Garonne
Direction Régionale du Travail et de la Main-d'oeuvre de la Région Midi-Pyrénées
Institut National de la Statistique et des Études Économiques (INSEE)
INSEE, Direction Régionale de Toulouse
Mairie de Toulouse
Ministère de l'Équipement
Ministère de la Reconstruction et de l'Urbanisme
Organization for Economic Cooperation and Development (OECD)
Préfecture Régional de Midi-Pyrénées
Ville de Toulouse

Journals and Periodicals

Annales du Midi
Auta
Bulletin municipal de Toulouse
Bulletin régional d'informations économiques, Midi-Pyrénées

Bulletin régional de statistique, Midi-Pyrénées
Les Collections de l'INSEE
La Dépêche du Midi
Economie et statistique
Etudes Statistiques
Le Monde
Le Moniteur des travaux publics et du batiment
Notes et études documentaires
Les Nouvelles industrielles et commerciales (NIC)
Le Progrès scientifique
La Recherche spatiale
La République du Sud-Ouest
Revue d'histoire de la deuxième guerre mondiale et des conflits contemporaines
Review
Revue française de science politique
Revue géographique des pyrénées et du sud-ouest (RGPSO)
Statistiques et indicateurs des régions françaises
Statistiques et études Midi-Pyrénées
TMP Magazine (Toulouse Midi-Pyrénées)
Urbanisme
La Vie Urbaine
Vingtième Siècle

Twentieth-Century Toulouse

Arnoldson, Gret, et al. *Les camps du sud-ouest de la France. Exclusion, internement et déportation 1939–1944*. Toulouse: Privat, 1994.

Ateliers Jean Jaurès. *Livre blanc, la culture à Toulouse et la région*. Toulouse: Privat, 1983.

Audibert, Vannina. *L'Evolution de l'emploi dans le secteur tertiaire public et parapublic de l'agglomération toulousaine*. 2 vols. Toulouse: Institut d'Études de l'Emploi, July 1973.

Baccrabère, Georges, and Georges Jorré. *Toulouse, terre d'envol*. Toulouse: Privat, 1966.

Beringuier, Christian, André Boudou, and Guy Jalabert. *Toulouse Midi-Pyrénées. La transition*. Collection Villes Clés. Paris: Stock, 1972.

Bertaux, Pierre. *Libération de Toulouse et de sa région*. Collection La Libération de la France. Paris: Hachette, 1973.

Berthaut, Philippe, ed. *L'Empal'Odyssée, traversées dans la mémoire d'Empalot, quartier de Toulouse*. Toulouse: Le Lézard, 1993.

Bonnaud, Jacques. *Panorama et structures économiques de la région Midi-Pyrénées*. Toulouse: Direction régionale du travail et de la main d'oeuvre, October 1976.

Chapman, Herrick. *State Capitalism and Working Class Radicalism in the French Aircraft Industry*. Berkeley, Calif.: University of California Press, 1990.

Cholvy, Gérard. *Histoire de Languedoc de 1900 à nos jours*. Toulouse: Privat, 1980.

Conseil d'architecture, d'urbanisme et de l'environnement de la Haute-Garonne and Ecole d'architecture de Toulouse. *Toulouse 1920–1940: La ville et ses architectes*. Toulouse: OMBRES, 1991.

Coppolani, Jean, ed. *Toulouse et son agglomération*. Notes et études documentaires, no. 4762. Paris: La Documentation Française, 1984.

———. *Toulouse aux XXe siècle*. Toulouse: Privat, 1963.

Coppolani, Jean, Guy Jalabert, and Jean-Paul Lévy. *Toulouse et son agglomération*. Paris: La Documentation Française, 1984.

Coutet, Alex. *Toulouse ville artistique, plaisante et curieuse*. Toulouse: Richard, 1926.

Estèbe, Jean. *Toulouse 1940–1944*. Paris: Perrin, 1996.

Fabre, Daniel, and Charles Camberoque. *La Fête en Languedoc*. Toulouse: Privat, 1977.

Faucher, Daniel. *Toulouse*. Paris: La Documentation Française, 1961.

Goubet, Michel, and Paul Debauges. *Histoire de la résistance*. Toulouse: Milan, 1986.

Gratias, Louis. *Le Nouveau visage de Toulouse*. Paris: José Corti, 1934.

Isaac, Guy, ed. *Midi-Pyrénées et le marché commun*. Toulouse: Université des Sciences Sociales de Toulouse, 1978.

Jaillet, Marie-Christine, *Les Pavillonneurs: la production de la maison individuelle dans la région toulousaine*. Paris: CNRS, 1982.

Jalabert, Guy. *Les Industries aéronautiques et spatiales en France*. Toulouse: Privat, 1974.

Lafont, Robert. *La Révolution régionaliste*. Paris: Gallimard, 1967.

Lagarde, Pierre. *Histoires et mémoire de Toulouse*. Marseille: Jeanne Laffitte, 1981.

Leblanc, Gratien. *La Vie à Toulouse il y a cinquante ans*. Toulouse: Privat, 1978.

Marconis, Robert. *Midi-Pyrénées, XIXe-XXe siècles. Transports, espace, sociétés*. 2 vols. Toulouse: Milan, 1986.

Pech, Rémy, et al. (Pambenel). *Politique en Midi-Pyrénées*. Paris: Eché, 1987.

Roubaud, Marie-Louise, ed. *Toulouse*. France Series, no. 4. Paris: Autrement, 1991.

Salies, Pierre. *La Vie quotidienne à Toulouse en cartes postales anciennes*. Paris: SFL, 1976.

Taillefer, François. *Atlas et géographie du Midi toulousain*. Atlas et géographie de la France moderne. Paris: Flammarion, 1978.

Teyssier, Francine. *L'Emploi public dans l'agglomération toulousaine*. 2 vols. Toulouse: Institut d'études de l'emploi, November 1970.

Vie, A. *Histoire politique de la municipalité Toulousaine de 1929 à 1939*. Toulouse: Privat, 1961.

History of Toulouse and Languedoc

Aminzade, Ronald. *Ballots and Barricades: Class Formation and Republican Politics in France, 1830–1871*. Princeton, N.J.: Princeton University Press, 1993.

———. *Class, Politics, and Early Industrial Capitalism, A Study of Mid-Nineteenth Century Toulouse, France*. Albany, N.Y.: State University of New York Press, 1981.

Armengaud, André, and Robert Lafont, eds. *Histoire d'Occitanie*. Paris: Hachette, 1979.

Armengaud, Roger. *Pays toulousain d'autrefois*. Lyon: Horvath, 1993.

Bonnaud, Pierre. *Terres et langues, peuples et régions*. 2 vols. Clermont-Ferrand: Auvernha Tara D'Oc, 1981.

Brunet, Roger. *Les Compagnes toulousaines, étude géographique*. Toulouse: Faculté des Lettres et Sciences Humaines, 1965.

Castor, Giles. *Le commerce du pastel et de l'épicerie à Toulouse de 1450 à 1561*. Toulouse: Privat, 1962.

Cholvy, Gérard, ed. *Le Languedoc et le Roussillon*. Civilisations populaires régionales. Roanne, France: Horvath, 1982.

Forster, Robert. *The Nobility of Toulouse in the Eighteenth Century*. Baltimore: Johns Hopkins University Press, 1960.

Frêche, Georges. *Toulouse et la région Midi-Pyrénées au siècle des lumières vers 1670–1789*. Paris: Cujas, 1974.

Johnson, Christopher H. *The Life and Death of Industrial Languedoc, 1700–1920*. New York: Oxford University Press, 1995.

Labrousse, Michel. *Toulouse antique, des origines à l'établissement des wisigoths*. Paris: Boccard, 1968.

Lafont, Robert. *La revendication occitane*. Paris: Flammarion, 1974.

Le Roy Ladurie, Emmanuel. *Histoire du Languedoc*. Paris: Presses Universitaires de la France, 1974.

Lerner, Henri. *La Dépêche, journal de la démocratie*. 2 vols. Toulouse: Privat, 1978.

Lewis, Archibald R. *The Development of Southern French and Catalan Society, 718–1050*. Austin, Tex.: University of Texas Press, 1965.

Lyons, Martyn. *Révolution et terreur à Toulouse*. Toulouse: Privat, 1980.

Mesuret, Robert. *Evocation du vieux Toulouse*. Paris: Minuit, 1960.

Nelli, René. *Mais enfin, qu'est-ce que l'occitanie?* Toulouse: Privat, 1978.

Schneider, Robert. *The Ceremonial City: Toulouse Observed 1738–1780*. Princeton, N.J.: Princeton University Press, 1995.

———. *Public Life in Toulouse, 1463–1789: From Municipal Republic to Cosmopolitan City*. Ithaca, N.Y.: Cornell University Press, 1989.

Sède, Gérard de. *700 ans de révoltes occitanes*. Paris: Plon, 1982.

Sentou, Jean. *Révolution et contre-révolution dans la France du midi: 1789–1799*. Toulouse: Presses Universitaires du Mirail, 1991.

Thomas, Jack. *Le Temps Des Foires: Foires et Marchés dans le Midi Toulousain de la Fin de L'Ancien Régime à 1914*. Toulouse: Presses Universitaires du Mirail, 1993.

Wolff, Philippe, ed. *Histoire de Languedoc*. Toulouse: Privat, 1967.

———. *Histoire de Toulouse*. Toulouse: Privat, 1974.

———. *Regards sur le midi médiéval*. Toulouse: Privat, 1978.

French Cities and the Urbanizing Process

Ardagh, John. *France Today*. New York: Penguin, 1988.

Barrère, Pierre, and Micheline Cassou-Mounat. *Les Villes françaises*. Paris: Masson, 1980.

Benevolo, Leonardo. *The European City.* Oxford, England: Basil Blackwell, 1993.

Bourdieu, Pierre. *Distinction: A Social Critique of the Judgement of Taste.* Translated by Richard Nice. Cambridge, Mass.: Harvard University Press, 1984.

Boyer, M. Christine. *The City of Collective Memory: Its Historical Imagery and Architectural Entertainments.* Cambridge, Mass.: MIT Press, 1994.

Carrière, François, and Philippe Pinchemel. *Le Fait urbain en France.* Paris: Armand Colin, 1963.

Castells, Manuel, et al. *La Rénovation urbaine à Paris, structure urbaine et logique de classe.* Paris: L'Ecole Pratique des Hautes Études, 1973.

————. *The Urban Question.* London: Edward Arnold, 1977.

Castells, Manuel, and Peter Hall. *Technopoles of the World.* London: Routledge, 1994.

Certeau, Michel de. *The Practice of Everyday Life.* Translated by Steven Rendall. Berkeley, Calif.: University of California Press, 1984.

Cohen, Jean-Louis. *Architecture et politiques sociales, 1900–1940.* Paris: Parentheses, 1985.

Direction des Archives de France, ed. *Reconstructions et modernisation, la France après les ruines 1918 . . . 1945 . . .* Paris: Archives Nationales, 1991.

Duby, Georges, ed. *Histoire de la France urbaine.* 5 vols. Paris: Seuil, 1980–1985.

Dunford, Michael. *Capital, the State, and Regional Development.* London: Plon, 1990.

Evenson, Norma. *Paris: A Century of Change, 1878–1978.* New Haven, Conn.: Yale University Press, 1979.

Foster, Hal, ed. *The Anti-Aesthetic, Essays on Postmodern Culture.* Seattle, Wash.: Bay Press, 1983.

Fourdstié, Jean. *Les Trentes glorieuses ou la révolution invisible de 1946 à 1975.* Paris: Fayard, 1979.

Gaudin, Jean-Pierre. *L'Avenir en plan: Technique et politique dans la prévision urbaine, 1900–1930.* Seyssel, France: Champ Vallon, 1985.

————. *Technopolis: Crises urbaines et innnovations municipales.* Paris: Presses Universitaires de France, 1989.

Hall, Peter. *Cities of Tomorrow, An Intellectual History of Urban Planning and Design in the Twentieth Century.* Oxford, England: Basil Blackwell, 1988.

Harvey, David. *The Condition of Postmodernity: An Enquiry into the Origins of Cultural Change.* Cambridge, Mass.: Basil Blackwell, 1989.

————. *The Urban Experience.* Baltimore: Johns Hopkins University Press, 1985.

Haumont, Nicole. *Les Pavillionnaires.* Paris: Centre de recherches d'urbanisme, 1975.

Hayden, Dolores. *The Power of Place, Urban Landscapes as Public History.* Cambridge, Mass.: MIT, 1995.

Jackson, John B. *Discovering the Vernacular Landscape.* New Haven, Conn.: Yale University Press, 1984.

Kopp, Anatole, Frédérique Boucher, and Danièle Pauly. *L'architecture de la reconstruction en France, 1945–1953.* Paris: Moniteur, 1982.

Kuisel, Richard. *Seducing the French: The Dilemma of Americanization.* Berkeley, Calif.: University of California Press, 1993.

Lavedan, Pierre. *Les Villes françaises.* Paris: Vincent Fréal and Cie, 1960.

Ledrut, Raymond. *L'espace social de la ville, problèmes de sociologie appliquée à l'aménagement urbain*. Paris: Anthropos, 1968.

Lees, Lynn Hollen, and Paul Hohenberg. *The Making of Urban Europe, 1000–1994*. 2nd ed. Cambridge, Mass.: Harvard University Press, 1994.

Lefebvre, Henri. *The Production of Space*. Translated by Donald Nicholson-Smith. Oxford, England: Basil Blackwell, 1991.

———. *La Révolution urbaine*. Paris: Gallimard, 1970.

Leontidou, Lila. *The Mediterranean City in Transition: Social Change and Urban Development*. Cambridge: Cambridge University Press, 1990.

Maspero, François. *Roissy-Express, A Journey through the Paris Suburbs*. London: Verso, 1994.

Piron, Olivier, ed. *Une Politique du logement, Ministère de la Reconstruction et de l'Urbanisme, 1944–1954*. Paris: Institut Français d'Architecture, Plan Construction et Architecture, 1995.

Rabinow, Paul. *French Modern: Norms and Forms of the Social Environment*. Cambridge, Mass.: MIT Press, 1989.

Roncayolo, Marcel. *La Ville et Ses Territoires*. Paris: Gallimard, 1990.

Roncayolo, Marcel and Thierry Paquot. *Villes et civilisation urbaine, XVIIIe–XXe siècle*. Paris: Larousse, 1992.

Ross, Kristin. *Fast Cars, Clean Bodies: Decolonization and the Reordering of French Culture*. Cambridge, Mass.: MIT Press, 1995.

Soja, Edward W. *Postmodern Geographies: The Reassertion of Space in Critical Social Theory*. London: Verso, 1989.

Stovall, Tyler. *The Rise of the Paris Red Belt*. Berkeley, Calif.: University of California Press, 1990.

Sutcliffe, Anthony. *The Autumn of Central Paris: The Defeat of Town Planning*. London: Edward Arnold, 1970.

Tafuri, Manfredo. *Architecture and Utopia: Design and Capitalist Development*. Translated by Barbara Luigia La Penta. Cambridge, Mass.: MIT Press, 1976.

Urry, John. *Consuming Places*. London: Routledge, 1995.

Vayssière, Bruno. *Reconstruction-Déconstruction. Le hard french ou l'architecture française des trente glorieuses*. Paris: Picard, 1988.

Verdié, Minelle. *Ces gens là, histoires du logement ordinaire*. Paris: Syros, 1995.

Voldman, Danièle. *La Reconstruction des villes françaises de 1940 à 1954. Histoire d'une politique*. Paris: L'Harmattan, 1997.

Wright, Gwendolyn. *The Politics of Design in French Colonial Urbanism*. Chicago: University of Chicago Press, 1991.

Zukin, Sharon. *Landscapes of Power, From Detroit to Disney World*. Berkeley, Calif.: University of California Press, 1991.

Index

Maziol, Jacques, 100, 110, 132–133, 236
Métropoles d'équilibres, 116–119, 120, 122, 125, 134, 137, 139, 206, 209, 214, 217, 230, 241, 266
Midi-Pyrénées region, 20, 56, 107, 136, 180, 181, 204, 210, 214, 224, 242, 244; creation of, 105–106, 113, 195; underdevelopment, 165, 166; foreign trade, 224–226, 228
Minimes, 48, 72, 83, 108, 147, 173, 186, 190, 196, 255
Ministère de la Reconstruction et de l'Urbanisme (MRU), 74, 77–78, 79–80, 83, 104, 193. *See also* Ministère de la Reconstruction et du Logement (MRL)
Ministère de la Reconstruction et du Logement (MRL), 87, 88, 96, 114
Monnet Plan, 159, 164
Montariol, Jean, 50–52, 80, 81–82, 86, 136, 245
Montaudran, 28; airport complex, 27, 36, 136–137, 140, 185–186, 187, 188–190, 192–193, 197, 231
Motorola, 208–209, 215

Nationale du Midi (SNCAM), 190–191, 192
Nicod, Charles-Henri, 60, 74, 77, 80, 90, 93, 94, 107–108, 114, 272
Nicod Plan, 74, 75–77, 80–81, 84, 85, 87–88, 90–91, 93, 95, 97, 163, 262
IXth Economic Region, 56, 57–58, 59, 64, 103–104, 155, 219
Noé internment camp, 34, 35

Occitan, 2, 3; early history, 12, 13–15, 16, 21, 23, 25, 28, 43, 44–45, 46; under Vichy, 59, 61, 154; modern interpretation of, 101, 103, 114, 148, 165, 173–174, 232, 259–260, 262
Occitania, 12, 13, 57, 166, 261
Occitanism, 43–45, 46, 58, 103, 173–174, 256, 259–260, 271, 273

Office National Industriel d'Azote (ONIA), 27, 32, 36, 49, 63, 69, 70, 123, 135, 141, 146, 152, 154, 160, 186–187, 211, 212–213, 214, 231, 238; housing programs for, 80. *See also* Azote et Produits Chimiques (APC)
Office of Urban Aesthetics, 97, 121

Palais du Capitole, 15, 16, 17, 18, 22, 32, 62, 76, 86–87, 100, 107, 110, 171, 174, 184, 222, 237, 262, 269, 272. *See also* City Hall; Hôtel de Ville
Pelletier, Emile, 106, 171, 222
Périllier, Louis, 104, 106, 165, 220. *See also* Inspecteur Général de l'Administration en Mission Extraordinaire (IGAME)
Petit et moyenne entreprise (PME), 242, 243, 248
Place des Carmes, 21, 22, 23, 149, 157–158, 254
Place du Capitole, 15, 21–22, 35, 39, 76, 81, 84, 95, 102, 126, 130, 149, 151, 157–158, 174, 175, 183–184, 222, 237–238, 240, 254, 255, 259, 272
Place Esquirol, 22, 23, 147, 183
Place Occitan, 8, 101–102, 261
Place Victor-Hugo, 92, 94, 149, 158, 261
Place Wilson, 76, 81, 92, 95, 251, 254, 263
Plan Courant, 83–84
Plan Directeur d'Urbanisme, 114–115, 117, 119, 120, 121, 122
Polygone, 182–183, 186, 204
Pompidou, Georges, 216, 239, 240–241
Popular Front, 29, 31, 45, 189–190
Poujadism, 175–176

Rangueil-Lespinet, 2, 117–118, 123, 124, 133, 137–141, 142, 143–145, 200, 204, 207–208, 210, 231, 243, 248, 268, 270
Ravanel, Serge (Colonel), 38, 62, 68